S0-BRM-897

Black, French, and African

Léopold Sédar Senghor as a newly inaugurated member
of the Académie Française.

Black, French, and African

A Life of Léopold Sédar Senghor

BENEDICTINE UNIVERSITY LIBRARY
IN THE KINDLON HALL OF LEARNING
5700 COLLEGE ROAD
LISLE, IL 60532-0900

Janet G. Vaillant

Harvard University Press • Cambridge, Massachusetts • London, England • 1990

R. YEBOAH-SAMPONG

841.9
S476
Wv/31

Copyright © 1990 by the President and Fellows of Harvard College
All rights reserved
Printed in the United States of America
10 9 8 7 6 5 4 3 2 1

This book is printed on acid-free paper, and its binding materials
have been chosen for strength and durability.

Library of Congress Cataloging-in-Publication Data
Vaillant, Janet G.
   Black, French, and African : a life of Léopold Sédar Senghor /
Janet G. Vaillant.
      p.   cm.
   Includes bibliographical references.
   ISBN 0-674-07623-0 (alk. paper)
   1. Senghor, Léopold Sédar, 1906–   . 2. Authors, Senegalese—20th
century—Biography.   3. Senegal—Presidents—Biography.
4. Negritude (Literary movement) I. Title.
PQ3989.S47Z95   1990
841—dc20   89-26767
[B]   CIP

To Henry, Marian, Derek, and Eliza

Acknowledgments

It is a pleasant duty to thank the many people who have helped me with this book. I began to write about the work of Léopold Sédar Senghor as a graduate student under the tutelage of Barrington Moore, Jr., who taught me the value of understanding complicated sociological theory and then finding simple language in which to express its insights.

When I set out into the field, busy people in Paris and Senegal met me with unexpected friendliness and interest, a reception that I attribute in part to their respect and admiration for the subject of this book. Those I interviewed or who offered help in other ways included Louis Achille, Sourou Migan Apithy, Michel Aurillac, Joanne Murphy Bâ, M. and Mme Marcel Baumlin, Nicole Bernard-Duquênet, René Brouillet, Mody Sékéné Cissoko, Léon Damas, Cissé Dia, Annette Mbaye Derneville, Birago Diop, Christiane Diop, Roger Dorsinville, Mother Gonzague Valot, Armand Guibert, André Guillabert, Dr. Linhard, Abdoulaye Ly, Kabirou Mbodj, Ségan Ndiaye, Théodore Ndiaye, Majib Ndaw, Claude Pompidou, Jacques Rabémananjara, Mme Alioune Sène, Blaise Senghor, Dior Senghor, François Senghor, Katrine Senghor, Lat Senghor, Pierre Senghor, Bakory Traoré, Jean Valdeyron, and Robert Verdier. Many gave of themselves far beyond the formal courtesies that might be considered the due of a foreign scholar. I thank them all, and especially appreciated the generosity of Hélène Senghor and Mamadou Dia. Others took time to help me to understand what it might mean to be African and French, among whom I would like particularly to thank Tahirou Diao, Ibrahima Diallo, and, most of all, Edouard Basse and Marie-Thérèse Senghor

Basse, who shared their reflections about their family and country and provided me with a home away from home in Dakar. President Senghor took time out of his busy life to see me many times, but never tried to influence my work.

Those who read parts or all of the manuscript, providing useful criticism and encouragement by turns, included Pathé Diagne, Suzannah B. Hatt, Nathan Huggins, Jill Kneerim, Martin Kilson, Robert Rotberg, and James Spiegler. Mercer Cook, who first met Senghor in the 1930s and later served as the American Ambassador to Senegal in the 1960s, played a special role by reading, commenting, reminiscing, and encouraging at a crucial moment. Saliou Mbaye guided me through the national archives in Senegal. In Paris similar roles were played by Mme Nathan at the archives of the National Ministry of Education, Michèle Le Pavec at the Bibliothèque Nationale, and Father Noël at the archives of the Congrégation du Saint-Esprit. Abdoulaye Lett assisted ingeniously with some of the photographs. For typing help, I am grateful to Carol Marshall, Ellen Lapenson, and Susan Zayre. A keen editorial eye at the service of a good brain was provided by my editor, Camille Smith.

I am grateful to the American Philosophical Society, the Wheaton (Massachusetts) College Faculty Fund, and the Bunting Institute of Radcliffe College for their support of parts of this work, and also to that extraordinary institution, the Russian Research Center of Harvard University, where many colleagues tolerated my aberrant interests and provided a congenial atmosphere in which to work.

I would like here to make special mention of a person who has been my teacher for as long as I can remember. Nancy L. Roelker introduced me to the pleasures of history and those puzzling and contradictory people, the French, and has supported me and my work for many years with her abundant energy, intelligence, and tact. And finally, I thank my family, who were a constant source of distraction in the hard times and always present to celebrate the good ones: my parents, and Henry, Marian, Derek, and Eliza, to whom this book is affectionately dedicated.

Contents

Illustrations

Campaigning in 1960. Senghor is at center right. To his right, Modibo Keita greets the crowd. Behind them are Lamine Guèye (in the dark suit) and Mamadou Dia (to his left). Courtesy Archives Nationales du Sénégal.

Dakar citizens line up to vote, about 1960. Courtesy Documentation Française.

Senghor (in the light suit) with Falilou Mbacké, grand marabout of the Mourides (to his left), on an Islamic pilgrimage in 1964. Courtesy Photo Info-Sénégal.

Senghor with his wife, Colette, and their son, Philippe-Maguilen, in 1961. Photo by Sauer, Scoop/Paris Match.

Presidents Senghor and Pompidou during Pompidou's official visit to Senegal, 1971. Courtesy Photo Info-Sénégal.

Senghor and Abdou Diouf at the ceremony transferring power to Diouf, 1980. Courtesy Photo Info-Sénégal.

Senghor in retirement. Courtesy J. René Jacques.

Dakar today. Courtesy Abdoulaye Lett.

Black, French, and African

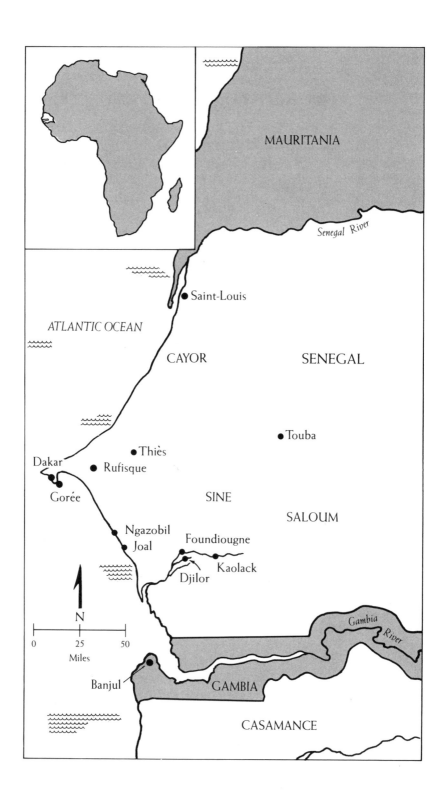

MAURITANIA

Senegal River

ATLANTIC OCEAN

● Saint-Louis

CAYOR

SENEGAL

● Touba

● Thiès

Dakar

● Rufisque

Gorée

SINE

SALOUM

● Ngazobil

Joal

● Foundiougne

Djilor

Kaolack

N

0   25   50

Miles

Gambia River

Banjul

GAMBIA

CASAMANCE

Introduction

Herein lie buried many things which, if read with patience
may show the strange meaning of being black here at the
dawning of the twentieth century. This meaning is not
without interest to you, Gentle Reader, for the problem of
the twentieth century is the problem of the color line.

—W. E. B. Du Bois, *The Souls of Black Folk,* 1903

In March 1984, the Académie Française welcomed into its exclusive
ranks Léopold Sédar Senghor, a man who was black, French, and
African, a prizewinning poet and a former president of Senegal. Membership in the French Academy is the highest honor France can bestow
on its statesmen and men of letters. At any one time, there are forty
living "immortals," as members of the Academy are called, each considered to have made an enduring contribution to the legacy of French
culture and statecraft. Senghor was the first black African asked to
join this distinguished company.

Paradox marked Senghor's life. The Academician outfitted with
brocade cutaway jacket and ceremonial French sword to be recognized
for his contributions to France had been born a colonial subject in a
dusty village in West Africa. He had passed his childhood among
villagers who spoke no French and neither read nor wrote. His rise
to world prominence and French honor might appear at first to be
proof of French generosity and the success of the French colonizing
mission in Africa. Yet Senghor gained notice because he challenged
French power and led his native Senegal to political independence.
He was the spokesman of Negritude, a theory of black cultural importance and autonomy, who argued that Africans must be free to direct
their own future. He wrote prizewinning poetry in which he expressed
his love for Africa and his anger at what France had done to his native
land. His poetry also told of his love for France and his guilt for
feeling tempted to desert his ancestors. He felt the humiliation suffered
by the black at the hand of the white. He also succumbed to the

charm of French teachers who persuaded African schoolchildren of the glories of French civilization and taught them that to be black was to be inescapably inferior. As he and his writing matured, Senghor recorded his evolution from a young African of promise, singled out by his French teachers for promotion and support, to a "New Negro," proud of his black heritage. His writings made up the stuff of a new ideology, and the poet and teacher moved into the political arena to lead a younger generation of Africans to their independence.

Senghor did not renounce his love of France as he called for black men to reevaluate their own culture. One of his proudest moments occurred when he and Charles de Gaulle stood side by side to preside over the ceremonies marking Senegal's independence. A lesser man might not have resisted the temptation to court popularity by blaming France for all Senegal's problems. Senghor stood firm, determined to find ways to reconcile his rich and contradictory heritage.

Later, to be sure, during his two decades as president of Senegal, some began to call him hypocrite, fake, a man with one side for his African constituents and another for his white French benefactors. Sometimes the gentle poet and intellectual in France acted as an autocrat with an iron fist in Dakar. Certainly at the height of his fame and power many of his countrymen cursed his name. But, as with all men pushed to the front of the historical stage, Senghor is far too complicated to be cast in a two-dimensional role suitable for easy judgment.

Senghor participated fully in one of the most important historical developments of our century, the transformation of a world dominated by white Europeans into a patchwork quilt in which many peoples are fighting to design their own futures. Sometimes this struggle against Western influence and domination is expressed, as it was in Senghor's case, in the vocabulary of race. At other times it finds expression in the language of Marxism, or of religious faith. Different languages and metaphors may influence the course this transformation takes, but not its essential nature. The holy wars of Islam, the class war of the proletariat, and the struggles of Negritude are all waged to throw off foreign domination and restore self-respect. This process, in one form or another, has influenced the lives of billions of people over the past fifty years. While the specific events Senghor helped to shape now lie in the past, the larger process of which they are a part continues to unfold.

Senghor provides a rare perspective on this transformation. He was one of its leaders and also a gifted poet and writer. He was able to express what he felt and wanted well before he reluctantly took the fateful step into politics. As a poet he spoke with an individual voice that defined and rejected the place prepared for the African by European civilization. He felt that he had a calling to speak for his people, and for all colonized people seeking to throw off the weight of colonial attitudes. As a writer, his chief subject was the meaning and implications of what W. E. B. Du Bois called the twentieth-century color line. It is a line that still exists in many places in subtle and not so subtle ways, between black and white in Europe and the United States and parts of Africa, and between white and yellow and brown in much of Asia. In Senghor's Africa, the color line reinforced the barrier between colonizer and colonized. Everywhere it helps increase the distance between the powerful and the powerless. Before the people of Senegal could move from colony to sovereign nation, they had to change the way they thought about white and black, about France and about themselves. Senghor was one of the first Africans to make this intellectual transition. His writings allow us to see the private man struggling with this issue before he became a public figure, and to watch poetry being transformed into abstract thought and ideology.

To what extent Senghor or any individual is able to deflect or redirect history's course, and to what extent he is caught up in an inexorable tide that sweeps him forward, is a tantalizing question for the student of history. A few great men who appear at times of change manage to articulate the needs and concerns of large numbers of people, to inspire them with hope, and to help bring forth new ways of life. A series of coincidences thrust Senghor into a place where his voice could be heard, and his words resonated among his people. They gave him their support, and he became their spokesman and leader.

It is still difficult to separate the man, Léopold Sédar Senghor, from his legend, a legend he cultivated and that was extended and embellished by both African and French for political purposes. Nor is it yet certain which will prove to be Senghor's most enduring accomplishments, whether he will be remembered primarily as a fine poet or a great statesman, or even how future historians will judge his political policies. What is clear is that Senghor is a valuable witness for a time of historic change. He played an active part in the events that led to the end of the French empire, and he wrote about the psychological and cultural processes that made this change possible.

As the twentieth century draws to a close, Du Bois's prophecy has proved its accuracy. The color line has indeed provoked concern throughout the century. Senghor is among those who have faced that line most directly, felt it, suffered it, challenged it, and transcended it. His testimony seems destined to endure, not because he was typical of his time, but because he is one of its most gifted interpreters.

1

Childhood

Léopold Sédar Senghor was born in Joal, a small coastal town in the French African territory of Senegal. His birth was recorded on October 9, 1906. At that moment, according to a tale now told by the Senghor family, a large baobab tree near the town cracked and fell to the ground. The great spirit that had inhabited the tree had identified a new person in whom to dwell. This story is now a secure part of family tradition. When it began to be told, however, is not sure.[1] It suggests some of the difficulty of sifting the facts from the myths about this remarkable man.

In a poem he wrote in his early fifties, Senghor himself suggests less remarkable beginnings, as well as some of the richness and complexity of his experience:

> Lord, you have made me the Master of language
> Me, son of a merchant, sickly and gray at birth
> My mother called me Impudent, so did I offend the beauty of the day.
> You in Your unequal justice have given me the power of the word.[2]

From the poet's point of view, greatness was not preordained from birth. He had no noble birth, no natural grace or beauty. He portrays his own mother expressing doubts about her new son by calling him Sédar, a name that means "impudent" or "he who is without shame." The name itself is ambiguous. Is Sédar without shame because, as the poem suggests, he is impudent, ugly, and puny? Or is he without shame because he will grow up into a man of great distinction who has every right to be proud of his accomplishments? What the poet tells us unequivocally is that he has been given a true gift from God: the power of the word.

Joal is in the modern state of Senegal, a chunk cut out of the bulge of West Africa. Senegal is a small country known best perhaps for its elegant capital city, Dakar, which reaches out into the Atlantic at Africa's most western point. The country has a territory of approximately 76,000 square miles, making it larger than England and Wales taken together, but only about half the size of California. Most of Senegal's people are Wolof by ethnicity and Muslim by religion, but there are several ethnic minorities, as well as Christians and animists, within its borders. Senghor's family, Serer by ethnicity and Christian by religion, was in the minority on both counts.

Senegal is not a rich land. At its northern border, the valley of the Senegal River is fertile when the swollen river recedes after the rains, but north of the valley the land is desert. That region, called the Sahel, is known for its droughts, its relentless sun, and the hunger of its peoples. Beyond the river valley to the south, in Senegal itself, the land is dry savannah. There, too, there is drought and sometimes famine. Farther to the south, the savannah gradually supports more growth and merges with forest in an area of moderate rainfall. There the land is richer, the rains more reliable. Throughout the entire area, agriculture depends on seasonal rains. When they fail, as has been increasingly true in modern times, people go hungry and the desert edges southward. Historical maps of the area reveal an ominous trend, for many of the great African empires of the past flourished in areas to the north and west of Senegal that are now desert. The fabulous city of Timbuktu is now surrounded by sand.

The region around Joal, which Senghor often invoked as the kingdom of childhood, is flat, dusty and hot in the dry season, its cover of acacia trees punctuated by great termite earth mounds and the giant baobab. This tree dominates the horizon. It plants its elephantine trunk solidly in the ground and depends for survival on short seasonal rains. These trees, like people, grow rapidly upward striving toward the sun in youth, and then, with age, add girth. Then their branches grow tough and gnarled, as if struggling for greater reach, and each develops a shape of its own. Bare for much of the year, the baobab puts forth leaves, flowers, and fruit in the few brief months of the rainy season. Its bark is used to make cord, its leaves are added to the staple food, millet, to enrich it with vitamins, and its fruit is used to make a sauce with medicinal properties. The versatility of the tree, its capacity to survive, its large size and longevity, and the remarkable individuality of each tree combine to make the baobab venerated by the Serer people. The first French visitors were also impressed by the baobab, and wrote home that the trees looked as if they had been there since before Noah's flood. St. Exupéry recognized the magic of the baobab in *The Little Prince*. Today botanists say that the baobab can live up to four thousand years. The Serer associate powerful ancestral spirits with the most ancient of the trees. Hence the family myth of the cracking of one such tree at Senghor's birth and the decision of its spirit to dwell in a young child predestined for greatness.

When Léopold Sédar Senghor was born, the French claimed a vast territory in West Africa that extended hundreds of miles into the interior, but their effective control was confined to a few coastal towns, and even there it depended on the cooperation of the indigenous population backed up by the threat of a small military garrison. Only traders, missionaries, and occasional members of scientific or military expeditions ventured into the pestilent interior. In the great majority of the inland villages such as Djilor, where Senghor spent his early childhood, the French impact was but indirectly felt. Even Joal, the coastal town to which Sédar Senghor's father brought his wife for the birth of her fifth son, had few French residents, and they in no way dominated the social life of the town. Joal was a thriving center of the peanut trade. Cultivators from the inland villages brought their peanut crop there to be weighed and sold. Native merchants such as Sédar's father and older brothers collected the farmers' peanuts and piled them up into towering mountains of peanuts, called *seccos,* which they then sold to large export companies based in Bordeaux. Between harvest time in November and the first seasonal rains in May, Senegalese boatmen would gradually deplete the seccos by transferring heavy burlap sacks filled with the peanuts to their dugout canoes rigged with sail. In these small but sturdy craft, they maneuvered south to the mouth of the Saloum River and upstream past the channel islands to the river port of Foundiougne. There the peanuts were reloaded into oceangoing vessels and taken to France. Oil from Senegal was in great demand among the soapmakers of Marseilles, who found it ideal for their blue-marbled soap. Pure peanut oil was also the cooking oil of choice for discriminating French cooks, who preferred it because it does not burn.

On this trade, men like Senghor's father, Basile Diogoye Senghor, grew rich. Diogoye Senghor—Diogoye means "the lion" in Serer—

was one of the clever and ambitious Africans who won the trust of the French exporters without losing the confidence of the Senegalese cultivators. As go-between, he translated each to the other. Through his hand flowed crops from the threatening and disease-ridden interior to the sea and then to France. Crops were exchanged for French money, for which the local population found increasing use. The reward for Diogoye's ability was wealth. He had money, which he lent to the cultivators in hard times; he owned fields and many head of cattle. In Joal he lived in a large house on the main thoroughfare, a house constructed of white limestone. Blind to the street, it opened on an ample courtyard. Behind his walls and green-latticed screens, Diogoye ruled over several wives and many children with the authority of the rich and successful patriarch of Serer country.

Chance had played an important part in Diogoye's decision to turn to trade. It was an unusual choice of occupation for a man of his generation. He had been a hunter in his youth, like his father before him. This was the traditional occupation for a man of his birth and family. He was reasonably good at it, and made an adequate living hunting the antelope and game birds that were abundant in the woods around Joal. One day while he was out hunting, a tragedy befell the young father, or so it seemed at the time: his gun misfired and the explosion severed his index finger. He could no longer hunt and so had no means of support.

There were at this time along the "petite côte," the coastal region where Diogoye Senghor lived, representatives of the French trading companies. One of them, a Monsieur Mourland, lived in Joal with his wife, a woman of mixed French and African parentage from Gorée. Mourland saw in Diogoye's misfortune an opportunity to recruit a good employee, and also to help a man in need. He offered Diogoye a job with his company. With no possibility of pursuing his traditional livelihood, and with a young family to feed, Diogoye accepted this offer. He became the African representative of Maurel Frères, a French trading company based in Bordeaux.

Once Mourland's trade in Joal was well established, he sent Diogoye to Djilor, an inland village some twenty kilometers from Joal, to encourage the cultivators there to change over from their traditional agriculture to growing peanuts as a cash crop for export. At first Diogoye had little success. As a man from the town and a stranger, he was viewed with suspicion. Ambitious, resourceful, even desperate, Diogoye used his knowledge of custom and human nature: he went to the headman of the village and asked to marry his daughter. He was accepted. From that moment his enterprise prospered. He began to divide his time between his village household and his other wives and children who lived in the big house in Joal.

This new wife, his youngest and last, was Gnylane Bakhoum. It was she who became the mother of Léopold Sédar Senghor. There is some question as to whether she was of Peul or Serer background.[3] People of both groups lived together in the village. Her brother, the beloved Toko Waly of Senghor's later poetry, was a shepherd. Gnylane Bakhoum Senghor was quiet and reserved. She greatly prized her peace and independence and must have been of resolute character, for she withstood her husband's repeated attempts to persuade her to move to Joal and live in the big house with the rest of his family. She preferred to run her small household in her own fashion, and not become entangled in the intrigue and rivalries that almost inevitably spring up in a large African household in which several wives and their children jockey for favor. In the village she could preserve her independence and also be useful to her husband, for she ran the business when he was in Joal.

Basile Diogoye Senghor was a success. He put together a considerable fortune and founded a large family, which he ran with equity and authority, so gaining the respect of all those who came into contact with him. He was known for his skill in divining and in predicting the future, as well as in enlisting the support of ancestral spirits on behalf of his own family. People came from throughout the area to seek him out for his healing abilities. Yet he was also a friend of the Europeans and practiced their religion, Catholicism. For his family, as in his trade, he acted as a go-between, a transitional figure between the traditional world of village Africa and the new world symbolized by the mountains of peanuts outside his store and the Catholic missions that were growing up along the coast.

The Christian community of Joal to which Diogoye belonged had a long and somewhat mixed history. Occasional missionaries, first Portuguese and then French, had passed along the coast in the sixteenth and seventeenth centuries, leaving fragments of their belief behind them. By the middle of the nineteenth century, there was a definite community of "Christians"—so they called themselves—in Joal. It was described vividly by the Abbé Boilat, who lived among them briefly in the middle of the nineteenth century. "To be a Christian of Joal," he wrote, "is to have numerous privileges. It is to be noble

. . . to be as free as the birds that fly along the river banks . . . it is the right to annoy and to be annoyed by no one."[4] The Christians of Joal claimed Portuguese ancestry, although, Boilat observed, they were indistinguishable physically from the other inhabitants of the place. Among the special privileges they claimed were immunity from all traditional control, and the rights of the white man. Of the latter, the most important was the right to drink hard liquor, a practice not known traditionally and forbidden to Muslims, the religion to which many Africans were converting at this time. In trying to convince Boilat they were really Christians, they argued that drinking alcohol set them apart from the Muslims and proved them worthy Christians. More practically, they had managed to monopolize all trade in liquor, tobacco, and gunpowder and so controlled an important source of wealth with which to sustain their elite position.

Of true Christianity, Boilat continued indignantly, they had no understanding whatsoever. The blessing had, by some curious evolution, come to be in the name of the Father, the Son, and an unrecognizable personality called Aspi Sisoti (presumably from *spiritu sancti*). They prayed to their father "quatre aux yeux" (four-eyed), perhaps from the phrase "qui êtes aux cieux," (who art in heaven) in the Lord's prayer, and muttered incantations in a cabalistic language known only to themselves which seemed to be a mixture of Serer and Wolof, two local languages, with a few words of Portuguese thrown in. In this account of Joal about the time Diogoye Senghor was born, Boilat mentions several "Christians" by name—Michel, Domingo, and Francisco—but no one by the name of Senghor. Whether Diogoye's father was among these Joal Christians is not known. The outstanding characteristics of this group, however, drunkenness, quick talking, deviousness, and trickery, are certainly not those for which later Senghors wished to be remembered.

By the time of Diogoye's adulthood, Boilat and other French missionaries had succeeded in establishing a more recognizable form of Christianity, but only in defiance of the "Christians" of Joal, who understandably resented the undermining of the spiritual power they had spuriously derived from the Western religion. To achieve their goal, the missionaries had to appeal to the traditional king of the region against the entrenched "Christians," and Boilat himself traveled to the interior to seek the king's permission to build a church and a mission in Joal. This support, combined with the judicious use of brandy to buy off the old "Christian" community and attract members to the new, won converts for the ever resourceful Boilat, who nonetheless apologized anxiously to his superiors for resorting to such primitive methods to achieve his Christian end.[5]

The Catholic missionaries active in Joal wisely continued to recognize limits on what they could ask of their followers. If the Abbé Boilat had had the flexibility to attract new converts with brandy, the missionaries of Diogoye's day were wise enough to accept men like Diogoye, who had several wives and continued to turn to his ancestral spirits for strength and guidance. They ignored any incongruity they might have noticed in the image cut by Diogoye as he set out for Mass in his top hat, stiff white collar, and tailor-made black European suit—followed by several wives and about two dozen children. Diogoye took what he liked from Christianity. He baptized his children in the faith, adding, for example, the Christian name Léopold to the Serer name, Sédar, by which Léopold Sédar Senghor has always been known, but he paid scant attention to Christian practices that did not suit him. Catholicism was successful among the Serer of Sine because it proved willing to coexist with vital and continuing traditional beliefs, as it has done in Mexico and many other parts of the world.

The annual celebration of First Communions provided a dramatic example of this creative weave of old and new. On May 24, 1913, the year Sédar was six, the records of the Joal mission indicate that more than 160 people gathered at the church in the morning to celebrate 27 who were taking their First Communion. In the evening there was a great procession accompanied by chanting and musical instruments in which all of Joal, Christian, animist, and Muslim, took part. The evening procession gathered at two points on the main street, one under the flamboyant tree next to Mme Mourland's house, the other across the street near the house of Diogoye Senghor.[6] It was an event that all the town celebrated with local music and chanting, and in which all were invited to play a part. This particular account confirms Diogoye Senghor's importance and the fact that his house was considered a landmark, located right across the street from that of the French commercial representative in the town.

Diogoye Senghor himself went to church and so showed respect to the Christian God. But he did not ignore the older gods of his family. He instructed his children never to kill or harm a serpent, for these creatures were, he believed, sacred, and closely linked to the prosperity of the Senghors. Family tradition records that whenever an important event occurred in the family, notably at every death, a snake or a large lizard would appear in the courtyard of the big house in Joal. It was important to set out milk and other tempting fare to please this creature. Diogoye also remembered his ancestors every year by sacrificing cattle to their spirits. After his death this responsibility passed to the eldest male member of the family, as his obligation to the common ancestor who would ensure the good fortune of all Senghors. This tradition must be continued, as one of Diogoye's grandchildren, a graduate of a French university and a resident of Paris, explained: "There are troubling things, things that are inexplicable, in Africa. It would not do to ignore this tradition of our family."

However determined to guard his family from the malevolent spirits of the Joal countryside and to strengthen the power of its protecting ancestor, Diogoye also saw the need for his children to prosper in the world of the French. Unable to read and write himself, beyond the crucial ability to add figures, he saw to it that his children went to the new schools set up by the missionaries. Perhaps this determination flowed from his powers of foresight and divination, to which his family always referred, for most Africans of his generation distrusted the missionaries and engaged in ingenious deceptions and delays to avoid sending their children to mission schools or the special secular schools established by the French for the sons of chiefs. Indeed, the missionaries and the French secular administration of the time complained that they had difficulty filling their schools. The village peoples felt no need for education. In Serer country, recruitment was particularly difficult. One schoolmaster reported that the Serer were very hostile to the French cause and, as they were also very primitive, did not wish to attend school.[7] As a go-between who had prospered, Diogoye Senghor felt differently. He sent his children to school to learn to be successful men of commerce.

Of course, the French missionaries who ran the schools had a different goal in mind. Their education was designed to create Christians, not traders. What French secular education did exist was intended to provide literate functionaries to man the lower rungs of the colonial bureaucracy and serve as clerks in the great houses of commerce. Africans were to be trained so that they could, and would, efficiently carry out the orders of their French superiors. As it turned out, the strong will of Diogoye and his sons prevailed over their French teachers on this matter. Diogoye realized his vision and saw his many sons become independent traders stationed throughout Senegal to form a family trade network. There was, nevertheless, one important exception. One of his youngest sons moved beyond his father's vision. Sédar Senghor rejected the world of commerce for that of letters, and later for politics.

Léopold Sédar Senghor, always called Sédar by his family and friends, was the fifth of the six children of Basile Diogoye Senghor and his wife from Djilor, Gnylane Bakhoum. Diogoye was an old man when this son was born in 1906, already father to more than two dozen children by several wives. Nonetheless, family tradition has it that at Sédar's birth his father predicted greatness for him: "The day when the giant birds go in the sky carrying people on their back and the day when the great snake can go from here all the way to Mali carrying people, that day my son will be one of the greatest men of Africa." In a day when airplanes and trains crisscross Africa, Diogoye's son is indeed one of its greatest men. This story has the ring of the apocryphal, but it is now a secure part of the tradition that has grown up to illustrate the foresight of the family patriarch and the fact that a great destiny was foretold for Sédar from the beginning. Such stories have come to surround Sédar Senghor as part of a legitimizing myth of preordained greatness. They place him within the realm of heroes sanctified by traditional means.

Although Gnylane Bakhoum had gone to the big house in Joal for the birth of her fifth child, she soon returned to Djilor, and it was in that village that Sédar spent his first seven years. Djilor was then and is today what urban Senegalese call scornfully "the bush." It was a small Serer village inhabited by illiterate cultivators, artisans, cattle-keepers, and a few traders who had learned to deal in the peanut trade. There was little visible French presence in the village apart from the growing tendency to grow peanuts for export rather than millet or other food for the local market. Serer villages like Djilor preserved their cohesion well into the twentieth century. Today these Serer villagers are still known for their simple agricultural virtues: hard work, stubbornness, and the skilled working of the land. The proud Wolof, the most populous ethnic group in contemporary Senegal, consider the Serer peasants in the pejorative sense of that word, dismissing their self-discipline and hard work as pedestrian. Be that as it may, the Serer developed a stable social order that successfully resisted both cultural and military pressures, and maintained their economic self-sufficiency. Early conversion to Christianity in no way destroyed traditional methods of sharing power and resources, methods that worked admirably to preserve a roughly egalitarian community.

The basic social unit into which Sédar Senghor was born was the family. This is true for peoples throughout West Africa. The Serer family is far larger than the European family, and includes all descendants of a common ancestor, those now alive and those now dead. The head of the family, the oldest living descendant of the ancestor, acts as a link between the living and the dead. Thus the family forms a great chain, which mounts from the youngest to the oldest living descendant of the family founder, through this family patriarch to those ancestors now dead, and, ultimately to powerful deities. Often an animal or a tree is integrated into this clan and, as were the snake and lizard by the Senghor family, treated with special care and respect by all its members. In defending this practice, the "totemism" much ridiculed by Europeans, Senghor later argued that the African's "famous totemism . . . is monstrous only in appearance. What is inhuman is to isolate man from his milieu, to domesticate the animal and the tree. In Europe this domestication goes to the point of a destruction which breaks the equilibrium of nature and engenders catastrophes."[8] In Africa, living and dead, man and creature, form and sustain important relationships that are both real and symbolic recognitions of their common participation in a single natural world.

The mother's family is particularly important among the Serer of Sine. It is the source of noble birth, and it also influences day-to-day relationships. In Djilor, Sédar was always Sédar Gnylane, or Sédar, son of Gnylane. From his mother came family membership and social position, and, according to village practice, from her brother would come rights to land and cattle. From his father might come movable goods such as furniture and personal possessions. Although patriarchal French law and Christian and Muslim traditions have all worked to weaken the matrilateral tie, Sédar's mother and her family played the decisive role in his early childhood. Only later did his father, Diogoye, succeed in establishing patriarchal control over his son.

The family and the village followed the traditions of the Serer. The Serer people were divided, as were other ethnic groups of the area, into three main social groups: noble, free, and slave. The nobles, or *guelowars,* were believed to be descended from the Malinké warriors who had conquered the area in the fourteenth century. When Senghor was a child in Djilor, the majority of the local population was made up of Serer freemen, but there were also slaves, who fell into several different categories depending on whether they had been purchased, captured, or born to slave parents.

The political and social organization of Sédar Senghor's people was a particularly equitable and successful one, which served to maintain peace in the area for several hundred years. No single element set one individual above all others from birth. To be king of Sine, a man had to be born the son of a woman of noble lineage, but also to have those personal qualities necessary to be selected by other freemen. He had to be acceptable to the leaders of the slave community as well. This arrangement both reflected and maintained a balance of social forces, and was built on consensus rather than force, blood, or divine assignation. The fact that hereditary right to social position passed through the mother's side of the family further inhibited the concentration of power, for it prevented a powerful and successful father from passing his position to his son unless he was able through marriage to ally himself with a noble family. Once chosen, the king ruled in consultation with representatives of both free and slave communities. Slaves made up his administrative staff. They therefore exercised considerable power, but they were ineligible to rule in their own right. Hence leadership among the Serer was the reward of the person able to balance interests and work out compromises agreeable to several different groups. The abilities to balance, compromise, and lead were synonymous. Such was the political culture of the community in which Senghor spent his childhood.

These institutions that dispersed political power were supported by other features of Serer life. Intermarriage among the different social strata, noble, free, and slave, was fairly common, and migrants from other ethnic groups were assimilated with little hostility. Sédar Senghor was identified by himself and others as a Serer, for example, and yet he had a Malinké grandfather from the upper Gambia and possibly a Peul mother, and also a father with a Portuguese name. Furthermore, the Serer did not develop the caste divisions based on occupation that had become common among the Wolof of Senegal by the early twentieth century. They therefore had fewer inhibitions than did other peoples of the region about turning from cultivation or cattlekeeping to other occupations. Diogoye, for example, became a trader without having to sacrifice his high traditional status. The result was a relatively egalitarian and culturally homogeneous society with few social distinctions that might hinder adaptation to a changing economy.[9]

Such were the varied traditions that surrounded Sédar as a small child. His own family made up a childhood world in which different claims had to be recognized, those of mother, uncle, and father. He had to learn early the ability to recognize what was appropriate to each, and to discipline his own wishes in order to live harmoniously within the group. Beyond his family lay the village and the Serer political kingdom, worlds in which leaders were recognized and admired for their ability to find consensus among representatives of different social strata. Harmony was the most important social goal. In the distance, Sédar also glimpsed his father's world, in which there was an intermingling of new and old, Europe and Africa. Senghor later drew on all these resources in developing his own personal and political style. When he became a student in Paris, he instinctively reached out to bring different groups of people together, and to find common ground among differing points of view rather than to out-argue or oppose them. Later, as president of Senegal, he tried to bring leaders of the opposition into his government whenever possible rather than alienate them further through exclusion. This is a political style quite different from that of many African politicians of his generation, and it proved the key to Senghor's longevity. No doubt he learned much about politics from observing Blaise Diagne, deputy from Senegal to the French National Assembly, whom he often visited while a student in Paris. Later he learned first-hand about political compromise and deal-making when serving as a deputy himself. Nonetheless, an equally powerful model for a conciliatory and consensus-seeking approach existed in the village of Djilor and among the Serer of Sine.

As a small child, Sédar rarely saw his father, a situation quite typical for Serer children of his generation. His earliest years were spent in and around his mother's house, watching her pound the millet to prepare the family's food, perhaps later tagging along with her or an older sister to fetch water or wash clothes. In the evenings he would listen to older brothers and uncles recount the day's happenings or tell tales of the exploits of his family, or of folk heroes, or of the Serer kings whom his family had served. He heard of one who had so chafed under a woman king that he left her entourage to settle in Mbissel, where he founded a new kingdom, and of another who had served as an important advisor to Koumba Ndofène Diouf in a victorious war againts Islamic invaders fought some forty years before Sédar's birth.[10] A descendant of this heroic leader, also named Koumba Ndofène Diouf, once visited Sédar's father. His presence made a strong impression on the child's imagination. In one of his later poems, Senghor celebrated the dignity and power of the traditional African king. The source of this vision is clear:

Koumba Ndofène Diouf ruled in Diakhaw, a proud vassal
And governed the administrator of Sine-Saloum
The sound of his ancestors and the royal drums proceeded him
The royal pilgrim traveled through his provinces, listening to
    murmured grievances in the wood
. . . . .
He called my father uncle. They exchanged riddles carried by
    greyhounds with golden bells
Cousins in peace, they exchanged gifts on the shore of the Saloum
Precious pelts, bars of salt and gold from Bouré, and gold from
    Boundou
And council high, like horses of the river . . .[11]

The vision of Koumba Ndofène Diouf ruling the white French administrator of the region lodged in Sédar's memory, as did the mysterious
ritual and opulence of Diouf's entourage. Sédar saw there a proud
culture, and one to which the French paid homage. That such a great
man should be on such close terms with his father confirmed Sédar's
sense of the importance of his own lineage.

The impressions of these childhood years surfaced later in much of
Senghor's poetry.

I remember the days of my fathers, the evenings of Djilor
That deep-blue light of the night sky on the land sweet at evening.
I am on the steps of homestead. Deep inside it is dark.
My brothers and sisters like chicks huddle their numerous warmth
    against my heart
I rest my head on the knees of Ngâ, Ngâ the poetess
. . . . .
And my father stretched lying on the quiet mat, but tall but strong
    but handsome
Man of the Kingdom of Sine, whilst all around on the *kôras,*
    heroic voices, the *griots* set dancing their mettlesome
    fingers
Whilst in the distance arises surging with strong warm smells, the
    classic murmur of a hundred herds.[12]

This atmosphere of peace and quiet splendor remained always with
Senghor. It lies at the core of what he called "the kingdom of childhood," to which he returned again and again for poetic inspiration.

If Senghor remembers his father as strong, as handsome, as noble,
the guardian of his childhood peace, he was also a distant father. Sédar
spent more time as a very small child following his mother's brother,

Waly, about in the fields. Waly, the shepherd, introduced Sédar to the world beyond the courtyard, to Senghor and Bakhoum ancestors from the Sine and the Gambia, and to the spirits of trees, rocks, and fountains.

> Toko Waly, my uncle, do you remember those distance nights when
>   my head grew heavy against the patience of your back?
> Or when holding me by the hand, your hand led me through the
>   shadows and signs?
> The fields are flowers of glow worms; the stars come to rest on the
>   grass, on the trees.
> . . . . .
> But You, Toko Waly, hear what is beyond hearing
> You explain to me the signs that the Ancestors give in the calm seas
>   of the constellations
> The Bull, the Scorpion, the Leopard, the Elephant and the familiar
>   Fishes
> And the milky ceremony of the Spirits along the unending shores of
>   heaven.[13]

His eagerness to be with Waly, to walk with him and ask him questions, led in the end to Sédar's being wrenched away from his fields. Early in the morning, before it was light, Sédar would wake and slip away from his own house without anyone knowing it. Through the fields he would hurry to where his uncle Waly slept. There he would wake his uncle, pressing him to get up and go out into the fields. At first Waly must have been surprised that a child of six or barely seven would come all that way through the dark alone so early. Perhaps he was a bit annoyed to be awakened from his own sleep. He would persuade Sédar to go back to sleep with him until it was time to go out into the fields. Then the child would follow his wondrous uncle, asking him about the trees and the birds, about how to do things and care for animals. At noon, when the sun was hot and dangerous spirits were apt to wander abroad, the two would gather the animals around them and seek the shade of the tamarind tree. Such days were far more exciting than those in his mother's house or in the shop in town. It was from Waly that Senghor first learned about his own world and the Serer ideal: to be a man of honor, self-respect, and self-mastery.

Sédar's mother was frightened the first morning she discovered that her son had disappeared. Initially upset, then worried by these odd ways, she eventually was simply annoyed as the habit persisted. It was

Sédar's father who put an end to this pastoral way of life. No doubt the patriarch Diogoye, who had already made merchants of his older sons, disliked the idea of this vagabond who preferred to dream or climb trees, or to trot through the fields behind an illiterate shepherd, rather than to stay at home or in the shop where he belonged, and especially a son who sneaked out of the house before anyone was awake to stop him. He had little thought to admire the courage or independence of such a son. A rivalry between natural father and maternal uncle, quite frequent in matrilateral societies such as the Serer, may have increased his displeasure. In any event, Diogoye determined to put a stop to these goings-on and "in order to punish me and to straighten me out, sent me off to the white school, much to the despair of my mother, who protested that at seven it was much too soon."[14] Sédar would go to school in Joal.

Sédar is said to have accepted the decision with equanimity. The rule of the lion, Diogoye, was not to be questioned. Nonetheless, one would expect a child of seven to be frightened at the prospect of leaving his family for an unknown town twenty-three kilometers away, there to stay with a friend of his father's whom he had never met. Sédar's older sister Dior recalls taking him to Joal in a horse-driven cart that belonged to the family, much like those which still occasionally pass up and down the main streets of Joal, jingling their bells to warn passers-by of their approach. Dior was surprised that her little brother showed no regret at all on leaving home.[15] He only seemed curious to see what lay beyond the village. All the way to Joal he sat silently in the carriage, gazing intently at all they passed: baobabs, acacia, flowers, birds, the giant termite hills of that land, the scattered houses, the shrine at Mbissel where lie the tombs of the Serer kings of Sine. In Joal, Sédar went to live in the household of his father's friend Bouré Diouf, who had been forewarned that Sédar was difficult and had promised Diogoye that he would put this unruly country child into a mission school. There Sédar would learn to take the place in the world his father had in mind for him. Sédar set out for his first class in the French school knowing not a word of the French language.

Seven years of childhood virtually without constraint, years free to wander the countryside, to dream, to learn, to ask questions of a wise elder, to listen in the evenings to the tales of his family, abruptly ended. In Joal, Sédar was entrusted to Father Léon Dubois, who introduced him to Christianity, to France, and more particularly to Normandy. He learned a few words of French, as well as Wolof, the language of Senegal's dominant ethnic group. This was not yet systematic education. Nonetheless Father Dubois laid a claim on Sédar, expecting the boy to do his errands and give his needs priority over those of his family. Senghor later recalled the "brutality" with which Dubois sent away one of his brothers who came to fetch him one day to help his father.[16] Sédar's first direct contact with a Frenchman brought with it a new type of discipline characteristic of a different way of life. The rupture with his childhood world was completed the next year, when Sédar was sent to board at a mission school run by the Fathers of the Holy Spirit at Ngazobil, six kilometers north of Joal.

In 1914 Ngazobil was a fine jewel in the missionary crown. It was the model and outpost of the order of the Fathers of the Holy Spirit. The Holy Spirit Order had been founded before the French revolution. In 1848 it had allied itself with an order founded by Father Libermann expressly to serve black people of Africa. He urged the missionaries "to be black with the blacks, in order to win them for Jesus Christ." The mission at Ngazobil had been established in 1863 by the bishop of all French missions, who was granted by the French civil authority a concession of a thousand hectares of land and a guarantee of military protection.[17] This fit the general policy of that most energetic and renowned governor general of West Africa, Louis Faidherbe, who at that time was trying to extend French control to the south of Dakar. Here church and state moved hand in hand, state granting to church part of a job too large for state to do by itself.

The mission grew rapidly at first. With the help of a few Christian Africans from nearby Joal, seven Fathers of the order first built a solid masonry building for housing and worship and then cleared land for cotton cultivation. This time, the 1860s, was a period of war and drought among the Serer of the Sine-Saloum, and refugees flocked to the mission for food and protection. They built houses nearby, and a Christian from Joal became headman of the growing village. Soon there were upward of two hundred Africans employed by the mission in growing cotton. Roads were laid out, a loading platform built, a trade school and a primary school established.

Setbacks at Ngazobil mirrored those of all French enterprises in this inhospitable climate. Yellow fever was endemic. Drought and clouds of locusts might strike several years in a row, devastating the fields. The patient monks were sorely tested. After several successive years of particularly severe locust infestation, the bishop from Dakar was called to Ngazobil. He gathered the missionaries and their villagers together, urging them to remember with humility that they were but instruments in the hands of God, whose ways were ever inscrutable. He then planted several large wooden crosses to mark the limits of the mission grounds, and solemnly pronounced the rarely used formula for exorcism, officially approved by Pope Benedict XIV. A few months later, a cloud of insects appeared on the horizon but passed over the mission fields to the forest beyond, and the mission completed its harvest. "Since then," one of the Fathers recorded, "our fields have been preserved from all ravages, and the yellow fever has not returned."[18]

By the time Sédar arrived as a student, the Fathers of the Holy Spirit had cleared a wide area of forest, formerly the province of lion and elephant, and transformed it into a populous settlement surrounded by fertile fields. The mission buildings, with their white stucco walls and orange tile roofs set up on a small promontory overlooking the Atlantic breakers, presented at first glance a neat miniature of the south of France. There was a small seminary, a novitiate, two orphanages, shops for metalworking and woodworking, two chapels, a primary school, and even a stone fountain at a spring where elephants came to drink. But this appearance of European prosperity belied the struggle necessary to maintain it in its tropical surroundings. Simple survival required stubborn determination on the part of the missionaries. They had to be almost entirely self-sufficient, for the rainy season made roads impassible, and travel at other times retained its adventurous side. Bush encroached on the fields, sickness and fever beset the Fathers of the order and the nuns who had joined them, and buildings crumbled away under the rains and the sun's heat. Wood fell victim to termites; mortar simply fell apart because the water with which it was mixed was too salty. Nonetheless, the missionaries struggled to "spread moral instruction and the love of work . . . and to establish regular family relations and property, the fundamental bases of any human society as well as of true religion."[19]

Academic instruction at Ngazobil began, and often stayed, at a rudimentary level. The missionaries knew both Serer and Wolof and used these languages in most of their teaching. The children chanted in rhythm the formulas of the catechism, usually in Wolof, and it was in this way that Sédar first learned to speak what is now the dominant language of Senegal. Once the children had learned the text, the missionaries began its explication using proverbs and stories of

everyday life as illustration. Because the colonial administration had
recently instituted a policy that put increasing pressure on the mission
schools to secularize their educational programs, the eight-year-old
Sédar also began to learn French, history, geography, and math. The
singing of hymns and canticles played a big part in the program,
because the missionaries had noticed that the Africans loved music.
Sédar remembered particularly one soaring soprano voice and the
music of the choir, which seemed to him then as an earthly echo of
what heaven promised the believer.[20] He enjoyed the singing and
continued to sing in a choir after he moved to Dakar.

At this time, there was considerable debate over the goals and
possibilities of native education. Most educators assumed that the
native could not fully assimilate the French language or give up his
former modes of thought. Some concluded that it would be more
sensible to give a rudimentary practical instruction in the native languages rather than to attempt the impossible task of teaching French.
But they were overruled: instruction in French became a priority.
"The French rightly regard their civilization as being of great cultural
value," wrote a young Harvard professor sent out to survey the condition of the French and British colonies in the 1920s. "They believe
that the natives, having learned the French language, will think like
Frenchmen and will thereby be bound by a cultural tie to the
'metropole.'" But the policy had its problematic side. One outstanding
French colonial educator, Georges Hardy, worried that the African
child taught French begins to live "in two separate worlds: the real
world from which he has come and to which he is passionately
attached by the language of the country; and an artificial world—a
temporary existence where he for the time being comes into contact
with the French language."[21] Most Africans in the schools gained only
a superficial understanding of French, and with it a thin cultural
veneer. Nonetheless a very small group, destined to become the elite
of the colony, developed emotional and cultural ties to France that
reinforced the colonial, political ones. For this group, including Sédar
Senghor, France's educational policy was a success, for it did bind
them to France. They came to love the French language and culture,
but they also suffered from living in the two separate worlds that
Hardy had identified.

The children entrusted to Ngazobil in Sédar's day were fortunate
in having Father Fulgence to oversee them. He was a man for all
seasons, said a nun who served with him, practical, energetic, and

ingenious in meeting challenges that ranged from broken equipment and insufficient water supply to the invasions of lizards into class-rooms. He rigged up a windmill, for example, to power a pump, and designed a system of water-tight catchment tubs to solve one of the worst problems the mission faced, that of a long dry season without water. He also invented a small press to squeeze cooking oil from the local peanuts. But he was especially admired for his bravery. The tale was often told how he had one night sought out and shot a huge lizard that had long terrified the nuns. Down-to-earth and practical himself, Father Fulgence saw to it that the children learned about their own world as well as that of their schoolbooks. They were required to help with all chores, from washing dishes to taking care of the animals and tending the gardens and fruit trees.[22] Later, in his informal talks with the villagers of the bush, Sédar Senghor was able to draw on this knowledge of local agriculture and animal husbandry learned at Ngazobil. He understood the patience and skill needed to eke out an existence from the soil.[23] Father Fulgence also loved to hunt, and spent his afternoons rambling over the countryside in search of monkey, duck, panther, and even elephant. He often took one of his pupils with him, and it was he who taught Sédar to shoot. Sédar developed this skill, as had Diogoye Senghor before him, but Sédar learned his skill from a priest of Ngazobil rather than from his own father. Somewhat later, when home on a short vacation with his cousins in Joal, he took great pride in shooting a duck to provide for supper.

Not all the Fathers were as broad-minded or good-humored as Father Fulgence. Father Ledouaron had a much narrower view of the proper education for black children and set a stringent policy of accepting only those children who had "sufficient moral and intellec-tual qualities and in whom it is possible to see signs of a special vocation." Sédar easily passed this test, as he was curious and hard working and assimilated new ideas quickly, but he could not entirely escape Father Ledouaron's sharp tongue. Father Ledouaron had grown peevish under his tropical responsibilities and took out his frustration on his pupils. He suffered isolation badly and was partially disabled by an intractable paralysis that no doubt increased his ill humor. His great pleasure lay in playing the organ, which he did very well. His great peculiarity, remembered long after his death, was an unusual taste for eating bats. It appears that he had little gift for fostering the growth of his charges. At one point his superior wrote that he showed "a tendency to criticize the blacks, his pupils, and sometimes discourage them with stinging words to which he himself attaches little importance, but which have an unfortunate effect on the seminarians."[24]

Sédar flourished in this new life and proved quick in his work. He was somewhat solitary, preferring his books to games with the other boys, more of a listener and a watcher than a child who confided his thoughts to others. He was particularly sensitive to criticism. He could not bear that anyone make fun of him and did not hesitate to "defend his honor." This sometimes led to fistfights. Later, he recalled with obvious pride numerous skirmishes with other boys, one of the most memorable of which took place the day of his First Communion.[25] Insults from teachers such as Ledouaron, however, required another strategy. Sédar reacted with self-control and the determination to work even harder to prove that such criticisms were undeserved.

Despite this somewhat mixed experience, Sédar took unto himself the vocation the Fathers had set for him. He decided to become a priest. Perhaps, as suggested by several of his more cynical cousins, he said this simply to get preferred treatment and escape some of the extra manual labor required of students whose vocations were less sure, but it is more likely that Sédar was motivated by honest conviction. He was a pious child, turned toward the church not only by the Fathers, who offered him access to a wide and exciting world through education, but also by the part of his own family he saw most often: the household of Hélène and René Senghor.

Shortly after Sédar entered the mission school at Ngazobil, one of Diogoye's oldest children, Sédar's half-brother René Senghor, moved to Joal with his young wife Hélène. Their household immediately became Sédar's family. It was too far to go all the way to Djilor for holidays, so Sédar stayed with the René Senghors in Joal. René was a man of commerce, following the path set out for him by his father. He had prospered, and with his growing success his stature within the family waxed as well. Diogoye came to depend more and more on his elder son for help in the upbringing of the younger children, a pattern common among large Serer families. René took increasing responsibility for Sédar's welfare. It was he who visited Sédar's teachers, inquired into his progress, and puzzled about the future of this studious half-brother. In several ways he was better placed for this task than Sédar's father. Not only was he younger and living near Sédar's school, but he knew the French world far better than Diogoye did, largely because Diogoye had seen to it that he should. Diogoye moved in two worlds, but stood more firmly on inland African soil than on the sands of the coastal cities dominated by the French. René, however, traveled comfortably from Joal to Dakar to the trading city of Rufisque. He had been to France. He kept a car. His French friends came to the house.

René, like his father, devoted his days to business, so Sédar found himself often in the company of his young sister-in-law Hélène. She and her story are essential to understanding Sédar Senghor.

Chance had played an important part in Hélène's life, as it had in Diogoye's, as it does perhaps in all lives. Her father was a Muslim from the Upper Gambia, a boatman.[26] He often stopped at Joal, where he met and married Hélène's mother, a Catholic Serer. When Hélène's mother married, she gave up her religion for her husband's, as was the custom, and moved to the trading center at Foundioung. Hélène's brothers and sisters were brought up according to the teachings of Islam: the girls kept at home to learn women's occupations, the boys learning Arabic and the Koran from the local Muslim teacher before entering the adult world of work. This was the world that provided the expected pattern for Hélène's life. But an odd circumstance intervened. Hélène's aunt, her mother's sister, had married within the Serer Catholic group. The aunt's husband, a man from Joal, had moved north to the city of Saint-Louis. This couple were greatly disappointed that they were unable to have children. Therefore, as was fairly common, the wife asked if she might take one of her sister's children to bring up, preferably a girl. Hélène was chosen and sent to live with her aunt in Saint-Louis. As a result, Hélène alone of her many brothers and sisters was brought up Catholic rather than Muslim, and attended a Catholic mission school, where she received the finest Western education then available in the colony. She did brilliantly.

Saint-Louis, built on an island at the mouth of the Senegal River, was then the center of French operations in Senegal. Hélène's schooldays there at the turn of the century coincided with the flowering of a distinctive Creole culture.[27] The African Creoles were descended from the first Frenchmen who had taken up residence in West Africa and settled with African wives. Unlike many other Europeans in Africa, these French fathers recognized their children, educated them, often in France, and supported their careers in commerce or the military, or as government functionaries, upon their return to Senegal. From such origins sprang a small, select, and closed group:

the great Creole families of Saint-Louis. They waxed rich on the Senegal River trade, married among themselves, took part in the administrative regulation of the town, and shared power with the metropolitan French. French and Creole alike assumed that Saint-Louis was an important part of a greater France and that the goal of Africans should be to become as much like Frenchmen as possible.

It was the children of this Creole elite whom Hélène joined at St. Joseph de Cluny, a school run by Catholic nuns. Although as a black child Hélène was in a small minority, she took eagerly to school. She passed her first examinations easily and went on to become the first African woman to pass the *brevet,* then the highest examination administered in the colony, and that she did with distinction. Like Sédar Senghor, who later became the first African to become a French university *agrégé,* she stood first in her class. Although girls and boys attended separate schools, they took exams together and competed for prizes with one another. Every year it was Hélène who won the prizes, including the Louis d'Or from the Alliance Française for top mastery of the French language.[28]

Among those Hélène beat out for these prizes was a Muslim from the Sudan, Lamine Guèye. He became one of her friends and was to play an important part in Sédar's later career. Guèye, born in 1891 in what is today Mali, had gone to Koranic school before entering the French school in Saint-Louis. He went on to study law, first in Senegal and then in Paris. After teaching for a few years, he entered the colonial service and served in Réunion and Martinique. He was a worldly and experienced man when he returned to Senegal in the 1930s to try his hand at politics. The colonial administration opposed him for this very reason, recognizing that he was one of the most sophisticated and well-educated Africans of his generation.[29]

Hélène's trajectory proved quite different from that of Lamine Guèye, however. Both her teachers and the examiners who came from Bordeaux to make sure that the local standard met that of metropolitan France were impressed with Hélène's intellectual promise. She was offered a scholarship to go to France to study. Her aunt was stunned; her father and mother refused to consider it. It was rare even for African men to get as far as the brevet, much less to Paris. Hélène recalls that the governor of the colony, Joost Van Vollenhoven himself, called several times at her school and talked with her family to persuade them to let her continue her studies. Van Vollenhoven was convinced that gifted Africans must be encouraged to get a thorough education, for he envisioned a future in which an African elite would govern the masses in close association with the French. Hélène seemed to be an ideal recruit for this select group. "Mademoiselle," he told her, "you are losing a great opportunity." Hélène was longing to go. Her education had taught her more of French history than of Africa. She had been taught that Africa was a blank page, fortunate in being able to receive the message of French civilization. Now she was being offered an opportunity to go to the source of this civilization. All the way to Paris? A fifteen-year-old girl? Her parents were adamant, and even her worldly aunt hesitated.

A temporary compromise was reached. Hélène began a two-year program at the local hospital to learn midwifery. In the third year she was to go to Paris. At the end of this apprenticeship, she bought her clothes and prepared to go. At the last minute, however, her parents again refused to let her leave. Hélène finally saw that she must give up her dream of Paris and make another life for herself. She began by teaching pupils privately at home. Then she was offered a position at a school in Dakar. But in Dakar there was an epidemic of plague. As a friend of the family put it, "It is fine post, Hélène. Take it if you want to die." She wrote the Inspector of Education that she did not want the position after all, and went to work in a shop in Saint-Louis. Through these disappointments, she was sustained by a strong religious belief, and a touch of fatalism. Perhaps God did not want her to go to France.

Hélène's aunt was a distant cousin of the Diogoye Senghor family. As a result, various of the Senghor children visited her in Saint-Louis. Among them were a number of Diogoye's children: Adrien, Pierre, Francis, and René. René and Hélène met, decided to marry, and moved back to René's home in Joal.

To a Saint-Louisienne like Hélène, Joal appeared to be a wild place, the bush. She was accustomed to the sophisticated life of the city. At first she simply stood at her window staring out to sea: "I cried and cried, thinking of what I had missed, of Paris, and felt homesick for Saint-Louis." She felt lonely and isolated in Joal. Diogoye's wives and other children treated her as a foreigner, as indeed she was to them by virtue of her education and intellectual interests. Such was her nature, however, that she gradually turned to the world around her. She met her cousins, tended the garden, and helped with René Senghor's shop. She also found some companionship with the missionaries who served the local church. They became frequent visitors at her house. Fortified by her Catholic belief and an optimistic temperament that taught her to look for some good in every situation, Hélène gradually made a new life for herself in Joal.

It was at this moment that young Sédar Senghor became a frequent visitor in her household. Sédar, then about twelve years old, was already at Ngazobil when Hélène and René came to live in Joal. After their arrival, he spent Sundays and holidays with them. For a while, he was the only child of this well-educated but lonely young woman. Later, he used to joke, he was the eldest of her seven. He chose this as his new family. It was a mutual attraction. Certainly Sédar provided great comfort to Hélène at a difficult time for her. He shared her passion for books and would inquire what she was reading, sneaking off with whatever book she put down when she went to do her chores. He also proved a good listener. Hélène first described for him the great city of Saint-Louis, and then the glittering Paris of her imagination. She told him about the success of her acquaintances, Blaise Diagne, Senegal's first black deputy to the French National Assembly, and Lamine Guèye, who was then at law school in Paris. Sédar became the focus of much of her intellectual and emotional energy, both solace for the present and a hope for the future. Her own children later shared this attention and were taught to look to Sédar as an example. They remember their mother's energy, her exhortation to work hard, her love of French culture, and her reminders that they were children of privilege and should use their gifts for others. Never were they to condemn anyone, for there was that of God in every man and only God should judge. Sédar received a firm Christian example in this family. Hélène's genuine belief reinforced the more formal teachings of the mission school.

Hélène became the confidante and teacher of Sédar's childhood and youth. Blocked in her own ambition, Hélène found in her gifted young brother-in-law an excellent companion and a receptive outlet for her enthusiasm and energy. She understood his excitement with books and fed his curiosity about the world. She and her husband spoke French at home with their children, in the firm belief that this was where the future lay, and that the more their children came to resemble and understand the French, the happier and more prosperous they would be. They shared the prevailing French goal of assimilation, as did virtually all educated Africans of their generation. Every one of their six children went to France to university, and today they are lawyers, doctors, and diplomats. With Hélène, Sédar could discuss his school life, his books, and his longing to know more about France in a way that was impossible with his more immediate family. How far already he had traveled from Uncle Waly and the Djilor household that looked to the countryside in Sine! Gnylane Bakhoum Senghor could neither read nor write, nor had she experienced this hunger for French and Catholic culture. In Djilor no one spoke French, there were no books, no Western schools, no expectation, indeed little understanding, of university or Paris education. Of the six Senghor children from Djilor, Sédar was the only one who received an advanced university degree. He was the one who brought honor to the family of Gnylane Bakhoum.

By now Sédar's family had recognized, not without some apprehension, that he was different. He seemed uncomfortable with children his own age. He rarely joined them in their play, but stole off with his books or else wandered in the fields or on the beach, as he had as a little boy with his Uncle Waly. Now he went alone. Commerce and trade interested him not at all. He lived for his books and for God. Like Hélène, he was very pious. He was determined to become a priest.

One day, during the rainy season, when food is always scarce, he stayed out late hunting. When he came back, he was dragging a large duck. "Now," he told Hélène proudly, still in his early teens but trying to act like a man caring for his family, "you will have food for a time." A similarly premature effort to prove he could do the work of a man led to a less happy result. One day at Ngazobil, when he was about fourteen, Sédar offered to take the horses down to drink. He insisted on taking the biggest, a large horse known as the "great jewel." The horse bolted. Sédar stubbornly refused to let go. His shoulder was dislocated, and the missionaries rushed him back to Joal in obvious pain. When Sédar told the story, he made a great point of emphasizing, to his family and the distracted missionary who felt responsible for him, that he had not let the horse run off. Already he seemed unusually determined to prove his ability to master the world and to become the Sédar who is without shame because he has no cause to be ashamed.

Sédar excelled at Ngazobil. He showed an enormous capacity for hard work and won all the academic prizes: slim green books from France, which he took home to Hélène's cool sitting room and read over and over. By 1923, when he was seventeen, it was time to move on. The Fathers suggested, and the family agreed, that he should go to Dakar for further education.

That fall, Sédar entered the newly opened Libermann Seminary in

Dakar.[30] It was run by the Order of the Holy Spirit, the same order responsible for the mission at Ngazobil. The governor general had authorized the opening of the seminary only that year, taking advantage of the receding influence of the anticlerical faction in metropolitan France. For the previous twenty years, religious education of any kind had been discouraged in the colony, as in France itself. Now the missionaries were able to select top students from their mission schools for seminary education in Senegal as preparation for future leadership in the African church. Ngazobil chose to send Sédar. His career did not work out as anticipated, but another student from Ngazobil, Joseph Faye, did follow the prescribed path and was ordained in the Cathedral of Notre Dame in Paris.

Sédar joined fifteen other students to form the seminary's first class. A picture taken that year of thirteen students shows him standing stiffly beside a sturdy French boy in a white middy blouse (see illustrations). He is one of the three black pupils, and of the three, the only one without a European-style jacket. He was the boy from the country, eager to prove his worth.

That same fall, on Armistice Day, the governor general of the French West African Federation, Jules Carde, laid the cornerstone for the new central Catholic cathedral in Dakar. Father Lalouse, director of the Libermann Seminary, took part in the dedication ceremonies. In his address, Lalouse described the cathedral as a monument to the sacrifice of those heroes who had spread civilization in Africa, a civilization that is "worth more than native customs, because it is Christian."[31] Such was Lalouse's firm belief, and the underlying assumption of the education offered at his school.

Sédar studied at Libermann Seminary for three years, preparing the curriculum for the French baccalaureate exam, with a particular emphasis on the Catholic philosophers. He greatly admired Thomas Aquinas, the standardbearer of system and logical clarity. Of his politics at that time, Senghor recalls that he, like his teachers, was a royalist, and of his future plans, that he wanted to become a priest.

Various accounts are given of the collapse of this religious vocation. Senghor's version is that he was something of a troublemaker at the seminary, and that he had a confrontation with Father Lalouse. According to Senghor, Lalouse took a particular dislike to him, called him pretentious and proud, and even warned his family that he would never amount to anything. Sédar, in turn, judged Lalouse a racist who treated black students differently from whites. African students were not allocated proper sheets for their beds, for example, and Lalouse called Africans savages. "As I had received a bourgeois, even aristocratic education, I reacted by affirming that we, too, had a civilization."[32] (It is interesting that Senghor chose to call his education aristocratic, not simply authentically African.) It is certainly true that Lalouse had no doubts about the superiority of French culture. He had made this abundantly clear in the speech he gave at the dedication of the cathedral. Recalling his conflict with Lalouse across a gulf of fifty years, Senghor with characteristic generosity acknowledged that Father Lalouse was not a bad man. He was merely a creature of his time, who honestly believed that French culture was superior to all others, and this, an older Senghor observed, was the typical colonial mentality.[33]

Whatever the details of the clash between Father Lalouse and a student he considered unduly proud and ungrateful, Senghor recalls a blunt interview between the two. According to Senghor, Father Lalouse called Sédar in shortly before it was time for him to graduate and go on to seminary in France, and informed him that he was not cut out for the priesthood. The school would not recommend him for further religious education in France. Father Lalouse had the power to make this decision, and by doing so he effectively blocked Sédar's path to the priesthood.

Sédar was shattered. He returned to Joal, Hélène Senghor recalls, and remained withdrawn and depressed. He would not go out of the house, but hid inside in the dark. He would not even read. On his first Sunday home, when Hélène came in to ask him to go with her to Mass, he refused. When she pressed for an explanation, and asked if he had lost his faith, he explained that it was the church that had rejected him. He likened himself to a defrocked priest. Hélène pointed out that he had never worn the cloth or actually been ordained. But, Sédar explained, everyone knew that he wanted to be a priest. He had intended to be a priest. He had worked hard to become a priest. The value of that calling and the habit of self-examination, as well as Christian teachings about sin and guilt, had been deeply ingrained in him from an early age. The place that he thought he had earned, and that people expected him to take, had been denied him. It was a blow to his faith in the church and in God, but it was also a devastating blow to his view of himself and the image he planned to present to others. He felt he had suffered public humiliation. How he appeared to others was already very important to Sédar. Hélène could not comfort him. She could only reassure him with the same argument with which she had previously comforted herself: if Father Lalouse did not believe Sédar to have the priestly vocation, it must be because he had had a revelation. Perhaps God had destined Sédar for something else.

It was, nonetheless, a severe setback. Sédar had sacrificed much and worked hard to achieve this goal of higher education and the priesthood. Many years later, after he had become president of Senegal, he and Hélène sat together at a dinner in the presidential palace. He reminded her of this bleak period, and that she had suggested that God might have had a different intention for him. She was able then to remember with him, "you see, you are more than a priest or a missionary. You have all the country on your shoulders. What more could you want?"[34]

As a much older man, Senghor was able to transpose this painful experience into a positive one. "When Lalouse gave the African seminarians their ancestral straw to sleep on instead of sheets, he was responsible for awakening the emotion that became the driving force of my adult life: I owe to him not the word Negritude . . . but the idea." That idea included the determination to prove Lalouse wrong, and to demonstrate that he possessed precisely those qualities Lalouse found lacking in Africans: organization and self-discipline. In achieving his maturity, Senghor succeeded in transforming the meaning of this severe early disappointment from a defeat into a constructive step in his development. He now added the recollection that he was later given a second chance at seminary education, which he refused: "I felt I would not there get the instruments necessary for the liberation of black Africa."[35] Not only had injustice planted seeds that flowered in his mature life, but the missionaries themselves had been forced afterward to admit they had misjudged him. What Hélène Senghor remembered as a setback, Senghor chose later to see only for its positive result: he had found a path more suitable for his talents and more useful to his people. It had become his own choice. He even added a footnote to the story that offered evidence of a personal quality of which he was justifiably proud. Though he remembered Lalouse as the person who had stood in his way, he also recalled that Lalouse had taught him many valuable lessons and took the time to visit Lalouse in his retirement.[36]

Senghor proved to have an ability to see and to create, at least for public purposes, only the most positive side of his experiences. His first serious disappointment was retrospectively transformed into a key step toward the discovery of his true vocation. Looking back many years later at his days at Ngazobil and his missionary education, Senghor paid tribute to the value of the lessons he had learned from the monks: "reasonableness, self-mastery, and a tendency not to be satisfied with mere talk."[37]

Turned away from the priesthood, but still eager for education, Sédar returned to Dakar to study at a newly opened secular school that offered secondary school courses. Some years later the school was named Lycée Van Vollenhoven, after the young colonial governor who, years before, had recognized Hélène's talent and urged her family to send her to France. Now, one generation later, Sédar was able to break through into a world Hélène had glimpsed but could not enter.

2

The French

When Senghor moved to Dakar, he entered a new world. In Ngazobil he had met the Frenchman's language and religion. Now, at secondary school, he plunged more deeply into the Frenchman's intellectual and psychological world. Even outside of school, living with relatives in Dakar, he remained in a social milieu with a distinctive Afro-French culture.

In the mid-1920s, Dakar was growing rapidly, just coming into its own as the capital of France's West African empire. Set up on the red coastal cliff at Africa's most western point, Dakar was ideally situated to serve as a key link in the communications chain from the pestilential interior to the coast, and from the coast over the ocean to Paris. The climate, too, was favorable. In the winter and spring Dakar is beautiful, dry and sunny. In early summer it turns hot and dusty from the winds that blow in carrying sand from the desert in the north. Then the sunsets glow yellow-red from the desert sand suspended high in the atmosphere. When the rains come the city is muggy and oppressive. In this rainy season, called the *hivernage,* French administrators and Senghor's expatriate teachers tried to return to France on home leave to escape the enervating heat.

When Senghor began his studies at the new French secondary school, the future for the empire and particularly for Dakar seemed bright indeed. The city was rapidly displacing Saint-Louis as the center of French commerce and administration. The port held impressive potential as a deep-water harbor. The French governor, imagining growing trade and a rich and enduring presence, had directed city planners to lay out a geometric street plan with spacious squares and wide boulevards. Tree-lined streets, squares, and parks modeled on those of Paris took shape, while an elegant neoclassical governor's palace topped the plateau above the native town. Not far away, a large central cathedral was under construction, the cathedral whose purpose, as Father Lalouse had explained at the dedication, was to serve as a memorial to the heroes of empire who had given their lives to bring Catholic civilization to Africa. French administrators filed reports that glowed with triumphs over disease, growing trade, and "the excellent attitude of the natives."[1] For many Frenchmen, Dakar and civilization-in-Africa were synonymous. Even today, the plan of the city and its elegant buildings remain as an enduring testament to France's grand ambitions on the African continent.

Dakar had developed a distinctive urban way of life in which French and African, Christian, Muslim, and animist lived peacefully side by side. Their attitudes and behavior toward one another had evolved slowly out of a long and complex history. Africans and resident Frenchmen were equally proud of their joint accomplishment. It was a history that had led to the habits and traditions to which Senghor was now introduced.

The oldest French settlement on the Senegal coast lay to the north at Saint-Louis, the city of Hélène's childhood, where the Senegal River joins the sea. Europeans had first entered the river in 1445. In 1659 a Frenchman founded Saint-Louis on an island at the river's mouth. This small settlement served as the center for French commercial activity along the coast for over two hundred years. Some years after the founding of Saint-Louis, a second settlement, Gorée, was established several hundred kilometers to the south. It, too, was set on an island. Such islands offered a modicum of protection from both mainland diseases and piratical European adventurers. When the island of Gorée grew crowded, its settlement spilled over onto the mainland. The satellite town was named Dakar, or "tamarind tree" in one of the local languages, for the trees that grew there in profusion.

Island settlements seem an appropriate symbol for France's primary purpose during this early period: to trade as one merchant with another, but neither to settle nor to attempt political domination. Although explorers ventured inland from time to time, it was not in a spirit of conquest. European travelers treated the local African rulers as they would treat royalty at home. One eighteenth-century African king, for example, sent his young son, Anabia, to France for education. There the boy caught the fancy of one of Louis XIV's favorites, so the king asked the philosopher Bossuet to instruct him in Christianity. Louis served as the boy's godfather and set him up with the income of a gentleman. When his father died, Anabia returned to Africa to rule his own kingdom.[2]

The first European traders made commercial agreements with the local rulers in accordance with the customs of the land. They paid a tax to guarantee the autonomy of their trading community and the right to operate peacefully under the local ruler's protection. In this, as in most ways, Europeans simply repeated patterns already established for relations among local peoples. Tradition also demanded, and the French complied, that traders pay a customs tax on goods passing through each African ruler's territory.[3] The relative power of the two local communities in these early days of settlement is illustrated by an incident in 1701. The Damel of Cayor, a powerful king of the region, captured the French governor of the colony, André Breu, and demanded ransom. French residents of Saint-Louis promptly paid it to secure his release.[4] Until the end of the eighteenth century, then, all evidence indicates that the relations between the African and the French were those of equals interested in a trade profitable to both, with the terms and modes of interaction set by African tradition.

The content of this trade changed over time. In the early seventeenth century, animal hides made up more than 50 percent of the total value of goods exported from the Senegal region, and were exchanged for iron and beads. It was not until the eighteenth century that guns joined iron and beads as important imports and slaves became the most valuable export. The slave trade was at its height between 1716 and 1788. Thereafter it fell rapidly, at first because of disruptive wars, and then as a direct result of new European laws making it illegal. For the most part, the slaves exported from the Senegal region originated in the interior, and were war captives. Relatively few belonged to the coastal ethnic groups. No representative of the Serer of Sine, the group to which Senghor belonged, was recorded in a sample of slaves exported after 1722, and the Serer as a whole provided only a very small percentage, 2.6 percent, of the total number of slaves exported from West Africa in the eighteenth century. The dislocation created by the slave trade appears to have been minimal among Senghor's people. After slavery was abolished, trade between Senegal and France took on a recognizably modern form: the export of raw materials, first gum and then peanuts, in exchange for manufactured goods from France.[5] Such was the trade on which Diogoye Senghor had prospered.

The official goal of French colonial policy during the late eighteenth century, the time of the flowering of the Afro-French community of Saint-Louis in which Hélène Senghor was educated, was assimilation.[6] Assimilation had both a political and a social and cultural dimension. In essence, it aimed toward a future when the colony would become an integral part of metropolitan France. The African peoples of Senegal were to become as much like Frenchmen as possible, in language, manners, and political orientation. This was certainly Hélène Senghor's goal, both for herself and for her children. Neither she nor her educated African friends ever questioned it.

The expectation that Africans could and should assimilate French culture was based on certain assumptions about man and society that prevailed in the eighteenth century, the period historians call the Enlightenment. It was assumed that all men were equal by birth, and that nurture not nature explained human variation. This was one of the fundamental assumptions of Senghor's teachers, confirmed by the teaching of the Bible that all men possessed souls and so were equal in God's sight. The radical belief in the equality of all men was combined with an equally firm conviction of the superiority of French culture. The first belief infused the Revolution of 1789; the second is perhaps even older. Michelet described it well in the *Introduction à l'histoire universelle* (Introduction to a Universal History), published in 1834.

> The Frenchman wants above all to imprint his personality on the vanquished, not because it is his, but because it is the quintessence of the good and the beautiful; this is his naive belief. He believes that he can do nothing that would benefit the world more than to give it his ideas, customs, and ways of doing things. He will convert other peoples to these ways, sword in hand, and after the battle, in part smugly and in part sympathetically, he will reveal to them all that they gain by becoming French.[7]

Both of these views pervaded Senghor's early schooling at Ngazobil, and both were further reinforced as he studied French history. Only years later did he understand the implications that had been evident to Michelet. As Senghor then put it: "[The Frenchman] wants bread for all, culture for all, liberty for all; but this liberty, this culture, and this bread will be French. The universalism of this people is French."[8]

In his years at school, however, Senghor understood the French Revolution as the ideal for all men, and French culture as a heritage that he too could enjoy.

French success in progressing toward the goal of assimilation was evident in Senegal at the time of the Revolution. In 1789, when all over France communities were gathering to draw up lists of grievances against the king and to elect delegates to the Estates General in Paris, the inhabitants of Saint-Louis also called an assembly. The *cahier de doléances* they drew up and sent to Paris began by identifying its authors: "Negroes and mulattoes, we are all French, since it is the blood of the French that flows in our veins or those of our nephews. This origin gives us pride and elevates our souls."[9] They then reminded the king of their past loyalty: When, in 1757, the local French garrison had surrendered Saint-Louis to the British, the native Saint-Louisiens had wished to continue to fight. As a condition of surrender, they asked for a guarantee that they not be obligated to fight against the French. When the French retook the island twenty-two years later, the Saint-Louisiens greeted them as liberators. This account seems to have been true. An independent British source of the time reported with dismay that the African and Creole natives of Saint-Louis remained loyal to France throughout the period of British control, and showed great liking for French values and institutions.[10] Clearly the French had succeeded in winning the Africans' affection and loyalty. At the time of the Revolution, the grievances of the Saint-Louisiens, as outlined in their cahier, were entirely economic and held no hint of resentment of the French presence. They took pains to express their loyalty to the king, and pleaded that he not forget their loyal little corner of the world, and his subjects there "who adored their sovereign . . . and every day at sunrise invoked the All-powerful to give him long life."[11] The document was signed by Charles Cornier, mayor of Saint-Louis. He was an African. The cahier was answered not by the king but by the Revolutionary National Assembly, which offered trade to all on an equal basis, abolished slavery, and granted citizenship to all peoples in the French colonies. In their small way, then, the Negroes and mulattoes of Saint-Louis took part in the French Revolution. They clearly felt themselves to be a contributing part of the French body politic. Senegalese to this day remember the cahier as evidence of their long tradition of experience with democratic institutions.

The Saint-Louis of the eighteenth century evidently considered itself socially and economically a part of the French system. About the middle of the nineteenth century, however, even as the Creole population of St. Louis was growing in wealth, influence, and cohesiveness, the balance of economic and material power began to shift dramatically in favor of France. Industrialization in Europe opened up an enormous gap between Europe and the rest of the world in terms of economic and material power. Along with their economic success, Europeans developed a new cultural arrogance, embodied in individuals as diverse in other ways as Cecil Rhodes and Rudyard Kipling, and no less widespread among the French, who spoke as if civilization and French civilization were one and the same thing. Michelet caught this spirit exactly. Europeans began to view the rest of the earth as a giant playground, a vast stage for their expansion and experimentation.

French ambitions expanded accordingly. Although many Frenchmen were indifferent to the idea of empire, others began to see a larger role for themselves in Africa. No longer mere traders, they would become governors of a vast colonial empire. The name given the empire, France d'Outre-mer (Overseas France) suggests the goal. Colony and metropole were not only to become manifestations of a single spirit but were to be ruled directly from Paris.

Numerous arguments were put forward in favor of imperial expansion, and these were still being repeated with only minor variation during Senghor's school days. Christian missionaries saw new opportunities to win souls for Jesus Christ. Humanitarians pointed out that a people superior in technical, scientific, and moral achievement had a duty toward inferior races. Both agreed that they had an obligation to bring French light into African darkness. Mission schools like Ngazobil were founded in this spirit. Unlike the British, the French did not claim a white man's burden but rather a specifically French mission. It was a question of spreading French civilization. And then there was the question of economic advantage. Ideas about their civilizing mission fit nicely with more mundane notions about the need to control sources of raw materials and to find markets for French industry.

Still others saw the colonies primarily as a training ground for young Frenchmen who would there develop the ingenuity, self-reliance, and habits of command necessary to make them the future leaders of a renewed France. The empire was to provide education for a new breed of French leaders who would restore French glory and rejuvenate the aging Fatherland.[12] Such arguments were accompanied by excitement about the potential of new technologies. One enthusiastic educator of Senghor's day put together an anthology that included a long excerpt from a novel by Emile Zola. Zola, who both deplored and admired the new industrial technology in Europe, gave rein to fantasy when his thoughts turned to the empire. He dreamed of a time when Algeria would be linked to Timbuktu by way of the Sahara and trains would bring everything from the old Europe across the infinity of sand, crisscrossing the empire to create "a new, immense France linked to the France-mother, the ancient fatherland at last . . . ready for hundreds of millions of inhabitants." Metropolitan France was to be the brain directing this vast corpus of empire.[13] Senghor was inculcated with such arguments in favor of empire, and came to believe them himself.

The West African empire that Senghor knew as a young man had been shaped by Louis Faidherbe, the governor appointed to Senegal in 1854. Tall, thin, and blond, Faidherbe wore steel-rimmed glasses that set off an equally steely gaze. Both an amateur scholar and a gifted administrator, Faidherbe was the model of a type that came to be known as chiefs of empire. One of his men recalls him as "a silent reproach to all who were not precise, just, logical, and regular."[14] This most energetic and capable of men undertook military campaigns to extend French control inland. For this purpose, he organized an African military unit, the Tirailleurs Sénégalais, to fight under French commanders. This unit later fought for France with distinction in both world wars. In the colony, Faidherbe's Tiralleurs enjoyed such an advantage in military technology—guns and cannons—that they easily pushed back African resistance. The French annexed the territories of the Walo and Trarza along the Senegal River to the north, and defeated Lat Dior in the south. Lat Dior, an African leader known for his intelligence, courage, and diplomatic skill, was compelled by this military defeat to sign a treaty. The loyalty that had been won by persuasion in Saint-Louis was now demanded by force. In spite of the treaty, the French continued to violate Lat Dior's territory, as construction of the Saint-Louis–Dakar railroad moved forward and peanut cultivation encroached on his lands. Lat Dior took to arms once again, and was finally defeated in 1886.[15] The French pushed inexorably on, and by 1900, after the defeat of the redoubtable Samory Touré in the Sudan, their West African empire stretched halfway across the continent and formed a territory only slightly smaller than the continental United States.

Faidherbe was not content just to conquer. He wished to rule. He established schools for the sons of chiefs and for Muslims who refused to attend Catholic mission schools. He set up a newspaper and even a small museum at Saint-Louis. Perhaps most important of all, during his administration the French made the decision to abandon once and for all any thought of European colonization. Kwame Nkrumah is said to have suggested that independent Ghana build a commemorative statue to the Anopheles mosquito, as it, the bearer of malaria, had saved Ghana from British colonization. Similar considerations moved the French. The document announcing the decision not to pursue a policy of French settlement in Senegal contained the observation that the climate there, unlike that of Algeria, was too unhealthy for French settlers. It suggested that the land be left for native cultivation and that the French concentrate on controlling the lucrative import and export trade.[16]

Faidherbe also established an administrative structure for his expanding colony that endured with little change right to Senegal's independence in 1960. It provided the political framework within which French and African regulated their mutual affairs. Each colony was divided systematically into regions, and the regions into circles. The commander of the circle—the first titles were military ones— supervised and transmitted orders to the village headman. Later other layers were added. The result was a highly centralized administrative system modeled on the administration of France, and, like that of France, directed from Paris. The governor, at the apex of the colonial pyramid, reported back to the Minister of the Colonies in Paris. At the turn of the century, a number of colonies—Mauretania, French Guinea, Ivory Coast, Dahomey, Niger, and Senegal—were grouped into the West African Federation. The position of governor general was then added as an intermediary between Paris and the governors of the colonies that made up the federation. The governor general of French West Africa was headquartered in Dakar, a fact that greatly enhanced the importance of that city, because all communications between the colonies and Paris had to pass through his office. Later, in 1910, a similar federation and governor general for the inland territories of Equatorial Africa was established.

Faidherbe's organization implied the direct rule of colonial territory by French administrators according to French rules. In fact, the situation was very different. Faidherbe judiciously supported the continued authority of local rulers and the Islamic marabouts, in part because he lacked trained Frenchmen to do the job. Perhaps more important, however, his own experience led him to conclude that "The first requisite is to administer the conquered populations well . . . Because of differences in race and religion, it is necessary to let them regulate their own affairs as much as possible."[17] Just who ruled whom was not always clear, as Senghor's poetic recollection of the French administrator paying homage to his royal ancestor suggests. Certainly, the administrator on the spot often found it necessary to modify directives from Paris, for what seemed logical and rational in Paris did not always suit actual circumstances on the ground.

An important and enduring distinction between two types of colonial jurisdiction, commune and protectorate, also dates from Faidherbe's administration. In the so-called communes, limited in the 1850s and 1860s to the towns of Saint-Louis and Gorée/Dakar (the town of Rufisque was later granted commune status, and Gorée and Dakar became separate communes; these make up the four communes of the early twentieth century), Faidherbe pursued a policy of assimilation and granted political rights to all inhabitants regardless of ethnic origin. Those born in the communes were considered citizens of France. Those born in the protectorate, that is, anywhere else in French Africa, were considered subjects under French administration. This administrative division coincided in large part with a different exposure to France and the new economy. Towns such as Saint-Louis and Dakar were fast becoming urban commercial centers with a distinctive Afro-French culture, whereas inland areas such as Djilor and Sine-Saloum still experienced French influence only weakly and indirectly. Village farmers were gradually beginning to produce peanuts for the export market and being drawn into the modern economy, but in places such as the Djilor of Senghor's childhood, the French presence had had little impact on the social structure or culture of the village.

In the areas of the protectorate, that is all of France's vast claim in West Africa with the exception of the four communes in Senegal, an African was a subject with no rights at all before French law. A rich merchant like Diogoye Senghor might work with a French firm and serve as patron to the French priests who ate freely at his table, but he remained a subject governed by a system of administrative law called the *indigenat*. Subjects could be seized and held without trial for acts not previously defined as crimes. They were forbidden to leave the colony, and could be summoned for forced labor as needed. In fact, the French administration conscripted thousands of subjects to build railroads and port facilities for little or no pay—an estimated 189,000 between 1920 and 1930. The conscripts were taken from their villages and sent wherever they were needed, often hundreds of miles from their homes. They worked not only on public projects but also in mines and construction for private firms.[18]

The children of Basile Diogoye Senghor, including Sédar, were all born in the protectorate and inherited their father's status. They were not citizens. Nor was there much they could do to change this situation. In theory, provision was made for granting citizenship on an individual basis to an African who mastered the French language and worked ten years for a French business or government office. In fact, the authorities grew increasingly reluctant to create new citizens. Between 1914 and 1922, a period for which there are statistics, only ninety-four subjects in French West Africa were naturalized as citizens.[19] For this reason, a resourceful African like Hélène Senghor found it worthwhile to travel to a commune, Rufisque or Dakar, each time she was about to have a child so that the child would be registered as commune-born. When one of her children was born prematurely, Hélène intrigued until she had him "properly" registered. All of her children were citizens. Sédar Senghor, whose mother lacked the understanding or motivation for such trips, was born a subject and remained a subject without any civil rights until many years after he had moved to Paris. This status later posed problems for Senghor, standing between him and his ambition to become a professor in Paris. It was a reminder that even he could not escape the limits of legal barriers erected long before he was born. This artificial division of the African population would become an issue in his first political campaign.

The division between two apparently contradictory policies, one for the communes and the other for the protectorate, reflected a basic ambivalence in France's ambitions for its African possessions. In metropolitan France, its political parallel was the zigzag course between revolution and empire. Enthusiasm for equality, rationality, and universalism, together with a belief in the perfectibility of man, alternated with periods of reaction, restoration, and a pessimistic acceptance of the irrational in human behavior. At such times of retrenchment, France turned to tradition and authoritarian rule both at home and in the colonies. In the colonies, these contradictory impulses manifested themselves in indecision as to whether Africans might eventually become fully assimilated vessels of French culture, black Frenchmen equal in every way to white Frenchmen, as Hélène Senghor and her family hoped, or whether African culture and tradition, and possibly the innate inferiority of black men, required that Africans remain perpetually dependent on France for guidance and tutelage, so that French and African might be associates in a common enterprise but never equal partners. This ambivalence was not resolved. It was most vividly demonstrated in heated debates over the question of whether Africans should be given an education identical to that given French children, or an education adapted to their presumed special capacities and needs. The first, assimilationist view was embodied in Senegal's communes; the second in the protectorate.

The world of the communes was first revealed to Senghor when he moved to Dakar. There Africans were accustomed to taking part in lively political debates and to vying with Frenchmen for seats on local councils. A plethora of parties and cliques published newspapers and broadsheets to put their ideas before the public. The local population had won and held these rights for a long time and, over the years, had established definite local traditions about what was and was not permissible. They were proud that their ancestors had participated in the French Revolution and that they were French citizens, even though it was not completely clear what French citizenship for an African entailed. Nonetheless, from the time of the decree of 1791, the citizens had elected local councils and mayors to administer their internal affairs. There had been times when local Frenchmen had tried to withdraw these rights. During the Second Empire of Louis Napoleon, the French governor and a number of French merchants who lived in the colony had circulated a proposal that would have created separate voting lists for African, Creole, and French. They hoped thereby to establish a quota system for native representation in the local councils. Fortunately for Senegal's future, this prototype of an apartheid policy was defeated, largely because a white Frenchman who was Senegal's representative in Paris lobbied the colonial ministry against it. This was an important defeat for the portion of the French community that wanted to break the power exercised over local political life by the native-born Creoles. The next French Republic guaranteed to the communes the right to govern themselves by the same regulations as did the municipalities of metropolitan France.[20]

The power of the African citizens within these representative institutions gradually grew. In the elections of the 1880s and 1890s, the Creoles dominated the politics of Saint-Louis and Gorée, while in the newer communes of Dakar and Rufisque, French merchants won most of the local council seats. Few black Africans were elected to any position until the turn of the century, and then it was in Dakar rather than Saint-Louis that they proved most successful. In 1898, a by-election for the fourteen-member Dakar municipal council led to the unexpected victory of three Africans. Five French councillors immediately resigned in protest, arguing that it was impossible to serve with so many "ignorant Africans." The crisis was resolved by the governor general, who illegally dissolved the council and then presided over an equally illegal delay in calling new elections until such time as the vacationing Frenchmen—for the election had taken place during the season of the hivernage—should return to the colony.[21] When the new election took place, the Africans were defeated. In spite of such aberrations, however, the basic tradition of a single, equal, and multiracial political system for the urban centers of Senegal was firmly established by the time Senghor was born.

In 1872, the Third Republic had made an important addition to the rights of the communes: they were granted the right to elect a deputy to the French National Assembly. Political participation for the colonies was thereby extended beyond local self-government to Paris, the true center of power. Such a right had first been requested by the Saint-Louisiens in 1791, but no action had been taken. Again, at the time of the revolution of 1848, the right to elect a deputy was requested, briefly granted, but then quickly withdrawn in 1852 by the Second Empire of Louis Napoleon. It took yet another revolution, that of 1870, to grant Senegal its first deputy. This proved an important victory for the colony. The first deputy elected was a Frenchman, Lafon de Fongaufier, the man mentioned earlier as the defender of Afro-French electoral rights and a single electoral list for Saint-Louis. French candidates dominated the deputy elections until 1902, but Creole candidates presented increasingly strong opposition. Both had to cater to the African majority of voters, a public relations challenge met more successfully by French than Creole until 1902. In that year François Carpot, a young, well-educated Creole lawyer, defeated his French opponent. Twelve years later, in a hotly contested election in 1914, multiple candidates divided the French and Creole votes. The beneficiary of this split was Blaise Diagne, a friend of the Senghor family, later a political mentor to Sédar Senghor. He became the first black deputy. Though there was little talk of race in the newspapers during Diagne's campaign, it was said that at rallies his supporters sang in Wolof, "If Blaise commands us, we will kill all the whites."[22] The presence of a Senegalese deputy in Paris in a position outranking the governor general proved its value to Senegal over and over again. The deputy could influence policy at the highest levels, put the African case before the French public, and, more important, provide a check on the great power of the colonial bureaucracy.

The deputy Blaise Diagne was the first African Senghor saw in a position that outranked Frenchmen. Diagne had won that place according to the Frenchmen's rules. This made a deep impression on Senghor, who studied Diagne's experience and example. Diagne had been born in Gorée in 1872. Brought up and educated by a Creole family who recognized his promise, he was sent to school first in Saint-Louis and then in Aix-en-Provence in France. He passed the difficult exam to enter the customs service within the colonial administration, and so gained one of the few positions then open to educated Africans. In the customs service he gained a reputation as a rebel, proud, hypersensitive to criticism or any slight to himself or to other Africans. Grudgingly acknowledged by his superiors to be intelligent and capable, Diagne nonetheless found himself frequently at sword's point with them. He was transferred from post to post, more than once with a note in his dossier that he should never be posted in that colony again. His position in the colonial service was becoming increasingly precarious, when he realized that he was once again on a collision course with the local governor where he was serving. Fortunately for Diagne, the governor decided to create a breathing space by granting him leave in Paris. There, in 1913, Diagne began to write and enter into public debates about the colonies. He discovered an appetite for political life and began to consider standing for Senegal's seat in the French Chamber of Deputies. He sent a friend to Senegal to test the local political climate and, learning that he had a chance, decided to run.

Diagne's subsequent victory astonished black and white alike, as no black African had ever before come close to victory. He won largely because of splits in the opposition and the fact that his opponents did not think him a serious rival. Even they, however, later admitted that Diagne had waged an impressive campaign. Unlike the other candidates, he set out on a vigorous program of speeches and meetings with small groups throughout his constituency. When a rival French candidate commented that it was impossible to appeal intelligently to illiterate African voters, Diagne calmly pointed out that a great proportion of France's voters were also illiterate, and that no one questioned their right to vote on that account. When the vote was in, and it was clear that a black African had won, a group of the French residents suggested to the governor that he find a pretext for annulling the election. After flirting briefly with this idea, the governor rejected it as "grossly immoral." Diagne took up his post as deputy to the National Assembly in Paris in July of 1914, on the eve of World War I.[23]

In his initial enthusiasm, Diagne pressed for the extension of communal privileges, and hence French citizenship, to the Africans of the protectorate. Although it was evident that the existence of two such different administrations for Africans was a potential problem, the French press promptly labeled Diagne a dangerous radical and demagogue. The war, however, pushed such concerns to the background and plunged Diagne into a different controversy. He was charged to oversee the unpopular conscription of black soldiers. The French promised full citizenship to anyone who fought for France. At this point, Diagne stumbled over what was to become a recurring problem for his and Senghor's generation: the question of how best to achieve equality for Africans. If Africans wanted French citizenship and the equality it implied, must they then participate equally in France's battles? There seemed to be no alternative. Diagne pressed ahead with the conscription of African troops. Many of them, formed into units that carried on the name of Faidherbe's Tirailleurs Sénégalais, fought and died on the fields of Flanders. Some educated Africans, especially the families of those conscripted with promises of citizenship that later were not honored, never forgave Diagne for what they believed to be his gross subservience to French interests. Others, like Hélène Senghor, whose brother suffered the rest of his life as a result of a gas attack during this war, supported Diagne's policy. Like Diagne, Hélène saw French citizenship for all Africans as a goal.

Diagne made his own addition to the evolving political culture of Dakar by methods Senghor observed and later copied. Through a wise choice of subordinates from many different ethnic and religious backgrounds and an uncanny ability to delegate the right responsibility to the right person, Diagne forged a single political party out of diverse groups of local interests. In so doing, he resisted any temptation to create blocs based on ethnic divisions, and so not only formed the first true political party in French West Africa but also set a salutary example for Senegal's future political development.[24] Appeals to one

ethnic group against another, an easy way to gain support in many
African settings, were not his style and have never been the style of
Senegal's politics. Later, when the French Socialist party, the SFIO,
asked Diagne to join them and transform his party into a local SFIO
branch, he refused. He realized that the problems of his district were
too different from those of France to be solved by a single policy
made in France to suit metropolitan conditions. He also realized that
if he merged his party with the SFIO he would lose his independent
political base and with it much of his personal power and freedom of
maneuver. The wisdom of these decisions was not lost on Senghor,
who later spent many long hours listening to Diagne talk about his
political experiences. Diagne was never defeated, and held his post
until his death in 1934. His African supporters greatly enjoyed
watching French officials kowtow to their leader, and local songs
praised Diagne as king of the white man.[25]

Such were the political battles and achievements of Senghor's childhood and youth, battles in which he played no part, but which set
the stage for his career and all subsequent politics in Senegal. By the
late 1930s, when Senghor joined the fray, local political papers had
circulations of several thousand, and squabbles and polemics were
commonplace.[26] By then, the Africans of the communes had acquired
considerable political experience.

During the years of Senghor's childhood and Diagne's tenure as
deputy, a growing number of Frenchmen began to question seriously
both the possibility and the desirability of attempting to integrate
their sub-Saharan colonies with France. In the first place, colonial
administrators began to appreciate the enormity of such an undertaking. In theory and rhetoric, assimilation had an appealing sound,
a logical simplicity that fit well with France's revolutionary tradition;
in practice, assimilation would be a gargantuan task. France's West
African territories held hundreds of culturally disparate peoples who
spoke no common language that would enable them to communicate
with one another, let alone with the French. In the 1840s and 1850s,
there had seemed to be an analogy between the administrative centralization of France at Paris and the future centralization of the empire
at the same point. An Inspector of Education had returned from
Brittany, for example, and commented that Breton children were "like
those of the countries where civilization has not penetrated: savage,
dirty, and unable to understand a word of the language."[27] By the end
of the nineteenth century, however, France's provincial children had

become "civilized," that is, had begun to meet Parisian standards of language and education, and to feel part of the French body politic. By contrast, little or no progress in this direction had been made in the African colonies. While the analogy of province and colony lingered, tempting the most ambitious to dream of world empire, it began to be challenged by the very administrators charged with creating it, as well as by intellectuals at home.

The growing awareness of the practical problems of bringing French culture and administration to the colonies was given theoretical support by a broad shift in European thinking about man and society that had implications for the colonial enterprise. This change began in the latter part of the nineteenth century and gained momentum in the early part of the twentieth. Eighteenth-century beliefs about the essential equality and similarity of all mankind began to give way to a new appreciation of the depth and complexity of national and cultural differences. Optimism about the power of knowledge to improve society was tempered increasingly by a new appreciation for the power of habit and the past. In the African case, the differences between its societies and France were dubbed those between primitive and civilized, inferior and superior. Even that most outspoken champion of political liberty, John Stuart Mill, noted parenthetically in his essay "On Liberty," published in 1859, that it seemed hardly necessary to mention that in the backward nations "where the race itself may be considered in its nonage," liberty as a principle had no meaning and that despotism, "provided the end be their improvement," was a legitimate form of government.[28]

The shift in French thinking about Africans is exemplified by the differences between the Abbé Boilat's observations of Africa, published in Paris in 1853, and the entry for "nègre" in Volume 11 of the authoritative *Grand dictionnaire universel du XIX siècle* (Great Universal Dictionary of the Nineteenth Century) published by Larousse in 1874. Boilat described in detail the characteristics of the different nations, as he called them, of the Senegal region. He marveled that such a variety of peoples, each with its own "physical type, temperament, customs, language and government" could develop and live in such close contact without fusing into a single people, and suggested that recent migrations might account for this. Each language, he noted with surprise, had its own order, logic, and precision, despite there being no Académie Française, no official grammarians, and no schools similar to those he knew in France. In his musings on this strange exotic world, Boilat wondered whether contact with France had brought progress, for the introduction of guns and hard liquor seemed to have had a pernicious effect on large segments of the coastal communities. Nonetheless, he, as a Christian, concluded that there was a need to win the peoples of Senegal away from Islam for Christianity. He urged, therefore, the founding of schools and suggested that Africans from the Antilles be recruited to serve in Senegal because they were "knowledgeable of trade and agriculture," and "conserve memories of their families and, above all, an innate love of their country," by which he meant Africa. Boilat seems curiously contemporary in this acknowledgment of the existence of a distinctive culture and history among Africans and of the fact that slaves in the new world had a special bond to a fatherland in Africa. There is no hint in Boilat that the African is biologically inferior, lacking in culture, or in any way essentially different from Frenchmen. On the contrary, Boilat assumes throughout that "these men are children of Adam, created in the image of God."[29]

A generation later, the *Grand dictionnaire universel* sounds a very different note. The dictionary itself represented a crowning achievement for Parisian classifiers and systematizers, who here anxiously brought together the most up-to-date information on subjects ranging from architecture through evolution to zoology, with the idea that the dictionary should serve as a standard reference work for all educated men for the foreseeable future. The unnamed authors of the authoritative entry for "nègre" explain that black people differ from white in more than skin color, and that they are almost as closely related to the orangutan as to the white species. After some other statements such as that black people hear and see better than whites and are able to become accustomed to misery no matter how dreadful, they conclude on a moralizing note, saying that the intellectual inferiority of black people imposes on the French the duty of aiding and protecting them.[30] The shorter Larousse dictionary, in general use when Senghor was a boy, limited itself to noting that the term "nègre" was given to inhabitants of certain countries in Africa "who form a race of black men inferior in intelligence to the white race, called Caucasian."[31] At the same time, then, that Senghor was studying the history of the Enlightenment and the French Revolution with its ideals of liberty, equality, and fraternity, he also came across this darker current in the French tradition. It surfaced repeatedly, often in combination with what he loved best about the French, as it had in Father Lalouse.

The new science of psychology, which made its debut in the late nineteenth century, also had relevance for colonial issues. One of its most outspoken and indefatigable promoters, Gustave Le Bon, who is best known today for his work on crowd psychology, set out to refute the "dangerous and erroneous idea" that all men are created equal. The leading eighteenth-century theorists had agreed with Helvetius that "education makes us all what we are . . . mental inequalities are the results of differences in education."[32] Not so, declared Le Bon. Addressing an international congress on the colonies in 1889—for he added an interest in colonial peoples to his interest in practically everything else—Le Bon argued that the idea that education could alter national habits and institutions is "one of the most harmful illusions that the theorists of pure reason have ever engendered."[33] Any policy based on this illusion would lead the colonies to decadence. Ten years later, Le Bon's colleague Léopold de Saussure spelled out a similar view in a book entitled *Psychologie de la colonisation française* (Psychology of the French Colonization). There he set forth in great detail the differences between the French and colonial peoples that resulted from "fixed and hereditary" differences in their mental make-up.[34] In slightly different form, these views reappeared in the work of the influential psychologist Lucien Lévy-Bruhl, who argued in 1923 that the mental make-up of primitive peoples was basically different from that of Europeans, and that these differences were hereditary and unchangeable.[35] Such were the "scientific truths" of Senghor's formative years.

This outlook easily lent itself to the position that there was no possibility of educating colonial peoples to think like, or become indistinguishable culturally from, white Frenchmen. The new science of psychology undermined the basic assumption of any policy of assimilation, namely that all people were born equal and the same. It could, however, be used to support a policy more compatible with belief in an unchanging primitive mentality, namely that of association. The proposal for such a policy was set out by Jules Harmand in a book published in 1910, *Domination et colonisation* (Domination and Colonization). There Harmand argued that assimilation should be repudiated as a long-term goal because "we can only raise the black and yellow races . . . by a gradual acceleration of their progress and not by a deviation from the ancestral road over which they have come."[36] He envisioned a cooperative future, a relationship of mutual benefit that at the same time "reserves with unshakable firmness all rights of domination." The goal was not to weaken but to strengthen French domination by making it less offensive and repugnant. A colonial congress convened in 1914, just before the outbreak of the war, adopted association as France's official policy. In its guise, continued colonial domination could be justified. It reflected the end of the revolutionary optimism and egalitarianism of an earlier period.[37]

Another intellectual development in France that confirmed the need for a new approach to relations with the colonies was the work of Emile Durkheim. This pioneer of sociology began publishing his studies of man and community at the turn of the century. In his *De la division du travail social* (The Division of Labor in Society; 1893), he presented a model of contemporary European society that emphasized that each individual performed a useful and interrelated function necessary to the smooth working of the whole. In all societies, he argued, men are interdependent. What changes in the course of evolution from pre-industrial to industrial society is the form of this interdependence. Social balance, stability, and individual well-being are, he hypothesized, closely related. In his famous study *Le suicide* (Suicide; 1897), he found evidence that even suicide, this most apparently individual of acts, can be related to general factors in society at large. Finally, in *Les formes élémentaires de la vie réligieuse* (The Elementary Forms of Religious Life; 1912), Durkheim illustrated more directly the connection between social stability and the shared values that are necessary for healthy human life. In the corpus of his work, Durkheim presented a new view of individuals and society functioning as a single interlocking system. He concluded that no element in the social equilibrium could be removed without affecting the others. This new vision of society had definite practical implications if applied to colonial policy. It led inexorably to the conclusion that to alter any single feature of a society would invite unexpected changes in others. To bring about desirable and predictable change would therefore be very difficult; rapid change might be destabilizing, and even dangerous. Each society, African and French, had established a viable social equilibrium based on a particular set of social practices and beliefs. Elements of the one could not be substituted, piecemeal, for those of the other.

In France, the views of these scholars influenced the work of some colonial administrators, such as Maurice Delafosse and Robert Delavignette. They set out to study African society, believing that added understanding would enable them to develop more effective social policies.

In the colonies themselves, however, policy was governed primarily by practical political considerations. In discussing educational policy, for example, practical, not theoretical, considerations carried the argument. From the vantage point of the administrator resident in Senegal in 1900, there were reasons both for and against providing widespread education for the local population. French education was an obvious prerequisite for any policy of assimilation. But of more immediate importance was the need for native employees to man the lesser posts in the administrative structure. It made sense to train Africans in the French language and in the rudiments of accounting and general administration so that they could fill these posts at low wages.

Others saw in widespread education in French the key to a firm and lasting domination of the land and its peoples. Camille Guy, the lieutenant governor of Senegal in 1902, chose a school prize day to extoll the benefits of learning French: "The French language is the language of the entire world, and you are not an educated or distinguished person, whatever your race, unless you know how to speak French . . . To speak French, my young friends, is to think in French . . . it is to be something more than an ordinary man, it is to be associated with the nobility and destiny of our country . . . Love France with all your strength because she loves you well." Governor General William Ponty was less grandiose, but more transparent: "The basic precondition of the success of our domination, of its continuation lies in the use of our language . . . by the local population." Such was the rationale for requiring that the Fathers of the Holy Spirit teach French to their pupils at Ngazobil. A few years later, in 1917, Governor Joost Van Vollenhoven, the same man who had urged Hélène Senghor to continue her education, put the question of educating Africans in a more complicated context. The mass of Africans, he argued, must evolve within their own environment, and for them and their well-being, steps must be taken to ensure that traditional society remain intact. A small group of gifted Africans, however, among whom Van Vollenhoven had identified Hélène, must be educated to stand above the rest because of their greater talent and ambition. This elite "must evolve more and more in our environment," and join with France to govern the rest of the population.[38]

It is worth nothing parenthetically that Van Vollenhoven's assumption that an elite must lead the mass was the common belief of his time and had been enshrined in the educational policy of metropolitan France. There secondary education was limited to children of the social elite and to a very small number of particularly gifted children from the middle classes. Van Vollenhoven was expressing an idea neither racist nor radical; he was merely transferring to the colonial situation an idea current at home. That cultural issues might complicate the situation in Africa did not preoccupy him. His was the old, eighteenth-century view. He did not question the ability of individual Africans to master the French way of life, nor question that this would be to everybody's advantage. It apparently did not occur to him that these Africans might thereby be cut off from something of value, namely their own culture and people.

Whatever the ideal, however, inescapable facts barred the way to widespread education for African children: enormous numbers, great distances, and a lack of people or funds to provide teachers and schools. The triumph of anticlericalism in metropolitan France in 1903 simply made matters worse. It resulted in a government policy that weakened and finally destroyed most of the mission schools in Senegal. Anticlericals in the cities busily attacked mission education, accusing the clerics of exploiting native children by making them till the fields and wait on tables. They forced the chief teaching order in Senegal to leave. Fortunately for Sédar Senghor, a few isolated missions outside the communes, such as those at Ngazobil and Joal, escaped the scrutiny of the anticlericals. In these outposts the missionaries continued to teach the catechism in local languages, provide practical instruction, and, as they had been directed, introduce the teaching of French.[39]

The course of anticlericalism in the colony typifies an important political reality of the entire colonial period. Policies made in France to suit French conditions were applied unthinkingly and without modification to the colony. Anticlericalism devastated colonial education. Its advocates also strengthened the hand of Islam. The departure of the teaching missionaries forced the closing of many schools, including a secondary school at Saint-Louis that had been in existence for more than fifty years. The colonial administration had to reorganize education from top to bottom.

The system of education that was then established signaled the abandonment of assimilation as a political goal for French West Africa, even if the official change in policy occurred somewhat later. The reforms of 1903 were hailed for their capacity to provide an education "adapted" to local needs. A network of village primary schools was to provide a practical education, complete in itself. Very few Africans would be encouraged to advance beyond it. A small group of particularly talented pupils would be chosen for admission to regional professional schools, to be trained either for administrative and commercial work or as primary school teachers. In defending this plan, one governor, Camille Guy, pointed out that the regional professional schools would deliver a technical and professional education to make of students "good agricultural overseers and foremen."[40] Three years later, the French author of a report on education in Senegal, A. Mairot, expressed the policy slightly more gracefully: "Respectful of the beliefs, the customs, the habits and the traditions of the African peoples submitted to this authority, the governor general wants in no way to assimilate the indigenous peoples." He prefers to leave the native in his traditional surroundings, to improve his well-being, and "to inculcate in the black Africans the ideas of justice and equality, [and] to give them a practical French education, appropriate to their mentality."[41] The patronizing tone is still audible, as is the assumption that only certain aspects of French culture can be mastered by an African.

In conjunction with this new educational emphasis, special texts were written on African geography and history, on agriculture and on other practical subjects adapted for the African milieu. The metropolitan curriculum with its emphasis on French history and literature was abandoned, although the schools continued to stress the teaching of the French language. Presumably nationalistic reasons for teaching French continued to sway educational planners. African history, as might be expected, was taught from the French point of view, that is, accompanied by reminders that France was more advanced and more civilized than Africa. Nonetheless, African schoolchildren did learn the geography of their own land and a bit of its history.

The textbooks in use after World War I, those of Senghor's generation, sent a variety of messages to African children. One of the most widely used was a reader, *Moussa et Gi-gla: histoire de deux petits noirs* (Moussa and Gi-Gla: The Story of Two Black Children), published in Paris in 1919. It tells the story of two native boys who travel with a European merchant through West Africa. This plot makes possible ample description of the country, and such sights as the river Niger and the ancient city of Timbuktu. Edifying commentaries accompany these descriptions. The children's attendance at a native festival in Dahomey allows the author to discuss human sacrifice and point out how much better off the natives are under French rule: "Thanks to the French, our children increase in happiness and security, and they are full of gratitude for those who have driven barbarism, massacre, and suffering from the country." A visit to the palace of the governor at Dakar occasions a lecture on the children's rights and duties:

> It is, on the one hand, an advantage for a native to work for a white man because the Whites are better educated, and more advanced in civilization than the natives, and because, thanks to them, the natives will make more rapid progress . . . know more things, and become one day really useful men . . . thus the two races will associate and work together in common for the prosperity and happiness of all. You who are intelligent and industrious my children, should always help the Whites in their task. This is a duty.

The helpful tasks then spelled out for African children include the cultivation of land, the bearing of arms, and a willingness to fight for France in the ranks of the Tirailleurs. The book, it should be repeated, was published in 1919, just at the close of a war in which the Tirailleurs Sénégalais had fought for France in Europe. Yet the book also sounds another note: "Goodness has nothing to do with color . . . is it not the same red blood that flows in the veins of the Blacks and of the Whites?"[42]

On balance, Senegal's schools in the 1920s compared favorably with those elsewhere in Africa. One scholar who surveyed schools in the British and French African colonies concluded: "Despite the use of the French language, the French educational system has adapted courses of instruction to the needs of the African much more successfully than has been done in any other territory in Africa. There is no teaching of Latin or of detailed French history in the French colonial schools. Texts and courses have been designed to fit native needs."[43] In short, French colonial education of the time seems to have been a success in the sense that it met the goals the French had for it. It inculcated loyalty to France, taught agricultural techniques to villagers, and provided the clerks and low-level administrators needed to keep the colonial system going.

These developments were not altogether to the liking of the local population, however, particularly the old Creole families of Saint-Louis. Guy's statement that African students should be educated to make good agricultural overseers and foremen infuriated them. Replacement of the public secondary school with a technical professional school adapted to "native needs," that is, those of overseers and foremen, was understandably seen as an attempt to deny the children of the local Creole elite the education necessary for real leadership. The Creoles interpreted this change as an attack on their rightful place in the colony. Louis Guillabert, a member of a prominent Creole family and a delegate to the Saint-Louis governing council, expressed the Creole point of view: "I would be of the opinion . . . that we follow the programs set out by the University of France. We are French . . . in creating a college or a lycée with exactly the same programs as in France, you will do a service . . . to the entire population." Galandou Diouf, who became deputy to the French National Assembly after Blaise Diagne's death, attacked the new education decree as racist. Lamine Guèye, who with Hélène Senghor was among the first to get a diploma under the new system and later experienced difficulties because it was not considered the equivalent of a French diploma, devoted his distinguished legal and political career to working for a French standard of education for Africans, and for true assimilation. The question of whether or not education should be adapted to meet distinctive African needs would be the subject of Senghor's first public speech. He, like those before him, would find it difficult to decide.[44]

Ironically, then, at the very time when some of the more knowledgeable and sympathetic colonial administrators were beginning to question assimilation policy in the name of African welfare and the preservation of the African way of life, well-educated Africans saw any deviation from the goal of assimilation as an attempt to deprive them of their rightful place as leaders of colonial life. A few thoughtful Europeans had begun to appreciate the value of African cultures and to see danger in their thoughtless destruction. They also worried about the consequences of driving a wedge between the bulk of the African population and the small elite that received Western education. They questioned assimilation, therefore, in terms of the interests of the African population. Other Frenchmen, more numerous, had no wish to create a well-educated, demanding African elite. Most African leaders, meanwhile, like Guillabert, Galandou Diouf, and Lamine Guèye, attacked any retreat from assimilation or the opportunity to receive a rigorous French education as a denial of African rights and a racist attempt to freeze Africans in servile positions.

They were surely correct that most French opponents of assimilation did not have the welfare of Africans in mind. French businessmen had no desire for real competition from well-educated natives. Jules Harmand, the theorist of association, argued that education adapted for

African needs and the policy of association would strengthen French domination by making it of mutual benefit to the two peoples, and so acceptable to the dominated. Georges Hardy, however, acknowledged that the educational reforms compromised the quality of education: "We have put much water in the wine of African programs . . . for the time being let [Africans] . . . remain in the cave of which Plato speaks so beautifully, and . . . look at the overly bright sun [of French civilization] only through its reflection in the muddy waters of African streams."[45] As with any issue of importance and complexity, the issue of education for Africans found men of good will on both sides.

There was one exception to the general plan for African education that provided a small opening for the native elite, a door through which Senghor slipped almost by chance. The ordinance of 1903 included a provision that in those "towns with a sufficient European or assimilated element" urban schools could be established in which "the course of study is to be that of the primary schools of the metropole." Staff in these schools was to be exclusively European.[46] Moving swiftly into this loophole, the French of Saint-Louis established an urban primary school for their own children and then, in 1910, reopened a secondary school to replace the mission school that had been closed under pressure from an anticlerical French government. This soon developed into a full lycée. To this school, the leading Creole families also sent their children. Somewhat later, in 1917, a group of French parents got together to open a private secondary school in Dakar. The governor general provided some support, but the bulk of the cost was borne by the parents. Many teachers served unpaid. One member of the faculty at the Dakar school, Father Aupiais, simply added duties as professor of Greek at the new school to his main job as chief cook at the hospital. By 1919, there were twenty-two students at this school: eleven European boys, ten European girls, and one lone African boy.[47] In 1925, eight years after its founding, the colonial administration decided to assume financial responsibility for the school, which then became a public lycée. As luck would have it, Sédar Senghor finished at the Libermann Seminary the next spring.

Recognizing the opportunity afforded by the existence of this new public school with high standards, Senghor's teachers recommended him for entrance. Had he finished Libermann Seminary two years earlier, he would have had no choice but to enter either the local seminary or a special school for Africans. Judging from the letters between Lalouse and his superior, it is almost certain that a desire to push Senghor forward toward higher education, rather than a determination to prevent him from entering the priesthood, motivated Father Lalouse to direct Senghor to the new secular secondary school.[48] What Senghor perceived at the time as a refusal to let him go directly to French seminary in fact pushed him through a door that opened onto a far broader vista. It was but chance that Senghor was able and ready for advanced secondary education at the very moment when good French education first became available free of cost to African children in Dakar. It was a rare opportunity, open to only a handful of Africans of his generation.

There were few Africans at the new lycée. It was intended for the children of the local French businessmen and administrators who wanted their children to follow a curriculum identical to that in France so that when they returned home they could continue their schooling without disruption. The school was not run with Africans in mind. When Sédar Senghor graduated, there were about fifteen Africans in a school of over one hundred, more in the younger classes than in his.[49] Pictures of his class and teachers reveal Senghor as a solitary black face. Senghor found himself the pioneering black in a predominantly white world, being taught the history and values of a country he had never seen.

While attending secondary school, Sédar and his younger brother, Charles Diène Senghor, lived with an aunt, Madeleine Vicine, who was married to a Chinese from Indochina. At school, Sédar made friends with the son of the school's director, Aristide Prat, and also with James Bruce-Benoît, who remained a close friend and later served as Senghor's secretary after World War II. Sédar and Benoît sang in the church choir and attended daily choir rehearsals. Benoît has recalled Sédar's determination to succeed in his new school, fueled by his fury at Lalouse for insults to him personally and to Africans as a group. He recalls Sédar's vowing to work as hard as he could to equal the best of the Europeans. For Senghor it was a question of honor, the honor of the Serer.[50]

And work he did. The year he arrived, Aristide Prat moved him up a class after two months and saw to it that he took the first baccalaureate exam in philosophy at the end of that first year. For the baccalaureate, French examiners came from Bordeaux to administer the orals to ensure that the colonial standard matched that of metropolitan

France. The students therefore learned much of French history, virtually nothing of Africa, and recited, as Senghor later recalled, the history of "our ancestors the Gauls, men tall, robust, with skin white as milk, blue eyes, and long blonde or red hair which they let hang on their shoulders."[51] Senghor's experience differed totally from that of most African schoolchildren of his generation, who received what continued to be somewhat euphemistically called "adapted" education. The few Africans of his generation who did receive and master a good French education went on to have a disproportionate influence on their times.

What effect such an intensive French education might have on an African child worried some French specialists. Georges Hardy, whose tall form and speeding bicycle were a familiar sight in Dakar during Sédar's school years, had already observed that such a child "lives in two separate worlds." For Senghor, this division grew wide and profound. Such a person was neither entirely of Africa nor yet of France. In those rare places where the teachings and values of the two cultures converged there was the possibility of satisfaction, but more often, as the Senegalese writer Cheikh Hamidou Kane wrote many years later, the experience was that of a "strange nature in distress in not being two."[52] To develop a stable, integrated personality that could encompass both worlds became the preoccupation of several generations of French-speaking Africans. For the moment, however, such complications did not cloud the excitement of Sédar's learning. He was making swift progress down the road traveled by Blaise Diagne, Hélène Senghor, Lamine Guèye, and a few other Africans who would have the opportunity to influence their country's future relations with France.

The graduation day of the lycée at Dakar was an important local event attended by businessmen, colonial administrators, and even Governor General Jules Carde. On the day of Sédar's graduation, July 7, 1928, one of the speakers directed her remarks to members of the graduating class. Mme Daniel, the history teacher at the school, congratulated those who had won prizes, but praised particularly those who had struggled hard to do their best. "The essential," she said, "is to go right to the limit of one's capabilities, and still look higher. Those who get all they want . . . set themselves too easy a task." Turning to the question of the French presence in Africa, she continued: "All achievement is the work of centuries. France has made some mistakes, but the overall result of the work of many hands is the creation of our beautiful overseas empire." In conclusion, she urged all present to work for the future success of the empire.[53] The exhortation to aim high was appropriate for Senghor; the talk of glorious empire a theme to which he was becoming accustomed and a cause he wished to serve.

The awarding of prizes was the crowning event of the day. That year, Sédar Senghor won every prize offered by the school: not only the academic prize in each subject but also the prize for the outstanding student. This prize was presented by Governor General Carde himself. Sédar had matched the standard set by Hélène. His sweeping triumph over all the French students gave rise to a legend passed on to subsequent African students about a black boy from the bush who had beaten out all the whites.[54] It served as their encouragement, for Africans at the best Dakar schools continued to be a small minority among the children of French administrators and businessmen for whom these schools had been founded.

Senghor had long seemed odd to his family because of his studious nature. Now, in secondary school, Sédar showed signs that he himself took this difference to be one of superiority. At one holiday gathering of the Senghor family in Dakar, he made clear what he expected from others. Two tables had been set, as was customary at such occasions, one for the adults and one for the children. Shown to his place at the children's table, Sédar refused to sit down. He did not belong with children. Admittedly he was no older than they, but he was now an educated person, a secondary school student in his late teens. He deserved to sit with the grownups. The adults would have none of this. Their table was already crowded. Rather than back down and sit with children, Sédar did without lunch.[55]

Watching Sédar's progress at school, the school director, Aristide Prat, had become convinced that his was an extraordinary mind. If he was to continue his education, he would have to go to France. It was in this context that the question arose again of Sédar's going to a Catholic institution so that his education could be financed by the church. But this option was not pursued. Whether it was ever a real possibility is not clear. This may be the moment Senghor had in mind when he said that he had turned the church down. There is in existence a letter from Father Lalouse to his superior, obviously sent in response to a query about the promising African boy. Lalouse writes that Senghor "might be attracted to the Catholic faculty in Paris," and wants to study law.[56] This exchange leaves the impression that Lalouse's superior could not have known why Senghor had left the

Libermann Seminary, or at least did not share Sédar's version of the reasons for it, namely that Lalouse had declared him unsuitable for church support. The details of this time are confusing. But the important practical issue was how to get a scholarship for further study. In the late 1920s there were scholarships for students from the colony, but most of them went to the children of French administrators. Those few scholarships offered to Africans were for the study of veterinary medicine, a subject considered useful and unlikely to encourage pretensions or troublemaking. Birago Diop, later a friend of Senghor's and the author of *The Tales of Amadou Koumba* and other stories, won such a scholarship to Paris from the Lycée Faidherbe in Saint-Louis about this time. He became a veterinarian—and a writer.

Aristide Prat did not give up easily. He was an unusual man and proved an impressive ally, the kind of Frenchman whom Senghor could trust and admire. Prat had graduated from the most elite of French educational establishments, the Ecole Normale Supérieure, studied for an advanced degree in letters, and later served as deputy in the French National Assembly. He had gone from this position to his current one, teacher of Greek as well as director of the Lycée and Inspector of Education for the French West African Federation. He was determined that Sédar Senghor, his most gifted African student to date, should have the opportunity to take the next step in his education. When Jules Carde hesitated to grant Sédar a federation scholarship, Prat threatened to resign and go back to France to publicize what had happened. Under this pressure, Carde relented and announced in July that the Federation of West Africa had awarded a half scholarship, 250 francs, to Léopold Sédar Senghor to study literature in Paris.[57] Senghor was the first black African to receive such a scholarship.

Senghor was elated, for, as he recalls ingenuously, "I, a classicist, had only scorn for the technicians and their subjects." Neither scientific or technical education nor religious education appealed to him. Senghor had learned the lessons of his French teachers well: art, literature, the classics, these were the subjects for gentlemen, not science or practical subjects such as veterinary medicine.[58]

Sédar's father, Diogoye the lion, was not very enthusiastic about this plan. School was all very well, in his view, for forming good merchants. Sédar's older brothers were now prospering as a result of their education. But enough was enough. At this time it was almost unheard of for a black African to go to school in France—that path was reserved for a handful of Creole Saint-Louisiens. Nonetheless, as was his custom, Diogoye called the family together in the big house with the green latticework in Joal to confer and make a decision. All the brothers came: from Dakar, Rufisque, and Joal. The patriarch's call could not be disregarded. More than twenty men of the family gathered to deliberate on the fate of the young brother and cousin who wished to follow a path new to family tradition. Diogoye was inclined to say no. He had never been to school himself, though he did recognize that his children's success lay in understanding the French world. But Paris seemed too far, and the advantages of such a course were unknown. It was time for Sédar to take his place in trade. Most of Diogoye's sons agreed with him. Not René, however, who was influenced by his strong-willed wife. Hélène saw the prospect of another life blocked on the threshold to higher education, prevented from having a chance to know French culture at its source. She pressed her husband to argue for letting Sédar go. After much discussion, and after each person had spoken his mind in the tradition of the African palaver, Diogoye made his decision. He would give his agreement: Sédar might go. But he would not pay the expenses. That would be up to René Senghor. René agreed to supplement Sédar's partial scholarship. It was a contribution he was happy to make. He and Hélène fully understood the opportunity Sédar had won. In many ways, Sédar's success was Hélène's as well.[59]

Before leaving for Paris, Sédar had to sign a document in which he agreed to serve the federation for ten consecutive years after the completion of his studies. His father signed it as well.[60] Once this was completed, Sédar set sail for Paris on the ship Medée II. Members of his family, friends from school, and Aristide Prat himself went down to the dock to see him off. Proud, stubborn, and hard working, Sédar Senghor left Africa with great expectations. It was 1928. He had just turned twenty-one.

3

Paris

A cold rain was falling in Paris the day of Senghor's arrival. The glittering city of his imagination quickly lost its sparkle. "Everything was gray," he recalls, "even the famous monuments. What a disappointment."[1]

Nonetheless, in October of 1928, Paris was sparkling with energy and optimism. Peace, political stability, and confidence in the future created a climate in which French business prospered. Economic growth had been steady since the end of the war in 1918, and France seemed the strongest and most prosperous nation of Europe. Its capital was the uncontested cultural center of the continent, and not only because of the French. The city had become a haven for creative people from many other nations, most dramatically for Russians fleeing the Revolution, but also for artists of other lands, fleeing, at least so said the Americans, the restrictions and monotony of their native cultural scene. Ernest Hemingway christened this Paris of the 1920s a "moveable feast," rich, colorful, full of spice and variety.[2] Sergei Diaghilev's Ballet Russe had settled at the Théâtre Sarah Bernhardt and mounted productions with choreography by George Balanchine, music by Igor Stravinsky and Sergei Prokofiev, and settings designed by artists of the caliber of Rouault and Bakst. Colette was publishing novels that captured the essence of womanhood, a charm and sophistication that seemed synonymous with being French, while Roger Martin du Gard chronicled the staying power of the French bourgeoisie in novels that streamed forth with an abundance that mirrored that of Paris itself. Maurice Chevalier was perfecting his special form of light entertainment in the music halls, and Edith Piaf was transforming her pain into music of great pathos and charm.

A large colony of American writers and intellectuals, Ernest Hemingway, F. Scott Fitzgerald, and the ubiquitous Gertrude Stein and Alice B. Toklas exemplified both the international nature of the Paris intellectual community and its high quality. But by the late 1920s, when Sédar arrived, the Americans were beginning to go home. Those who remained still gathered at Sylvia Beach's lending library, Shakespeare and Company, to borrow and talk about books. Across the street, Paul Valéry, André Gide, the novelist Jules Romain, and lesser-known poets gathered to read aloud from works in progress, and often invited the Americans to join them.[3] It was a small, intense, creative world in which writers took an interest in one another. The troubling minor themes of the 1920s, such as the iconoclasm of Dada and the Surrealists who challenged prevailing assumptions of smug bourgeois rationalism, did not yet seem important.

Paris could still absorb and enjoy eccentrics like Nancy Cunard, the rich and beautiful English poet who astonished her aristocratic mother by consorting with a black American and collecting African art. Cunard ran a private press that published whatever caught her fancy. Books ranging from Ezra Pound's poetry to Louis Aragon's translation of Lewis Carroll's "The Hunting of the Snark" carried her imprint, the Hours Press. After the failure of this venture, she stubbornly struggled to publish her own book, a remarkable collection of articles designed to address what she called "the problem of color." Published finally in London in 1934, Cunard's nine-hundred-page anthology, *Negro,* brought together articles by some fifty contributors, French, English, American, and African, who wrote about the black experience in America, the West Indies, and Africa. Historical essays about black Africa and vivid accounts of racial injustice were set side by side with discussions of African art, West Indian music, and black American poetry. Contributors ranged from white writers such as Pound, Theodore Dreiser, and William Carlos Williams, to black activist Americans W. E. B. Du Bois and Walter White. Figures important to the Harlem Renaissance, notably Alain Locke, Langston Hughes, Countee Cullen, and Sterling Brown, were also represented, as were Africans who would later be active in the movements for independence, such as Nnamdi Azikiwe and A. A. Ademola. Where translation from French to English was needed, Samuel Beckett or Louis Aragon provided a graceful pen.[4]

This volume attests to a growing, serious interest in Africa and the African diaspora among cosmopolitan intellectuals in France. Painters such as Picasso were fascinated by the stylized African art they saw in the new ethnographic museum in Paris. A few of them began to collect African art. For most Frenchmen, however, knowledge of black America or of Africa was limited to events like Josephine Baker's opening with the Revue Nègre at the Théâtre Champs Elysées, or the great colonial exposition of 1931, a sort of world's fair of the French empire, in which entire African villages were constructed on the outskirts of Paris.

It was widely believed by the French that Paris drew no color line. Certainly Nancy Cunard's experience was that she and her black American companion, Henry Crowder, caused less scandal in Paris than London.[5] An unfortunate incident of some years earlier, when an African lawyer practicing in Paris, Tovalou Houénou, had been refused service in a Montmartre restaurant—reputedly, it was said by way of explanation, at the request of American patrons—was forgotten or judged an aberration. After all, when Tovalou had pressed charges against the unfortunate restaurant owner, had he not won damages in court and had not the prime minister, Raymond Poincaré himself, come to his support? Had not René Maran, a Martiniquan in the colonial service, won the Prix Goncourt for his novel *Batouala,* a story of the African village, in spite of its preface attacking the colonial administration? The fact that Tovalou thereafter became a political activist on behalf of black people was conveniently forgotten, as were the facts that René Maran had been forced to resign his post in the colonial service and that his novel was still banned in the colonies. Few Frenchmen knew that a professor lecturing on Shakespeare's *Othello* at the Sorbonne had remarked from the podium that the play was flawed because it was unbelievable that Desdemona could have loved a black man. But the story of that incident had spread like wildfire through the small West Indian community.[6]

This turbulent and exciting world of culture and the arts was invisible to the newly arrived Sédar Senghor, who saw only the gray exterior of the city and felt that he had been somehow deceived. His was not an uncommon experience. Others of his classmates, students from the provinces brought up on an evocative literature of Paris as the center of glamour and intellect and force-fed on the frustrated ambition and imagination of their provincial teachers, also imagined a dream city of marble palaces, warmth, and welcome. Many of them felt, as did Senghor, a terrible disappointment and apprehension, even fear, as they first breathed the city air, which seemed cruel and indifferent to their hopes and dreams. Paul Guth, a classmate of Senghor's, vividly recalls his initial amazement at seeing haggard, hollow-eyed Parisians rushing from place to place among blackened, dark buildings. Many students' anticipation quickly froze to foreboding.[7]

As he began attending lectures in the crowded amphitheaters at the Sorbonne, Senghor grew increasingly depressed and confused. The French university system of the time took pride in the liberty granted its students. Senghor was accordingly left largely to his own devices, to attend lectures and study at will. Like many newcomers to the city, he felt isolated and bewildered. Fortunately a friendly professor, Alfred Ernout, took an interest in him and advised him to leave the Sorbonne and enter the boarding section of the elite Paris secondary school, Lycée Louis-le-grand. Senghor did as Ernout suggested, and signed the school register in December. He was the last person to enter that year. Asked to write his name and nationality on the list, he wrote: Léopold Sédar Senghor; French. Such he believed himself to be.[8]

Louis-le-grand was then considered to be the best lycée in France. It was also one of the oldest. Founded in 1563 by the Jesuits as the Collège de Clermont, it had survived struggles between Jesuit and crown, changing its name but not its location or traditions, for more than three hundred fifty years. Different times required different names: among them Collège Egalité during the revolution of 1789, Lycée Impérial under Napoleon III, and finally in 1873, Louis-le-grand. In the seventeenth century, the school educated primarily the sons of the great aristocratic families—Soubise, Rohan, Conti, and the like. In the eighteenth, it extended itself to give scholarships to boys of outstanding talent—Robespierre attended Louis-le-grand on scholarship, and, ironically, returned there to prison on the ninth of Thermidor. By the end of the nineteenth century, Louis-le-grand served not only the well-born but the most talented students from all over France as selected by competitive exams. Among its graduates were the first great administrator of Senegal, Louis Faidherbe, the writers Molière, Victor Hugo, Alphonse Daudet, and Charles Baudelaire, several members of the Rothschild banking family, and the Marquis de Sade. More recent graduates included Georges Sorel and Emile Durkheim, the socialist leader Juan Jaurès, and the man serving as French prime minister when Senghor arrived, Raymond Poincaré. Such was the luster of the tradition that Senghor now joined.[9]

At the lycée, Sédar entered a special class called *khâgne,* a boarding section that attracted top students from all over France and a few from the empire. Khâgne had been established at the end of the nineteenth century to prepare students for that most rigorous of all French academic competitions, the exam for the Ecole Normale Supérieure. The Ecole Normale Supérieure supplied professors for the French university system and most of the best secondary schools, and also served as the most reliable stepping stone to high posts in the French government. Entrance to the school virtually ensured a successful career thereafter. Senghor must have been pleased to compete for the school that had graduated his patron and headmaster in Dakar, Aristide Prat. It was generally agreed that the best place from which to attempt the exam was the special preparatory class at Louis-le-grand. In khâgne, Senghor found that more than half of his classmates were prizewinning students from the provinces of France. They, like him, were new to Paris, and, like him, accustomed to success.

At first there was a cacophony of accents and physical types: Queffelec from Brittany, Valdeyron from the border country near Spain, Pompidou from the Auvergne, Louis Achille and Jules Monnerot from Martinique, Khiem from Vietnam, and Senghor, the African, from south of the Sahara. Each taught the others about his province and described its landscape and charms, no doubt with a touch of homesickness. Senghor talked of his province, Senegal. What they all shared was ambition, past success, and excitement at the possibility that their academic ability might carry them to the top. They had a single goal: to win a place at the Ecole Normale Supérieure and with it the guarantee of a high government or academic post. The first year, known in student slang as *hypokhâgne,* was considered a year of acclimatization, a time to get used to the intense pressure of preparation for the exam. For the final year they moved on to khâgne. Khâgne held about eighty students in an immense classroom that looked north, separated by a narrow street from the Collège de France. It included those who had failed the exam in the previous few years and were trying again, as well as the entering group. Each student heightened in the others the sense of competition. Those entering khâgne saw in the three- and four-year repeaters the stigma of defeat, likening them to "veterans of the retreat from Russia or old gladiators who satisfied their masochism by exposing all their wounds and scars." These veterans were the bearers of the folklore of khâgne. They warned, for example, that classics students would do well to memorize the names of Greek toys, for examiners had stumped numerous past students on this obscure vocabulary. Under this common pressure and obsession with the exam, provincial differences fell away to be replaced by the camaraderie of the trenches.[10]

In this atmosphere, Sédar Senghor thrived. He found a material security and a clear direction that, he recalls, were not unlike those of a military barracks. This was a common analogy—the barracks, the convent, or the prison—and indeed the school had been a prison for Robespierre over a century earlier. The huge stones of the school and courtyard stood impervious to the life that had passed and continued to pass through the school. The students who gathered in twos and threes in the gray courtyard to discuss history, a philosophy question, or a Latin text, left no visible trace. Rarely did they mention anything personal. The dormitory itself, with rows of beds side by side, offered no privacy and reinforced the sense of monasticism and of timeless devotion to learning. Indestructible iron grills covered the downstairs windows, windows designed, so it seemed, to bar exit rather than to provide connection to the world outside. Little sunlight penetrated the dark interior of the school. Up at 6:00 A.M., the students attended class and study hall with only a short recreational break and time out for meals. Lights were turned out at 10:00 P.M. Silence was expected in the classrooms, and to drop a book was considered a serious offense. A roll of drums marked the beginning and end of class. Only twice a week, on Sundays and Thursday afternoons, were the students free to go out into the city. For the most part, then, "we were in Paris at the heart of a bright and exciting capital but isolated from it as on an inaccessible island for seven-eighths of our existence."[11] It was indeed a Spartan regime, particularly compared to the warmth and laxity of Sédar's former school in Dakar.

The intellectual fare was as rich and varied as the physical fare was stark and limited. Required to study several foreign languages and the classics as well as French literature, philosophy, and history, the students ranged through space and time with an ease that telescoped history and lent an immediacy to the eighteenth, seventeenth, or fifteenth century that rivaled that of the present. Discussions about contemporary French policy in Morocco, for example, quickly led to comparisons with the situation in Canada in 1763; Poincaré's policy was likened to that of Charles Gravier, Count of Vergennes, the French Minister of Foreign Affairs who had secretly aided the Americans during the American Revolution. Past and present flowed together.

One of the students' favorite teachers, Jean Bayet, would get them discussing with equal intensity a recent play by Jean Cocteau or a question that had preoccupied Henri IV, namely whether or not the Cathedral of Notre Dame should be torn down as an affront to French classicism. "Fragile indeed," recalls one student of the time, "were our ties with the world of the living."[12]

Senghor dug into his work with satisfaction. He had much to learn and the will and ability to learn it. The regularity imposed by the school program reinforced his own self-discipline and suited him well. He felt he had not read widely enough and was behind the others, and so threw himself into the study of French literature and culture. His teachers commented on his great effort and hard work.[13]

What he learned in classes was complemented by what he learned from his fellow students. Each, as the saying went, was a genius in his own way, and most would go on to make a mark in French life. Friends Senghor made at Louis-le-grand included Georges Pompidou, later president of the Republic, Pham Duy Khiem, the Vietnamese writer and diplomat, Robert Verdier, a prominent socialist leader, René Brouillet, a distinguished Inspector of Finance, Jean Valdeyron, journalist, publisher, and later Minister of Cooperation between France and Senegal, as well as the writers Maulnier, Robert Merle, Paul Guth, and others.[14] These men remained friends in part because they all prospered, but also because presence in khâgne guaranteed lifelong membership in one of the most exclusive and influential, if informal, groups in France: the old boys of Louis-le-grand.

Several of these friends recall that Senghor as a student had a special quality that set him apart from the others. It had nothing to do with ambition. They all had that. Nor was Senghor like the other black students, the gay and worldly North Africans, who bragged about their amorous conquests and their familiarity with the hidden pleasures of the city. Quite the contrary, Senghor was then what the students called a *tala*: a person who goes faithfully to Mass on Sundays. His was a living faith, his friends felt, not simply a habit he was loath to break. Unusual as church attendance was among the others, the quality and authenticity of Senghor's piety gained their respect and stuck in their memories. It was combined with a radiant calm that "made you feel peaceful yourself in his presence" and protected him from the barbs of even the crudest students. There were, inevitably, occasional tense moments. Once a fellow student made a racial slur at Senghor's expense, and was removed quickly from the room by Senghor's friends. Senghor, for his part, learned to take such remarks in stride. On another occasion, walking in the Luxembourg Garden, Senghor and a friend heard a child say loudly to his mother, "look at the little Negro." The woman was obviously embarrassed and slapped the child, but Senghor managed to smile at them both, as if to say that he understood that the child was only commenting in a way natural for someone his age.[15]

Senghor's serenity in all circumstances—one friend used the word "sweetness"—seemed to be one of his outstanding characteristics during his secondary school days. His French friends never suspected the first impression that Senghor had had of them: "Their worry for their careers, the sense of money and the taste for things of the flesh was for me a perpetual subject of astonishment . . . We didn't react the same to the teachings of our professors, nor to art."[16] Such thoughts Senghor kept to himself. Even as a young man in his early twenties, Senghor was able to construct an impeccable facade to meet his friends' expectations as to what a black Frenchman should be. They, in turn, accepted him for what he seemed to be: polite, quiet, self-contained, at ease in their world. They saw him, not unkindly, as a symbol of the fairness and success of French civilization and colonial policy. They also accepted him as their friend. Robert Verdier invited Senghor to stay with his family in a little village at Saint-Mandé in Val d'Isère during the summer holiday. This provided Senghor yet another view of France and the French. Verdier senior was the head of the local boys' school and, with his wife, exemplified the well-educated provincial family. In this small town, few had ever seen an African. When he went for a walk with the Verdiers in the evening, Senghor drew stares from the children. Whatever discomfort this may have caused him was more than matched by the welcome of the Verdiers. Many years later, when the elder Verdier died, Senghor wrote to Robert Verdier recalling the family's kindness and how much he had enjoyed being welcomed into a French family.[17]

On school Sundays during the term, Senghor often went from Mass to lunch at the house of Blaise Diagne. This impressed his friends, for Diagne was an important figure, a member of the French Chamber of Deputies, and a well-known man about town. The most distinguished Senegalese then living in Paris, he was the logical person to serve *in loco parentis* for a promising student from his territory. Diagne's friendship with Hélène Senghor, who had named one of her sons for him, added warmth to this relationship, with the result that

Sedár Senghor was a frequent visitor in the Diagne household and spent some of his summer holidays with the deputy, his French wife, and various of their four children. Diagne provided Senghor with a model of African success in France, and of the rewards that awaited the well-behaved black Frenchman.[18]

Blaise Diagne was then a controversial, albeit successful, figure. Tall, elegant, an outstanding orator, he was enjoying the fruits of his success. His duties as deputy required that he spend most of his time in Paris and move among the rich and the powerful. On his infrequent visits to Senegal, he was one of the few blacks received by white society there. W. E. B. Du Bois commented disapprovingly that Diagne was a Frenchman who is "accidentally black." The French referred to him affectionately as "our blackest deputy." The Diagne Senghor met was an elder statesman, a man in his mid-fifties remote from local concerns. He had a big apartment at a good address, took vacations in the mountains, played the odd game of tennis, and enjoyed rich dinners and wines with his friends. He lived a life indistinguishable from that of other prominent Frenchmen. In keeping with this personal style, he proclaimed to the world, "We French natives wish to remain French, since France has given us every liberty and since she has unreservedly accepted us on the same basis as her European children. None of us wishes to see French Africa given over exclusively to Africans."[19] His was one path open to Senghor.

Senghor knew that Diagne had demanded and received the respect of Frenchmen in both Africa and France. He also knew that Diagne was widely criticized at home for being subservient to French business interests. By the time Senghor met him, Diagne had lost much of his early combativeness. When first elected, he had fought for increased rights for Africans and had successfully resisted attempts by the colonial administration and Bordeaux merchant houses to whittle away long-held privileges. Now, he appeared far too accommodating to these interests and, as young Senegalese saw it, too remote from African realities. He seemed to be caught up in Paris issues and the French political game. To be sure, he was good at that game. He served in eight cabinets under various heads of government, and twice as undersecretary of state for the colonies. At Diagne's table, Senghor met many important and politically influential figures of the day and, through their conversation, gained informal knowledge of the political scene. Such occasions added one more facet to Senghor's learning about France and its culture. It seemed then of minor importance to the aspiring academic. Only years later, after he had himself joined the political fray, did Senghor recognize that he had gone to "political school with Diagne."[20]

More and more, Senghor's learning began to take place outside the classroom. As is true for many students, what he did learn and retain from the classroom was a method for approaching problems rather than any specific knowledge. He gained the habit of posing questions in a certain way, of analyzing what was given, of weighing the value of each point in turn before trying to reconstitute the whole. He learned to seek clarity, objectivity, and what was practical. At the same time, "week after week, year after year, I was able to advance my understanding of the Greco-Latin genius of which French civilization is a principal heir."[21] This was a knowledge gained from his books, from fellow students and, increasingly, from the world of Paris beyond the doors of Louis-le-grand.

In the fall of 1930, Georges Pompidou entered khâgne. Senghor later remembered his first impression of this young man who became first his deskmate and then a life-long friend, observing that when you go to a foreign land for the first time, "everyone looks alike. All the white students in khâgne looked alike. Pompidou contrasted with the others. He was taller . . . and had bushy eyebrows." Pompidou for his part befriended the "two exotics," Pham Duy Khiem from Indochina (Vietnam) and Sédar Senghor from Africa. Pompidou was popular with everyone and a recognized leader of the class. He made many friends and counted Senghor among the closest. Theirs seems to have been an easy friendship. Once when Pompidou was expecting a visitor and could not meet him at the train, he sent Senghor, assuring the friend that Senghor would stand out in any crowd.[22]

Pompidou guided Senghor into the world of contemporary Paris and gave him "a taste for the theater and museums. And also the taste for Paris." This comment is of interest, for it suggests that Sédar's first impression of Paris as a dark, forbidding city had lingered, and that for his first two years at Louis-le-grand he had lacked such a taste. Pompidou ushered in a new era, one in which Senghor spent less time at his desk, fewer Sundays with Blaise Diagne, and more time roaming the streets with his new friend, "long walks under a warm rain or the blue-gray mist. I remember the sun in the streets in spring, and in autumn, the soft gold light on a patina of stones and faces."[23] The cold rain of his first year does not dominate Senghor's memory of this later period. And his time with Pompidou is the time he later chose to remember most warmly of all.

Many years later, the two men found their lives and concerns again intertwined as both pondered the future relationship between the colonies and France in the late 1950s, Senghor as deputy from Senegal, Pompidou as a close advisor to de Gaulle on the new French constitution. Pompidou pushed to see to it that the constitution would include reference to the independence of overseas peoples, and he later participated in the secret discussions that led first to the Evian Accords, then to Algerian independence, and eventually to independence for all of France's sub-Saharan colonies. Again in the 1960s, they found themselves working together, this time as presidents of two independent countries. The special quality of this friendship is suggested by a letter Pompidou wrote to Senghor in 1968, almost forty years after their first meeting: "I evoke with nostalgia Louis-le-grand . . . Now we are both heads of state. What an adventure!"[24] No doubt Pompidou's early friendship with Senghor helped make him sensitive to Africa's aspirations for independence in a way de Gaulle was not, just as Senghor's with Pompidou provided him an ever open window on the French perspective.

Senghor has recalled that under Pompidou's guidance he began to read more widely among recent French writers. Hitherto he had confined his reading quite closely to the prescribed school program, doubtless because at first the schoolwork was difficult for him. Now he felt confident enough to branch out. In some ways Pompidou was a discouraging friend, because he mastered his schoolwork so quickly while Senghor, by his own account, had to struggle like an ox. But Pompidou opened Senghor's mind to new facets of French culture. One result of what Senghor called his new life as an intellectual vagabond was that he studied less hard for his exams. Yet from Pompidou, he "learned more . . . perhaps, than from any other of my teachers."[25]

Among the first writers who caught Senghor's interest was Maurice Barrès. Between 1929 and 1934, Plon was republishing Barrès's works that had been originally published before the war. His taste for tradition, the earth, and cultural roots was enjoying a new vogue. Senghor still recalls the impact of Barrès's novel *Les déracinés* (The Uprooted).[26] Set in the province of Lorraine, it tells the story of a group of schoolboys who are taught to scorn local tradition by misguided, and misguiding, young professors sent out from Paris. The teachers, ignorant of the Lorraine to which they have been sent by the educational bureaucracy, pride themselves on being universalists, devotees of reason. They try to convince their pupils that reason is

the key to understanding, and that what is universal is by that fact
alone more valuable than what is local or individual. Barrès shows
that the teachers have cut themselves off from their own roots and are
totally insensitive to the importance of tradition, the soil, and local
culture. The result of their teaching is confusion. In contrast, Barrès
offers as the true hero and aristocrat a young man living on land held
by his family for generations, and brought up to respect the age-old
traditions of his locality. He is the bearer of the morality and culture
of France and of national vigor, what Barrès calls the national energy.

Barrès's clear statement of the importance of traditional and provincial loyalty struck a responsive chord in Senghor: "For me, the voice
of Lorraine, the call of Lorraine . . . was the call and the voice of the
land of the Serer; the blood of Lorraine, the blood of the Serer. In
reading Barrès, I thought about the lessons of my father. I became
one with my land and with the values of its civilization."[27] If but
recently a monarchist, as he had learned to be among his politically
conservative teachers in Dakar, Senghor felt now even more justified
in regretting the passing of the "nobility" of his province, the *guelowars* of Sine. Memories of Africa were often in his mind at this
time. His teacher of philosophy, André Cresson, commented one day
in class: "When your friend Senghor speaks to me in almost all of his
themes of Africa, land of songs, he touches my heart and I question
the benefits of a civilization that consists in shutting him up in a Paris
boarding school."[28]

Senghor also began to read some of the poets who were then
popular with the intellectuals of his generation. Of them, he preferred
Claudel, Rimbaud, and Baudelaire to the more cerebral Mallarmé,
Valéry, or Verlaine. Each of the three had a special message for
Senghor.

Rimbaud had startled bourgeois France of the late nineteenth century by declaring himself a Negro and leaving France with much
fanfare to spend the rest of his life in Africa.[29] His life became as
important a part of his legend as his poetry, and may first have caught
Senghor's eye. It was Rimbaud's imagery, however, that proved of
more long-lasting influence. Born in 1854 and brought up in a small,
dull town in northeastern France, Rimbaud began writing poetry
when he was fifteen. That same year, he impetuously boarded a train
for Paris in search of poetry and excitement. Having no money to pay
for his ride, he was put in jail. Fortunately he was bailed out and sent
home, but he simply ran away again. This time he wrote to the poet

Paul Verlaine, who took him in, and there he stayed for two stormy years. In this brief time, Rimbaud wrote most of his finest poetry, notably "Une saison en enfer" (A Season in Hell), which he called his pagan or Negro book, and "Les illuminations" (The Illuminations). He then declared he would write no more poetry. As a result, his reputation rests on poems written before his twenty-second birthday. He left France and wandered, often on foot, through Europe and the Middle East to Egypt. He became the first European to explore the Ogaden area, and finally settled on the coast in what is today Ethiopia. There he lived by trading guns and doing such other merchant business as he could pick up. The rest of his life was spent in this self-imposed exile, until an illness that would prove fatal forced him to return to France. From Ethiopia, in letters to his family (which Senghor probably did not know about), he expressed in more discursive form the ambivalence about Europe and Africa that marked his poetry.

"Une saison en enfer" is a long narrative poem that sets out the reasons for the poet's embrace of the persona of Negro. In style it is iconoclastic, consciously breaking most of the stylistic rules and regulations that had long governed French verse. The poem treats a classic theme, namely the poet's descent into himself in search of an authentic self. When Rimbaud looks within, he sees a plethora of conflicting elements in his heritage—Gallic, peasant, Christian—which pull him in conflicting directions. He also finds an irreconcilable inconsistency between his sensibility as a poet and the reality of his life in a hypocritical, morally pretentious bourgeois society. He feels anger and disgust, both with himself and with the culture that has made him what he is. He then makes his decision: he will reject this pallid, corrupt society and that part of himself which it has shaped. He will go back and join the Negro in a pagan world that does not know Christianity. The Negro may live in a world innocent of right and wrong, but at least he is free from the hypocrisy of so-called civilized man. From that world, the poet can make a fresh start. In words memorable to his and future generations, he declared, "I am a beast, a Negro" and attacked France as full of fierce, miserly maniacs. He avowed that the noblest thing he could do was to abandon a continent where madness prowled and to enter into the kingdom of the children of Ham. Then, and only then, might he be saved. But first he must acknowledge his dark side.[30]

Rimbaud, the poet, in his new persona as Negro, watches the white Christians approach Africa. They go ashore with their guns and force people to "submit to baptism, to wear clothes, to toil."[31] The Christians have come from a society in which pretense and falsehood confuse every action. In Africa, they can still find a vitality and an innocence that would make an honest life possible. But they do not. Instead they infect Africa as well. Yet Rimbaud knows that he cannot solve his own problems simply by rejecting Europe for Africa. He continues to yearn for the Christian God. It is a hunger implanted by his personal baptism and two thousand years of Christianity. At one moment he prays for God's help and deliverance from a personal hell. At another, he despairs of reconciliation with God, and sees the identity of the beast/Negro as his only authentic one, one that offers salvation from the fate of false pretender, but at the cost of damnation.

The most unusual aspect of this poem, considering that it was written in 1873, is the imagery with which Rimbaud depicts the struggle between two parts of himself, or two possible selves. This he conceptualizes as a struggle between Negro and white, an innocent Africa and a corrupt West. With the withering honesty of the young, Rimbaud unmasks and condemns himself, and France, for hypocrisy at home and cynicism in the colonies, for forcing on Africans a dialect that stifles the drum, and for corrupting a whole people for commercial and military ends.[32] But this same clear vision prevents him from transforming Africa into an Eden. Africa is alternately attractive, offering the poet "spicy" lands, and repellent, a soggy, "sodden" place; it is not corrupt, but it lacks the higher moral dimension possible only with Christianity. The Negro remains the beast/Negro.

Clearly Rimbaud was not preoccupied with the actual relationship between a real Africa and a real France, or with the true nature of the African. He used the two as geographical symbols to express an inner struggle. In his poetic world, he created a landscape in which Africa and France occupied clearly defined territory. In this world, in certain moods, the poet rejected the land conventionally assumed to be superior, France, for that conventionally despised, Africa.

There is, of course, a long European tradition of looking to other lands and peoples with a wishful eye that sees "realities" that are not at all descriptions of real people, but rather projections of the viewer's fantasy. The non-Western man, in this case the African, becomes a model of what the European thinks he himself was in happier days, in the past, or what he might one day become. What the European sees in the African tells as much about his own needs as it does about the people he observes.[33] Rimbaud found the African both savage and innocent, if not the perfect man, at least more honest and less corrupt than the European. In many ways, Rimbaud shared French stereotypes of Africans, such as the assumption that if they were not Christian they could have no morality at all. What set Rimbaud apart from the usual theorizer was that he fused symbol and reality in his own life. He abandoned France for Africa and lived as if his symbolic world and the real world were one and the same. He thus greatly strengthened the credibility of his vision. He also expressed this vision in poetry of rare power. Once in Africa, Rimbaud became somewhat disillusioned by the reality of what he found, but never sufficiently so to return to France until he was mortally ill.

Senghor's fellow students read Rimbaud for his extraordinary imagery and the violence and boldness with which he challenged the assumptions of his elders. Surrealist spokesman André Breton considered Rimbaud the precursor of a whole new movement in the arts.[34] All recognized that Rimbaud was a great stylist and innovator. But Senghor saw more. He saw a vision of bourgeois France not unlike his own. He saw a contrasting image of Africa that contained much that was positive, both like and unlike his own recollection of home. Rimbaud provided a way of thinking about the contrast between Africa and Europe that was more complicated than that of the usual Frenchman. The fact that Rimbaud's subject was a moral and psychological conflict he felt within himself and within French culture, not the contrast between two different cultures, did not destroy the power of the images he constructed. What Rimbaud intended as a symbolic contrast of Negro and French had a concrete dimension for Senghor.

About the time he was reading Rimbaud, Senghor experienced a short-lived religious crisis. Later, recalling the reasons for it, he commented that it was part of a general disillusion with Europe. Three years in khâgne had taught him that Europe possessed no universal recipe, and had its dark as well as its bright side. While living in Africa, it had been possible to believe the assurances of his teachers that in France the Christian message was honored. Troubles with a seminary director or a teacher in Dakar could be attributed to aberration, or to the effect of isolation on a peevish individual. In the real France, he now saw, "the idea was not linked to the act, the word to deed, the morality to life."[35] The contradiction between the teachings of Christianity, which Senghor had embraced with youthful idealism, and its rather sordid reflection in the life of Paris was borne in on him. He was tempted, as he put it, by despair, one of the most serious of

Christian sins. His disillusion at this point focused on the hypocrisy of French life, the quality that had pushed Rimbaud to find its opposite in an imagined Africa. Unlike Rimbaud, however, Senghor was able in the end to see his way through this despair to a reconciliation with God. Either this period of lost faith was brief or Senghor kept it to himself, for his friends from Louis-le-grand remember only the devout and sincere believer who attended Mass every Sunday. He was not one to share his troubles with others.

The devoutly Christian poet Paul Claudel helped Senghor to retrieve a viable Christianity as, later, Pierre Teilhard de Chardin was to confirm it. Claudel offered, Senghor later said, a new plane on which to be a Christian. Claudel, too, had found Rimbaud fascinating. He had discovered in Rimbaud not only rebellion and despair but also an honest, if desperate, search for God. Claudel went so far as to name Rimbaud as a religious inspiration responsible for leading him back to God. Rimbaud's influence on Claudel did not carry over to poetic style, however, for Claudel perfected a traditional, almost biblical style for a poetry that was profoundly Catholic in tone and content. To Senghor, immersed as he was at this time in the study of the classics and educated from childhood to know every word of the Catholic Mass, Claudel's style felt familiar and comforting. In Claudel Senghor found a sensitivity to each and every object in God's creation that was not only Christian, he thought, but profoundly similar to that of the African.[36]

However much Rimbaud may have jolted Senghor, or Claudel have provided comfort, it was the poetry of Baudelaire that Senghor loved best. Among his most vivid memories of khâgne are those of Pompidou reciting Baudelaire. "I hear him still, reciting to me 'The Flowers of Evil' in a grave voice, a bit muffled, monotonous. It was the tone of an incantation, the very tone of the bards of Senegal."[37] His friends remember Senghor himself reciting Baudelaire. Such was Senghor's interest in this poet that in preparing his Diplôme d'Etudes Supérieures, he chose a Baudelaire text for his analysis and also wrote his qualifying essay on exoticism in the work of Baudelaire.

Baudelaire's chief poetical work, Les fleurs du mal (The Flowers of Evil), is a collection of poems written over a long period of time, which expresses a variety of moods and attitudes. What holds them together is Baudelaire's overriding concern with the search for beauty, a search always hedged in by his preoccupation with the problem of good and evil and his discomforting suspicion that the divine and the bestial are so close as to be inseparable. To find the beauty and meaning he believed to lie behind the surface logic of the external world, Baudelaire sought escape in drugs and alcohol from the censorship of intellect. He thus explored his sensuality in fact as well as in imagination. This rich soil gave root to Baudelaire's poetry. From it grew poetic flowers of pain, disillusion, and great sorrow, but also of great beauty. *Les fleurs du mal* grew out of the struggle between flesh and spirit, as Baudelaire reached for an honest morality with which to counter the hollow conformity of "civilized" life.

Many of Baudelaire's poems are addressed to a beautiful woman, a woman of color. She provides the symbolic bridge to carry the poet from the flat reality of his actual life in Paris to an exotic world bright with flowers and perfumed with tropical spices. This brilliant world is no simple paradise, for it beckons the poet to a slavery of the senses that both attracts and repels him.

The woman who inspired Baudelaire was Jeanne Duval, a West Indian woman of mixed blood from Santo Domingo. She was the poet's mistress, companion, and obsession for eighteen years. In praise of her and in contemplation of the contrast between her tropical childhood and her Parisian adulthood, Baudelaire wrote a poem of special poignancy for any exile, and especially for an exile from tropical Africa. He wrote of her dark body and velvet eyes, of the hot luxurious landscape of her island childhood, and of his wonder that anyone would leave such a paradise for a place like France where sad-eyed people shivered in a land of dirty fog, hail, and snow.[38]

The exotic world conjured up by Baudelaire readily fed Senghor's nostalgia for Africa, inspired as it was by a woman of color and filled with the colors, smells, and even the tamarind tree of the tropics. Cresson, Senghor's philosophy teacher, had remarked on the descriptions of Africa that crept into Senghor's papers. Study of Baudelaire's poems provided Senghor with an opportunity to let his imagination wander south and dwell in the world of his childhood.

Senghor's favorite among these poems, which he memorized and chanted aloud for the benefit of his friends, was "La chevelure" (To Her Hair). The poem begins with the poet gazing at the black woman's hair, which triggers his imagination. Reflecting on its abundance, he finds his room filled with echoes, and soon he flees to hot Africa, a land of perfumes and noises, skies that quiver with heat, and air scented with coconuts, musk, and tar. The black woman's hair provides "an oasis" and a key to unlock and free the "wines of memory."[39] For

Senghor, this poem also provided an oasis and a key to unlock his treasured memories of Africa and a temporary refuge from thoughts of Paris.

About this time, Senghor himself began to write poetry. In his first poems, memories of childhood form his chief subject. Many are frankly nostalgic evocations of his childhood in village Africa:

Joal!
I remember
I remember the woman in the green shade of the verandas
. . . . .

I remember the funeral feasts smoking with the blood of fattened
    sheep
The noise of quarrels with the rhapsodies of the griots
I remember the pagan voices chanting the Tantum Ergo
And the processions of palms and the triumphal arches
. . . . .

I remember, I remember . . .
My head full of rhythm
What a dreary route throughout the days of Europe where now and
    then
Appears an orphan jazz that weeps, weeps, weeps.[40]

Here Senghor presents a contrast not unlike Baudelaire's, between the warmth and luxury of Africa and the cold, austere life of Paris. For Senghor, however, unlike Baudelaire, the setting of village Africa is unequivocally attractive and whole. It does not include the temptation to evil or self-abasement. In another poem, one of his best known, Senghor writes in praise of the beauty of the black woman. He evokes her sensuality. This sensuality is a clear, physical, and healthy quality that altogether lacks the suggestion of danger and self-annihilation that hovers over Baudelaire's tropical world. The woman is neither dangerous nor demanding, but a simple physical presence.

Naked woman, black woman
Clothed with your colour which is life, with your form which is
    beauty
In your shadow I have grown up; the gentleness of your hands was
    laid over my eyes
And now, high up on the sun-baked pass, at the heart of summer, at
    the heart of noon, I come upon you, my Promised Land.
And your beauty strikes me to the heart like the flash of an eagle.[41]

For Senghor, the poetry of Africa and of childhood contained an element of escapism. For such a poetry, however, he found approval in Baudelaire's critical theory. If Senghor reached back to the kingdom of childhood as the inspiration for his poetry, Baudelaire had observed that this was true of all great artists: "The character, the genius, and the style of a man is formed by the apparently commonplace occurrences of his childhood."[42] By this assertion, Baudelaire gave Senghor permission, indeed encouragement, to let his imagination run to the kingdom of childhood. Baudelaire confirmed Senghor's growing sense that childhood experience must form the basis for the development of a personal voice. This notion had already found support in Barrès, in the argument that tradition and native soil were the source of all national energy and creativity.

One other aspect of Baudelaire's literary criticism is worth notice, in light of the fact that Senghor not only loved his poetry but chose to study and write on his work. Baudelaire believed in a system of what he called correspondences between visible objects and an inner and more significant meaning for which the objects were a signal or sign. He was a Swedenborgian, insofar as he thought that outward appearances, the objects of the everyday world, are but the tangible shell of a greater and more important intangible reality. In Baudelaire's view, every object in the natural or visible world corresponds to a more vital reality in the invisible spiritual world. The great poet or artist is the person who can decipher this relationship. The poet does not create so much as translate the code. He illuminates these correspondences.[43] This idea must have made sense to Senghor. Several years later, describing the world view of the African, he chose the same word Baudelaire had used, *correspondance,* to describe the relationship that Africans know to exist between objects in the material and spiritual worlds.

The poet as translator was an idea that Baudelaire and Senghor shared. Rimbaud, in his own way, also viewed the poet as translator, but he worked from the opposite direction. He did not contemplate the physical shell of the Negro to understand what lay beneath it, but, on the contrary, created a vibrant symbolic Negro to house the qualities he found in his inner world. He was interested in the image of the Negro for what it might be made to signify. Baudelaire thought he was working from outward appearance to find the spiritual world it signified. He did not create Jeanne Duval entirely from his imagination, but her image developed its vibrancy as a metaphor for the world of warmth and color that dwelt in his imagination. Together Rimbaud and Baudelaire contributed to the creation of a vivid role for the Negro in the French consciousness. Each began with a private vision that he wished to bring to life, and then chose the Negro as its vehicle. Their symbolic purpose did not prevent Senghor from connecting this imagined Negro to the African he actually knew. Senghor felt the power of their images and saw the Negro through their eyes as well as through his own. Years later, he declared that Rimbaud had recognized the values of Negritude, that special vitality and authenticity of the Negro and his civilization that sets him apart from an aging and artificial Europe. He also credited Rimbaud and the philosopher Henri Bergson as key figures in the cultural revolution that enabled France to break out of its eighteenth-century fixation on the power of reason, a narrowness of vision that had led French nineteenth-century culture to a dead end.[44]

While reading the poets and writers popular with his generation, Senghor also continued to prepare for his exams. Throughout this year of "intellectual vagabondage," 1930–31, his grades showed steady improvement. His teachers recognized his "serious and hard-working effort," and one even commented that he showed "a quality of depth," a rare professional lapse in the usual laconic "rather good's" and "improving" that sprinkle the grade books at Louis-le-grand. The quality of Senghor's thinking was beginning to manifest itself, particularly in literature and history, where he stood in the top third of his class. Nonetheless, he failed the entrance exam for the Ecole Normale Supérieure that spring. While many of his classmates decided to stay at Louis-le-grand to try again, Senghor decided he was too old to take another year and would go on to university to study for a teaching diploma.[45]

The day of his graduation from Louis-le-grand held special poignancy for Senghor, because the main speaker took as his subject the French empire. Interest in the colonies was high in 1931, largely because of the May opening of the vast colonial exhibition on the outskirts of the city at Vincennes. The exposition was intended to educate Frenchmen about their empire. It included reconstructions of entire villages to show the life and diversity of peoples from such distant places as Indochina and India, New Caledonia, the Antilles, Madagascar, and French Africa. Thousands of Parisians flocked to the exposition, as much to marvel at their own nation's accomplishments as to learn about the peoples over whom they held sway.

The exposition was the occasion for a series of officially sponsored books on the territories. The book on West Africa, written by Robert Delavignette, was illustrated with pictures of half-naked women with jugs on their heads, men fishing, and other people dancing or lying about listlessly under shade trees. Its text suggested a more subtle, if still stereotypical view of African life.[46] This book, like the exposition as a whole, piqued interest in the empire while simultaneously confirming widely held beliefs about French greatness and the relative backwardness of others. A spate of novels and travel books were published to take advantage of the current vogue for the colonies. Such writings were devoured by a public drawn to a new and titillating type of escape literature.

The nature of popular thinking about the colonies is suggested by the success of Edith Piaf's teary tribute to "Mon Legionnaire," the man who had left her to go off to explore distant lands, and one of Senghor's classmates, Paul Guth, who recollected he spent a full year in his "exotic stage," reading everything he could about the colonies and doing the Charleston, a dance made popular by Josephine Baker.[47] The best-selling novelist Roger Martin du Gard created a heroine who was fascinated by the "barbaric dances" of Africa she saw performed in Paris. She admired the African dancers for their sensuality, criticized her French companion for his lack of energy and imagination, and explained to her friends: "It's only over there one can really live." There one had the right to be oneself.[48] Such were some of the stereotypes about the colonies and their inhabitants. Most Frenchmen continued to think of Africa, if they thought of it at all, as a romantic, primitive place, and based their opinions on fanciful travel literature and popular novels.

Students at Louis-le-grand studied about the colonies from an anthology of excerpts from a number of different French writers. Senghor would have read of Senegal that it was a land where "naked children armed with reeds long as lances . . . climb up on huge termite mounds" to protect the fields from monkeys and brightly colored tropical birds. This same book included a selection from one of the heroes of empire, Marshal Lyautey, who urged young men to come out to the colonies, there to join a "more and more numerous group of initiators, strong men" who would be able one day to overcome the inertia of metropolitan France. Such men would reawaken a "spirit of fertility . . . commerce, and enterprise" and lift France out of its current doldrums.[49] The colonies, in short, were to provide a training ground for future leaders of France. That the training ground might be scarred by the crude maneuvers of the French trainees was never recognized as an issue.

Paul Reynaud, then the Colonial Minister, opened the exposition by explaining that its goal was "to give to the French a consciousness of their empire . . . Each one of us must feel himself a citizen of the greater France." Thereafter the words empire and greater France (la plus grande France) became part of the French political vocabulary. Another official declared: "France is an indivisible whole. The old France of Europe and the young France overseas have grown slowly closer . . . have mixed with each other and have become inseparable." Men began to dream of a France with a hundred million inhabitants. Novelists, adventurers, businessmen, politicians, missionaries, patriots, and moralists all found something of value in the idea of empire.[50]

It was in this context that a geographer, Duplessis-Kergomand, had been invited to address the parents and students at the Lycée Louis-le-grand graduation and prize day in July 1931. It was an important event for the intellectual community of Paris, presided over by an important official from the University of Paris, as well as the director of the school and a representative of the diplomatic corps. It was a day on which Senghor could expect to enjoy his achievement. He had not passed into the Ecole Normale Supérieure, but he had done well. His name was on the honor roll for excellence in his studies. On this particular graduation day, he was going to have the opportunity to hear an address on a subject close to his heart, namely the French empire. What he heard may have surprised him. It could not have pleased him.

After outlining the qualities that made French colonization unique, namely the devoted attachment of the colonial peoples to France in gratitude for the gift of peace and prosperity to their primitive lands formerly plagued by civil wars and terrible epidemics, Duplessis-Kergomand urged the graduating students to consider careers in colonial service. The goal of colonization now, he pointed out, is no longer conquest but the extraction of raw materials, trade with France, and the education of the natives. "You will love these big children, the Blacks, and . . . the Yellow people," he continued, "as parents love their children, as the master loves his pupils."[51] Listening to this exhortation, Senghor may have wondered where he fit into this vision of the future.

Graduation day provided in capsule form the mixed experience

Senghor had had since he arrived in Paris: on the one hand, success and recognition, even prizes for excellence; on the other, an undercurrent surfacing from time to time in a racist remark from a fellow student, the thoughtless comment of a child, or an insulting literary description of African life. Unless he were to forget entirely who he was, he had to accept the fact that he was different and did not truly belong. As he moved on to the Sorbonne to continue his studies, Senghor took with him this mixed experience. French tradition had a definite place for the Negro, that of the big friendly child or the lazy but passionate primitive. A few French writers, self-critical and in rebellion against bourgeois society, had suggested a somewhat different role for the Negro. Yet even they, Baudelaire and Rimbaud for example, created an image of the Negro that embodied some of these same stereotypes.

Recalling his time at Louis-le-grand many years later, Senghor mentioned that he often thought of his teachers and former friends, "from whom I have taken my best quality, the spirit of humanity that permits me to place honors in the right perspective." Elsewhere he wrote, "the most important lesson I received from Paris was less the discovery of others than of myself." He discovered himself by recognizing what he was not: he was not a white Frenchman. He was attracted to French culture, and he felt "a great weakness for France." But when he listened to his own voice he heard, like it or not, that, "civilized for a long time . . . I speak its language well, but with what a barbarous accent!"[52]

If Senghor had learned what he was not, he was not yet certain what he was. The search for what he was could no longer be avoided. It led Senghor to what he called his "Negritude." He came to this discovery in part through self-examination, in part by learning how others saw him, and in part by participating in a special milieu that crystallized in Paris in the mid-1930s. Students from all over the empire, men of color as they liked to call themselves, drew together out of a shared sense of being set apart. This perception temporarily obscured the great differences among them. They gathered to discuss why and how they differed from the French. It was in this setting that the idea of Negritude was born.

4

The Milieu of Negritude

The few years after he left Louis-le-grand were crucial ones in Senghor's intellectual development. Both his intellectual and his personal horizons expanded dramatically. He began to find his way toward a mature understanding of himself as a black man in the Frenchman's world. It was a journey made easier by friendship with other black men who were following a similar path, but, however exciting, it took courage to face unpleasant realities. At times, the strain threatened to destroy his precarious inner balance. To find his way, Senghor had to create a new view of himself that would allow him to draw on both his African and his French experience.

After graduating from Louis-le-grand, Senghor enrolled at the Sorbonne to study literature as preparation for becoming a teacher. He moved out of the dormitory, where he had slept one among many in two long rows of monkish iron beds, and into a newly completed student hostel at Cité Universitaire. His hostel, The Fondation Deutsch de la Meurthe, was named for an oil tycoon whose desire to establish a great philanthropic work had led to the creation of a "student city" near the middle of Paris. By bringing students from all over the French-speaking world together, the founders of Cité Universitaire hoped to promote understanding and unity. Prior to its construction, students had had no alternative but to live in hotels scattered throughout Paris. The Fondation Deutsche de la Meurthe was built in Anglo-Saxon style as filtered through the French imagination: its buildings had quaint pointed roofs and vine-covered walls. Modest as Senghor's quarters were, they were luxurious compared to those at Louis-le-grand. Of their advantages, the greatest was privacy.

At the end of his first year at the Sorbonne in the spring of 1932, Senghor succeeded in getting the Diplôme d'Etudes Supérieures. It was for this degree that he submitted an essay on exoticism in Baudelaire. He also prepared Baudelaire as one of the authors upon whom he was examined orally. In the course of the year, he had a brief stint as a practice teacher as preparation for his intended vocation. The report that his supervisor, M. Roland, wrote for the scholarship office painted a clear picture of a conscientious, conventional young man, abiding by all the rules in his teaching: M. Senghor "knew how to appreciate the class as a whole . . . (and has) an actively experimental method, going always from the concrete to the abstract, using abundant and appropriate familiar images that are simple and expressive, sometimes attaching himself to a single pupil and leading him patiently to find the correct answer." M. Roland concluded, "I think that M. Senghor will be a remarkable teacher. He has a profound pedagogical sense. He himself told me that he had a real vocation for teaching. I think he was not mistaken when he told me that."[1] This report helped ensure Senghor further scholarship support for his studies; it also indicates that he was pursuing a path conventional for an aspiring French intellectual. But he was an African.

With the idea of becoming a university professor or at least a lycée teacher, Senghor set out to get the difficult *agrégé* degree in grammar, the equivalent of the American Ph.D. No African had as yet obtained it. Why he chose grammar rather than letters is not altogether clear. This course had a reputation for being somewhat easier than literature, and it would allow him to pursue his interest in languages. It may also be that he shared the feeling of many of his fellow students that the study of literature at the Sorbonne was musty and out of date. Certainly the morale among the literature students was low. Senghor gave as his reason the fact that he wanted to do research on the native languages of Senegal, as indeed he did some years later.

When seeking to qualify for this course of study, Senghor had rather a rude shock. In the enrollment book at Lycée Louis-le-grand, he had listed himself as of French nationality. Now the Sorbonne administration discovered that he was not legally a French citizen and so was not eligible to take the qualifying exams for the agrégé. He was a subject, born outside of the four communes of Senegal. He had never thought to apply for a change in status. By the 1930s, French residents in the colonies had begun to fear rising political and economic competition from Africans, and the colonial administration was making it difficult for subjects to become citizens. At this point, Senghor turned to Blaise Diagne. Whatever he may have felt about Daigne's politics, Senghor was too bent on his goal to let such reservations prevent his asking for help. With Diagne's intervention, an exception was made. Senghor was naturalized as a French citizen in June of 1933. Once again, the advantage of having an elected deputy in Paris who outranked the colonial governor showed its usefulness. The one drawback was that Senghor the citizen was obligated to do French military service. At the time, this seemed a small price to pay for the right to seek to qualify as a professor. With characteristic determination, Senghor then set his mind on the agrégé exam, his next goal.

As a student at the Sorbonne, Senghor had the opportunity to meet many new kinds of people and the leisure to follow up on his intellectual interests. School discipline no longer restricted his comings and goings, nor was he held to a steady rhythm of productive work, books that had to be read, essays that had to be written. He still had exams and papers to worry about, but semesters were long, and his time was more his own. It was now possible for him to pursue a wide variety of friendships, to study or talk late into the night, and engage in the heated conversations that students carry on without end in the cafés that surround the Sorbonne. It is characteristic of Senghor that he threaded his way among various groups and schools of thought, seeking to understand what each might offer of value, without fully identifying with any. He developed cordial relationships with the French intellectual establishment, with socialist students, with colonial administrators, and with the black colony resident in Paris, without ever losing the conviction that none of these worlds fully described himself.

In September of 1931, the autumn after he moved to the Cité Universitaire, Senghor met Aimé Césaire. These two quickly became, each for the other, friend, sounding board, support, teacher and pupil by turn. Césaire, like Senghor, was an outstanding student from overseas. He had come from Martinique to prepare at Lycée Louis-le-grand for entrance to the Ecole Normale Superiéure. Like Senghor he experienced the shock of arriving in Paris full of hopes and anticipation, and confident from past success, only to find the French uninterested in him and unexpectedly alien. He too was a person of great talent, and he too was to combine the careers of poet and political figure. The two formed a special bond and remained life-long friends. Although they later diverged in their political views—Césaire spent a number of years in the Communist Party—these disagreements never destroyed their friendship or their mutual respect. As in his relationship with Pompidou, Senghor saw to it that political differences did not sever personal ties.

The quality of this friendship and its importance for both men was summed up some forty years later by Césaire. The occasion was a trip to Martinique in 1976 by Senghor, then president of Senegal. Césaire, himself the mayor of Martinique's capital city, Fort-de-France, offered the official greeting. He recalled:

> For forty years, we have lived in parallel . . . leaving each other, as life went, but nonetheless never truly separating. Was this surprising? After all, our adolescences were entirely blended. We read the same books, and often the same copy, shared the same dreams, loved the same poets. We were torn by the same anguish and, above all, were weighed down by the same problems . . . our youth was not banal . . . It was marked by the tormenting question, who am I? For us, it was not a question of metaphysics, but of a life to live, an ethic to create, and communities to save. We tried to answer that question. In the end, our answer was Negritude.[2]

Césaire's fond remembrances are confirmed by such evidence as a copy of Leo Frobenius's African ethnography inscribed to Senghor from Césaire, as well as by the recollections of their friends.[3]

It testifies to the apparent success of France's colonizing mission that the two would-be scholars from distant parts of the world met first in Paris in the narrow street in front of Louis-le-grand. Césaire had arrived about two weeks before, and was going to register for hypokhâgne, an experience Senghor well remembered. He was, as Senghor had been three years before, new to the city, a bit lost, a bit ill at ease in what seemed then a severe and unfriendly place. From that moment the two were friends. Each was drawn to the other not just by color but because both had a growing preoccupation with the problem of color as such. Senghor was the first African Césaire knew well; Césaire was the first black man Senghor had met who, well-educated, young, and ambitious, shared his awareness of being set apart.[4] Together they began to ponder the problem: If I am so very different from the French, who then am I? In temperament they were totally different, Césaire volatile, excitable, and combative, Senghor measured and cautious, already a bit professorial, ever in search of the middle way. Yet they proved to be kindred spirits.

Césaire shared his excitement about meeting "a brilliant African in the Quartier Latin" with an old schoolmate from Martinique, Guyana-born Léon Damas. In theory, Damas was in Paris to study law, but in fact he was enjoying the Bohemian life, writing poetry and attending courses at the Institute of Ethnography. Both he and Césaire had begun to feel dissatisfied with their total immersion in French culture, and had grown curious about Africa. Senghor was their first direct contact with it. As Césaire put it, "in meeting Senghor, I met Africa."[5]

Damas and Césaire opened new vistas for Senghor. Through them he met the West Indian colony in Paris, notably the Nardal sisters, Jane, Paulette, and Andrée, and their cousins, the Achille family, also from Martinique. Louis Achille, Jr., was about Senghor's age and, like him, wanted to be a teacher. Louis Achille, Sr., had been a professor at Howard University in Washington, D.C., spoke English as well as French, and had many contacts with black American intellectuals. It was natural for black Americans traveling to Europe to arrive at the Achilles' apartment with a letter of introduction from one of Louis's colleagues at Howard. Visiting Americans found the Achille household congenial, "typically French . . . cordial and cultivated."[6] Paulette Nardal was often called upon to entertain them, and would tour the city, organize a trip to Versailles, or perhaps arrange an evening at the Folies Bergère. There the black American singer Josephine Baker was among the most popular performers in a variety show that included skits and songs as well as dancing. Such entertainment was considered the epitome of civilized, French nightlife: American jazz was taking the city by storm. The black Americans, in turn, found Paris invigorating and liberating, almost entirely free from the restrictions that hemmed them in at home.

The Achilles' apartment overlooked the Jardin des Plantes, not far from the Sorbonne. It was convenient for students as well as for the touring Americans. Senghor, like many of his new West Indian friends, was a frequent guest. The Americans who passed through ranged from the dean of Howard University to Mercer Cook, a black American professor of French and one of the first to publicize in the United States the work of French-speaking blacks. Senghor also met members of an older generation of West Indians such as René Maran, who had won a prize some ten years before for a novel set in Africa, *Batouala*. It was here that Senghor first began to learn about the writers of the Harlem Renaissance and the New Negro movement in the United States. In time, he began to meet the black Americans, who were always welcome in the Achilles' bilingual household. He discovered with surprise that there was a whole world, even if a small one, that was as preoccupied as he was by the question of color.

There were also more informal gatherings of young people at Paulette Nardal's apartment. She and her sisters, accomplished musicians, invited friends on Sundays for dancing and talk to the accompaniment of the new American music. Senghor occasionally joined them, but he seemed stiff and ill at ease. He was no dancer, and quite the opposite of the stereotype of the loose and easy-going black African.

Some of the members of this group began publishing a journal, *La Revue du Monde Noir* (The Review of the Black World) in the fall of 1931. In its purpose and substance the journal marked a new departure for French-speaking blacks. It was based on the assumptions, novel for the time, that all black people, regardless of national origin, language, or culture, formed a natural grouping that had common interests, and that education, research, and cultural activities were a primary means of bringing this community together. In keeping with this aim, all articles in the review appeared in both English and French. Knowledge of one another, so went the thinking, would transform a potential community into a real one. The goal was nothing less than the creation of a new worldwide black consciousness. The editors also stated that they had no intention of being racially exclusive or separatist.

The first issue included a statement of purpose:

> to give to the intelligentia of the blak [sic] race and to their partisans an official organ in which to publish their artistic, literary, and scientific works. To study and to popularize . . . all which concerns NEGRO CIVILIZATION and the natural riches of Africa . . . [and] to create among the Negroes of the entire world, regardless of nationality, an intellectual and moral tie which will permit them to better know each other, to love one another, to defend more effectively their collective interests and to glorify their race.

Serving the black race was not the sole aim of the review: "By this means, the Negro race will contribute along with thinking minds of other races and with all those who have received the light of truth, beauty, and goodness to the material, the moral and the intellectual improvement of humanity."[7]

The list of contributors to *La Revue du Monde Noir* reads like a who's who of important black writers and thinkers of the next few decades. It was distinguished from the group around Nancy Cunard by the absence of well-known French literary figures and by the relative youth of its members. Young West Indian writers such as Louis Achille, Andrée Nardal, Etienne Léro, René Maran, Gilbert Gratiant, and René Menil contributed fiction and poetry, as well as articles on black music, art, and folktales; Félix Eboué, a Guyanese who had served in the colonial administration in central Africa and was then a student at the school for colonial administrators in Paris, retold several folktales he had collected among the Banda of central Africa. Eboué later became the governor of French Equatorial Africa and an important supporter of de Gaulle during World War II. He also became Senghor's father-in-law.

The editors of the review printed excerpts from the work of leading ethnographers, notably Maurice Delafosse and Leo Frobenius, two men whose work later shaped Senghor's thinking about African society. There were articles about black America, such as a description of education at the Tuskegee Institute, and about the experience of black Americans in Liberia. And finally, seemingly most important for Senghor at the time, the review contained a sampling of the work of two contemporary black American poets, Claude McKay and Langston Hughes. Langston Hughes's "I, Too" appeared in the third issue: "I, too, sing America. I am the darker brother." The black is forced to eat in the kitchen, but one day he will sit at the table. Then white Americans will see how beautiful he is, and they will be ashamed.

Senghor remained on the periphery of this project, but spent time with its editors and writers. It is almost certain that he first encountered the new black American poetry in this review. He did not know about the Harlem Renaissance before he met Césaire, and Césaire has confirmed that he himself first read the poetry of Hughes and McKay in the review.[8] Soon thereafter, Senghor was reciting poems by Hughes, McKay, Jean Toomer, and Countee Cullen by heart, and struggling to read articles in English written by W. E. B. Du Bois and Carter Woodson in The Crisis and Opportunity, the journals of the National Association for the Advancement of Colored People (NAACP) and the National Urban League respectively.[9]

Senghor was deeply impressed by Alain Locke's edited volume The New Negro (1925), which he read at this time. The New Negro had been a landmark in the cultural awakening of American blacks. Its title, suggesting a new beginning, impressed Senghor so much that he later took this same term in French translation, le nègre nouveau, to refer to the new man with new attitudes he hoped to see among

French-speaking blacks. His deliberate choice of the word *nègre,* rather than the more respectable *noir,* suggests both the influence of the Americans and Senghor's wish to signal a break with past attitudes. Indeed, Locke's book may also have given Senghor the idea for his own anthology of French-speaking black writers, which he published in 1948. Locke had pulled together selections from many of the writers of the Harlem Renaissance, and included an introduction to analyze their significance. The Harlem Renaissance had earned its name from the fact that most of its participants lived and worked in the Harlem section of New York City. A diverse group of poets, social critics, and writers were loosely united by an overriding central purpose: the determination, as Langston Hughes put it, to reject all inferiority complexes and express themselves without shame or fear.[10] They believed a positive self-image was a necessary first step toward achieving equality in American life. If Negroes were able to become thinkers and doers, they argued, reasonable men would have to recognize them as equals.

Alain Locke himself was a Harvard graduate, class of 1906, Rhodes Scholar and Ph.D., who was then a professor of philosophy at Howard. *The New Negro* was a scholar's look at the black writing and research of the Harlem Renaissance, and its title was chosen to call attention to a remarkable new departure. Locke also asked an ever provocative question: Why had this outburst of creativity occurred in this place at this time? In answer, he pointed out that there were now many more educational opportunities for Negroes than ever before, but even more important, that in the 1920s Harlem and a few other northern cities had become centers of migration for energetic rural Negroes from many different parts of the country. Transplanted, they were transformed. In Harlem, Americans met West Indians and even Africans. Their world stretched, and their minds stretched with it. This expanded awareness led to a totally new outlook.[11] According to Locke, the Harlem Renaissance was the result of social and intellectual developments in the United States that created an urban Negro milieu. It was precisely this sort of milieu that was now emerging in Paris.

The concept of the New Negro with pride in himself and his heritage, determined to create his own culture, appealed immediately to Senghor. That American blacks had made such a bold declaration and begun to act accordingly by writing poetry, literature, and history allowed him to think that French-speaking blacks might do likewise. The work of Anglophone and Francophone blacks had previously been separated by language. Now both English and French speakers worked to close this gap. Mercer Cook, for example, put together an anthology of French-speaking black writers to use in his advanced French literature seminar at Howard University.[12]

La Revue du Monde Noir devoted itself entirely to cultural matters. The editors took care not to speculate about the possible social or political implications of what they were doing, or to tie individual works to a specific historical and social context. Nonetheless, the Paris police watched the group carefully and sent notes to the colonial administration about its contributors. One of its editors, Louis-Jean Finot, was described as possibly dangerous, a "Jewish Negrophile married to a black violinist." The review's statement of purpose was thought worth summarizing for the police archive, as were other reports speculating about possible links to Communists and other black activists such as the American Garveyites.[13]

Two articles in the review's sixth and final issue were exceptions to the policy of avoiding subjects with social or political implications. The first of these was called "La poésie ethnique" (Ethnic Poetry) in its French version, but the English version was entitled "Racial Poetry." Whether this inaccurate translation indicates that the English speakers were more militant than the French speakers is not clear. In the article, A. G. Perier reviewed a book in which a former colonial minister warned that one day the colonies would fight metropolitan France with its own weapons, by which he meant modern technology. Perier suggested that a somewhat different counter-thrust was already under way as the "penetration of Negro art and literature into the white world constitutes a far reaching offensive."[14] Perier did not develop this idea further.

The second article with political implications was Paulette Nardal's "The Awakening of Race Consciousness."[15] Nardal identified three stages through which race consciousness had evolved in the Antilles and the United States. In tracing this development, she never questioned that race, rather than cultural, linguistic, or historical factors, was the salient cause. But neither did she suggest that all members of the black race, including the Africans, would pass through similar stages. Indeed, Africans were not mentioned at all.

When blacks first arrived on the American continent, Nardal begins, they were forced to assimilate the language and culture of white Americans. Their only possible mode of expression was one imitative of American English. The second phase in their development began with the slave revolts, and was accompanied by a literature of moral protest. This literature appealed to white sympathies by making claims in terms of white morality; that is, it remained within the white American tradition. Then, at the turn of the century, Aframericans (Nardal's term) moved to a new stage, in which they began to create their own independent culture. This stage was divided into two streams. The first, exemplified by writers like Paul Laurence Dunbar, used a mixture of dialect and English to create what Nardal calls the school of racial realism. The second, associated first with W. E. B. Du Bois, continued the literaure of moral protest. Du Bois advocated equal civil and political rights for blacks and whites. Unlike Dunbar, however, who worked in a linguistic idiom specific to blacks, Du Bois wrote with eloquence in the literary style and language of educated white Americans. At the present time, Nardal concludes, the most avant-garde black writers, men such as Claude McKay and Langston Hughes, have abandoned dialect in favor of the forms of traditional American literature, but their themes are those of their race and its experience.

According to Nardal, the Antillean development had been slower and somewhat different. The Africans brought to the West Indies were not interested in their African heritage. After the abolition of slavery, their chief concern was to gain equal rights, and, as individuals, to rise in the social hierarchy. In keeping with this spirit, the writers of the late nineteenth and early twentieth centuries chose styles and themes that made their work indistinguishable from that of metropolitan French writers of the same period. The generation of the 1920s finally produced a few isolated writers interested in the life of the islands, but almost no one other than René Maran identified race rather than an exotic corner of France as his subject. Most of the writings of this generation were imitative, and mingled indistinguishably with a popular branch of the French literature of the time, which took as its subject exotic peoples and places. The theme of racial solidarity, Nardal argues, is new and was first touched on by individuals who left the islands to live in Paris. As a result of being uprooted, West Indians in Paris began to develop a new, modern outlook. That new outlook is the inspiration for the *La Revue du Monde Noir*. Now young West Indian poets are beginning to treat characteristically racial themes and, in this sense, are reaching the phase reached by the American blacks at the turn of the century. Their evolution is occurring extremely rapidly, and will be illustrated, she promises, by some remarkable new poetry in forthcoming issues of the review. As it turned out, the review ceased publication. Nonetheless, many of its young contributors and others from the Antilles, notably Aimé Césaire and Léon Damas, later did publish poetry that embodied precisely the concerns and attitudes Nardal described.

In her article, Nardal suggested some reasons why a new racial consciousness was developing in Paris. Like Alain Locke in his analysis of the Harlem Renaissance, she believed migration and the experience of entering a new social environment to be the stimulus. Many of the West Indians who moved to Paris had come for higher education and so were already a sensitive and articulate group. Nonetheless, it took the experiences of leaving home, living at the center of French culture, and meeting men of color from diverse backgrounds to push these young people to think about themselves in a new way. What Nardal did not point out was that the shock of being uprooted and transplanted was not reserved for the West Indian students alone. It affected an African like Senghor even more deeply.

Nardal's observation about the effect of living in Paris was confirmed by both Césaire and Senghor. Césaire wrote that "in Paris, at the same time that I discovered culture, I better understood the reasons for my own malaise. I became conscious of belonging to the basic category of Negro [nègre]. My poetry was born from that confrontation." Senghor acknowledged that he had been profoundly drawn to the French and their culture, and not until he was a student in Paris had he recognized how different his intuitive reactions were from theirs. It was this sense of being different, Senghor agreed, that drew the overseas students together.[16]

One of the most detailed discussions of this experience came later from Frantz Fanon, a controversial, Antilles-born psychiatrist who was active in Algeria in the 1950s. Fanon's *Peau noir, masques blancs* (Black Skin, White Masks) provides a lengthy discussion of the inner struggles of the black man in the white man's world. The problem faced by a man from the Antilles in Paris, Fanon wrote in 1952, is that the Antillean does not think of himself as black. He thinks of himself as French. When he reads in his schoolbooks about the white explorer who goes out to civilize the savages, the Antillean identifies with the white explorer. As far as he is concerned, Negroes are people who live in Africa. Subjectively and intellectually, he lives as a white. It is when he goes to Europe for the first time that he realizes that when the French speak of the Negro they mean him, and not just the Senegalese.[17]

Fanon emphasizes that in Paris the French imposed the Negro

identity upon the West Indian for the first time. The West Indian's new focus on race was not simply the result of his being uprooted, but was directly related to the way others, namely the white Parisians, saw him. The fact that Parisians lumped together all Negroes regardless of their place of origin, education, or social position influenced blacks themselves to do likewise. They then began to minimize the many important differences that did exist among them, and to focus their attention on what seemed in the Parisian context to be the overriding consideration, the color of their skin. It became easy for them to think in terms of race alone, and to ignore the "details" of local culture, education, and social or economic differences. As they did, they followed the lead of the French. Paulette Nardal did not appear to be conscious of this effect, although her whole approach confirmed it.

In closing her article, Nardal set an agenda for the future. Black students should investigate their own special heritage. They should stop writing papers and themes on French subjects, as indeed Senghor was in the process of doing in his study of Baudelaire. Students must instead study black history, and write the ethnography and poetry needed to serve as a foundation for future pride in the black race. This view was shared by Nardal's young friends. Aimé Césaire wrote a paper on the theme of the South in black American literature;[18] Damas set about studying African survivals in the West Indies; Senghor, ever the good academic, enrolled in courses on African ethnography and studied African languages. Birago Diop, one of the Senegalese of Senghor's generation sent to France to study veterinary medicine, recalls that Nardal influenced his decision to retell and publish African tales about Kotje Barma, the trickster and wise man of West Africa.[19] While it would be foolish to find in the review or Nardal's article the cause of, or even the primary influence on, this rapid growth in racial awareness among French-speaking blacks in Paris in the early 1930s, it is nonetheless true that the review pointed the way and provided the first outlet for its expression.

Ephemeral student publications followed quickly in the footsteps of *La Revue du Monde Noir*. Several attempts were made at one called *L'Étudiant Martiniquais* (The Martiniquan Student). A manifesto called *Légitime Défense* (Legitimate Defense) was published in June 1932, a few months after the collapse of the review. The students who published *Légitime Défense* were tired of what they called the moderation and superficiality of the review. They called for more connection between literature and politics. They demanded a radical break with Western bourgeois culture, interestingly enough for reasons much like those given by Rimbaud—it was degenerate, tired, too materialistic—but they added Marxist rhetoric and advocated the overturn of capitalist society. Their focus was not so much on race as on the sins of the French bourgeois establishment. In this they echoed contemporary French radicalism, which also spoke in the language of Surrealism and Marxism.[20]

Senghor took no part in this militant turn. The review, with its emphasis on culture and the unity of black people everywhere, better fit his approach and his temperament. He did take part in the creation of an organization of West African students in Paris toward the end of 1933 and French police reports occasionally noted his presence at a student rally, but the student organization concentrated on the material and individual welfare of students, such things as housing and scholarships. Senghor, already recognized as a leader by the African students, served as president. Ousmane Socé Diop, a Senegalese who had come to Paris about the same time as Senghor and who later became a novelist and politician, was the assistant secretary. The students scrupulously avoided obvious contact with a small group of radical black men of the older generation who were closely watched by the French police.[21]

Probably because of his friendship with Césaire and Damas, but also because of his interest in developments among black Americans and the influence of the review, Senghor encouraged contacts between African and West Indian students in Paris. By so doing, he revealed what was to become the hallmark of his political style, the will and ability to bring together and reconcile people formerly opposed. Logical as this particular move may seem in retrospect, it was not attractive at the time to either group. Traditionally the French West Indians had scorned Africans as barbarians. As Fanon pointed out, the West Indians did not think of themselves as black at all, but as French. They had been brought up in a culture—the French culture—that saw blacks as inferior. All of their history textbooks, and even literature, when it discussed blacks at all, implied this conclusion. To be black themselves was, therefore, unacceptable. They reserved blackness for Africans.

Senghor himself had experienced the West Indian's contempt for Africans. Some of the Antillean students, especially the women, made fun of him behind his back as a black savage from the bush. After World War II, when he married Ginette Eboué, his Guyanese mother-in-law often expressed her belief that Africans were half savage. She had a particular animus against Senghor and ridiculed his poetry in front of other people.[22] In her disdain for an African, she was typical of middle-class West Indians of her generation.

The Africans, for their part, associated West Indians with the colonial administration. The only West Indians they were likely to have met in Africa were men like René Maran or Félix Eboué, who were serving with that administration. Africans did not consider West Indians superior, but rather thought of them as petty bureaucrats, supporters and lackeys of the French.

Good Senegalese that he was, Birago Diop was astonished when Senghor invited him to lunch and suggested that they should make an effort to get to know the West Indian students in Paris. Birago recalls Senghor pursuing his point in a soft-spoken, reasonable, and ultimately persuasive manner: "Remember they have reasons to hold a grudge against us. It was our elders who sold theirs." Senghor was no doubt unduly charitable in identifying this as the reason West Indians avoided the company of Africans. Nonetheless, his argument carried the day. So convincing was Senghor that Birago found himself hosting a lunch for Damas, Césaire, and others. They met at his hotel, the Colonial Hotel, so called because it was at the edge of the Bois de Vincennes, near the site of the colonial exposition of 1931. They continued to meet there, even after some street disturbances provoked by the French right prompted the timid owner of the hotel to rename it the Concordia. They also often met informally at the apartment of Marthe Lamine Guèye, a West Indian married to a prominent African, or in one of the many restaurants in the Quartier Latin. Their talk was not of politics but rather of culture, and more specifically of the past and future of black culture.[23]

The West Indian students who had become interested in problems of race, and in their black as opposed to their French heritage, were eager to learn about Africa from the Africans. Their attitude was well described by Claude McKay in *Banjo* (1929), a novel that had great vogue among the students at this time. McKay was in a position to know a great deal about the attitudes of different groups of blacks. Born in Jamaica in 1889, he lived in the United States as a young man and became an important figure in the Harlem Renaissance, publishing both poems and fiction. He then moved abroad and spent most of his later years in France. Several of his poems appeared in *La Revue du Monde Noir*. Thus he came to know the black milieu at several different times and places—in the West Indies, in Harlem at the time of its cultural flowering, and now in Paris. In *Banjo* he assembled his observations with such accuracy and persuasiveness that its characters were quoted to prove points in arguments and discussions. Both Césaire and Senghor could recite long passages by heart. Indeed, when Senghor suggested to Birago Diop that one reason for the coolness of West Indians toward Africans was that African grandfathers had enslaved West Indian ones, he was merely paraphrasing the musings of Ray, the protagonist of *Banjo*.

McKay suggested a number of reasons why the West Indians felt superior to the Africans, but he also noted, through his spokesman, Ray, that the West Indians and "Aframericans" felt a mixture of humility and envy when they heard the Senegalese speaking together in their own language. These Africans possessed a "wholesome contact with their racial roots." The Africans gave West Indians something they had lacked, a sense that it was possible for black men to have a world of their own.[24]

The West Indians' interest in Africa seems to have been forced upon them rather than freely chosen. As Rousseau pointed out long ago in his *Discourse on Inequality,* when men enter society and gain its benefits they also come to live in the eyes of others. The power of these "eyes of others" to force an undesirable identity on West Indian students was confirmed by their experience in Paris. Senghor, too, referred to the impact of "being seen by the corrosive eye of the white."[25] Once forced to give up the idea that they were French, the West Indians had to look to Africa for a cultural heritage. Hence Césaire's excitement at meeting Senghor. As one West Indian put it, Senghor was for him and his friends a cultivated person who was also African and who showed them a way to deal with Europeans as with equals. "We found at last an African intellectual who carried in himself all the dignity of Africa, and it was this quest for dignity that we were pursuing." Césaire put it more simply when he said that in meeting Senghor he felt that he had met Africa. The West Indian students began to probe Senghor for information about their newly discovered heritage. This pushed Senghor to articulate precisely what that heritage was. It also put pressure on him to embody what they took him to be, the personification of the dignity of Africa, just as earlier he had tried to meet the expectations of his French teachers by becoming the perfect black Frenchman.[26]

During these years when Senghor was impressing the small black community in Paris with his serenity and academic accomplishments, he had many worries that he kept to himself. His friends did not suspect that this model of African dignity, generosity, and apparent success was in fact constantly worried about his precarious financial situation, and was no stranger to failure. This other side appears in Senghor's correspondence with the colonial administration. His first letters, sent directly to the governor general, serve as a reminder of the extent to which Senghor had already attracted the attention of important colonial administrators. Senghor was always careful to submit the respectful letters necessary to keep them interested in his progress and willing to continue his support. He wrote not only to the governor general but also to the Inspector of Education for the colony. The letters show the respectful tone of a supplicant well aware of the importance of satisfying his patron.

Most of the available letters for the period 1930–1931, when Senghor was still at Lycée Louis-le-grand, describe how hard he was working and how disappointed he was to fail the exam for the Ecole Normale Supérieure. After deciding not to take the exam again, because, he wrote the Inspector of Education, the competition was simply too tough and he was too old to spend more time on it, he requested financial support to go on for his teaching degree. Blaise Diagne wrote several times on his behalf.[27] This request was granted, the work completed, and the requirements for the Diplôme d'Etudes Supérieures duly met. Senghor then asked for, and was granted, support to continue studying for the agrégé exam. This was the time at which Diagne intervened to get Senghor his French citizenship.

Early in 1932, Senghor began to express anxiety about his financial situation. His first problem arose from a confusion over the proper level of his scholarship. Instead of getting 6000 francs as he had expected, he received only 1000. In a letter dated March 31, 1932, he wrote asking, "will you please send me by air"—a phrase then scratched out and replaced with the more formal "would you have the kindness to send me by air"—the needed money. His father, he wrote, was very old and suffering in the current economic crisis in Senegal. Having many children to support, he was unable to give his student son any financial help. With this worry over money, Senghor continued, "it is hard for me to get into the spirit necessary for difficult work," and in a footnote he added, "Here it has been two months that I have been unable to pay for my room. I think I am in danger of being put out into the street."[28] Two weeks later he wrote again, repeating that he could not get up the energy to work. In the meantime, the administrators in charge had discovered that the problem was the result of a typographical error, in which the figure 1 had replaced the figure 6 by mistake. But it was early May before the governor general wrote to the director of the Cité Universitaire to say that the federation would be responsible for Senghor's lodging, and sent additional money directly to Senghor. Senghor thereby learned, painfully, how dependent he was on the whim of the colonial administration, and if not the stroke of a pen, the hammer of a typewriter. He might work with all the discipline and energy at his command, but his future was still at the mercy of the colonial administration.

Once this financial crisis was settled, Senghor decided to go home. In July he wrote the Inspector of Education, Albert Charton, of his plans. After expressing thanks for the scholarship money that had at last come through and made such a visit possible, Senghor wrote that he had not seen his parents in four years. He felt the "need to immerse myself in the atmosphere of my native land."[29]

What Senghor found at home that summer could not have pleased him. His father was old and close to death. Whatever fortune he had once possessed had been dissipated by the infirmities of old age, drought in the land, and the effects of the world depression on the peanut trade. There was the added problem of an invalid brother who had been gassed in World War I while serving in the French army with the Tirailleurs Sénégalais. Senghor's mother was now poor. To see the position into which his family had fallen must have been a shock. They were hardly the wealthy aristocrats his French friends had been led to believe. Senghor must have suffered from the sight of the collapse of his childhood world. Indeed, four months later his father was dead. To Hélène Senghor's children, however, Sédar Senghor was a breath of fresh air and a glimpse of what could be theirs if they followed the path their mother was setting out for them. They remember long walks with their uncle on the beach at Joal, and his reciting poetry by the black American poets.[30] By October 1932 Senghor had left the family and was back in Paris.

That fall, Senghor was often ailing. He first fell sick during the boat crossing from Africa to France, and spent his first three days back in Paris in bed. A letter to the Inspector of Education described his illness and struck a plaintive note. It also contained the increasingly familiar request for money for the books needed to begin his studies. Senghor described himself as working hard, spending afternoons in the Bibliothèque Nationale, but unable to get as good a start as he would like on his preparation for the agrégé exam because he needed to buy books. He concluded, "Please send my scholarship money at once."[31] Perhaps more than any other, 1932–33 proved to be a year of hard work with little visible reward. Senghor failed the agrégé exam in the spring. Because he did not lack by much, his teachers supported his decision to try again. It was quite common to fail on the first try.

The next fall, Senghor was again pleading for financial support. Again his professors were happy to recommend him, and again, the money eventually came through. A vivid indication of his state of mind that fall and winter is a letter dated Christmas Day 1933. Christmas was an important day for the devoutly Christian Senghor, normally a happy day associated with renewal, family, and friends. And yet this Christmas he wrote the Inspector of Education a gloomy letter. He had been sick all month, he wrote, and working constantly. After this somewhat self-pitying beginning, he abruptly changed key to describe his future plans and new interests. He had been auditing the course of Mlle Homberger on black African linguistics and soon would start going to the lectures of Henri Labouret on African eth-nography.[32] The letter poignantly reveals a young student away from home on Christmas Day, lonely and sick. This particular young man, momentarily self-pitying, comforts himself with dreams for the future. Apparently Senghor suffered bleak periods throughout his life. He learned to recognize them and to remember that they would pass. He developed a method for working through them: "I let myself go into it and slow my life down to a more moderate pace. I do something methodical, organized, and useful. At the end of a certain time, it lifts. Physical exercise has also played an important role for me."[33] Even in times of depression, Senghor was able to maintain the self-discipline and perspective to master his emotions. This Christmas letter showed that he was planning ahead and able to share those plans with someone who could help him. He was beginning a formal study of African culture. This turn to African linguistics fitted logically with his con-centration on grammar for his degree, but his interest in ethnography suggests a new focus. It was in this same year that he made his first attempts to bring West Indian and African students together. This rather long period of depression and discouragement apparently proved also to be a time in which new ideas were incubating in Senghor's mind. As its end, his goals were set.

When he became a French citizen so that he could compete for the agrégé degree, Senghor also took on the responsibility of doing French military service. The question of when and how he would do this now began to press upon him. His first plan had been to enter the service in the fall of 1934, presumably after passing his agrégé exam the previous July. When July came, however, and he failed the exam for the second time, he had to reassess his situation. The goal of becoming a scholar and university professor was about to elude his grasp, because there was a rule that no one could present himself more than twice for this exam. He now had an offer to teach in a high school in Poitiers. If he accepted it, he would at last be self-supporting. In a discouraged moment, he seriously considered this option. It would have put him far from Paris, however, and cut him off from any chance of continuing his linguistic and ethnographic studies. It also seemed probable that he would be inducted into the military sometime that autumn, and so would not be able to complete the academic year at Poitiers in any case.

It was then that Senghor discovered, after some investigation, that students from overseas could be exempted from the prohibition against more than two attempts at the agrégé exam. He wrote to the governor general pointing out that students from the colonies had this special grace, and asking his support. In this effort to persuade the governor general to come to his aid yet another time, Senghor enlisted the help of his professors. Several wrote on his behalf, one to emphasize that Senghor knew his subjects well and that his failure had been simple bad luck. Another commended his hard work and model behavior.[34]

By the early fall, Senghor had worked out an ingenious plan to solve his many problems simultaneously. First, he had written to the new Inspector of Education who had replaced Charton, expressing his relief in discovering that scholarship holders from the colonies were allowed to attempt the exam a third time. With that in mind, he had been working all summer preparing the books required for the next competition. He had also looked into the matter of his military service, and after some confusion resulting from "functionaries who in typical manner do not know their own rules," had found out only in September that he must spend a full year in military service starting that very autumn. His last hope, then, to avoid losing a whole year and the momentum he had developed, was to work for the exam at the same time that he did his military service. He would be free evenings and able to study. So, he concluded, was there a possibility that the federation would continue his scholarship so that he could take private lodgings and have a quiet place to study in the evenings? His father had died in January 1933, completely ruined. He himself was already in debt. "I send you a timid, oh, so very timid, SOS . . . I have told my embarrassing situation in detail, counting on your goodwill as my protector."[35]

Such a suppliant attitude seems out of place in the confident young man who had arrived in Paris in the fall of 1928, and in the charming, assured person whom friends saw at evening get-togethers or in the cafés of the Quartier Latin at this time. They believed Senghor came from a rich family. He often paid the bill, and he had a reputation for being generous with money. This was the man who seemed to have everything under control, who three years before had appeared, smiling, to guide Césaire through labyrinthian Paris and now acted as his rock of support. Senghor was the one with contacts, the one who invited Birago Diop to a good meal and proposed that Africans try to develop links with the West Indians. In direct contrast to this outer image of success and ease, however, Senghor keenly felt his vulnerability. He was haunted by financial worry and depression. These were problems and doubts he buried within himself. Often lonely, constantly reminded of the precarious nature of his dream of becoming a professor and of his dependence on the goodwill of powerful bureaucrats he had never met, he reacted with self-discipline, persistence, and hard work. This is what the others saw. They saw what he wanted them to see. It was an achievement of self-control, fueled by ability and pride. Senghor was very proud, but not so proud that he could not ask quietly and persistently for what he really needed.

He was also cautious. Encouraged by a Martiniquan friend, he attended several meetings of a Catholic group of laypeople devoted to bringing members of different races together. Such an effort might have been considered suspect by the French police, and Senghor worried that this might be the case. He seemed very nervous at these meetings and soon ceased to attend them. He had no intention of jeopardizing what was almost within his grasp.[36]

A week after Senghor had sent his rather desperate letter about studying for the agrégé exam while doing his military service, the questions first raised in July were answered. He had the good news that the federation would continue to give him financial support. He also had some bad news, for he had not been posted to a military base near Paris as he had hoped, but to Verdun in the east. Any possibility of attending courses or having regular access to good libraries was thereby closed. After another flurry of letters, Senghor managed to produce what turned out to be a decisive medical certificate detailing his bad health. His urgent request for a post closer to Paris was granted, and by December he was back in Paris. As a French citizen, he had been recruited into a French company where he was the only black. Now, to satisfy his demand for a place near Paris, he was assigned to a regiment of colonial infantry. He did not complain, for the change suited him well. He began by working alternately in the kitchen and the library until, rising in status, he became the officers' librarian. There he had time to read and to study at night to prepare for a third try at the exam.

At last, in August 1935, Senghor was able to report the triumphant news that he was an agrégé of the University of Paris in Grammar. He had passed the exam. The title, agrégé of university, was one that professors and ambitious French parents considered synonymous with intellectual superiority. Senghor now had the distinction of being the first black African to hold it. He had accomplished the goal for which he had worked with determination for four long, often miserable years. He wrote happily of his success to the Inspector of Education, mentioning in the same letter that he was planning to be married to "a young woman of color." A police report of the time had noted that he was against mixed marriages.[37] This particular young woman of color seemed a perfect choice, but she chose to marry someone else.

The correspondence between Senghor and the men who controlled the purse strings of his fellowships offers a rare glimpse of the person behind the facade he carefully constructed for both his French and his African friends. During this time, he kept his personal struggles carefully hidden from everyone who knew him. None of his friends has left even a hint of Senghor as troubled or discouraged. On the contrary, they invariably describe him as self-assured, smiling, and generous with both time and money. The only bit of evidence they recall of this darker side, though they did not interpret it as such, is their recollection of Senghor as suffering from bad health. He was never strong, they recall, often sick. Neither the climate of Paris, nor, later, that of Tours seemed to agree with him. The only chink in his facade may have been bouts with psychosomatic illness. When recalling this period more than forty years later in a series of interviews intended to serve as an autobiography, Senghor passed over any difficulties, saying only that he had been pleasantly surprised that he did so well on his written exam on his first attempt at the agrégé and had failed the oral only because he had not prepared for it properly. He also commented that he had lost only one year in that he was doing his obligatory military service.[38] As was his habit, Senghor did not remember—or did not choose to recall for others—discouragement or failure.

The year Senghor passed his exam, 1935, was also the year he published his first article. It appeared in yet another ephemeral publication, *L'Etudiant Noir* (The Black Student). The title of this publication was significant as an assertion that the tribalism of black students in Paris should come to an end. It indicated that the time had come to stop identifying oneself as Martiniquan, Guyanese, or African, and to identify with black students in general. Who actually took the first step toward this important change or had the idea for *L'Etudiant Noir* is not altogether clear. Perhaps it was Césaire, who had recently been elected president of the Martiniquan Student Association. Senghor was then his counterpart as president of the West African Student Association. Césaire recalls that he had the idea for a new publication and immediately thought of Senghor. As they were such close friends at the time, this seems a plausible sequence of events. Senghor gives Césaire credit for the idea, as he does for originating most of their joint enterprises. Indeed Senghor almost always gives credit to others for any enterprise in which he was involved. Be that as it may, neither could have achieved the step without the other. The one and only issue that remains available of *L'Etudiant Noir* came out in March 1935.[39]

L'Etudiant Noir is important for several reasons. First of all, it represents a clear decision by a group of young students to continue in the direction suggested by *La Revue du Monde Noir,* rather than in that of the politically oriented and Marxist-inspired *Légitime Défense.* Its editors chose to stress the unity of all blacks, and to focus on cultural issues. It is also important because the central figures of the later Negritude group, Senghor, Césaire, and Damas, were involved in its organization and planning. It was here that Sédar Senghor published his first article, and it was here that he tentatively set out for the first time the themes that were to preoccupy him for much of his life. He had reached the moment when, after reading the work of others and discussing his views with friends, he was ready to express his own point of view in print.

For a number of years, scholars talked enthusiastically about the tremendous importance of *L'Etudiant Noir* without, as Damas rather wickedly pointed out, ever seeing a copy of it.[40] As a result, its importance was exaggerated, particularly insofar as *La Revue du Monde Noir* had not been carefully analyzed. *L'Etudiant Noir* was therefore credited with being a totally original departure. In fact, although it provided a forum for new voices, its themes and approaches clearly built on those of earlier periodicals. Some of the same people were involved. Paulette Nardal collaborated on *L'Etudiant Noir,* as did Gilbert Gratiant, a West Indian writer who had contributed to the earlier review. Now that these and other journals are available, the affiliation and development from ephemeral publications of the 1920s such as *Race Nègre* and *Cri des Nègres,* through *La Revue du Monde Noir* to *L'Etudiant Noir,* is clearly visible.[41] The latter remains important nonetheless because it brought together the individuals and the ideas that were to mobilize a whole generation.

L'Etudiant Noir, like several earlier black student publications, contained some material purely topical in nature, such as student concerns about scholarships. It also contained articles by Césaire, Senghor, and Gratiant that focused on wider problems. Césaire's contribution was a harsh assessment of the attempt by black individuals to assimilate French culture. Senghor's article was superficially more cautious, but actually an equally far-reaching call to open discussion of the nature of black culture.

Césaire, like Paulette Nardal before him, traces the development of black/white relations through several phases. To an extent greater than she, he stresses the dependence of black attitudes on white ones. In the first stage of the black/white encounter, he maintains, whites treated blacks as beasts. In the second, whites turned kindly and indulged blacks as if they were big children—the attitude reflected in the speech at Senghor's Louis-le-grand prize day. In this phase, blacks were allowed to go to white schools and encouraged to imitate whites. As a result, many blacks grew so accustomed to pretending they were whites that they could not go without their coats and ties. They simply could not take off the veneer of white culture that had cost them so much to acquire. This black man was proud of himself, and looked down on crude, uneducated blacks as his inferiors. This is the view of the contemporary West Indian who scorns Africans. But, Césaire argues, such a man is deceived at the deepest level. This black man is a copy, a fake, scorned by those he imitates even as they encourage him to try harder: "If assimilation is not a madness, it is most certainly a stupidity, for to wish to be assimilated is to forget that no being can change its biological type, its true nature."[42] With these few words, Césaire starkly condemns several generations of "progress" for educated West Indians. They have wasted their time in a struggle for what is ultimately an impossible protective coloration. Quite simply, the color of their skin remains unchanged. Black hands and faces are visible even when black bodies are draped in coats and ties. As for Césaire's view of the future: the new generation has turned its back on this outdated approach. They will write and contribute to history. They will not play the role of mimic but be themselves. They seek neither slavery nor assimilation, but emancipation.

Gilbert Gratiant, another Martiniquan student, chose to write more specifically about the problems of his island. There everyone except for a tiny minority is a *métis,* a person of mixed blood. The dilemma for the Martiniquan is that he is at the same time "completely (that is the mystery) French in his thinking, spirit, and culture," and "sincerely but confusedly . . . African." Therefore, Gratiant concludes, the Martiniquan has to reject both assimilation and the return to the African origins. He has "to return to the natural condition of Creole civilization, a state of equilibrium between two civilizations" created in a country that was originally neither one nor the other.[43] Gratiant put the situation of the métis bluntly, and denied himself the easy pleasure of romanticizing his African roots or pretending that all could be solved by a return to a past that Martinique never knew.

Senghor characteristically took a more scholarly and indirect approach to the problem. To an extent, he hid behind the writings of another, René Maran, choosing as his title, "L'humanisme et nous: René Maran" (Humanism and Us: René Maran). Maran was a man who caught Senghor's imagination as a model for the French-educated black man. He had been born of Guyanese parents in Martinique in 1887, but lived in France from the time he was very young. He received all of his education in Bordeaux. Having passed the necessary exams, he, like Blaise Diagne and Félix Eboué, chose one of the few careers open to the educated black, the colonial service. He was posted to Ubangi-Shari in the French equatorial federation, the second of the two administrative divisions into which France had divided its West African possessions early in the century. Up to this point, Maran was the assimilated black man par excellence, and might have been expected to fulfill all African preconceptions about how West Indians behave in Africa. Maran, however, turned out to be different. While in Africa, he decided to write a novel to describe African life. Toward this end, he kept a journal and observed as accurately as he could the manner and style of village society. In the novel that resulted, *Batouala*, Maran portrayed, in a somewhat romanticized but extremely attractive way, the life of village Africa. This picture mirrored closely French preconceptions about idyllic native life in an exotic corner of their empire and was, to this extent, an unremarkable addition to a growing literature of exotica then popular in France. Maran seemed to see Africa through French eyes. For *Batouala* he won the Goncourt prize for 1921. Some said, churlishly, that the French jury chose his novel to show its gratitude for the contribution of the Tirailleurs Sénégalais in World War I. These are the uncontroversial facts about the book. It caused quite a stir, however, because of its preface.[44]

In the preface to *Batouala,* Maran delivered a devastating critique of the French colonial administration. He said that he wanted to draw attention to the fact that the colonial administration did not heed its own rhetoric about a civilizing mission. On the contrary, it was totally corrupt and served, if at all, only to carry out the orders of French financial and business interests. By connecting this critique to a novel, Maran hoped to bring the problem to the attention of French public opinion and so to produce some effort at reform. In his argument, he made no mention of the question of race or of any special quality of African civilization. He spoke solely in terms of the accepted French values of equity and justice, hoping to appeal to the French on their own terms. Unfortunately for Maran, the book had its success, but it was the success of a scandal. He was attacked in the press and forced to give up his post in the colonial administration. The book was banned in the colonies. Many years later, in the late 1950s, the issues Maran had raised were still so embarrassing to a segment of the French public that a French publisher who wished to reprint the novel asked Maran to change the preface for republication. This Maran refused to do.[45]

In making his argument for colonial reform, Maran spoke not as a member of the colonized group, not even on its behalf, but rather as one Frenchman urging another Frenchman to put their common house in order. He spoke as an insider. By the time Senghor met him in the 1930s, however, Maran had decided that he had misunderstood the true problem. Race was a big issue, if not the main issue, and had to be approached head-on. By then, Maran was a well-established man of letters with several more novels and collections of poetry to his credit. The students of Senghor's generation looked up to him as a successful writer and a wise survivor of an older generation. Maran, for his part, was in the process of rethinking his position as a black man, totally French by culture as he surely was, but equally surely unacceptable in most French society. The book in which he explored this problem most fully was *Un homme pareil aux autres* (A Man like Others). Jean Veneuse, Maran's protagonist, is a man closely modeled on Maran himself, and, in turn, provided a touchstone for others. Frantz Fanon, for example, used the Jean Veneuse character to illustrate the psychological problems typical of the assimilated black in French society. In effect, Maran provided a case study almost clinical in its accuracy of the anomalous and ultimately self-destructive situation of the black Frenchman. From at least the early 1930s when Senghor met him, Maran had struggled to confront and resolve this dilemma on the personal level and to stem the "current of hatred and jealousy that almost carried me off." He felt increasingly cut off from the mainstream of society, discouraged, and even defeated. Yet he saw the publication of his case history of Jean Veneuse as a social duty. He tried to reassure himself that one day the world would recognize that his writings had served France, his country, and his race. He felt a keen loyalty to both worlds.[46]

Senghor's article, ostensibly about humanism but based on Maran, has a contradictory effect. On the one hand, by his very choice of Maran as subject, Senghor revived the still-living memory of the incident that had first brought Maran to public attention, the controversy surrounding *Batouala*. On the other hand, the article does not once mention this book or the scandal it caused. It is mild and scholarly in tone, lacking altogether the undercurrent of emotion and militancy that mark Césaire's piece on the follies of assimilation or Gratiant's on the anguished métis. The argument that Senghor puts forth is balanced, carefully considered, and so stated as to avoid sounding the alarm. It is written as if it were just another assigned essay required for an academic degree. Senghor was a cautious young man. He had no intention of burning any bridges to academic respectability.

Senghor starts his article, somewhat pedantically, with a definition of his terms. As with the clever student, his choice of definition determines much of his argument. The essence of humanism, he begins, is man's self-knowledge. For black men, then, humanism is a "cultural movement that has the black man as its goal, and Western reason and the black soul as instruments of research . . . it requires both reason and intuition."[47] Insofar as there are few blacks of unmixed blood, even in Africa, he continues, it must be that to be black is more a matter of psychology than of blood. And then, in an apparent non sequitur, he adds, "to be black is to recover the human being crushed under the wheel of inhuman conventions," for the black has remained human at a time of increasing artifice and mechanization. Black writers have already produced works of naive strength that have not yet received the recognition they deserve. René Maran provides a case in point.

In these few short statements that do not follow in any logical way one from another, Senghor foreshadows much of his later thinking: blacks have a psychology basically different from that of whites; blacks need to investigate their own heritage; and blacks have retained profound human values that whites have lost. He also reveals his characteristic style: these potentially provocative declarations are couched in a language that is abstract and scholarly, that of one French scholar speaking calmly to another in a tradition they share.

Senghor's analysis of the particular nature of René Maran's achievement is also significant. Because of his French education, Maran has seen Africa through the eyes of the white. His systematic note-taking in preparing to write *Batouala* illustrates that he has learned the method and objectivity valued by Europeans. His European culture here plays a positive role, for he is able to "penetrate rationally" the language and customs of the native people. But what makes his real understanding of the African village possible is that he has a black soul: Maran intuitively understands the spirit of the village. His kinship with that spirit is illustrated by his writing style, which uses the alliteration, onomatopoeia, concise elegance, and stylized repetitiveness that mark the African oral tradition. These qualities, Senghor adds, are also found in Greek and Roman classics. Mention of the latter connection, perhaps explained by the fact that Senghor was then a student of classics, may also explain why Senghor was drawn to the classics in the first place, namely that he sensed a kinship between the literary expression of the three preindustrial peoples, African, Latin, and most of all Greek. Whatever the reason for his love of the Greeks, Senghor obviously enjoyed finding parallels between African culture and another culture admired by the French. The important point he wants to make about Maran, however, is that he exemplifies black humanism.

How does Maran, child of Bordeaux, French by education, Martiniquan by birth, come to embody black humanism? Senghor explains: Maran has learned from the French an intellectual method characterized by an objective and systematic way of thinking; he preserves, because of his blackness, a special quality of intuitive understanding, the black soul. The latter quality would appear to be his simply by virtue of his blood and birth, and to be unrelated to personal experience; the implication is therefore a racist one, that race in itself is the determining factor, but Senghor does not state this explicitly. Maran's interior life, Senghor continues, has been made up of dramatic duality "between reason and imagination, mind and soul, white and black." Maran's strength is that he has managed to move beyond this duality of Frenchness and blackness to reach a point where he seeks only to be true to himself. He neither follows fashion nor cuts himself off entirely from contemporary life. For refreshment, he reads the classics, which have formed his mind and permitted him to discover his own resources. From Senghor, this is high praise indeed.

The key to understanding the force of this compelling description of Maran, the black humanist, is that Senghor seems to be describing himself, or at least himself as he would like to be. He had been searching for an image of himself that could bear the weight of his experience and yet would not diminish him. Maran, or what he imagined Maran to be, provided Senghor with just such a vision. In this detailed and admiring description of the ideal black humanist, he set out the manner of man he wished to be.

One interesting sidelight of this focus on Maran is that Maran's achievement had cost Maran dearly, as Senghor could have known if he had chosen to pursue clues in his possession. Two months before this article appeared, Senghor had written to Maran and received in return a copy of Maran's first published collection of poetry. Of the collection, Maran wrote to Senghor that it contained the poems of his schoolboy idealism. "I then cherished the high-minded desire to be an honor to my race and to illustrate it by illustrating myself. I have since lost the best part of my enthusiasm. The freed Negro [*nègre*] in general aspires only to become a slave again, for the sole purpose of having himself tolerated by European conformism . . . you will discover in it [the poems] one side of the mirror with two faces of my adolescence, and some of its enchanted dreams . . ."[48] Senghor preferred not to question what had led to Maran's loss of enthusiasm for being an honor to his race. He apparently did not wish to learn about Maran's struggles with anger and disillusion, or to recognize how close Maran lived to the edge of despair.

After Maran's death in the early 1960s, Senghor wrote a memorial essay entitled "René Maran: Precursor of Negritude." In it he acknowledged for the first time in print the degree to which he identified with Maran. Of Maran's days of schooling in France, he noted, in spite of many solid friendships with "his white schoolmates . . . he could not defend himself from the solitude which is the lot of all the transplanted. Against it, he found refuge in authenticity, the pride in his race that is the first condition of Negritude. Solitude and pride, these are the two spurs that would make of him a man of culture and integrity."[49] The likeness to Senghor's experience is striking. Solitude was familiar to Senghor in Paris, both the physical solitude of a lonely student and a sense of isolation from his African home. Solitude and exile are important subjects of his early poetry. Pride is a quality that had marked him from his schoolboy days in Dakar, when he stubbornly insisted on being seated at the table with the grownups because he was an educated person. Then his pride was an individual sense of entitlement to a place he had earned by hard work and talent, and had nothing to do with race. Now, in Paris, when he found that the French grouped him automatically with other black men and judged the group as a whole to be inferior, pride led him to reject the idea that any group to which he belonged could be inferior. The twin spurs of solitude and pride that lacerated Maran until he found refuge in this authenticity just as surely cut into Senghor and forced him to seek a new understanding of himself and his place in the world.

Senghor's article about Maran in *L'Etudiant Noir* is remarkable on two counts. It contains, in embryo, the outline of his later thinking. It also sets out his ideal, for any black man perhaps, but more important, for himself. It indicates that by the time it was written, in the middle of 1935, Senghor had resolved a number of important personal and intellectual issues. He had not solved them once and for all, but he had begun to acquire a vision of who he was and the path he would like to take. He had also chosen his prose style, a rather pedantic professorial one that masked the fact that some of what he was saying had radical implications. He had no wish to alarm the French establishment. His goal was not to oppose them but to become one of them. This same year he began to express himself in poetry. He was twenty-eight years old.

As he searched for the best ways to express and confirm his new ideas, Senghor found the companionship of his West Indian friends to be one of his most valuable resources. He was also able to draw on the complex traditions of French literature and culture and on his knowledge of a new literature produced by black Americans. It was not that his experience exactly paralleled that of the Americans, but rather that their example gave him the conviction that a new perspective could be achieved. The challenge was to achieve this new perspective on both an intellectual and a personal level.

Having at last passed his exam, Senghor was qualified to teach. Once his education was complete, however, according to the terms of a document he and his parents had signed when he received his scholarship, he was obligated to serve the colony for ten years. The French ministry of education, apparently unaware of this obligation, assigned him a post at the lycée in Tours. Senghor quickly developed a plan. He wanted to study African linguistics and ethnography, subjects that would allow him to combine academic and personal interests, and to work for the highest French degree, the Doctorat d'Etat. Tours was close enough to Paris that he could go up easily to audit lectures and use the libraries. With this plan of combining teaching and study in mind, he wrote to Governor General Boisson, who was then serving in an interim capacity, that "Conforming to the spirit of your government, which wishes that the native . . . should find his tradition and renew it . . . in the light of the French genius," he was asking permission to stay two more years in France to finish his linguistic studies and to study Negro-African ethnography.[50] He also asked for a small subsidy to help pay for a room in Paris so that he could stay there overnight when he had time free from his job in Tours. This letter is rather amusing, in that it illustrates how well Senghor had mastered the art of telling the administrators what they wanted to hear in order to persuade them to do what he wanted them to do. In this particular case there is an added twist. Boisson, the interim governor general who received the letter reminding him of his own idea about Africans finding their own tradition, later headed the Vichy regime in West Africa. Boisson then carried out a policy totally in keeping with Vichy and Nazi views about basic differences between the races. When he encouraged African students to do research into their own cultural roots and traditions, Boisson hoped this research would help Africans to know their proper place. He little suspected where this new interest would lead. In 1935, happy to support an African who wished to move in this direction, he granted Senghor's request.

Senghor moved to Tours to teach classics and French. There his duty was to ground French children in their European heritage; at the same time he began, really for the first time, to dig into his own.

5

Coming of Age

On the eve of World War II, Tours was a calm little town in the Loire Valley slightly to the south and west of Paris. The people of the region were known as bon vivants, lovers of good food and wine. They were sunny, like their rich and fertile countryside. Tours is, and was when Senghor arrived, a town typical of provincial France and the French heartland. Senghor particularly enjoyed the fact that it had been a Roman settlement, Cesarodunum, and remained rich in signs of its Roman and early Christian history.[1] It encompassed, therefore, all he thought best in French culture.

In the fall of 1935, the forty-four children who arrived for their first day in sixth class met an unexpected sight. They knew they were getting a new teacher, an agrégé from the University of Paris, who was better educated than many of their other teachers. They expected him to be poised and well-prepared. When they entered their ground-floor classroom, the found a man who seemed confident and well-educated but who was black. They had never seen anyone like him before. Senghor sympathized with the awkward situation of the director of the school, who must have wondered how best to present the new teacher to the students' parents.[2] As it turned out, Senghor quickly won the children's confidence as an excellent classics teacher. He set out to teach Latin as a living language and managed to avoid the monotonous declension of nouns and verbs that had characterized his own learning of the classical languages.

Senghor soon became part of the town's intellectual community, to which a lycée teacher naturally belonged. He attended the frequent informal parties teachers held at their houses, befriended their children, joined them on weekend expeditions, donned a costume to take part in the Christmas skit, and even served as witness at a colleague's wedding. He became a great favorite for his humor and good nature, and in no way appeared ill at ease in the general company. Soon affectionate anecdotes were told about him. He was, for example, a bit excessive in his concern for physical fitness and a great believer in regular exercise. His friends called him "Ghor," as had Pompidou, a word which means male or the courageous one in Serer and is also, more obviously, a shortened *Senghor*. Inverted as *ruug*, it became the Serer word for vital spirit or soul. One day when swimming with his friends at a favorite spot in the River Cher, Ghor ran up with an exaggerated look of excitement, strutting a bit and exclaiming that everyone was staring at him because he was so handsome. Of course many people were staring at him, quite clearly, but they were staring because he was black, not because he was handsome. It was a charming joke that brought them together with laughter. As far as the teachers were concerned, Senghor was a real addition to their company. He showed none of the sensitivity to slurs, real or imagined, that plagued many of his black contemporaries. He made it clear, nonetheless, that though he might play the clown occasionally, it would be on his own terms. His good humor and ability to make fun of himself were totally consistent with his obvious self-respect. He always dressed neatly, was restrained at parties and celebrations, and lived frugally from day to day.

Senghor's position among the rest of the townsfolk was less certain. Occasionally one of the prominent families of the town asked him to dinner or tea, notably a man who had served in the colonial service in Indochina. Such invitations were relatively rare, but then, they were rare for other teachers as well. From time to time a parent or child would refer to him as "the black one," which his friends found mildly annoying, but Senghor remained unaware of this or at least chose to ignore it.

Senghor's arrival in Tours coincided with a time of growing alarm among French intellectuals over the rise of political extremism throughout Europe. Intellectuals as a group were growing increasingly active politically, and those in Tours were no exception. After the Italian invasion of Ethiopia, Senghor joined the Committee of Intellectuals Against Fascism, a group that tried to provide information about what was going on in Spain and Germany. Speakers were invited from Paris to bring the latest news about these and other developments. Senghor also became active in the local branch of the Socialist party and was elected an officer of the teachers' union. He joined a number of his colleagues in teaching at a free night school sponsored by the trade unions to improve the general educational level of the workers of the town. One evening each week he taught French literature to a small but determined band of workers, choosing authors such as Balzac and Zola who were likely to appeal to them. Such activities, typical for his time and milieu, indicate how totally immersed in French life Senghor seemed to be.

Senghor did occasionally discuss with friends his interest in Africa. At such times, he spoke with a scholarly voice rather than a personal one. He talked about Serer grammar, the verbal system of the Peul, or the courses and books on African ethnography that he had begun to follow with interest. Occasionally he urged a colleague to read a new book. To one of his frequent hostesses, for example, he gave a copy of a book by the ethnographer Maurice Delafosse. But there was nothing strident about this interest. Indeed, the recipient of this book recalls that she paid little special attention to what Senghor said in those days, because at the time "it seemed just talk, like that of all the other young people we knew." Indeed, no one who has written or spoken about their impressions of Senghor at this time recalls thinking that he would have a brilliant future.[3] Senghor's interest in Africa seemed natural enough, certainly not excessive. If he talked about the relationship between the colonies and France, it was always to the effect that it must evolve gradually. He might make fun of the textbook he had used in Africa as a child in which he learned about his blond, blue-eyed ancestors, the Gauls; he might express annoyance when someone referred to the Africans as a junior race; but he never left the impression that he resented France as a whole for its treatment of Africans. Whatever may have preoccupied him within did not ruffle the surface. The French of Tours, like the West Indians of Paris, remarked on his calm and good nature.

Senghor was not unaware of an element of pose in what he did. In a poem he later wrote about his days in Tours, he addresses his students with affection to tell them things about himself they could never have known:

You, my lambs, my delight with eyes that will not look upon my age
I was not always a shepherd of fair heads on the arid plains of your
    books
Not always the good official, deferring to his superiors
· · · · ·

The poetesses of the sanctuary have given me suck
The king's *griots* have sung me the authentic legend of my race to the
    sounds of the high *koras* . . .[4]

The poet wants to tell his students about the age-old culture of his
African childhood, a rich nourishing world of which French children
know nothing. He marvels at the contrast between it and the French
milieu in which he is living, and at the fact that what is real and
present in his mind is completely invisible to those with whom he
spends his days. Elsewhere, in a poem entitled "Le portrait," he writes
of his "sweet Touraine":

. . . the springtime of Europe
Is making advances to me
Offers me the virgin odor of its earth
The smile of its sunny surfaces.

This world attracts him, but

It does not yet know
The stubbornness of my rancor, made sharp by winter
Nor the demands of my imperious Negritude.[5]

Senghor's early poems describe this division between the world in
which he lives from day to day and the world he knew as a child and
in which he continues to live a rich inner life. They illustrate convinc-
ingly that he could not be adequately described by the serene face he
turned to his colleagues at Tours, to Pompidou, or even to his African
and West Indian friends. It is also worth noting parenthetically here
that this poem of 1936 contains what seems to be Senghor's first
published use of the term "Negritude" as a synonym for those qualities
which drive him from within.

During this time at Tours, the colonial administration continued to
keep an approving eye on Senghor's progress. It was, after all, still
supporting him financially so that he could keep a room in Paris for
his trips there to pursue his linguistic and ethnographic studies. In
December of Senghor's first year as a lycée teacher, the Inspector
General of Education for French West Africa gathered materials for a

report on Senghor to the governor general. In the report he wrote, "His intellectual qualities are truly French . . . he has a methodical mind, serious rather than brilliant. I have the impression that he will be a professor rather than an orator . . . on the personal side, he is pleasant and appealing, always correct . . . modest, reserved . . . a special person." In conclusion, he recommended that the governor general continue his interest in Senghor and encourage his linguistic studies: "I can easily see M. Senghor a professor of oriental languages."[6] And finally, he pointed out that the federation had already invested a lot of scholarship money in this young man, and so should continue support until Senghor could fill a role for which he seemed ideally suited. Tours should be simply an interim position.

Senghor's own plan at this time fit rather well with the plan that was being worked out for him. Still eager to deepen his study of African ethnography and linguistics, he began to work on a thesis on African languages with the goal of becoming a professor at the University of Paris. He was also becoming a poet. He was not at all shy about reading his latest poems. He read them to his West Indian friends in Paris and also to little gatherings of his colleagues in Tours, chanting in a singsong voice which, he said, imitated the rhythm of the oral poetry of Africa. Sometimes he was teased for this style of delivery, but as usual he did not seem to take offense, or, perhaps more accurately, he was able to repress whatever irritation he felt.

Because he was taking courses on linguistics and African ethnography, Senghor went up to Paris often during his three years at Tours. There he met a growing number of Frenchmen active in the worlds of university and letters, and in the colonial administration. He also found in his reading and courses on African ethnography much that excited him.

It is ironic that Senghor had to turn to the work of European ethnographers to learn about his own culture. But he was not one to let this apparent contradiction prevent him from using whatever they could offer. The work of Maurice Delafosse immediately captured his interest. Excerpts from Delafosse's writing had been published in *La Revue du Monde Noir,* and the many books and articles he had published between 1912 and 1917 were widely available and still well respected.

Maurice Delafosse had spent a long and distinguished career in the French colonial service.[7] He was born in 1870 and received a rigorous classical education before being posted to West Africa. On his first trip out, before World War I, he developed a passion for this strange land and its people. He set about learning African languages, and then turned to the study of African history and ethnography. He traveled widely, observed with care, and kept voluminous notes. On the eve of the war, he was recalled to Paris to take the chair in African languages at the school for colonial administrators. From that position, he put his formidable energy to work informing the French public about Africa. In his first book, *Haut-Sénégal-Niger* (1912), he told the story of the great empires of Ghana and Mali that had flourished long before Africa had had significant contact with Europe. While across the street, at the venerable Sorbonne, Professor Seignobos was teaching his students that Africans were big children incapable of governing themselves—the prevailing view of the time, and the one with which Duplessis-Kergomand instructed Senghor's graduating class at Louis-le-grand considerably later—Delafosse was quietly refuting this notion with careful scholarship. He was telling his students that Africans had a complex and integrated culture of their own, and had organized extensive empires. The reward for Delafosse's painstaking work and honesty was that William Ponty, then governor general of West Africa, considered him too independent and dangerous, and criticized him for expressing opinions contrary to official policy. In part for this reason, Delafosse was removed from his university post and sent back to Dakar. He was delighted. His tendency to take the independent path, however, again got him into trouble. Like Governor Van Vollenhoven, the young administrator who had encouraged Hélène Senghor to go to Paris to study, Delafosse opposed the large-scale conscription of black troops to fight France's wars in Europe. This put him at odds with Senegal's deputy, Blaise Diagne. He also criticized Diagne's policy of introducing benefits for the assimilated citizens of the four communes at the expense of the village Africans of the protectorate. What was even more outrageous, he challenged the very foundation of France's assimilation policy, namely the assumption that Africans had no distinctive culture of their own. Delafosse went too far when he openly accused Diagne of pursuing policies favorable to the assimilated elite of the communes in order to gain their votes and to further his own political career, and not because these policies were in the interest of the country as a whole. Diagne was furious. He intervened with the colonial administration to block Delafosse's promotion, once again illustrating the power of the deputy over the colonial administration. Delafosse returned to Paris, where he taught and continued to publish articles and books based on his many years in the field. He died in 1926.

The basic legacy of Delafosse's work was very simple and very important to Senghor, one in keeping with the more general theories of society developed by Emile Durkheim. Delafosse argued an idea startling in its day, namely that Africa had its own civilization, its own aspirations, and its own needs. Africa has, he argued, a culture as ancient as that of France. If at first African behavior seems irrational to a European, further observation will reveal that the Africans have a completely rational reason for what they do. Insofar as African societies have their own internal dynamic and cohesion, Delafosse concluded, no one should deny them the right to maintain their own civilizations. Hence his opposition to recruiting troops to fight French battles and to Diagne's policy of promoting assimilated Africans at the expense of those without European education. In the name of equality, and in an arrogant belief in the superiority of their own civilization, he wrote, Europeans had suppressed native institutions. Delafosse also worried that the French were creating in Africa a caste of the privileged few who might neither serve nor understand the mass of the population.[8] Such were the views of the man Senghor found to be "France's greatest Africanist, by which I mean the most attentive."[9] Senghor also found a Frenchman who had risked his career to serve France and Africa as he saw best.

Senghor's study of ethnography was just beginning. If Delafosse was the first Frenchman to make a serious study of African history and culture, and so provided Senghor with much factual detail about traditional African society, the German anthropologist Leo Frobenius gave Senghor something of equal importance. Frobenius suggested a new way of thinking about culture as such, a way that fit nicely with Senghor's evolving thinking about the relationship between Africa and Europe. A collection of Frobenius's essays was translated into French in 1936. Both Senghor and Césaire pounced on it. Senghor's copy is inscribed by Césaire with the date, December 1936. So excited were they by what Frobenius had to say that they learned great chunks of it by heart. "We still carry the mark of the master in our minds and spirits, like a form of tattooing carried out in the initiation ceremonies in the sacred grove," wrote Senghor many years later. Frobenius provided a broad sweep and a theoretical frame that opened a new perspective for them both. "All the history and prehistory of Africa were illuminated . . . we learned by heart Chapter Two of the first book . . . 'What Does Africa Mean to Us?,' a chapter adorned with lapidary phrases such as this: 'The idea of the barbarous Negro is a European invention.'"[10] This work could only add to Senghor's confidence that his thinking about African culture was in line with that of the most advanced Europeans.

Frobenius was born in Berlin in 1873, and began publishing his findings about Africa in the 1890s.[11] He was a precocious and unconventional scholar. His early work disturbed his professors so much that they rejected his doctoral thesis, entitled "The Origins of African Culture." As it turned out, their disapproval did not deter their determined student. Frobenius managed to mount twelve large expeditions to Africa between 1904 and his death in 1935. There he proved an indefatigable collector, his energy and range of interests matched only by his enthusiasm for note-taking and cataloging. He trained painters to accompany him to reproduce accurate facsimiles of the art he discovered, and students to help in the gigantic task of describing and classifying the information he found. His collection method was that of the omnivore: take note of everything because evidence is fast being destroyed. There was no way to be sure, he thought, what might interest future generations or what might later prove to be of value. He put together enormous archives on mythology, as well as photographs and drawings of the rock art he discovered in the Sahara and South Africa. Unlike Delafosse, Frobenius took no interest in the contemporary problems of Africa and its colonizers. He was a scholar, scientist, theorist, and interpreter of the past. He was determined to find the data to prove that civilizations previously thought to have no history because they had left no written record, had in fact experienced development and evolution and were an important part of world history. He was one of the first cultural anthropologists to move beyond the collection and description of ethnographic facts—the work at which Delafosse excelled—to suggest a structure for organizing those facts. He proposed a theory of culture and history that would unify the work of the anthropologist with that of the historian.

Frobenius began with an assumption taken from the great German historian-philosophers Herder and Hegel, namely that each culture is an entity in itself, separate from the individuals through whom it presents itself at any given time. He likened culture to a living essence, a being that possesses a unique form and personality. He further proposed that insofar as each culture is unique, there is no way to place cultures in a hierarchy. Each has a different essence, what he called a "paideuma" or cultural soul. His conviction of the singularity and wholeness of African culture increased with time: "The more I traveled about Africa and observed its different cultures," he wrote, "the more conscious I became of what was typical and organic rather than unique and individual . . . familiarity with the dark continent," he added, "gave me a keener insight into the form of modern European culture."[12] Africa was one. Africa was unique. Europe was different. To range them in hierarchy with respect to each other made no sense. They could not be compared in this way. These ideas were what Senghor and Césaire wanted to hear.

A third man whose ideas had a great impact on Senghor at this time was Robert Delavignette. Delavignette was Senghor's contemporary, a French colonial administrator in the tradition of Maurice Delafosse, competent, well-trained, respected, and full of love for his adopted land, Africa. Early service in West Africa awakened in Delavignette, as it had in Delafosse, a lifelong sympathy and interest in all things African. He had been a student of Delafosse, and he took the older man's discoveries as a foundation on which to build. Delavignette had written the very sympathetic, albeit romanticized, account of African life for the colonial exposition publication of 1931. He served in the colonial administration and then as director of the colonial school in Paris, where he trained a generation of colonial officials. His books ranged from the frankly poetic *Soudan-Paris-Bourgogne* to an authoritative history of French West Africa. These books were widely read. To both French and African Delavignette represented humane colonialism at its most sensitive and generous best. If any one person can be identified as the shaper of French public opinion about the colonies in the 1930s and 1940s, it is he.

What Delavignette envisioned for the colonies was very simple and is encapsulated in the somewhat awkward title of his book, *Soudan-Paris-Bourgogne*. He hoped for a future in which Soudan, like Bourgogne, would be a province of a vast empire centered in Paris. How he differed from the French colonizers of the past can be neatly summarized by a phrase from this same book. He hoped to make possible for many others an experience he had had, when, far up in the bush of Soudan, he had sat down in the evening with an African ruler and "tasted the sweetness of being different and together."[13] France and Africa would live together in harmony, each respecting and enhancing the unique qualities of the other. It was a view that attracted Senghor greatly, a view very different from that which held that Africans must become more and more like Frenchmen. Both Senghor and Delavignette believed that a future association based on mutual respect was both desirable and possible. Each supported the other. Delavignette opened official doors for Senghor and introduced him as an expert on Africa and a spokesman for the new African generation. Had all French and all Africans thought as they did, the history of relations between the two countries might well have taken a different course.

These three Europeans provided Senghor with ideas and perspectives that suited and influenced his own. Delafosse confirmed Senghor's conviction that Africans had a rich and distinctive culture; Frobenius provided a new way of thinking about culture in general and its manner of evolution, which confirmed the value and integrity of each and every culture; Delavignette offered a positive view of a future political relationship between Africa and France. Study of their work provided Senghor with the authoritative facts and theories that he needed to achieve scholarly respectability for his own ideas. He was beginning to find support for a new view of his African heritage within the French scholarly establishment. To serve the one did not require desertion of the other.

In the course of his visits to Paris from Tours, Senghor maintained and developed old ties of friendship as well. He continued to see Césaire, and other West Indian and African students with whom he shared his ethnographic discoveries. He took special pains to show he remembered his old friends and cared about their work. When Ousmane Socé Diop's novel *Karim* was reviewed by René Maran, for example, Senghor sent a copy of the review to Socé. Senghor was also beginning to meet French intellectuals, of whom Emmanuel Mounier and the Catholic group around the journal *Esprit* struck a particularly responsive chord. They, too, had set out to separate what was durable and valuable in French culture from the unpleasant developments in interwar France. They criticized contemporary science as detached from wisdom, and economic structures that tried to adapt man to the machine rather than the machine to man, and they deplored the concentration of human effort on serving strictly materialistic goals. They had a clear sense of their enemies: individualistic materialism, collectivist materialism, and the false spiritualism of fascism. Their goal was to foster the renaissance of personality and community, hence Mounier's term "personalism."[14] In Mounier's personalism, Senghor found a Frenchman's critique of contemporary French society that paralleled his own.

Senghor also managed to continue his friendship with the newly married Georges Pompidou, whom he visited during Easter holidays in Marseilles, where Pompidou had a teaching job. He spent other holidays at Pompidou's father-in-law's house at Château Gontier, a small town in the Mayenne. Château Gontier, and the friendship of Pompidou, his wife, Claude, her sister, Jacqueline, and the rest of the Cahour family provided Senghor a home away from home during these years. He signed some of his most important poetry from Château Gontier. As had now become the rule rather than the exception, Senghor lived in several different worlds at the same time, and kept each carefully separate from the others.

The diversity of levels on which Senghor existed is most evident in the poems he wrote during his years in Tours. Most of them were not published until later, but it seems clear that it was during this often lonely period that Senghor first realized his vocation as a poet. His earliest published poems provide a revealing glimpse of the emotions and concerns that preoccupied him then and would continue to preoccupy him in the future. Senghor has emphasized that in 1935, the same year he moved to Tours, "I discovered myself such as I was."[15]

This coming of age was not an altogether happy one. It was accompanied by moments of doubt and even despair. Looking back, Senghor recalled it as a time of fervor and perpetual tension. He, Césaire, and a few other black friends with whom he met during his trips to Paris resisted taking the easy road of assimilation, becoming the educated black Frenchmen so dear to sentimental colonial bureaucrats. They accepted a call to live life honestly and dangerously, and saw themselves as New Negroes with a mission to spread the word. The struggle to express what they felt led, according to Senghor, to "literary work which was morally, how shall I put it, physically and metaphysically lived right up to the edge of madness." Their inner turmoil was experienced as illness. Césaire actually had a nervous collapse in the fall of 1935. The breakdown was attributable partly to overwork in preparation for the Ecole Normale competition, but it also coincided with Césaire's attempt to absorb the shock of his encounter with Paris and, through Senghor, with Africa.[16]

Senghor has written that Césaire and he suffered through this period together. To a point their anxiety stemmed from the same source. Césaire's attempt at cure mirrored Senghor's, though each was filtered through the prism of a different temperament and personality. There was the further difference that Senghor, unlike Césaire, had a personal memory of a real Africa. Césaire saw Senghor as the more fortunate of the two for this reason. Looking within, Césaire discovered emptiness, whereas Senghor discovered warm memories of another world. Nonetheless, as they came to know each other, each began to see that his individual dilemma was not simply a personal misfortune or the result of undue sensitivity, but the effect of a structure created by a historical relationship between black and white developed over hundreds of years. The Afro-French society of Senegal, the transplanted and mixed culture of the Antilles, as well as the promises and conditions of French education for blacks, had left a difficult legacy. Césaire and Senghor discovered that the educated black man trying to live in France suffered from this situation in the extreme.

The severity of this strain was illustrated dramatically for them by the suicide of a black French-speaking writer, the Malagasy poet Jean-Joseph Rabéarivelo. Rabéarivelo's death received considerable publicity in the Paris press. His last diary, published in the *Mercure de France,* revealed that in taking leave of life he had left "a kiss to the books of Baudelaire," Senghor's favorite poet. This event shook Senghor and his circle, who identified Rabéarivelo's situation with their own. Both Senghor and Damas wrote about it. Damas observed that the suicide was partly the result of "despair brought about by a sense of the uselessness of all effort, by uprooting and exile in the very land of his ancestors [he was in Madagascar at the time of his suicide], . . . but also illustrated the drama of a man who has crossed very quickly, too quickly, the stages of civilization. Rabéarivelo aspired high, not just to be the equal of the white, but to be an intellectual. Yet he became a being apart, neither fish nor fowl, and suffered for it." Senghor reflected on Rabéarivelo's suicide somewhat differently. He saw it as one possible outcome of the failure to make peace within one's own personality. When a man has become French by education, he feels himself an outcast in his own land. This makes Rabéarivelo's suicide understandable.[17] Senghor was determined to integrate in himself the best of both worlds and to be comfortable in both. He understood that this would be impossible without the reevaluation and acceptance of the core values of the Africa of his childhood. This was a part of his basic identity, the remnants of childhood that must be preserved. It would require the creation of a new person with a new voice. The voice would be neither French nor African, for the man was neither French nor African. It would be that of a new historical personage, the French Negro. The whole quest, as Senghor put it, was "nothing but a quest for ourselves."[18] It was no idle or vain goal, but a vital necessity.

The examples provided by Césaire and Rabéarivelo suggest that

Senghor was not being overly melodramatic when he spoke of his quest for a new identity as "a question of life and death." The price of failing to achieve equilibrium, he wrote in his reflection on Rabéarivelo, is despair.[19] And, elsewhere, discussing Rabéarivelo and suggesting that he himself was no stranger to this despair, "I would never commit suicide because I think it is giving up. It is the acceptance of defeat. For me, suicide is cowardice. And the fault I scorn the most is cowardice."[20] Despair is also one of the most deadly sins for the Christian, as suicide is considered a crime against God. Senghor's deep Christian belief and his long Christian education helped provide the framework for resisting Rabéarivelo's choice. They promised Senghor that an alternative was possible.

Poetry gave both Césaire and Senghor, and their friend Damas, a language and form in which to express the problem and to reach toward its solution. In Césaire's case, recovery from a psychological breakdown coincided with his sketching out the first draft of a long prose poem, *Cahier d'un retour au pays natal* (Notebook of a Return to the Land of Birth). In Senghor's, it led to the discovery of a vocation for poetry that allowed him to recognize himself "such as he was" and to write the poems that make up his first published collection of poetry, *Chants d'ombre* (Songs of, or from, the Shadows). In both cases, it led, as it had for the heroes of Maurice Barrès who had so attracted Senghor in his student days, to a return to the traditions of their homeland.

Césaire's *Cahier* is transparently autobiographical. It presents in poetic form an account of a metaphoric return to his native land, a trip mirrored by Césaire's actual trip to Martinique in the summer of 1936. He looks open-eyed at his island and accepts the fact that this is his only home. Senghor has emphasized repeatedly how close in their thinking he and Césaire were at this time; thus Césaire's account is valuable for what it suggests about both men. Césaire sets out to assess his native island with an objective eye for the first time. He sees a people who are browbeaten, disease-ridden, and poor. He sees a land that is ugly, with a stench of poverty, "rotting under the sun." He sees hunger and suffering, a place where the river of life has been blocked up and lies, torpid, in its bed. He accepts this as the reality of his home and of his personal past. He sees also that he is connected by virtue of his black skin to the experience of all black men, black men of Africa, Haiti, Virginia, Georgia, and Alabama. He accepts their history as his—the ugliness and ignorance, the poverty and disease, the slavery and cannibalism. This is a real and inescapable part of the black experience. Both the exotic Negro of French invention and the black Frenchman are myths created by white Europeans. To the rest of the world, he now hurls a challenge: "Adapt yourself to me. I do not adapt myself to you." He will cheer for those who are nothing. They at least are not cynical or corrupted by the exploitation of others. This does not mean that he hates other races, only that he will exalt in his own. He accepts unconditionally his membership in a race with a grim and degraded past. In the future he will stand up, as he has not done in the past, and other Negroes will stand up with him. Exoticism and illusion are not fit food for a man. They cannot nourish his growth. Man must stand on what is real. No matter how unpleasant that reality is, only it can provide a steady foundation. For Césaire, in this poem, the progression is simple. First, he will recognize the location of his true homeland; second, he will look objectively at it; and third, he will accept it for what it is. Then, and only then, can he move forward. No more self-deception or seeing himself reflected in the eyes of others.[21]

Senghor saw his task as somewhat different. If Césaire and the black population of Martinique had in fact lost all traces of their distant African heritage and been left only with poverty and slavery, he had not. Senghor argued that blacks had been *taught* for centuries that they had thought nothing, built nothing, painted nothing, sung nothing, and that they and their culture were nothing, the "tabula rasa" of French mythology.[22] This was the stuff of his schooldays, when his French teachers had reminded him over and over again that they had driven barbarism and sickness from his country and had brought him the benefits of civilization. But while he was learning this from his French teachers, he had also known something else, something that he had for a time discounted. He had a direct experience of the African village, of Djilor and Joal. This knowledge contradicted the French doctrine that Africa was a blank page, totally without culture. What Senghor had now to do was to stop pretending either that the French teaching was correct or that it did not exist. He had to acknowledge that most Frenchmen considered blacks inferior men whose best hope was to become discolored Frenchmen. He finally realized that he could never achieve self-respect as long as he continued to pretend that he and the French saw no difference between him and them. Like Césaire, Senghor resolved to confront these attitudes and teachings with another reality. He, too, would make the metaphoric and symbolic trip home.

The poetry Senghor wrote in Tours reflects this resolve. It evokes and examines his childhood heritage and accepts it as an inextricable part of his own personality. The subjects of these poems, their shifting emphases and rich ambivalence, provide a glimpse of Senghor's inner self and the associations that rang through his memory at this time. While it is always dangerous to assume that the voice of a poem and the actual voice of a writer are identical, in Senghor's case the connection seems close indeed in these early poems.

The first theme Senghor takes up is that of exile. Its direct connection to his life as an African student in Paris is clear. He expresses feelings of isolation among strangers, of unease, and of a keen, almost unbearable love for the absent one, Africa. The theme of exile and return, providing opportunity for loving descriptions of home and immersion in memories of childhood, is an understandable one for any student far from home. For Senghor it had a special significance. Immersing himself in memories of childhood, sharing them with sympathetic West Indian friends, and writing about them provided Senghor a source of pleasure and companionship.[23] It lent dignity and wider significance to what otherwise might have been solitary daydreaming or a grim quest. Césaire and others, hungry to learn about Africa, encouraged him to continue in this direction.

Senghor writes lyrically of his childhood home, Joal, and the nights of Sine:

> Woman, lay on my forehead your perfumed hands, hands softer than fur
> Above, the swaying palms rustle in the high night breeze
> . . . . .
> Listen to its song, listen to our dark blood beat, listen
> To the deep pulse of Africa beating in the mist of forgotten villages.[24]

Working on these poems in his room, Senghor could travel home in his mind's eye and give outlet to his nostalgia. He could write of his beloved uncle, Waly, his mythic and noble father, the dignity and riches of traditional kings, and the peace and calm of evenings in the still villages. Such was the inspiration for one of his most often quoted poems, a poem written in praise of the beauty of the black woman and of the Africa she embodies:

> Naked woman, dark woman
> Firm-fleshed ripe fruit, sombre raptures of black wine, making lyrical my mouth

Savannah stretching to clear horizons, savannah shuddering beneath
   the East Wind's eager caresses.
Carved tom-tom, taut tom-tom, muttering under the Conqueror's
   fingers
Your solemn contralto voice is the spiritual song of the Beloved.[25]

Senghor celebrates the particular texture and physical presence of a
concrete place and time, the Africa of his childhood. It is a pure and
integrated world that is, to use his own phrase, innocent of Europe.

Into some of Senghor's evocations of Africa, however, creep signs
of the European. Even as he remembers Joal with the beautiful women
in the cool shade of verandahs, King Koumba Ndofène Diouf, and
the rhapsodies of the griots, he also hears with pleasure pagan voices
chanting the "tantum ergo," and sees the Catholic religious processions that gather by his grandfather's house in Joal. They, too, are
part of his remembered Africa.[26] They appear in the poem as totally
compatible with the rest. Both elements are part of a harmonious
memory.

These poems are consistent, affectionate, and whole. The merging
of Africa, paradise, and childhood is complete. If Baudelaire taught
that all great poets are inspired by childhood, Senghor happily bears
him out in finding in the kingdom of childhood his chief poetic
inspiration. Such an imaginative return also offers the poet an opportunity to relive a period when his experience was integrated, before
he felt the impact of the French in Africa or the adult experiences of
dislocation and division. With a flash of insight, Senghor acknowledges that childhood and Africa are linked with Eden in his memory,
there confused and inseparable.[27] Like Eden, his childhood Africa
offered him a place of perfect harmony between man and his surroundings. Perhaps even more important for Senghor, it was the time of
emotional peace and internal harmony. In Eden man and God lived
in accord. Man did not yet know sin, which cuts him off from an
integrated communion with God. In Senghor's imagination Eden and
the Africa of his childhood are one and the same, what he calls the
kingdom of childhood, to which he can return at will for inspiration.

When Senghor writes of his present situation and feelings, however,
the poet's attitude and mood become far more complex and varied.
He finds no single consistent stance toward the French world, at least
not in his early poems. Even the notion of exile becomes more complex. At times, the poet focuses on the physical exile that leads to
solitude and isolation. But he finds that his solitude is deeper than

mere physical absence from Africa. He is further isolated by specific qualities of French life. Even this, however, is not the full measure of his separation. He suffers most of all from "that other exile harder on my heart, the tearing of self from self / from the language of my mother, from the thinking of my ancestor, from the beat of my soul."[28] This wrenching of self from self leads to an almost overwhelming sense of being two.

The poet realizes that he has internalized both his African and his French upbringing, and finds the two sets of values and behaviors to be at odds. The colonial administrator and educator Georges Hardy had warned that French schooling could lead Africans to live in two separate worlds and that this could have dire results. For most African children, the French world was but an artificial and temporary existence, while their real world remained securely that of Africa. For Senghor, however, the balance was far more even. He loved France and French culture. He also loved his native Africa. If he was to find a new voice as a French Negro, he had to resolve this problem of twoness. For him, the French Negro could not be the black Frenchman of colonial policy, the Frenchman who happened to be black. That black Frenchman was doomed forever to second-class citizenship. Nor could the French Negro be the African innocent of Europe. Senghor would have to be a black man first, who then acquired French culture and put it to work for his own purposes. It was too late to reject his laboriously acquired French education, nor did he wish to. A linguistic solution of this dilemma, simply by fusing together two words, an adjective and a noun, "Negro" and "French," and announcing oneself a "French Negro" or a "New Negro," was a declaration of intent, but only a first step. What might seem but a small shift in emphasis required in fact a basic redefinition of the nature and possibilities of the black man.

This theme of separation, internal fracture, and the search for wholeness adds a more sombre dimension to the theme of exile. This is the note that dominates Senghor's first published collection of poetry, *Chants d'ombre* (Songs of, or from, the Shadow). So long as he felt these inner divisions, he could not rest. As he explored their nature and consequences, he was comforted by knowing that his painful experience was shared by men like Césaire and Maran, as well as by men who had lived before him and whom he knew only through their writings, such as the black American Dr. W. E. B. Du Bois. Senghor was astonished, he later wrote, to discover such kinship in the writings of Du Bois, a man living so removed from himself in both time and place. In expressing what he called his constant sense of twoness, Du Bois had put the problem of the black man in a white man's world with stark clarity. His writings further convinced Senghor that all black men shared a common experience.

W. E. B. Du Bois was born in Massachusetts in 1868, almost forty years before Senghor's birth. The worlds in which the two men grew up bore no resemblance. They did share, however, the experience of moving at a very young age into a world dominated by whites who had certain preconceptions about black people. Du Bois grew up in the little New England town of Great Barrington, Massachusetts, and received a Ph.D. from Harvard University, an institution whose relative prestige among Americans rivals that of Louis-le-grand and the Sorbonne among the French. He, like Senghor, was able to excel according to the white man's standards. Yet though Du Bois got a degree from Harvard and studied in Europe, when it came time for his adult career, race became the decisive factor. Du Bois had to look for employment, as did another black Harvard graduate, Alain Locke, at a black institution such as Fisk, Howard, or Atlanta. Similarly, Senghor was constantly reminded in small ways that, despite his unusual success in the French system, he was not French and never could be. Biology and birth proved decisive in such matters. When Du Bois published *The Souls of Black Folk* in 1903, three years before Senghor was born, he was in his mid-thirties, a gifted and successful young man who appeared to have a promising scholarly career ahead of him. In his book, Du Bois describes the position of the black man in America. Living in the American world, he observes,

> yields him [the Negro] no true self-consciousness, but only lets him see himself through the revelation of the other world. It is a peculiar sensation, this double-consciousness, this sense of always looking at oneself through the eyes of others, of measuring one's soul by the tape of a world that looks on in amused contempt and pity. One ever feels his twoness—an American, a Negro; two souls, two thoughts, two unreconciled strivings; two warring ideals in one dark body, whose dogged strength alone keeps it from being torn asunder.[29]

Du Bois, like Senghor in his poetry, identifies several dimensions to the problem of "twoness," and of the black man in the white man's culture. On the first and most obvious level, the black self seen through the eyes of whites is an inferior person in every way. He has invented nothing, has done nothing, and is nothing. He can be only an object of contempt, curiosity, or pity. As the dictionary Senghor used at school put it, Negroes are inhabitants of Africa who form a race "inferior in intelligence to the white race called Caucasian."[30] But there is a second part of the problem, both more subtle and more intractable. The educated black American not only is seen by others as inferior but also sees himself as inferior, for he sees with eyes shaped by white values and culture.

Du Bois offers a precise description of Senghor's experience. Though African by birth, Senghor had become French by education. He was taught to see Africans as French people saw Africans. No allowance was made for the fact that he himself happened to be African. Nothing in his education encouraged or even allowed him to have a clear sense of himself as an educated black person. According to his French culture, to be black and educated was a contradiction in terms. There was no such person. Hence the sense of twoness. It was not simply a question of being buffeted by the insolence of others. The struggle was between two warring parts of the self. Under these circumstances, to become an integrated, single person with a clear voice was a difficult achievement, and yet to fail was to pay an enormous price. The suicide of Rabéarivelo illustrated just how high that price might be for a sensitive person. Given Du Bois's powerful description of an experience Senghor felt to be his own, it is small wonder that Senghor later called Du Bois one of the fathers of Negritude and firmly believed that the essential black experience was shared by black men everywhere.

Senghor explored this experience of twoness in his early poetry. The poet discovers first one and than another rift in his personality. At the most obvious there is a division between the outer self he presents to the world, that of the dutiful teacher who "smiles but never laughs," and an inner self, brooding about his African roots. The outer self, carefully constructed to hide emotion, is calm and serene; the inner self is in turmoil. This dichotomy is the subject of Senghor's first extant reliably dated poem, "Jardin de France" (French Garden):

Calm Garden
Grave Garden
Garden with evening eyes
Lowered for the Night
. . . . .
White Hands
Delicate motions
Soothing gestures

. . . . .
But the tom-tom's call
   bounding
      over continents
      and mountains
Who will quiet my heart
Leaping at the tom-tom's call
   Violently
      Throbbing?[31]

Here the calm, French surface is barely able to contain the African
heart that stubbornly leaps to the beat of the drum. The stolid measured rhythms of being in the French world contrast stylistically with
the flowing energy of the lines describing the inner African being,
reinforcing the explicit content of the poem. It is a contrast parallel
to that of the later poem "Portrait," in which the poet expresses the
discontinuity between his inner world and that of the French in which
he lives, but also acknowledges the appeal of the French world. The
spring of Touraine is sweet and makes advances, totally unaware of
the poet's "imperious Negritude." The poet makes no attempt at
reconciliation of any kind. He is simply descriptive.

At times, the poet wishes only to bury his African side. When he
first arrived in Paris, for example, Senghor shared the French view
about Africans' lack of contribution to world culture: "Had our black
skins allowed it, we would have blushed for our African birth . . . the
[African] people made us secretly ashamed."[32] This is the attitude of
his schoolboy verse written in imitation of the French romantic poets,
an attitude that later made him so ashamed that, as he wrote to
Maurice Martin du Gard, he destroyed this early work. It is an attitude
he admitted openly only after he had cast it off. In a poem entitled
"Totem," he writes of being pursued by a heritage he cannot shake:

In my inmost vein I must hide him
My Ancestor with the skin storm-streaked with lightning and
   thunder
My guardian animal. I must hide him
Lest I burst the dam of scandal.

And, elsewhere, "it pursues me, my black blood, right into the solitary
heart of the night."[33]

Even as he is trying to hide his ancestor, and so to escape his black
blood, Senghor realizes that this is impossible. The advantage may be,

as the poet suggests in "Totem," that the ancestor protects him from his naked pride that might lead him to develop the "arrogance of the lucky races," and from the weakness of civilized man. These arguments are not altogether convincing. The poet seems to be casting about for some consolation for his inescapable blackness. It is a great effort. Senghor had to "hypnotize himself," he said later, to find all that belonged to white Europe, its reason, its art, and its women, ugly and insipid.[34]

The arrangement of the individual poems in the *Chants d'ombre* collection reflects what Senghor calls the order of their general inspiration, if not the actual dates of composition.[35] The progression from poem to poem therefore parallels his own evolution, at least as he later came to see it, and the stages he went through in his growing self-awareness.

The first poem in the collection, "In Memoriam," finds the poet in Paris in his room, alone, apprehensive about the crowd of men "with faces of stone" who await him in the street below. To escape them, and to avoid going down into this world, he dreams of Africa, his race, and the dead ancestors. With images of African power, he builds a protective wall between himself and the world outside. At the end of the poem, he reluctantly gives up this secure fortress and goes out into the world, where he resolves to live with "his brothers with the blue eyes and hard hands." Several short poems that convey similar attitudes are followed by the poems singled out above for their clear, unambivalent evocation of the nights of Sine, Joal, and Djilor, the beauty of the black woman and of Africa, and the comfort and strength of the ancestor. In one poem, however, entitled "Le message" (The Message), the ancestor accuses the poet of ignoring the family songs, of learning new languages, and of memorizing an alien history of other ancestors, the Gauls. The poet is accused of becoming a doctor at the Sorbonne, bedecking himself with diplomas and surrounding himself with piles of papers. The ancestor questions why he has done this, and whether it has led to happiness. Return to me, the voice urges.[36]

At this point in the poetic cycle, the poet finds himself once more in Paris. But now his attitude is somewhat different. In "Neige sur Paris" (Snow on Paris), Senghor evokes the sterility and cold of the city. Whiteness and snow bring death, not purity or innocence. The poet is no longer content with seeking refuge in memory. Rather, he is ready to accuse the white hands "that whipped slaves / . . . that slapped me / . . . that delivered me to solitude and hatred / . . . that cut down the forest of palms which dominated Africa / . . . to build railroads / They pulled down the forests of Africa to save Civilization," because they were weary with their own failures and shortcomings. The expression of anger and bitterness is new. The poet feels these emotions strongly and no longer needs to hide them. Nonetheless, Senghor pulls back from closing even this single poem in anger. He ends with a prayer to the Christian God, and with the resolve not to use up his hatred on "the diplomats who bare their long canine teeth and who, tomorrow, will barter black flesh." He promises that he will achieve reconciliation in the warmth of God's sweetness and embrace his enemies as brothers. Even though he is angry with the Europeans' ravaging of Africa, he still recognizes their God as his God and accepts the Christian goal of reconciliation.[37]

The poet now considers contributions that Africans can make to the European world. If the Africa of the empires has died an agonizing death, Europe, too, is suffering. Like the good Samaritan who gives up his last garment for another, the African will give life to the dying European world. He will provide the leaven for the white flour, the grease for the city's rusty steel, "For who would teach rhythm to a dead world of machines and cannons? / Who would shout the cry of joy to wake the dead and the orphans to the dawn? / . . . / We are the men of the dance, whose feet gain strength by striking the hard earth."[38]

This new stance is not firmly held. Triumph is followed by defeat. At times, as in "Totem," he still wants to hide his ancestry. He writes of false starts, setbacks, frustration, and depression. In two poems that come at this point in the collection, "Ndéssé ou 'Blues'" (Ndéssé or Blues) and "A la mort" (To Death), Senghor records a youthful surge of life and promise that is blighted, confused, left without outlet or direction: "My wings beat and bruise themselves on the bars of a low sky." A child races gaily after a ripe fruit. It rolls under a palm tree, and the child is flattened abruptly to the ground. The poet is pressed down, stopped, smothered. He feels a vivid loss of well-being. Disappointment and the chilling winter rains, too, are the poet's inescapable companions.[39]

In the next long poem, "Que m'accompagnent kôras et balafong" (Let Me Be Accompanied by Kôras and Balafong), Senghor returns to the theme of Africa the unspoiled, where Africa, Eden, and childhood merge in an eternal present. In this realm, man is always whole.

It is a wholeness that encompasses both Christian and African worlds
and lies at the center of Senghor's being. In his original plan, this was
to be the title poem of the collection.[40] The poem recalls, in loving
detail and long, hypnotic rhythms, the Africa of childhood. It states
the poet's dilemma: Must he choose? It is no longer a question of
rejecting the call of his ancestor for the inviting world of the French,
or of forgetting Europe in the warm embrace of his native land. Either
choice would diminish the poet. He finds that he is "deliciously torn
between these two friendly hands / . . . these two antagonistic worlds /
When mournfully—ah! I no longer know which is my sister and
which my foster sister" (p. 30). He feels deep love for both. Not to
choose but to hold them simultaneously in his desire: "But if I must
choose at the hour of the test / I have chosen my distressed people,
my peasant people, the whole peasant race throughout the world / . . .
To be your trumpet!" (pp. 30–31). And with that choice, the poet
heralds a new mission, listening to the new voices and the song of
"seven thousand new negroes" (p. 35). And yet it is still not really a
choice, for he takes with him to this Africa a friend from the Breton
mist. In Europe he will play the trumpet of Africa for European ears.
In Africa he will introduce the good European. Senghor aspires to be
like Maran, to whom the poem is dedicated. The poet will combine
the strengths of both traditions to serve his people. What makes this
poem extraordinarily successful is that it is in itself a tour de force of
harmonized styles and symbolic references, an extraordinary blend of
classical, French, and African allusions. It resounds with the music of
the African instruments that are called for as accompaniment, as well
as with classical echoes of Virgil and pious Aeneas, the Roman exem-
plar of filial piety. It also evokes the Christian Eden and God's promise
of redemption to those who are worthy. The effect is a rich harmony,
the enhancement of each by the other, for which Senghor yearned in
his own life.

The next few poems speak of the difficulty of departure, of giving
up the physical and emotional comfort of Africa to return, as he must,
to Europe. The poet does not doubt that he must return. The collection closes with a poem that appears from internal evidence to have
been written during World War II. It is called "Le retour de l'enfant
prodigue" (The Return of the Prodigal Son), and is dedicated to
Senghor's nephew, the son of Hélène Senghor, Jacques Maguilen
Senghor.[41] Here the theme of deserting the ancestors, of guilt and
the need for forgiveness, is explored directly. Tired from years of

wandering and exile, the prodigal son has returned home, to the herdsman who shared his childhood dreams, and to his ancestors who have withstood the passage of time unchanged. He seeks from them pure water to wash away the mud of civilization that clings to his feet. He seeks peace, guidance, and strength. In this search, the poet makes a pilgrimage to the ancestral tomb, the Elephant of Mbissel, the tomb Senghor had first visited as a child on his trip from Djilor to mission school and had recently revisited on his trip to Senegal, the tomb where his father now lay buried. Prostrating himself, the poet invokes the African idiom of praise, to the ancestor and his noble lineage, to the greatness and riches of the kings of Sine. He thanks his fathers, who have not allowed him to fall into hatred when faced with "the polite insults and discreet allusions" he has had to endure (p. 50). To them he confesses his apparent disloyalty and friendship with the princes of form. He has eaten bread that was bought with the hunger of others and has dreamed of a world "in brotherhood with my blue-eyed brothers" (p. 50). It is true. Senghor did thirstily drink in French culture, enjoy European friends, and imagine a life of success and general acceptance in the European world. He did neglect his ancestor. He hid him. He pressed on to become an accomplished intellectual, one of the princes of form. For this, the poet now begs forgiveness from his family, the ancestors, and the land. He has recognized that, like the mythic Greek wrestler Antaeus who was invincible as long as his foot touched the earth, his strength depends on contact with his native soil.

Having thus humbled himself and praised his ancestors for their power and endurance, he invokes the most glorious of them and entreats them to hand on to him the knowledge of the great wise men of Timbuktu, the will of the conqueror Soni Ali, the wisdom of the Keita, kings of Mali, the courage of the *guelowar,* conquerors of Sine, and the strength of the *tiedo,* the fierce armed slaves. He offers to give up his life in battle if he must, but in return he asks that the forces of past heroes live on in him, that they make of him their "master of language . . . their ambassador" (p. 51).

This prodigal son, unlike the son of the Biblical parable, does not wish simply to be forgiven by his father. He does want forgiveness, indeed the very title of the poem implies that he will be forgiven, but he also wants something more. He wants his father's blessing on his future life in a different world. Senghor wants to serve his people, not just as the trumpet that blares out his people's virtue and strength, as

he had put it in "Que m'accompagnent kôras et balafong." He wishes
now to be an ambassador, the man who represents and explains his
people to alien lands, a trumpet that will play a melody Europeans
can understand. In closing the poem, the poet evokes both the emotions that pull him back and the sense of duty that propels him
forward. First the familiar evocation of childhood, the security and
refuge, "to sleep again in the cool bed of childhood," and then the
reluctant departure: "Tomorrow, I will take up again the road to
Europe, the road of the ambassador / Longing for my black homeland" (p. 52). This poem, meditative and reflective, calm and measured
in tone, expresses a firm determination to take on a mission on behalf
of his people. The poet sees his calling as one that requires not simply
self-expression, the strident note of the trumpet, but interpretation,
the diplomatic skill of the ambassador. He must express his experience
and that of his people in a way that can be understood by people of
another world and culture. He embraces the duty of becoming a
spokesman whose message is intelligible, not simply a poet who allows
himself the self-indulgence of beautiful words without regard for his
audience.

It is noteworthy that the poet never suggests that his Christianity
may be one of his sins against his ancestors. Why should they not be
jealous of his worship of an alien God? Instead the poet blends traditional and Christian imagery so that each reinforces the other with
grace and fluidity, proof in itself, it might seem, that the choice to
serve his ancestor is in harmony with loyalty to his Christian self. Style
and meaning are fully adapted to each other. The model for the African
Prodigal Son is taken from the Christian Bible. This confident and
successful synthesis would seem to reflect the deep level of Senghor's
faith and the degree to which he felt it to be compatible with the
values of Africa. Of all that he had learned from the French, the
Christian belief was most deeply rooted in his personality. The sound
of tantum ergos chanted in African rhythms blended with his earliest
childhood memories. He found nothing discordant in this. He knew
Christian belief to be an essential part of French culture as well, albeit
one deserted by most intellectuals of his own generation. Nonetheless
in Christianity Senghor found a system of values he felt to be acceptable in both his worlds. Perhaps this explains why it proved such an
effective anchor for him throughout his life. It not only was the first
formal intellectual discipline he met in his seminary education but also
provided the music, catechism, and values of his earliest schooling. In

a phrase to which he returned again and again, Africa-Eden-Childhood, he asserted the identity of Africa, the original Christian paradise, and his childhood self. To be a Christian was a way to be whole, to serve both African and European and to replenish the dogged strength which, to use Du Bois's phrase, was necessary to hold warring selves together. Looking forward to the future, Senghor also found in Christianity the promise that reconciliation is not only favored by God but always possible in the world God created.

In the collection taken as a whole, Senghor traces an evolution that bears every mark of being his own. There are many shifts of mood along the way in the poems, as there undoubtedly were in his own life. Admiration for the French, love of their culture, fear of them, and the desire to hide his African ancestor alternate with their opposite, refuge in Africa, the paradise innocent of both Europe and the industrial world. The poet is angry at the French for what they have done to Africa. Elation at finding an apparent solution, the return to his African roots, is followed by despair at finding that it is not truly a solution at all, but only a momentary respite. The poet finally reaches a position he hopes to make his own, that of ambassador of his people to Europe, trumpet of his people to the French world, and a Christian. This persona need not feel the guilt of desertion because he will serve his people. At the same time he will also be free to continue the life of an intellectual in Paris.

This interpretation of *Chants d'ombre* is supported by a letter Senghor wrote to René Maran shortly after it was published. Thanking Maran for reading the collection, he continued, "no approval could be more precious than yours . . . By your double culture, French and African, you were more qualified than any other to judge these songs in which I wanted to express myself authentically and integrally, where I wished to express the 'conciliating accord' that I force myself to realize between my two cultures."[42] Elsewhere he wrote: "It is exactly because Eden-Africa-Childhood is absent that I am torn between Europe and Africa, between politics and poetry, between my white brother and myself . . . As for me, I think that to realize myself as a man, it is essential for me to overcome negation, to bridge the chasm."[43] To build these bridges and unite his disparate selves was the task Senghor had to take on in order to become whole. In the most basic way, he had no choice: he was the two. But the difficulty of achieving the integration and perspective from which to begin his adult work required all the strength and self-discipline he could muster.

He still felt as if he teetered precariously over the chasm. His chosen self was not yet natural for him. It was a solution to which, as he put it, he "forced myself."[44]

In a letter he wrote during the war to Maurice Martin du Gard, Senghor explained how important language and poetry had been to him during this period. He had begun writing verse in the style of the French romantics while still at lycée. Later, while at the Sorbonne, he had been influenced by the Surrealists and also had begun to learn about Africa through the writings of ethnographers and "above all Negro-American poetry. I even met some Negro-American writers. These discoveries were true revelations for me which led me to seek myself and uncover myself as I was: a Negro [nègre], morally and intellectually interwoven with French. I then burned almost all my previous poems to start again at zero. It was about 1935." By the gesture of destroying his previous work, so theatrical and uncharacteristic, Senghor dramatized his determination to break sharply with his past. "Since then, I have wanted to express something. It is this 'New Negro,' this French Negro that I had discovered in myself." Here Senghor used a literal translation of Alain Locke's term, until then not used in French, choosing the pejorative nègre rather than noir.* Furthermore, Senghor continued, in order to express this new departure, he could not use the classic French verse form but had to create a new verse form to convey "the Negro rhythm while respecting the order and harmony of the French language."[45] As a poet, he would use a new style to express his new voice.

The words of the psychologist Erik Erikson, who studied what he called the identity crisis both among his young patients and in some historical figures, express what Senghor experienced during this time: "There is a moment in life when each youth must forge for himself

---

* I have translated the French nègre as "Negro" throughout this book, and noir as "black." In the United States of the 1930s, the word "Negro" did not carry the negative connotations that it has since the 1960s, whereas in France the word nègre did. The alternative translation of nègre, "nigger," seems too strong. French-speaking West Indians of this time, according to Frantz Fanon, considered nègre a word to refer to Africans, not themselves. If they were asked to describe themselves, they would answer "French," or "from the Antilles" or use the word noir. Fanon, Black Skin, White Masks, trans. Charles Lam Markham (New York: Grove Press, 1967), pp. 147–149; A. James Arnold, Modernism and Negritude: The Poetry and Poetics of Aimé Césaire (Cambridge, Mass.: Harvard University Press, 1981), pp. 261–263.

some central perspective and direction, some working unity out of the effective remnants of his childhood and the hopes of his anticipated adulthood; he must detect some meaningful resemblance between what he has come to see in himself and what his sharpened awareness tells him others judge and expect him to be." And historically great men, Erikson continues, "although suffering . . . through what appears to be a prolonged adolescence, eventually come to contribute an original bit to an emerging style of life: the very danger which they have sensed has forced them to mobilize capacities to see and say, to dream and plan, to design and construct in new ways." Such young people then experience a "kind of second birth." Sometimes the creative person will experience more intensely what is shared to a lesser degree by a number of his contemporaries. When this is true, and if he is able to find a solution that makes sense to others, and if he is sufficiently gifted to express this hard-won new perspective in words that resonate in his contemporaries, he may become a leader of his generation.[46]

Senghor wrestled for several years with this question of his identity and his place in the world. He had tried to become what the French admired, a dutiful black Frenchman. Yet in Paris he realized that he was no Frenchman, and that the way French students approached life was, for him, "a perpetual subject of astonishment." He also realized that most Frenchmen considered him first and foremost black, and that for them, to be black was to be inferior. In his first stage of self-discovery, Senghor and his West Indian friends met this French racism with a racism of their own. They accepted the racist premise that black men were basically different from whites, but rejected the way in which Europeans evaluated this difference. Yet even as he was pursuing this discovery of his Negritude, Senghor was confused by his continued attraction to the French, to their culture and their world. He felt at home among his French friends and did not want to give them up. He spent time both with them and in the company of the students of color. Each group welcomed him, but each saw only part of what Senghor felt himself to be. This put him off balance. His intellectual solution remained at odds with his emotional experience, and he suffered from a real depression.[47]

Even his friends seemed not to sense that his surface equilibrium was not the natural expression of a man at ease with himself but rather the hard-won result of enormous self-control. Any doubts, hesitations, or self-revelations that might have allowed his friends to share his intimate experience remained strictly hidden, then and throughout the rest of his life. When he did describe his inner troubles, it was always from a distance, as something that had been felt in the past but since mastered and placed into its proper perspective. Only one of his contemporaries, Marc Sankalé, a Senegalese physician who knew him in Paris in the late 1930s and early 1940s, sensed this other side. Drawing perhaps on his powers as a clinician, Sankalé observed that Senghor domesticated his body with demanding daily exercises and a frugal regime and applied the same discipline to his mental life and his personal life. Every minute of his time was used for some necessary activity. Sankalé was intrigued that such a methodical, orderly person would write a poetry marked by reverie, escapism, and fantasy. He found Senghor contradictory, both eloquent and withdrawn, lively and solemn, and noted what he called a mystical fervor in his exaltation of Negro-African culture, a fervor that had something "pitiful about it." Senghor wished himself to be heart, mouth, and trumpet of his people, Sankalé continued, but his was not a real Africa. Though Senghor, the poet, acknowledged that he had fused Africa-Eden-Childhood in his imagination, Sankalé implied that this confusion was not simply a poetic convention but a basic and even desperate need. As a result of his strong will, Sankalé concluded with no small admiration, Senghor had become "the complete Man he wanted to be."[48]

The effort Senghor put into this enterprise was no secret to Senghor himself, even it if remained hidden to many of his admirers. Almost twenty years later, in 1950, he published a confident article in which he discussed the future of French Africa. He ended this article on a personal note, choosing one of the most powerful metaphors a Christian has at his command, that of rebirth:

> May I be permitted to end by evoking a personal experience? I think of those years of youth, at that age of division at which I was not yet born, torn as I was between my Christian conscience and my Serer blood. But was I Serer, I who had a Malinké name—and that of my mother was Peul? Now I am no longer ashamed of my diversity, I find my joy, my assurance in embracing with a catholic eye all these complementary worlds.[49]

Such was the confident integrity of the mature Senghor at his most assured. But the continuing strain of this achievement was a constant companion. A few years later, when he was in his mid-50s, Senghor wrote:

In fact my interior life was, very early, divided between the call of
the Ancestors and the call of Europe, between the requirements of
Negro-African culture and the requirements of modern life. These
conflicts are often expressed in my poems. They are what binds them
together.

Meanwhile, I have always forced myself to resolve them in a
peaceful accord. Thanks to the confession and direction of my
thinking in youth, thanks, later to the intellectual method which my
French teacher taught us.

This equilibrium . . . is an unstable equilibrium, difficult to maintain. I must, each day, begin again at zero, when at 6:30 or 7:00 in
the morning I get up to do my exercises. In effect, this equilibrium
is constantly being broken. I must not only reestablish it but still
perfect it. I do not complain about it. It is such divisions and efforts
that make you advance by one step each day, and that make for
man's greatness.[50]

The achievement, maintenance, and expression of this balance
became the task of Senghor's maturity. Above all, he wished to avoid
sharp conflict or rupture with France, with Africa, with friends, and,
most important, within himself. In his poetry, he often addressed the
themes of wholeness and integrity and their connection to the preservation of vitality. In his scholarly life, he worked to analyze and
describe African culture in order to increase African self-knowledge
and French understanding. Later, in his political life, he took on an
additional and enormous task: to persuade his countrymen and the
French of the validity of his vision. He then threw his considerable
energy into seeking first cooperation and then independence from
France without rupture or total separation. And finally, after Senegal's
independence, he tried to further the interests of independent Senegal
in a close and special relationship with the former colonial power. His
public goals represent his determination to create in the outside world
a situation congruent with the balance he had had to create within
himself.

6

Spokesman

Throughout the early and mid-1930s, while Senghor was teaching at Tours, resolving personal issues, starting to write poetry, and beginning ethnographic and linguistic study at the Sorbonne, he remained essentially a private person. Most of his writings were known only to his friends, who saw in his poetry and essays the literary aspirations they all shared, rather than an early sign of unusual talent or possible future importance. So far, Senghor had published only one article in an ephemeral student magazine, *L'Etudiant Noir,* and had had a few poems published in *Cahiers du Sud,* a literary magazine where he had a friend on the editorial board. These had attracted little notice. As for his impact on his own people in Africa, it was virtually nonexistent. Beyond the legend he had created at Lycée Van Vollenhoven as the boy from the bush who had won all the prizes, little was known about him. It had been almost ten years since he had left Dakar.

In September 1937, this anonymity came to an abrupt end. That month Senghor made two public speeches, one in Dakar and one at an international congress in Paris. Both caught the attention of important people. In Dakar, he impressed an audience of colonial administrators and young Africans by challenging certain long-held assumptions of the local elite. In Paris, he aroused the interest of a distinguished audience of French officials and intellectuals gathered to consider the future of the colonies. Together the two speeches heralded a new stage in Senghor's life, one in which he moved increasingly into the public spotlight. They also foreshadowed the role he was to play after the war.

During the academic year 1936–37, Senghor was corresponding regularly from Tours with the Inspector General of Education in Dakar, Albert Charton, as well as with the newly appointed governor general, Marcel de Coppet. He continued to keep them informed of his plans and expressed his views about African education, such as his concern about the procedures for taking and grading the baccalaureate exam in the colonies, which, he thought, provided too many opportunities to tinker with the results. His correspondence indicates that he was still in touch with the African student community in Paris and indeed seems to have served as their spokesman to the administration. In one of these letters, as so often in the past, Senghor referred to the poor health that kept him from his work. It was made worse by the "damp climate of Tours that is deceptively unhealthy beneath its apparent mildness." Perhaps this was a metaphor for his growing ambivalence toward France.[1]

Because of his interest in education and the good impression he continued to make both at Tours and with the colonial administration, Senghor was invited to take part in the International Congress on the Cultural Evolution of Colonial Peoples to be held in Paris in September 1937. He readily accepted the offer, which included a trip to Senegal during his summer vacation to do preliminary research. The congress would provide a forum in which to present his developing ideas; it also provided an opportunity to return home, his first visit in five years.

In the late 1930s the atmosphere in Senegal was changing rapidly. French West Africa had a new governor general, de Coppet, appointed by the Popular Front government in 1936. This government was a coalition of the left drawn together by fear of the rising power of French fascism. It had won the general election of 1936 on a program designed to bring together all progressive men of goodwill. De Coppet was very much a man of this stamp. He quickly gained a reputation among local Africans as a person who understood and respected their interests. As a young man, he had been reproached by none other than Van Vollenhoven himself for being too liberal and too much a "negrophile." René Maran, on the other hand, wrote to Delavignette that the nomination of de Coppet was an error, and that they would soon regret it because he was not much of a worker and enjoyed playing the grand seigneur. Furthermore, he was pro-Islam. Nonetheless, his appointment raised high hopes in Dakar.[2]

In keeping with the new atmosphere, Senghor was invited to give an additional talk about education in the colony at a public meeting sponsored by the Franco-Senegalese Friendship Society in Dakar. It was scheduled to take place at the end of his summer visit.

De Coppet instructed his subordinates that Senghor was to be given all the courtesies appropriate for a distinguished visiting scholar, the necessary documents, free transportation, and easy access to the schools he wanted to visit. Senghor's plans included visits to Dakar, Joal, and Thiès, and to schools in the countryside of Sine-Saloum, to gather data for his upcoming report.[3]

This was Senghor's first trip home since the death of his father five years before. He made a pilgrimage to his father's grave. This experience surely contributed to the emotional intensity of several poems he wrote soon thereafter, notably "Le retour de l'enfant prodigue" (The Return of the Prodigal Son). While this poem reaches for its meaning beyond the personal loyalty of son to father, it gains much of its power from its connection to this personal event. Senghor also renewed ties to his mother, to Hélène Senghor, and to his many nieces and nephews. Hélène's son Lat, then a small boy, remembers walking with his uncle on the beach at Joal and hearing Senghor reciting by heart the poems of Langston Hughes, Claude McKay, and others. For Lat and for Hélène's other children, Senghor was a hero and an example, about whom they had heard a great deal. She had often showed them pictures of Senghor in Paris with the son of Blaise Diagne, and talked of the great vistas his education had opened before him.[4]

One small incident that occurred during this visit serves as a reminder of Senghor the stubborn child who had become the determined adult. Senghor had been spending a few days in Joal with his family and was due to attend a reception at Gorée Island. The plan was to go from Joal to Gorée in a boat captained by Uncle Waly. They set out from Joal, with the old man at the helm. The boat was small, the wind began to rise, and the sea grew ugly as a squall threatened to overtake them. The little boat, with Senghor, Waly, a nephew, and Senghor's school friend James Benoît, nearly foundered, and had to turn back. As they approached shore, the travelers heard singing from the church in Joal, as if "rejoicing at our safe return," and all felt relieved as they stepped safely onto dry land. But Senghor was not satisfied simply to be safe. According to Benoît, he insisted on setting out once again, in spite of the storm, this time over land. The road was deep in mud, frequently blocked by puddles that had become ponds, and visibility was obscured by driving rain. Nonetheless, Senghor pressed on, made it to Dakar, caught the ferry for Gorée, and arrived at the reception less than an hour late. There he was celebrated royally. No one had expected him to make it through the storm from Joal. To his hosts he said simply that he had promised to come, and that he was a man of his word.[5]

In this and other small ways during his visit, Senghor exhibited the personal style that he would carry with him into his later political career. Though there is no evidence whatsoever that he had at this time any thought of returning one day to go into politics, he could not have cultivated the ground more effectively than he did by his simple, unpretentious attention to the people he met in the course of this visit. He also revealed an instinctive talent for handling the press and making judicious public statements—an ability he later developed into a high art—in an interview he gave to the local daily, *Paris-Dakar*. Asked about his views of France, and goaded by his interviewer, who referred to another student recently returned from France, Ousmane Socé Diop, as a man with obvious political ambitions "with whom we understand you are not always in agreement," Senghor replied blandly that he could not speak of France or the French in general. He knew only the university milieu. It had taught him to appreciate the intellectual rigor of his teachers, and the hard work and good organization of his fellow students. "All have a critical turn of mind, a quality eminently French." More on the French Senghor would not say. Asked for his opinion about the current situation in Senegal, he was equally circumspect. He explained that he had come to do a study of primary education and to investigate current attitudes of the African bourgeoisie toward rural schools. "I have the impression," he continued, "that the Franco-African cultural movement must succeed, and will succeed, in spite of the imperfections revealed in its practice." And then, pressed to comment specifically on the local political scene, he parried adroitly, saying he could not possibly comment on it in depth after such a short visit, he could only "guess at things." He added that it pained him to see Senegalese divided among themselves, and that he hoped for "a gathering together of the Senegalese that will begin with the young people"; with a smile, he added, "of course, there are some old people who have remained young and many young people who have already grown old."[6]

This lengthy interview reveals Senghor's natural political talent. He was too wary to be trapped into making impulsive and possibly inflammatory statements. He instinctively knew how to charm an interviewer without providing the controversial statements that all interviewers hope for. This confirms the impression left by his earliest writings and correspondence with his colonial patrons, namely that Senghor learned early to be sensitive to what would please and what displease. He was not one to be drawn into arguments he did not choose, or to seek the limelight by raising controversy for its own sake. It seems the more certain, then, that when Senghor did speak out on matters of importance to him, and in ways likely to cause dispute, he did so in full control and knowledge of his probable impact. He learned and understood quickly the sources of political controversy in Senegal, as his speech at the international congress in Paris was soon to show.

Senghor's public lecture sponsored by the Franco-Senegalese Friendship Society was one of a series held at the new Chamber of Commerce building in Dakar. Senghor seemed an ideal person to be one of their speakers, a professor rather than an orator, a man whose intellectual qualities even the Inspector General of Education called truly French. He would not be a rabble-rouser. If his West Indian friends in Paris found in Senghor the embodiment of Africa, the colonial administration found in him the living model of the obedient black Frenchman. For the Friendship Society, he represented an ideal commingling of the two. To the people of Senegal, he was a visible demonstration of the heights an African might scale if he applied himself to his books and mastered the French examination system. Without a move on his part, Senghor conveyed a powerful message. He was cast in the role of symbol. He was on display, expected to satisfy the preconceptions of others.

De Coppet invited Senghor to dinner before his speech, and sent his limousine to pick him up.[7] In that era, such hospitality was an extraordinary mark of respect for an African, and word of de Coppet's gesture quickly spread around Dakar. Such a courtesy in itself would have made his address an unusual occasion. When Senghor arrived at the Chamber of Commerce, a huge neoclassical building on Dakar's central square, the hall was packed with more than a thousand people. Most of the important people in the colony were there: administrative officials, French businessmen, prominent African politicians. Young students crowded in at the back. Others milled around outside waiting to catch a glimpse of Senghor as he entered and left the building, or to be the first to know from their friends what he had said. There was a general sense of anticipation as well as a certain smugness among the French as they settled down to listen to the black Frenchman from

Paris. The audience listened to him with an almost religious attention for more than an hour.[8]

Senghor was introduced by the president of the organization, an African, Papa Guèye Fall, who spoke of the courage and tenacity of a man "who had left the bush of Sine to climb the ladders of learning." He was to speak on a question of interest to them all, "The Problem of Culture in French West Africa." It was an ideal topic for a young academic and promised to be suitably abstract and unthreatening.[9]

Picking up on Fall's introduction, Senghor identified himself as a humble Serer from the Sine, thereby suggesting to the Africans in the audience, most of whom were from the Wolof or Toucoleur ethnic groups that predominate in the Dakar region, that he sprang from a group they considered dull and prosaic. City Africans, citizens of the communes, considered the Serer of the protectorate mere peasants, hard-working country folk rather than urbane cosmopolitans like themselves. Nor did Senghor make any attempt to suggest that his family was of noble lineage. Such distinctions were still very important in African society, and the more usual African style was to brag about noble ancestry rather than to minimize it. Senghor thus chose to begin with exaggerated modesty and humility.

He then defined the word "culture." He seemed a bit pedantic, perhaps, but his audience would not have thought this odd in a university agrégé. Here, as he had done in his article on René Maran's humanism, he injected a somewhat unusual note into his definition, a note that here, as there, was crucial to his argument. Culture differs from civilization, he said. Culture endures in a people through various manifestations in different places and times. Culture is "a racial reaction of man to his environment that tends toward an intellectual and moral equilibrium between man and his surroundings" (p. 12). Senghor's choice of an anthropological rather than literary definition reflects his growing interest in this field and his debt to Frobenius. His insertion of the word "racial" was his own variation, an addition that led him away from contemporary French convention, certainly from Durkheim and his school. Obviously conscious of this departure, he added, as if to acknowledge its importance but not to dwell on it, "race is a reality, I do not mean racial purity. There is a difference that is neither inferiority nor antagonism" (p. 13). He then moved quickly to more familiar ground, defining education as the means by which a child learns the culture, accumulated experience, and present civilization of his people.

Professorial and definitional duties over, Senghor turned to education in Senegal, and discussed in some detail various aspects of rural education and the role of the primary school. The key to understanding the goal of all education in the colony, he argued, is the recognition that the child lives in a society that is not only West African but also French. The African child must understand both, must develop a "two-minded" or bilingual existence. Senghor thereby presents as inevitable and necessary the cultural division that had given him such pain. Even in primary school, then, African children must learn French. Up to this point, Senghor was merely reiterating arguments well known to his audience and confirming their preconceptions about the value of a French-oriented education. Moving easily from French and classical references to local African ones, he was providing, in effect, intellectual entertainment of a high caliber, amusing his audience within the confines of what they already knew and believed.

He then came logically to the question of secondary education for Africans. With the high standards the colony had already achieved, he had no quarrel. Ever diplomatic, he praised teachers and students alike for their impressive results on the baccalaureate exams. But the secondary schools now followed a curriculum virtually identical to that in France. They, like the primary schools, must recognize that the African child lives in a milieu neither wholly African nor wholly French. They, too, should develop two-mindedness and bilingual knowledge, providing instruction about Africa as well as France. High school graduates will form the elite, and that elite "is called to be an example and intermediary. What credit, if it is cut off from the roots of its race? What competence if it does not know its own people?" As if to dispel any doubt as to what he had in mind, he continued, "the intellectuals have a mission to restore black values in their truth and excellence" (p. 18). The true bilingualism of the "New Negro" (he here again used the direct French translation of the American term) will permit the use of French for science and native languages for stories, poetry, and theater. There can be no civilization without a written literature that expresses it, and how can one imagine a native literature that is not written in a native language (p. 19)? (In 1963, when Senghor edited this speech for republication, he indicated that he no longer believed that only local languages could express local culture.)

At this point, there was whispering and commotion in the hall. And why not? By urging the study of local culture, Senghor was challenging the basic assumption of several generations of the African elite and the "best" and most generous of the French, namely that the goal of educated blacks was to know France, use French like native Frenchmen, and become as much like Frenchmen as possible. This was a point of view that Senghor knew well. He had acknowledged it at the beginning of his speech, when, warming up his audience by using the dialectical style of a legendary African wise man, Kotye Barma, he asked an imaginary African Everyman what he would like the black West African to be in the world of tomorrow. "A Frenchman," his hypothetical African had answered (p. 12). This was the goal Senghor now challenged. All he asked, he said, was to raise the possibility, particularly for the young, that the solution to the problem of culture in French West Africa was not simply to intensify learning about France.

The sources for Senghor's idea, extraordinary for Dakar in 1937, are clear from his speech, and even more so given knowledge of the Paris circles he had just left. In the speech he cites first Robert Dela-vignette, who would have been well known to his Dakar audience as an administrator and a writer of impeccable credentials, as someone who had enjoyed "the pleasure of being different and together" (p. 13). Senghor's own definition of culture implies that any culture worthy of the name cannot derive all its inspiration from foreign sources. His West Indian friends, he continues, have assured him that the French West Indians boast many diplomas but little culture. West Indians have written books, but because their literature is only a pale copy of French literature, it does not contribute to true culture (p. 20). In support of his conviction that black writers can indeed create a rich literature that is their own, he refers to Dunbar, McKay, and Hughes, who have made of the black American dialect "a thing of beauty" (p. 19). In conclusion, he quotes Claude McKay's Ray, in *Banjo:* "To plunge right into the roots of our race and build on our own foundation, that is not to return to the savage state. It is culture itself" (p. 21).

The full impact of Senghor's talk is hard to ascertain. Its complete text was published in local newspapers without comment. Several men who were present recall that it caused consternation and controversy among French and Africans alike, both of whom were convinced that progress would be made only through total assimilation. As for Senghor, he did not stay to elaborate his point. He firmly rejected an offer from de Coppet to become Inspector General of Education in

West Africa, saying that he knew he could not prevail over the conservatism of the colonial establishment.[10] He went back to France to teach, to study ethnography, and to make further contacts in French university circles. He still planned eventually to return to teach in Senegal.[11]

It is worth noting here, in the light of Senghor's explanation of why he turned down de Coppet's offer, what sort of support he might have had from de Coppet. The governor general published an article at this time outlining his plans for educational expansion and reform. In it he explained that he intended to provide education for more natives so that they could participate in the colonial administration. "I have too much confidence," he added "in the black race to think they will limit their ambition to imitating us." They are too creative not to find new ways to create a new civilization. "Only one assimilation is interesting: an active assimilation." And in conclusion, de Coppet referred to Senghor and assured his readers that there would soon be natives to lead their people on a new way, "perhaps parallel to ours, perhaps different."[12] It would seem, then, that Senghor's thinking about schooling for Africans was totally in line with that of at least one faction of the colonial service. It seems likely that Senghor was not worried about lack of support for his views, but that a career in education in Africa simply did not appeal to him in 1937. He still wished to be a scholar and an intellectual.

Nonetheless, years later, many of the young men who had crowded in at the back of the hall for Senghor's speech in 1937, the lycée students and intellectuals of the coming generation, recalled that they had been deeply impressed by his words, unable to believe that a man of his experience and accomplishment would stand up for the study of the African heritage.[13] He had planted the seed for a new development of culture, even though conditions were as yet unfavorable for its growth. When Senghor returned to Africa to run for political office after World War II, there were those who remembered this speech and rallied to his banner because of it. Senghor was, from that time forward, on record as a man who saw the importance of African culture for its own sake, and who argued that an African who lacked pride in his own culture could not take pride in himself. On the details, Senghor changed his mind, but on the importance of culture and the African past, he did not.

In Paris, on the afternoon of September 26, 1937, three weeks after delivering this discourse on the problem of culture in West Africa,

Senghor was at the podium again. This time he spoke to the delegates
at the International Congress on the Cultural Evolution of Peoples.
To be asked to address this group was a great honor. The conference
was sponsored by the French government, and participants included
top officials of all the ministries concerned with the colonies, namely
foreign affairs, colonies, interior, and education. It drew eminent
French scholars such as Paul Rivet, professor and director of the Musée
de l'Homme in Paris, Marcel Griaule from the Ecole des Hautes
Etudes, Henri Labouret from the Ecole Coloniale, and Marcel Mauss,
a professor at the Collège de France. Present also were colonial administrators such as Robert Delavignette and Senghor's long-time correspondent Albert Charton. Invited scholars came from the French
Antilles, Belgium, Portugal, England, and the United States—the well-
known American Africanist Melville Herskovits and a representative
of Harvard's Peabody Museum were also on the official list. There
were, by contrast, only a handful of Africans, about ten among the
more than one hundred participants.[14]

The official purpose of the conference was to bring together scholars
and administrators responsible for colonial policy to discuss the implications of the rapid changes taking place in the colonies. The very
existence of such a conference testified to the increasing acceptance of
the new scholarly field that the French called ethnography, an acceptance based on the premise that the findings of scholarly ethnologists
who studied overseas peoples would enable administrators to shape a
more effective colonial policy. It now seemed clear that Africans were
not, after all, a people without culture, a *tabula rasa* awaiting the
imprint of French civilization. The situation was infinitely more complicated than it had seemed at first.

Senghor presented his paper on the afternoon of the first day of the
conference. He spoke directly after the Comte da Costa-Lobo, a representative of the Geography Society of Lisbon. Costa-Lobo had
begun his paper with elaborate praise of France for its exemplary
guidance of colonial peoples. He followed his excessively long introduction with a brief discussion of Portugal's educational efforts overseas. He argued the familiar Enlightenment view that all men belong
to a common humanity, and so should have the same moral rights.
All men are equal, indeed the same, everywhere, he said, and because
Europe has developed the highest and best culture, it follows that all
men should receive a European education. Using the examples of dead
civilizations that no one would think of trying to revive, such as

ancient Greece and pre-Columbian Mexico, he continued that it would be equally impossible to conserve traditional African civilizations or their languages. Portuguese-speaking Brazil and the English-speaking United States were the models for emulation. He looked forward to a time when the African and his respective European benefactors would share a common civilization, that of Europe.[15] His speech expressed what was a noble dream in its way, created by the idealism of a bygone age.

Senghor followed Costa-Lobo and expressed a diametrically opposed view. Even his tone was different, according to the official record, for he bypassed entirely the custom of beginning with effusive praise for France. No such courtesies softened the impact of his remarks. Senghor spoke on a specific topic, one that indicated that he had indeed spent his time in Senegal doing research on primary education as the governor general had specified, and had also studied the attitudes of the African elite toward recent educational innovations. His title told his argument: "La résistance de la bourgeoisie sénégalaise à l'école rurale populaire" (The Resistance of the Senegalese Bourgeoisie to the People's Rural School).[16] Of more than thirty papers given at the conference, it was the only one that signaled in its title anything but a cool scholarly summary of the state of cultural evolution in one or another colony. Under the circumstances, namely the distinction of his audience, the formality of the setting, and the tone of what had preceded him, to present his paper in this way was a brave act.

Senghor's remarks bore signs of the thinking he had expressed shortly before in Dakar, but also suggested that he understood the political overtones of educational issues in Africa. He began with the commonly repeated fact that the new rural primary schools had been very popular among the country people of West Africa. He then added his own observation that these same schools had met with almost unanimous opposition from the Senegalese bourgeoisie. Why this difference? Why did the most well educated, in the European sense, of West Africans and those who set the tone for intellectuals throughout the West African Federation oppose the new schools? It was striking that a group that normally disagreed about virtually everything was unanimous on this issue. All the newspapers directed by Senegalese were of one mind. Senghor then made a second observation, namely that the handful of Africans who, like himself, had been educated in France rather than Senegal tended to support the schools. To explain these apparent contradictions was the purpose of his paper.

The colonial administration, he explained, had set up the rural primary schools to provide a practical agricultural and technical education for rural children. This the Senegalese bourgeoisie applauded. What they opposed absolutely was that these principles of education, together with the periods of manual or agricultural work required in their curriculum, be applied to urban schools. Rural schools adapted to African circumstances were fine for village children. They were not suitable for city children, the offspring of an educated elite. What the Senegalese bourgeoisie wanted for its own children was an education identical to that in metropolitan France. A thorough French education, they argued, should be available to the citizens of the four communes.

This position, which had both a political and a cultural rationale, had its roots in the history of the communes, above all of Saint-Louis. It was also connected, Senghor pointed out, to an assumption shared by the metropolitan French and the Senegalese they had educated, namely that to be cultured and educated was to know classical and French philosophy, history, and literature. Such a notion of education and culture rejected the practical and the need for any knowledge of Africa. It implied that Africans need learn nothing about their own philosophy and history. The Senegalese bourgeoisie's rejection of the new primary schools for their children was, according to Senghor, an understandable result of their own schooling, which had succeeded in making them share the French view of culture and education.

The Senegalese elite, Senghor suggested, was also wary of the new schools for another reason, one with political and economic implications. To get a good job under the present circumstances, meaning a job with the colonial administration or a French company, one had to have a diploma identical to that given in France. The elite believed, with some justification, that urban schools should therefore direct their children toward full assimilation from the very beginning. "Adapted education" or learning about the specifics of the African situation could only take up time better spent on subjects that would help the child get a job in the modern sector of the economy. Adapted education, as Georges Hardy had put it some years before, meant putting much water in the wine of a good French education.

As if to justify the worries of the Senegalese bourgeoisie, Senghor added, the governor general had recently stated that there were not enough openings in administration or business to provide jobs for the increasing number of African graduates. The administration had used this fact as a reason for introducing "professional schools," in other words, vocational education. The worries of the Senegalese bourgeoisie were even more understandable when the official journal, *Annales Coloniales,* could suggest that vocational education should be the only education in the colonies because native hostility toward the French was directly related to the natives' level of instruction. Citing this comment, Senghor found it quite reasonable that Lamine Guèye, an eminent spokesman for the African elite, should warn against a growing trend to limit access to a rigorous French education. A limit on education appeared to the Senegalese elite as a first step toward limiting the traditional rights of the citizens of the communes, and their access to positions of responsibility. Indeed, as Senghor told it, the situation threatened to repeat that of turn-of-the-century Saint-Louis, where, after the closing of the mission schools, the French administration had tried to limit access to education and so restrict opportunities for the advancement of the local population. Then, too, the indigenous elite had fought for a "French education" for their children, and for many of the same reasons.

Senghor closed his talk by suggesting that there was another position, one he did not identify as his own, but one that was certainly compatible with his statements in Dakar three weeks before. A few Africans supported the notion of a Franco-African rather than entirely French education. They saw both cultural and social advantages in an adapted education. Most of these men were well-educated students in France. Yet they also shared the political goal of the Senegalese bourgeoisie, that is, they too wished to see Africans participate more and more fully in the administration of the colony. They wished to adapt education to meet special African circumstances without lessening its quality. Having completed his analysis, Senghor finished with a disclaimer: he had tried to explain, not to justify, the resistance of the Senegalese bourgeoisie to the new rural primary schools.

This speech is worth outlining in such detail for a number of reasons. First of all, it indicates that the determination of the African elite to have an education identical to that in France was still strong in the late 1930s, as it had been in Saint-Louis at the turn of the century, and that there were shrewd political reasons for it. In the early twentieth century, Louis Guillabert had argued eloquently against "adapted education," which he believed to be the thin edge of a wedge that would prevent Africans from getting the education necessary for real leadership. He saw it as a stratagem by which the French locals hoped to undermine the rightful position of the citizens of Saint-Louis. He believed then, as did the prominent lawyer Lamine Guèye a generation later, that education was the only reliable route to true equality with the French. Anything less, and Guillabert and Guèye could both cite the odd official statement to support their allegation, represented a deliberate effort on the part of the colonial administration and French businessmen to limit African influence in the colony.

Senghor's speech also indicates his skill in adapting his presentation to different audiences. In front of the Senegalese elite in Dakar, the group whose attitudes he now explained sympathetically, he had called for a Franco-Senegalese education and for Africans to develop their own culture. Now, to a predominantly French and European audience, he pointed out that there were very good reasons why the Senegalese elite was opposed to adapted education, to a Franco-Senegalese education as it was then practiced. He appeared now to support the views of men like Hélène's old friend Lamine Guèye. It had not taken him long in Senegal to learn that there were important political and historical reasons why the elite insisted that education for their children be identical to that in France. He saw that this view was based on a totally reasonable reading of administrative policy. What he therefore stressed to his audience in Paris was that, although the Senegalese might be divided on the issue of adapted as opposed to totally French education, they were united in their wish for a greater role in the administration of their own country. He implied, but did not say, that no Senegalese wanted the policy of adapted education to serve as a Trojan horse for introducing second-rate education into Senegal. From his vantage point in Paris, it had seemed obvious to Senghor that African education should encourage Africans to study their own world. After a visit to Senegal, he had quickly understood that it was impossible to discuss educational policies in the colonies without considering their political implications.

Many speakers at this conference expressed their doubts about the policy of assimilation. Several pointed out that it was common for a partially educated indigenous elite to have unreasonable scorn for "savage ways," and argued for the value of adapting education to the realities of life for African children. One of these was a Frenchman, Charles Béart, who was encouraging his students at the William Ponty teacher training college in Dakar to write and mount plays based on traditional motifs. Others at the conference suggested that uprooting Africans too suddenly from their traditional milieu would be dangerous and lead to a loss of moral orientation, suffering for the individual, and trouble for France. There was even a European who pleaded that Africans must somehow be helped to avoid "our errors" on their march to progress.[17] Many participants in the conference, therefore, challenged the assumption that assimilation must be the overriding goal of colonial education; many others supported assimilation as the sole rational and humane purpose of colonialism. There were knowledgeable individuals of good will on both sides. What distinguished Senghor's argument, then, was less its thrust than its concreteness, its tie to the reality of the situation in Senegal, and, most of all, its sensitivity to the fact that there were political as well as cultural issues at stake.

At this conference, discussion of educational and cultural issues often turned into attempts to answer one basic question: what should be the long-range goal of Europeans in Africa? Should indigenous cultures be respected and developed, or should the goal of colonial policy be, as Costa-Lobo dreamed, the progressive assimilation of colonial populations into European culture? The debate focused on morality, totally ignoring crucial questions about practicality. Senghor contributed persuasively to the general discussion, and with such authority that the published proceedings of the conference refer to him as the spokesman for one of the two main positions on this issue, the one that opposed total assimilation as a desirable policy objective. Senghor challenged the idea that the advanced nations had the right to force uniformity on mankind. He put his argument in moral terms, proposing that to teach the blacks of Africa the Greco-Latin humanities on the pretext of civilizing them would be to abuse the genius of their race. "To apply to them the mold of a civilization that is made neither by them nor for them and for which they are not suited would be to commit an error of orientation, a true injustice, to end up finally in the production of a cultural métis, a half-breed encased in a veneer that is not assimilated because it is not assimilable." Those truly interested in Africa must do research to understand the direction in which black civilization had set out so that it might continue in this direction at a faster pace. Some colonial administrators such as de Coppet and Delavignette basically agreed with this idea. Scholars like Delafosse, Durkheim, and Frobenius had gathered information to support it;

some of their successors present at the conference would have been sympathetic. The official rapporteur who summarized Senghor's remarks, however, was quick to point out that the conferees as a whole could not agree "with this seductive argument." Not only was the term "black civilization" meaningless and the notion of a black race a myth, he claimed, but it was not now a question of the arts and poetry but of providing food for an underfed people, medicine to combat disease, and education for the illiterate.[18]

The congress passed several resolutions. It found no difficulty in concluding that understanding colonial peoples was a precondition of good policy, and that, as a result, scientific research on the colonial peoples must be supported and encouraged. But it had great trouble reaching agreement on anything else, including the relative place of indigenous and European culture and the desirable goal for colonial policy. Ambivalence and disagreement on these issues were reflected in two somewhat contradictory resolutions. On the one hand, it was recommended that centers be created to encourage native arts and trades. On the other, it was resolved that no woman should be forced into a marriage that she did not want and that marriages of girls under the age of puberty should be altogether forbidden, for the reason that some of the natives had sufficiently evolved under French tutelage that, "Christian or not, they should not be subjected to customs contrary to the principles of French civilization."[19] These two resolutions, set side by side, illustrate the continuing ambivalence of the French toward native practices. Here they resolved it simply by distinguishing between two realms of native culture, that of the arts—to be encouraged—and that of certain social practices offensive to the French—to be discouraged.

Senghor made a fine impression on this occasion, his public debut among the French establishment. Both in Dakar and Paris, Senghor was henceforth a man whose opinions on Africa were sought out and respected. Up until this point, while the governor general or the Inspector General of Education might ask his opinion on specific, narrow issues such as the administration of the baccalaureate exam, Senghor's relationship with them had been that of student to patron. He wrote letters and answered their questions. Now he was ready to speak in public. For the moment, he was careful to speak as a scholar, explaining the views of others, rather than as an independent voice expressing his own.

September 1937 marked an important watershed for Senghor. He made his first important statements of what was to become his characteristic point of view. These statements were important because of the distinction of the audiences to which he presented them, and because he now presented publicly for the first time a position that would remain basically unchanged throughout his life. At this time, too, others stated for the first time the major and most persistent objections to his argument, namely that there was no such thing as a black race with a distinctive culture of its own, and that too much emphasis on matters of culture made little sense when people were starving. Given his natural caution, Senghor's decision to speak out in public was doubly significant. If two years before, by his own account, he had been reborn to a new life in which he understood his authentic voice as a poet, now he felt secure enough in his intellectual position to speak for the public record. He continued to do so in ways that satisfied his need for self-expression without jeopardizing his position with the French. Thus he maintained the support of both his West Indian friends and a substantial wing of the French establishment. Nonetheless, the French police kept a watchful eye on his contacts with suspected radicals. When in the fall of 1938 a number of West Africans tried to organize a new student movement in Paris, the police were pleased to report that Senghor declined to do anything for them.[20] Senghor was not yet ready to risk losing official French support, nor did he want to choose between his French supporters and duties to his own country.

While in Dakar, Senghor agreed to write for de Coppet a detailed evaluation of educational policy in French West Africa. Early the next year, he sent a long letter, twenty-two pages, to de Coppet in which he explained that he had purposely presented his ideas to the Senegalese public only at a theoretical level, but that they clearly implied a policy that "is exactly that of the governor general." He thought that the African elite had a "false idea of culture; on the other hand, their social aspirations are legitimate." Ways must be found to teach young Africans about their own world without in any way lowering the standard of their education. In setting a literary exercise, for example, there was no reason to give an African student a text from French literature when he might study one by a colonial writer such as Pierre Loti or René Maran. Furthermore, education in France was also much too abstract. Both should teach less about wars and famines and more about culture and social history. Remembering his own struggles to study amid the noise and confusion of his relatives' household in Dakar, he suggested establishing voluntary study halls for the older students and trying to enlist parental support for the education of their children. In closing, he reminded de Coppet that "the West African humanism of which we dream should permit whites and blacks to meet each other and come away from this encounter the richer for it, with a stronger personality." This memorandum shows Senghor at his best, both idealistic and practical, as well as tactful, remembering to assure his powerful patron that he, de Coppet, had already set out the broad outlines of the correct policy.[21]

The two long poems in *Chants d'ombre* "Que m'accompagnent kôras et balafong" and "Le retour de l'enfant prodigue," illustrate clearly the connection between Senghor's new public role and the resolution of his private concerns. Both were written after his public appearances of 1937. Their meditations about the poet's relationship to his father, his ancestors, and his people had led to a resolve to be his people's trumpet and to serve as their ambassador. This is precisely the path he had now begun to follow.

Senghor loved words, put them together easily, and used them well, but writing for its own sake was not, he believed, a sufficient vocation. It is revealing on this score that Senghor remembered one particular detail about his early education and his confrontation with Father Lalouse at the mission. Lalouse had insulted him by saying that Africans were "merely responsive to the hollow sounds of words without putting ideas behind them."[22] This remark lodged in Senghor's mind as if it were a challenge. One of the most important lessons he had learned from his French education, he later said, was not to be satisfied with words alone. Perhaps he believed Lalouse's criticism to be true, and remembered it so clearly for that reason. Be that as it may, he made an early resolve always to have logic, evidence, and research to back up the graceful words that came so easily to him as poet and writer. As interpreter, then, he would have to master the evidence that would attract not just the ears, but the minds, of the French.

Senghor now had a clear conception of his own role for the future. He had resolved some of his personal conflicts by accepting the fact that he was a French Negro, not a Frenchman whom some misfortune had caused to be born black. This freed the energy and enthusiasm of his youth for the task of urging others to share this view of the world. The attention and support he had had from de Coppet, the respect he had gained at the Paris congress, and his growing recognition as a spokesman for Africa were confirming his view of himself as the ambassador of his people. That he took himself very seriously as a representative of his people is suggested in a letter of thanks to de Coppet in which he wrote, "you have helped my people through me."[23]

In an odd way, Senghor had chosen a role similar to that played by his father, Diogoye Senghor, at the turn of the century. Then, Diogoye the trader had served as go-between for economic exchanges between African cultivators of the interior and the French merchant houses along the coast. Chance had thrust Diogoye into that role; skill had enabled him to play it well. For Sédar Senghor, too, there was chance—that Ngazobil was near his home, that Hélène came to live in Joal, that a public secondary school was created in Dakar just when he was of an age to enter it. And for him, too, there was the skill, the intelligence, and the drive that enabled him to seize these opportunities. By the 1930s and 1940s, the modes of contact and the issues at stake between African and Frenchman were far more complex than they had been in Diogoye's day. But Senghor, like his father, mastered the language of the French establishment to the level required at his time in history so that he could play the difficult role of interpreter of French to African, African to French.

7

The War Years

The war cut across Senghor's life as it did across all of France. In the fall of 1939, he was called up to serve in the regiment of colonial infantry he had joined several years before. He greeted this call with a certain sense of relief, for mobilization offered him a respite from trying to reconcile his growing militancy about Negritude with his continued love of French culture and enjoyment of his French friends.[1] During his physical examination, however, the military doctors found his eyesight so bad that he should not serve, so he was sent home. Meanwhile, the French army, reputedly the strongest in the world or at least second only to Germany, did nothing while the Nazis crushed Poland. By April of 1940, German advances into Denmark and Norway had put the French on guard. Senghor was called up again. On May 10, 1940, German troops began their move into Belgium and the Netherlands, and only a few days later they crossed into France. Senghor's unit was sent to defend a bridge at Charité-sur-Loire, a small town south of Paris, not very far from Vichy. Four days later the unit surrendered to the Germans. Although the French had already sued for peace, Senghor and his fellow soldiers were put into a prisoner-of-war camp.

The eighteen months Senghor spent in the camps marked him deeply. As is characteristic of the way in which he habitually recasts the events of his life, he has recounted only the positive side of his war experience. Even a frightening incident right after his capture is transposed into something of value. As soon as the Germans had taken Senghor's unit prisoner, they pulled the blacks out of the ranks and lined them up along a wall. Senghor quickly understood that the

Germans intended to shoot them on the spot. Just as the firing squad was at the point of firing, "we called out, 'Vive la France, Vive l'Afrique noire.'" At that very moment, the Germans put down their guns. A French officer had persuaded them that such slaughter would be a stain on Aryan honor. Which he cried first, "Vive la France" or "Vive l'Afrique noire," Senghor says he cannot remember. He only remembers feeling intense loyalty to his two homelands at what he thought to be his final moment. Looking back at this dramatic experience, Senghor realized that it had crystallized his sense that he was a child of Africa and of France. It also gave him an odd new feeling of power and freedom. Forced to face the possibility of a senseless death, he recognized his own mortality. The only question was how and when the end would come. Thereafter, he has written, he no longer feared to risk his life, if need be, in his cause. He was able to tap that special energy that is freed when one accepts that death is inescapable and as likely to occur for trivial as for important reasons. He also remembered that it was a French officer who had saved him.[2]

In the camps, Senghor was moved frequently, from Charité-sur-Loire, to Romilly-sur-Seine, to Troyès, to Amiens, and then to Poitiers. He learned to live with deprivation and uncertainty. The Germans developed a policy of shooting a certain number of POW's at random to retaliate for attacks on Germans by the Resistance. Although the worst of these reprisals occurred after Senghor's release, the policy as he knew it was a constant reminder of his total vulnerability. And yet what Senghor recalls of prison is that it was a time of moratorium on any activity or external commitment, in some way a relief, a time of leisure and reflection.

The Germans moved into Paris on June 14. They raised the swastika above the Arc de Triomphe and set up machine guns trained down the large avenues of the city.[3] The French government retreated to the south, first to Bordeaux, and then, pursued by German troops, to Clermont-Ferrand. The politicians finally settled at the mountain watering spa at Vichy. There, ample hotels provided space for a makeshift government presided over by the eighty-four-year-old hero of World War I, Marshal Pétain. By summer's end, the Germans occupied the northern two-thirds of the country.

Pétain's announcement on June 17 that he was seeking an armistice with the Germans was greeted all over France with a flood of relief. The bloodletting of World War I was still fresh in memory. With such considerations in mind, Pétain and his supporters decided not to fight

on, either on French soil or, as they might have, from French North
Africa. Few saw any merit in the ideas of an obscure colonel, Charles
de Gaulle, who pointed out that the French fleet and the army units
taken off the beach at Dunkirk remained intact and might regroup
with existing garrisons in North Africa to continue the fight. De Gaulle
was refused a hearing. Pétain instead sought an armistice agreement
as a means to keep the French unified. He was determined to keep
empire and metropole together under French administration. Many
felt that a fight to the finish might lead to civil disorder, and disorder
to revolution. This was the lesson they had learned from the First
World War and the Russian experience of 1917. The French leaders,
therefore, welcomed the armistice as a guarantee of order in the short
run, and a prelude to a respectable and harmonious peace agreement.
It was widely assumed that Britain would go down in defeat in a
matter of months. Everyone expected Churchill soon to sue for peace;
the war would be over. So thought the French. The government did
not even bother to worry about central heating for their summer hotel
offices at Vichy, so sure were they that they would be back in Paris
before the cold weather.[4]

German and French alike would have been astonished if someone
had suggested what in fact took place: The German occupation of
France lasted four long years. The armistice agreement established two
zones, a northern zone administered directly by the Germans, and a
southern zone, to be run by the French, centered at Vichy. France
was drawn more and more deeply into the Nazi war effort, and, in
the end, northern France became a battle zone. Even the most basic
of France's objectives in signing the armistice, the avoidance of war
on French soil, was not met. Germans fought Englishmen and Americans on French territory, and Frenchmen attacked and betrayed
Frenchmen, as bitter division split the nation.

Only recently has the story of active French cooperation with the
Nazis begun to be told. After the liberation of France, it seemed that
every Frenchman had been a resistance fighter from the beginning.
The story of the war was presented as one of heroic resistance by
the great majority of Frenchmen, and of supine collaboration by a
malevolent few—one or two outstandingly evil and energetic men.
Pierre Laval, Pétain's right-hand man for much of the war, became
the prime scapegoat, a man of apparently superhuman ability who
singlehandedly had managed to cajole, persuade, and deceive an entire
nation. Only gradually has such a view given way to the solemn

recognition that France had been reluctant to enter the war against Germany in the first place, and that the majority of Frenchmen, leaders and led, believed at least at first in the advantages of collaboration. Indeed this word was invented by the French themselves to describe their relationship with the occupying force as an honorable one between equals. Such had been their innocent hope when they signed the armistice agreement in 1940.

There were many intellectual currents in prewar France that fed this swell of support for collaboration with Germany, currents that had influenced Senghor as well as the rest of the intellectual community in Paris in the 1930s. Many of the same pressures that had crushed the Weimar Republic, namely economic depression, ineffectual parliamentary institutions, and a sense of continuous decline, had also built up in France. The fact of European decadence was generally accepted, and discussion of its causes and possible cure was a staple of French intellectual discussion.[5] Bourgeois capitalism seemed worse than immoral: it simply didn't work. Some French criticisms of the time sounded very much like attacks on modern industry and modern life as such. Contemporary life was said to be unsatisfactory because it dehumanized man, required regimentation and conformity, and rewarded mediocrity. Several of the best expressions of this anti-modernism appeared in films that had wide popularity, notably René Clair's *A nous la liberté* (Liberty for Us) and Charlie Chaplin's *Modern Times*. These films graphically depicted machines and industry as the enemy of a humane life. These ideas swept France in spite of the fact that the French economy was actually lagging behind its industrializing neighbors.[6] Perhaps for this very reason, wide segments of the French public continued to resist change, resented the confusion of their own parliamentary representatives, and longed for strong leadership.

It was in this mood that French intellectuals turned to new philosophies and other cultures. Indeed, one of the strongest arguments for empire included the idea that experience there would forge the energetic leaders that France needed. This partially explains why Martin du Gard's heroine is drawn to the primitive vitality of Africa and why artists such as Picasso became fascinated by the energy and fresh vision of African art. Surrealism's attack on reason as such, as well as the flirtation of interwar France with Marxism and fascism, drew on the same sources. One of the few positive voices was that of the Catholic Emmanuel Mounier, who had drawn Senghor's attention.[7]

What role this crisis of self-confidence played in France's defeat is difficult to assess. Memories of the slaughter of World War I doubtless further sapped the will to resist. Military miscalculations were also important. What is clear is that when the army went down in defeat, no one cared to muster support for the Third Republic. The government was dissolved and power handed over to Pétain without a murmur of protest.

Henri Philippe Pétain, Marshal of France, seemed to symbolize a simpler time. He was the Hero of Verdun, the last surviving Marshal of French victory in World War I. Under German tutelage, he began to speak of national revolution and renewal. Just as few Frenchmen had mourned the demise of the quarrelsome parliamentary regime of the Third Republic, many now saw in Pétain's leadership an opportunity to move forward after decades of stagnation. Civil servants marveled at how much easier the budgeting process had become now that there was no meddling by elected members of parliament. Partly as a result of false hopes and self-delusion, and partly as a result of the human instinct for survival, a group of odd bedfellows were drawn to the Vichy regime. They ranged from frankly fascist intellectuals such as Senghor's former classmate Robert Brasillach and Pierre Drieu la Rochelle, who saw in Vichy and in fascism the sole means of reducing decadence, to conservative Catholics who saw in Vichy the means for France to return to the traditions of its past glory. Vichy also attracted the loyalty of technocrats tired of Third Republic muddle-headedness, as well as their opposites, those who longed for the harmony and simplicity of the preindustrial past. Vichy policies reflected these contradictions. On the one hand, Vichy supported the Catholic church and organized youth groups to promote the moral education of the young. It published paeans to family and peasant as the backbone of France. It also gave free rein to the technocrats. And it played to French xenophobia. Laws were passed against Freemasons and Jews. The government set up a local version of the concentration camp in which it interned undesirable aliens. The new laws had relatively little impact on the day-to-day experience of the Africans living in France. To be sure, Hitler in *Mein Kampf* had referred to Africans as "half-monkey," but most Germans were no more racist than the French.[8]

In the summer of 1940 the majority of Frenchmen had high hopes and genuinely supported collaboration. They were shocked and disappointed when the Nazis rebuffed their offers to participate in the building of a new Europe, and decided not to grant concessions in exchange for French good behavior. The Germans did not permit the reunification of the two zones of the country, or liberate the prisoners of war. On the contrary, their demands grew more and more imperious. Food for the French population grew short as more and more supplies were exported to feed German factory workers and soldiers. As the tide of the war began to turn, the Germans lost patience with the charade of French autonomy. They ruled France more and more blatantly as the occupying power. There was less and less talk of renewal, of simple peasant virtues, or of hearth and family, and more and more concrete evidence of the Nazis' contempt for the people they had conquered. Brutal treatment of the civilian population became commonplace.

Because he had been called up as a private second class into a colonial unit, and because of German methods of camp management, Senghor spent much of his time as a prisoner among raw recruits mobilized directly from Africa. Through them, he renewed contact with the thinking of his compatriots. There were long evenings in the barracks huddled together around the warm stove, seeking diversion in talk of home. There were new friends, among them the two sons of Félix Eboué, the black governor of Chad. There were "literary evenings" for telling tales and reciting poetry, and even music on a makeshift kôra, the traditional Senegalese lyre. Enforced inactivity gave Senghor the opportunity to consider how he, an African, found himself caught up in Europe's quarrels. He began again to wonder about the mainspring of a civilization that could drive itself into such murderous conflict.

In the camp at Poitiers, Front Stalag 230, Senghor wrote many of the poems that make up his second published collection, *Hosties noires* (Black Hosts or Black Victims).[9] The tone of *Hosties noires* differs sharply from that of *Chants d'ombre*. Since some of the individual poems in *Hosties noires* were written before others published in the first collection, it is clear that Senghor consciously crafted the two collections so that each would focus on certain themes and present a unity of mood. *Chants d'ombre* groups lyric, meditative, and nostalgic poems that chronicle the poet's personal evolution. It records the poet's discovery of his vocation as poet and his personal preoccupations. The poems of *Hosties noires* turn to public themes and historical issues. This collection strikes a militant note. This was Senghor's express intention, for, as he put it, *Chants d'ombre* was intended to record stages in his personal development, while *Hosties noires* contained his thoughts on war and captivity.[10]

The very title *Hosties noires* was carefully chosen for its double meaning. It can be translated into English in two ways, either as "black victims" or as "black hosts"—host in the sense of the sacrificial host of the Catholic Communion. The title suggests therefore that black people have been both victims and sacrifices for European causes. Their bodies, like the body of Christ sacrificed and symbolically consumed by the Christian congregation in the Communion feast to gain them God's forgiveness, have been sacrificed to the purposes and benefit of Europeans. This meaning is explicit in a poem that is a prayer for the Tirailleurs Sénégalais, the historic unit of Senegalese troops that fought for France in two world wars. The poet prays that God will receive the bodies of black African soldiers, which are offered alongside those of the peasants of France. This is a sacrifice to France, but also with France. It is a sacrifice willingly made so that the black child and the white child may walk hand in hand in the "confederated France" of the future.[11] At a more mundane level, the poet also knows that the Senegalese soldiers have volunteered at least in part so that as veterans they may have the rights and privileges of French citizenship, the reward traditionally promised the black soldier by the French colonial administration.

This theme is repeated in "Au gouverneur Eboué," a poem dedicated to Eboué's sons, whom Senghor had just met. Félix Eboué, the governor of Chad, became legendary as the first French official to cast his lot for de Gaulle. For a time, his African territory was the only territory de Gaulle could claim for a Free France. Senghor notes that Eboué provides an eloquent symbol of the ironies of French colonialism. Here is a man of African descent, a native of French Guyana and therefore a child of the diaspora, who has become the ruler of Africans by virtue of power vested in him by the French. Then, at the time of France's trial, this twice-transplanted African proves more loyal than his French colleagues to the French traditions of patriotism and liberty. He alone of the French colonial administrators seems to understand the implications of collaboration with the Nazis and to possess the courage to move out on his own. Senghor honors Eboué for giving voice to a thousand people and a thousand tongues. Through Eboué he also honors Africa, which is the *hostie noire*, the black victim-sacrifice-host offered to keep human hope alive.[12]

The theme of African service to France and sacrifice for France

dominates the collection. At best, the African gains through his sacrifice a sense of participation in creating the world of the future. The
poet hears a "catholic Marseillaise," which resounds to call men of all
shades and colors to join together, people of roast coffee, banana and
gold, or the color of rice fields, and the nomad, the docker, the miner,
and the Jew.[13] But there is another side. Often the eager recruit, the
Tirailleur Sénégalais, finds that his sacrifice is neither understood nor
rewarded.[14]

Later in this collection, Senghor writes of an incident at the end of
the war, then fresh in memory and most profoundly disturbing to any
hopes for Franco-African harmony—the events at Thiaroye. Thiaroye
was the site of a repatriation center for Senegalese troops. It was close
to Dakar, but outside the city. After being shipped home from France,
the African troops were gathered at Thiaroye to await discharge.
There, on December 1, 1944, at least twenty-four Africans were killed,
eleven wounded, and another thirty-four put into detention. What
actually happened remains obscure. Africans claimed that the French
were trying to cheat them out of pay earned during the war. They
merely objected to this unfairness, and in return were fired upon. For
several days before this, however, rumors had been circulating in Dakar
that there was danger of a black uprising. Some Frenchmen felt that
a frightened French commander, determined to show that the postwar
administration of the colony would be firm, lost his nerve and fired
on the Africans to make of them an object lesson. Whatever the events
that triggered the violence, the deaths outraged the black population
of the colony. Black leaders led by Lamine Guèye were further angered
that the events were hushed up. No word about them appeared in the
local press. In his poem "Tyaroye" (sic), Senghor expresses his disillusion: "is it thus true that France is no longer France," that the
bankers have hired the soldiers, and that the African blood spilled so
recently for France has been forgotten? The poet vows that the Tirailleurs shall not have died in vain at Thiaroye, but as witnesses for
Africa and the world of tomorrow.[15]

Alongside these poems on general themes and public events, Senghor also writes of the feelings of the individual prisoner. There is the
humiliation of a proud man who finds himself begging for a cigarette
butt, the fear of one who suddenly realizes that he may not live to see
his children grow up or ever again feel the joy of a harvest dance, and
the special loneliness of an African soldier far from home. Beside these
painful experiences, experiences no doubt drawn from his own, the

poet places the fortitude of the simple African soldier. Senghor devotes one poem to the name and honor of just such a soldier, Mbaye Dyôb. It is a *taga,* or praise poem, written in the African tradition. Mbaye Dyôb has no noble ancestry to praise, no great heroic achievement to be recounted, but he has faced hunger, cold, and the humiliation of captivity. He has remained loyal. He is a man of duty.[16] In another poem, dedicated to Jacqueline Cahour, the sister of Claude Cahour Pompidou, Senghor praises the women of France, for courage, faithfulness, and loyalty to the spirit of the true France. And finally the poet invokes his own mother, the mother who grows pale as the bush blown dry by the Autumn wind, the mother for whom he was to have been a joy and celebration, "the flourishing green palm of her old age." To her he must tell the bitter truth: he is no longer a man with authority, the marabout with his disciples. He is a weak victim of the European war. He is now nothing but a child who remembers her warm breast and sobs at his cruel fate. He must swallow coarse millet, the food of slaves. He begs her to come to his aid, that he may call forth the old tales and the pride of his fathers.[17] From her, from "the black girl with the rosy heel" in whose veins flows the message of Africa, and from the black American soldiers, black brothers who join him in the springtime of peace, the poet gathers the strength and hope that infuse the final poem of *Hosties noires,* "Prière de paix" (A Prayer to Peace).

This poem, which follows directly the poem of anger and disbelief over Thiaroye, is dedicated to Georges and Claude Pompidou. It is a poem of reconciliation and forgiveness, in which Africa is likened to the crucified Christ. Africa has suffered slavery, torture, and war, the burning of forests, the hunting down of its children, and the transformation of its men into "boys." Knowing this, the heart of the poet has bred the serpent hatred. Yet that serpent must be controlled. The poet prays to the Lord to forgive France, a France that has both fallen away from Him and "crucified Africa." May God erase from his memory "this France that is not France, this mask of pettiness and hatred for which I have nothing but hatred." The poet has a great weakness for the France that he knows to exist beneath this mask. This is the people which brought him "Your Good News, Lord," but it is also the people whose missionaries "tracked down my priests like game and wrecked their sacred images." He will hate the evil of France and love its good. The poet closes by asking God's blessing for all people, "beneath the Rainbow of Thy Peace."[18] Senghor concluded his collection thus, with a poem that offers to God both the suffering of Africa at the hand of the European and the African's willingness to forgive France for the benefit of peace. He is ready to start again and to build afresh.

In *Hosties noires,* the poet is no longer the searcher of the *Chants d'ombre* poems. In this second collection, the poet has begun to live his vocation, and to serve, as he vowed he would, as the trumpet of his people. It is on behalf of the Tirailleurs that he writes, on behalf of those killed at Thiaroye, on behalf of the African host devoured in sacrifice, and on behalf of Africa's suffering, which, like the suffering of Christ, can yet be redemptive.

In the German POW camps, Senghor had time not only to write poetry but also to consider anew the implications of his "drunken plunge" into the kingdom of childhood and his triumphant discovery of his African past. The triumph of Nazism and the horrors it engendered, he writes, "brought me to my senses." They helped him to recognize the danger of any racism, even one called forth to combat the racism of others. If before the war he had at times wanted to reject everything of France and exult in his newly appreciated blackness, "After two years of captivity . . . two years of meditation, I came out cured. Cured of . . . racism."[19] No doubt this time of imposed reflection deepened Senghor's hold on an intellectual position that supported what he felt to be true. The poetry of *Chants d'ombre* reveals that his love of France was too profound simply to be cast out, while Africa provided the nourishment he needed for survival. This dual loyalty broke through in his cry of "Vive la France, Vive l'Afrique Noire," and more soberly in *Hosties noires.* In the POW camps, Senghor had found solace in the companionship of fellow black prisoners, in hearing their tales and listening to the kôra. He had also found, "often at dusk, in the moment of the low and shiny tide of the soul, I felt the need of comforting. Well, it was enough for me to read some pages of French prose. In this French-style garden, I found everything in its exact place, illuminated according to its size. And, once again, everything within me regained its place and its assurance, its human size in its own light."[20] The French garden in his early poem of that name had been distinguished by this same calm and measure. Then, however, he had felt himself a dangerous misfit in such a place, fearful that his African passion would disrupt this attractive but alien order. Now, with his growing maturity, the French garden has become a comfortable place of refuge and solace, a place for gaining perspective and security.

During his captivity, Senghor also read. His minuscule library included Virgil's *Aeneid*, Pascal's *Pensées*, Plato's *Dialogues*, and two of Goethe's works, *Faust* and *Iphigenia*. He took advantage of his free time to learn enough German to read Goethe in the original. He also read and reread the classical writers. If Frobenius had encouraged Senghor to think that each culture was unique and separate, another German, Goethe, now seemed to argue that too great a separation was dangerous. Senghor found in Goethe a warning about the dangers of cultural isolation, of turning too much in on oneself. Thinking about his reading and seeking the lessons of the war, Senghor realized again the central importance of balance and equilibrium. Goethe seemed to provide a modern restatement of the wisdom of the Greeks. There must be a balance of forces. The energy of black Africa must be harnessed. But it was not enough to try to build the new Africa solely on the foundation of the old. The scientific discoveries of Europe must be integrated and joined with the strengths of Africa. Senghor saw Goethe as a northerner reaching for the south and a culture with which to balance his own, just as he, Senghor, reached from south to north for a similar equilibrium. Writing in 1949 about what he had learned from his wartime reading of Goethe, Senghor summed up Goethe's message to him in words that echoed Robert Delavignette's expression of pleasure in being different and together: Goethe had tasted the sweetness of the sea where waters mingled together, the *mer métissé* (crossbred sea), the Mediterranean.[21]

Senghor found this same lesson in the Greeks. Although he had been reading Greek texts with his lycée pupils, and had studied them for long hours with his teachers at the Sorbonne, he now saw for the first time that Greek civilization was not a triumph of the Indo-European spirit but rather an example of the great creativity possible when two peoples of different biological and cultural heritage fuse their genius. The golden age of Greece was the joint creation of pre-Hellenic and Hellenic peoples. Pondering this fact, Senghor grew sure that the great civilizations were not those which, like the Nazis, sought purity, but rather those which, like the Greeks, embraced biological and cultural diversity.[22]

This new viewpoint transformed the implications of the old. An exclusive focus on black Africa and a rejection of all things European was not only impossible, it was not even desirable. Senghor now expressed his goal in a phrase he was to make famous: "to assimilate, not be assimilated." Africans must assimilate actively and judiciously the best of what France had to offer. They must at the same time remain true to their own distinctive culture. In an article written during the war and published in 1945 with a dedication to Delavignette, Senghor argued that Africans must learn more about the customs and languages of traditional Africa.[23] They must do so quickly, because African traditions were being rapidly transformed by contact with Europe. It was important to assimilate European techniques to the African setting and purposes, but such assimilation would be possible only when the African setting was known and African purposes clear. Instruments imported from Europe must be adapted to work African soil. It was a matter, Senghor argued, of grafting new ideas onto the healthy roots of tradition, rather than uprooting the old plants to set in the new.

Senghor takes his argument for the benefits of diversity and cultural borrowing one step further. Just as Africa can learn from Europe, so Europe can learn from Africa. Black Africa has an obligation to know itself, not only for its own benefit, but also so that it can bring its contribution to the rest of humanity. Africa must now bring to France the spiritual force to renew a culture that has been ruined by an undue materialism. Here Senghor's diagnosis of France's malaise and its needs began to echo that of some French intellectuals of the 1930s and most closely that of the French Catholics of Mounier's *Esprit*. With such ideas, Senghor was beginning to move beyond analyzing the past, or evaluating the present, to suggest directions for the future. He now talked not only of Africa but of the French and European future.

Conditions in the camp were hard. Senghor had never been physically strong. Indeed his preoccupation with exercise and personal moderation and perhaps even his extraordinary self-discipline were in part a reaction to his recognition that he lacked a robust constitution and had to husband his energies. Through the intervention of friends and at the recommendation of a French doctor who discovered he had a "colonial disease" of undetermined origins, he was released from the camps on the pretext of illness in February 1942.[24]

Senghor returned to a Paris stricken by privation. By the winter of 1942, any euphoria the French may have felt when they managed to avoid the German blitzkrieg had disappeared. Although the Nazis still had supporters among the French, both among intellectuals such as Brasillach who had long held fascist beliefs and among opportunists who saw in collaboration their chance for power and position, many who had at first supported them had begun to understand what the Nazis really stood for. Their treatment of French Jews provided a dreadful example. At first the Jews were harassed in small ways, forbidden in Paris, for example, to use public telephones. In May 1942 all French Jews were required to wear the yellow star; in July the Germans arrested more than twelve thousand "foreign" Jews in Paris and deported them to concentration camps. In August the Vichy regime followed suit, arresting 4,000 stateless Jews in their zone and turning them over to the Germans. That same summer, on June 22, the anniversary both of the signing of the armistice agreement and of Germany's invasion of the Soviet Union a year later, Pétain's minister Pierre Laval broadcast a speech in which he declared his hope for a swift German victory.

But in November 1942 the Allies made a successful landing in North Africa. Even though Vichy quickly broke diplomatic relations with the United States to demonstrate its loyalty to Germany, the Nazis moved into the unoccupied zone to protect the Mediterranean coast. The charade of Vichy autonomy was over. A few months later, in early February 1943, the German army suffered its first major defeat at Stalingrad. The tide had begun to turn.

Life for the intellectuals of Paris during the occupation was full of contrasts. Food was short, heating fuel scarce, clothing and virtually every other amenity either not available, severely rationed, or, if available on the black market, wildly expensive. In her memoir of the war, Simone de Beauvoir describes the days she and her friends spent writing at cramped tables in cafés in order to keep warm because there was no heat in their rooms. Paradoxically, the occupation was also a period of great creativity.[25] Picasso, Braque, and Giacometti were at work in their studios. Jean-Louis Barrault, who dominated French theater in the decades after the war, revealed his great talent as mime and actor, and mounted an extraordinary production of a new play by Paul Claudel, "The Satin Slipper." Jean Anouilh's somewhat ambiguous version of *Antigone,* a play about personal values and civic loyalty, played to full houses. Jean-Paul Sartre wrote his two best plays, *No Exit* and *The Flies,* and Antoine de Saint Exupéry published *War Pilot.* Filmmaking flourished as well. The war years were arguably the most creative period in French culture in the twentieth century. Why this should have been true is a puzzle. Perhaps it was their very powerlessness in social and political life that gave French intellectuals the added energy for creative work. Perhaps it was a need to express individuality at a time when the nation as a whole was compelled to be silent, or perhaps it was a basic human response to limitation and calamity. Whatever the reasons, the arts flourished in occupied Paris as they had not done for many years.

This was the atmosphere into which Senghor emerged from the camp. Though he was beginning to meet influential members of the French intellectual establishment, he was by no means a participant in the round of meetings and parties of which Beauvoir and Sartre were central figures. Senghor was still a lycée teacher, with the advantage that he had now been assigned to a school on the outskirts of Paris. He was an earnest young scholar, bent on completing his dissertation for the highest French scholarly degree, the Doctorat d'Etat. He had chosen as his subject a linguistic study of several of the African languages spoken in Senegal. In 1943 and 1944, evidence of his scholarly work appeared in the form of two articles on the grammar of the Wolof and Serer languages in the *Journal de la Société des Africanistes*. A third article, on the use of the conjunctive article in Wolof, was published in the same journal in 1947.

During these years Senghor maintained his contacts with African intellectuals and students. He welcomed virtually all of them at his rooms at 8 rue de Lamblardie, not far from the Porte Dorée. There was by now a small group of younger African students for whom Senghor was an elder example and model. He played the role well, inviting them to visit and talk, and leading a study circle in which he encouraged the young to learn about their own cultures. He also urged them to look to the future and consider the relationship of their cultures to the rest of the world.

Although always friendly and attentive, Senghor rarely spent time in the restaurants and bars frequented by African and West Indian intellectuals. If, walking down the Boulevard Saint-Michel, he saw a group of friends in a café, he would wave, or perhaps even stop to shake hands all round, but almost never would he join them. On the contrary, he would disappear for extended periods of time. Then he would turn up again, or invite a group to his rooms, warm and gracious as ever. He was now a busy man, determined on accomplishment. This pattern of frequent eclipses was one his West Indian friends had noticed before the war. Then, as now, some of the time they did not see him was spent with French friends, but most of it was taken up by hard work. Now he spent a lot of his time with his old friend Georges Pompidou, Pompidou's wife, Claude, and Claude's sister, Jacqueline. Jacqueline had served as Senghor's wartime "godmother," sending him letters and packages while he was in the POW camps. It was to her that he dedicated a poem in praise of the devotion and courage of the women of France. The four of them often played bridge together in Pompidou's Paris apartment, talking about where and how to get good food at a time when it was truly scarce. At the end of the evening Senghor would join thousands of other Parisians in hurrying to get the last metro home.[26] They often spent vacations together at the Cahours' family house at Château Gontier.

This pattern of disappearances enabled Senghor to get his work done. He was always free for his African student friends, if an occasion was planned ahead. He was there to serve as godfather, witness a wedding, or celebrate the successful completion of an exam. But his time was a precious commodity, not to be wasted. One student who remembers "The Elder," as he called Senghor, recalls that he was always available in time of need, but that everything was planned and under control. He remembers Senghor as always serious, hard-working, and frugal. Senghor had learned several languages and also found the time to learn the essentials about anthropology, botany, history, and economics.[27]

Senghor often met his African friends at a center for colonial students set up by the Nazis. There students from the French colonies were provided with a comfortable meeting place that had two large floors with conference room and library, all conveniently located at 184 Boulevard Saint-Germain. The Germans encouraged the overseas students to gather and study their home cultures. Such activity fit well with Nazi theory about the inescapable ties of blood and soil. No doubt the Germans anticipated that their kindness might also create an opening wedge with which to split colonial loyalties from France. The students apparently did not concern themselves with such ulterior motives. They simply enjoyed the relatively lush surroundings provided them, where they could be warm when fuel was short, watch free movies, and receive supplementary food rations, no small consideration in the winter of 1943 when food was scarce and expensive. The center's good coffee and fried bananas were remembered many years later as among its greatest attractions. At Christmas the center even organized a party with presents for children that was presided over by a high official of the Vichy colonial administration.[28]

Regardless of the reasons for its existence, the center became an important gathering place for the Africans in Paris. A group gathered around Senghor's compatriot Alioune Diop. In this "circle of Father Diop," as it was called, young Africans discussed many of the issues dear to Senghor. There were also formal occasions to which the students invited outside speakers, among them Senghor himself. Later, in July 1943, the center began to publish a bulletin entitled *L'Etudiant de la France d'Outre-mer: Chronique des Foyers* (The Student of Overseas France: A Chronicle of the Clubs). It took as its motto a quotation from St. Exupéry, "I do not like it when they injure or damage human beings." In their statement of purpose, the editors explained that the journal was designed to allow students from overseas to share their experiences with one another, for "many students want to know their own civilization better, a civilization they have left too soon."[29]

The lead article in the first issue, written under the pseudonym of the West African sage Kotye Barma, outlined the problem faced by the student from overseas. This student is a "being in transition, mentally a hybrid. Neither native, since his French education has made him so different from his ancestors, nor European, since he has been brought up elsewhere," he is a person without a stable self. First he admires the little white students in his class; next he is impressed by the heroes of French literature and history. When he goes to France, he is at first overwhelmed, but also happy and hopeful. He works hard. But then he comes to feel an inner emptiness. Often he does not realize that he has been uprooted from his world until he learns that he is not well adapted to European civilization. He then has a crisis. He has three choices: to resist, to capitulate, or to adapt. At worst, the result can be suicide. Even at best, he experiences confusion and pain. To this problem, its sources, and its possible solution, Kotye Barma explains, the new publication will turn its attention. Evidently the new generation of students was trying to articulate and face together problems that Senghor, in an earlier time, had had to face alone.

Senghor participated actively in the regular Sunday meetings at the center, and contributed poems and articles for the bulletin. He published four poems in the first issue, "Masque nègre" (Negro Mask), "Libération," "Porte Dorée," and "Visite," and one in the second, "A la mort" (To Death). "A la mort" is one of the most pessimistic poems Senghor ever published, a poem that lacks his usual serene faith in the possibility of redemption and harmony. Senghor did not publish any of his recently written war poems in this bulletin. Possibly he feared they might cause trouble with the German administration, or, more likely, he did not wish to publish anything critical of France at the time of her humiliation and defeat.

Even as Senghor was beginning to serve as elder and guide for a new generation of students, he continued to pay homage to the men who had guided him, René Maran and Robert Delavignette. Reviewing for the *Chronicle* a new novel by Delavignette, Senghor praised him for his realistic portrayal of a model French teacher in Africa. This is the Frenchman who uses French reason to work for the creation of an imperial community. Senghor also says admiringly that Delavignette has written a political book in the best sense, a contribution to understanding and a model for imperial humanism. Delavignette, it would appear, was the kind of political person who made politics seem attractive to Senghor, and a Frenchman with whom he would like to work to develop the "imperial" community.

Senghor also wrote a review of Maran's *Pionniers de l'empire* (Pioneers of Empire). Maran had suffered during the war for refusing a German order to write a critique of French colonial policy. He had written that the elementary duty of every Frenchman, for so he still considered himself to be, was to avoid doing anything that the occupier might use against his country. In his review, Senghor highlights Maran's distinction between politics and culture. To be French above all is an excellent political slogan for Africans, but as a cultural goal it is nonsense. The two realms must be kept distinct. Senghor quotes Maran: "The work that is the most profoundly national, the most particular, ethnically speaking, is also the most human and that which can touch most deeply a foreign people." Senghor then praises Maran as a model, as a writer who has mastered French language and thought and put both to work in order to reveal the sensibility of his own people. "His phrase unites the French order and the black order . . . This Guyanese writer has found and realized himself by returning to his ancestral sources." In this context, Senghor also meditates about the role of heroes and leaders. The destiny of peoples is forged, Maran has said, "by the powerful hands of a few leaders of men . . . These individuals are great because, beyond their own ambitions, they have the higher ambition to serve their king, country . . . and sometimes their god."[30] High praise indeed for what a single leader could accomplish. Perhaps Senghor was beginning to wonder if he himself could play such a role.

Of his inner life, little was visible to those who remember him during this period. Now, as before, his ability to present to the world what he wanted the world to see, a confident, competent, generous young scholar, was impressive. This public, self-created persona seemed to be all there was. The only discernible clues that he might be more than he seemed lay in his poetry, and even there he was able to transpose emotion into art. What others saw was the public face Senghor had laboriously created.[31]

In French West Africa, too, the war had been a time of division and change. When Germany attacked France, the radio call to the African army reserve was picked up by drums and spread to the distant back country. Some eighty thousand African Tirailleurs rallied to the French flag and were sent to the front, both in France and in North Africa. Senegal's deputy to the French National Assembly, Galandou Diouf, warned his African constituents: "If by misfortune we lose this war, it is not Paris that Germany will demand but the colonies."[32] Lamine Guèye joined his political opponent Diouf and the French administration to urge all Senegalese to forget their differences and unite for the war effort. The Imam of Dakar led the faithful in prayer for the victory of French armies and was joined by Islamic priests throughout the land. Popular support for France's war against Germany was high in Senegal, illustrating the widespread feeling that the fate of Senegal was tied to that of France.

In the beginning of June 1940, the Dakar newspapers echoed the metropolitan press, reporting on the exemplary courage of the French army. As the month progressed, however, they began to write of strategic and well-managed retreat, and then, toward the month's end, published Pétain's call for an armistice. The first reaction of the Dakar populace was to reject it. Governor General Cayla declared that he would not yield an inch of territory, and on June 20 the local daily, *Dakar-Matin*, published de Gaulle's ringing call to all true patriots to continue their struggle against the Germans.

But French West Africa was not ready for a unified rally to de Gaulle. While many local organizations such as army veterans, students, and locally elected councils declared for de Gaulle, the colonial administration was divided. Strengthened by the decision of the French military commanders in North Africa to join Vichy "lest France in its misery be cut in two," the pro-Vichy forces in Dakar pressured Governor General Cayla to retract his declaration for de Gaulle. Faced with stiff opposition from his own staff and from the highest-ranking military men in the colony, who were, after all, the ones who would have to lead any defense, Cayla acquiesced. He was removed from his post by a decision of the Vichy Council of Ministers and replaced by

Pierre Boisson. Boisson received a newly created title, that of High Commissioner to the colonies. He took office at the very moment that Félix Eboué, as governor of Chad, was leading his colony over to de Gaulle. What the Vichy government had claimed it could avert, namely the division of the French empire, thus occurred at the very inception of the Vichy period.[33]

Knowing that he had some following in Dakar, and spurred on by Eboué's support, de Gaulle continued to hope that Senegal might come over to his side. The port at Dakar was a tempting prize. Wishful thinking and a lack of accurate intelligence led de Gaulle and the British into an ill-starred expedition intended to tip the balance. Early on the foggy morning of September 23, 1940, while a few French and English warships stood off the harbor of Dakar as they had been doing intermittently throughout the summer, an airplane flew over the city and began to drop leaflets urging the population to come over to the Gaullists and fight to save the colony from the Nazis. At 6:40 A.M., two planes landed at the airport. Their passengers were quickly arrested. At about the same time, an emissary from de Gaulle came ashore in a small boat. De Gaulle expected the populace to rally to his support. It did not. After a few skirmishes, the battle began to escalate. De Gaulle's warship started to shell the town, but there was still no sign of the expected support for his cause, and the Anglo-French force withdrew. Boisson used this adventure as a pretext to arrest several dozen men suspected of being Gaullists. He further declared that de Gaulle was a pawn of the British and that he, Boisson, would never be a party to the dismemberment of the empire or its separation from the legitimate authority of France, namely the Vichy regime. He further accused the Gaullists of exaggerating the German menace as a pretext for bringing the French colonies under the control of its traditional rival for empire, Great Britain.

The result of Boisson's determined loyalty to Vichy was a curious interlude in Senegal's history. His real enthusiasm for Pétain's program of national renewal was evident in the Dakar newspapers. Pétain, the hero of Verdun, was portrayed as the guardian of peace and integrity. His stolid face and white moustache soon became familiar from frequent appearances on the front page of the local daily. Newspapers heralded the rebirth of a new and more vigorous France that drew its energy from rural and traditional virtues based on blood and soil. On a more local note, Africans were reminded of France's grandiose ambitions: the French language and culture were expanding their influence and stretched throughout the world, to Quebec, Louisiana, and Belgium, as well as to Indochina and Africa, and thousands of students were going each year to study in Paris and returning to their homes to take part in the building of a greater France. The administration organized the week of July 15, 1941, as a time to celebrate the French empire. Educated Africans were asked to submit essays on the work of the French in Africa. These essays included such comments as "The French colonization is one of man's most beautiful achievements, since it is good and just." Another wrote that because France as a country had evolved further than Africa, it had a duty to colonize those less evolved.[34]

Governor Boisson, anxious to enlist the enthusiasm of young people in the French cause, established a new newspaper, *Dakar Jeunes* (Dakar Young People). Its primary purpose was to serve Vichy interests. Its front pages repeatedly urged people to work hard for France, to remember their place as beneficiaries of the radiance of French culture, and to grasp their fresh opportunity for building a vast new empire that would restore "pride and hope to . . . many young people still weighed down by defeat." Illustrations told the story even more directly. The front page of the new journal's first issue held a large picture of two healthy boy scouts, one black, one white shaking hands.[35] Subsequent issues featured pictures of the peasants of the Lorraine and the Vosges, bringing in the harvest and milking cows. Such pictures were accompanied by pronouncements by Marshal Pétain, who praised the peasant for preserving deep roots in the soil of the fatherland. In the metropolitan Frenchman far from home, such pictures no doubt did stir patriotic feelings.

How to touch the same note among Africans? To do so seemed important to the regime. If on the one hand, Boisson wrote, it is important to grant the African native elites the opportunity to play a part in their own administration while making sure they recognize that their best guides in this endeavor are Europeans, it is also imperative that colonial policy put an end to the dangerous isolation of the young educated Africans from their own people. "This will be our best guarantee against their falling victim to all kinds of outside solicitations," which will take advantage of their disappointments and transform their legitimate aspirations into hostile claims that will sooner or later be expressed in political and racial ways. Boisson truly believed that educated Africans should be encouraged to maintain ties to their own cultures. This was the same Boisson who had responded favorably to Senghor's request before the war to be allowed to stay in France and study ethnography, the better "to find his tradition and renew it . . . in the light of the French genius."[36]

Following Boisson's lead, the editors of *Dakar Jeunes* decided to sponsor a writing contest. Readers were invited to submit essays about the countryside and its influence on the spirit of those who inhabited it—about the connection, as it were, between blood and soil. The best essays would be published. Imagination about France proved fertile, and many essays on its varied provinces appeared. Almost inadvertently, it would seem, some of the contributors turned out to be Africans. They began to write of their homeland, the African countryside, and to consider those values which tied them to the African soil and to their own villages. It was not long before discussion of specific localities and cultures began to be replaced by more general reflection.

Under the umbrella, then, of a Vichy-inspired call to revive local rural traditions, young Africans began a far-reaching discussion about the nature of indigenous culture and its prospects for the future. Carried on in the inside pages of *Dakar Jeunes,* tucked discreetly between pictures of Bordeaux winegrowers and French athletes, it attracted the participation of many of French Africa's newly educated elite: Ousmane Socé Diop, a friend and ally of Lamine Guèye; Emile Zinzou, later president of Dahomey; Fily Dabo Sissoko, later deputy from the Sudan; and other young people then little known, such as Joseph Baye, Fatou Sow, and Mamadou Dia.

This discussion was characterized by one writer as "of pressing interest to every educated African."[37] It began with an article by Ousmane Socé Diop entitled "Cultural Evolution in West Africa," an obvious echo of Senghor's Chamber of Commerce speech. Socé presented two main positions, that of men like himself who believed assimilation to be both inevitable and desirable, and that of those, like Senghor, whom Socé called anti-assimilationist. Socé quoted at great length from Senghor's earlier speech, largely to disagree with it. Senghor had argued that "to teach the blacks of Africa the Greco-Latin humanities . . . would be to spoil the genius of their race, to turn them away from another possible humanity more in keeping with their . . . congenital aptitudes. To apply to them the mold of a civilization that is neither made by them nor for them" would be wrong. On the contrary, Socé Diop argued, Senghor is the one who is wrong, because all civilizations are mixtures.[38] By 1942 Senghor would have agreed with Socé's argument, for his thinking was changing. But it was not the agreement or disagreement between these two men that was of primary importance. It was the simple fact that discussion of the desirable future relationship between the French and African cultures had been placed squarely on the public agenda. It was also significant that Senghor's name and early ideas were again being presented in Senegal.

The heat and intensity of the reaction to Socé Diop's article, which seemed on the surface to be a discussion of rather abstract cultural problems, may be partly related to the fact that all local politics had been suppressed by the Vichy regime. Cut off from the give-and-take of local politics, to which they had become accustomed, young educated Senegalese were thrown back on ideas and theories. Unable to act for the time being, they considered cultural questions with added fervor, questions remarkably similar to those Senghor had addressed during his student days in Paris.

A series of articles in *Dakar Jeunes* began with a number of personal testimonials about the effect of an education that included intense exposure to two very different cultures. Many who wrote to the newspaper had spent their childhood in African villages and had also received a bookish French education. They had experienced the desire for "French refinement" and believed that no African could ever be as refined as the Europeans. Yet to choose between these two worlds, several agreed, would be to tear out a part of themselves.[39] The experience, and even the words, that Senghor had articulated some ten years before were now being repeated by many members of a new generation, both in Paris and in Senegal.

Two distinctive voices stand out. One is that of Joseph Baye, who pointed out that "the mixing of culture should not be a goal but a means." French education should help Africans to develop their own culture. What was important was "an unshakable will to remain black, to assimilate without letting ourselves be assimilated." Here Baye used the very phrase that Senghor was to make one of his hallmarks: "to assimilate, not be assimilated." A similar view was expressed in a different way by a young school teacher, Mamadou Dia, who was later to become Senghor's most important political colleague: "The question is not can we, but ought we, to run to the Sorbonne when we can build here . . . I share Senghor's worries . . . under the ruins of empire are hidden a patrimony as yet unexplored . . . in descending to the profound springs of our history . . . we will realize ourselves

. . . the cost if we do not do this [would be to] . . . stifle the genius of our race."[40]

Although contributors to this discussion continued to pay their respects to the French, and to thank them for their encouragement of "this reawakening of Africanism," French administrators did not like the turn the reawakening had taken.[41] At the William Ponty School, for example, the school administration had encouraged theatrical productions based on African folklore. Now African writers in *Dakar Jeunes* suggested that the theater develop more serious themes based on African history. Lat Dior and Samory, two leaders known for their opposition to French occupation, were suggested as suitable subjects for new plays. Mamadou Dia wrote, "the literature of a country should be a reflection of the national conscience, a mixture of virtues and moral ugliness . . . we do not need to prettify Africa, even if the crudeness of its features astonish the European, even if he is ready to laugh at us." In answer to Dia, Charles Béart, the director at Ponty who had encouraged plays based on folklore, responded that the newspaper was called "Dakar Young People," not "Dakar Baby," and added that Africans who said they wanted to write serious plays and were told they lacked the skill acted like children who cry when grownups do not give in to their every whim. In fact, he continued, most Africans "speak French poorly and can not even understand the concepts of tragedy and irony." How could they write serious plays?[42] This insulting article, not surprisingly, infuriated the African readers of *Dakar Jeunes*.

Administrators began to write worried notes to one another. A police report described the African elite as "overheated" by such discussions; a political officer wrote to the Minister of Information that he did not think such material was necessary to get young Africans to read *Dakar Jeunes*. The Minister of Information in turn put pressure on the newspaper's French editor to stop the discussion. In May, after five months of such exchanges, *Dakar Jeunes* published a notice that it could no longer print contributions to the debate about French and African culture because they were "either too abstract or too schoolboyish" to be of general interest.[43] While a few additional articles on the indigenous theater and African ethnography appeared, both Boisson's regime and *Dakar Jeunes* soon fell victim to the Allied invasion of North Africa. Senegal lent its support to de Gaulle and Boisson was replaced; *Dakar Jeunes* was renamed *Afrique en Guerre* (Africa at

War) and became virtually indistinguishable from the main French-edited Dakar daily. Nonetheless, like Pandora's box, *Dakar Jeunes* had loosed something new that would not be forgotten. The colonial police continued to keep an eye on its contributors, intercepted their mail, restricted the distribution of newspapers in the colony, threatened activists with dismissal from their jobs when they tried to organize professional groups, and even tried to prevent activists from continuing their education.[44] Some of the administrators were ready to take harsh steps against those they considered radical. Although Senghor's name and views had played a prominent part in stirring up this ferment, he himself was not among those mentioned in local police or political files.

Except for this unexpected and contradictory development, Senegal's Vichy regime brought a definite move to the political right. Discriminatory practices were introduced that had, until then, not existed in the four communes. They ranged from disproportionately long jail sentences for Africans accused of being Gaullists, while Frenchmen similarly accused were usually released, to separate lines for black and white shoppers in Dakar stores and separate cars on local trains. Boisson suppressed local representative councils, favoring traditional leaders and chiefs at the expense of the French-educated elite. Food shortages and rationing exacerbated the situation.[45] After Boisson had been replaced, the new governor of Senegal wrote privately to the governor general that two years of Vichy rule had led to a deterioration in the relations between the French and Africans living in the colony and that he himself was determined to combat racism of any kind.[46]

The Senghor family was directly affected by Boisson's policies. René Senghor, Hélène's husband, was accused of being a Gaullist sympathizer and arrested. He was later released, but in the meantime the administration took away the ration card that had enabled Hélène to claim her allotment of rice, bread, sugar, and other scarce staples. Her reaction was one Senghor heard over and over again from her and others when he returned to Dakar after the war: surprise and then anger at the French for their maltreatment of Africans loyal to France. She petitioned the administration again and again, reminding them that her brother had died for France at Verdun as had other members of her family. Even now she had several relatives under arms. How could the family's reward for loyalty and devotion be discrimination in their own country?[47] Hélène's anger and her conviction that the French had betrayed their trust were as straws in the wind.

In Senegal, then, as well as in France, the war proved a watershed. The French were never again able to find the high ground from which to survey and maintain their empire.

8

Brilliant Apprentice

The triumph of de Gaulle and the Allies brought with it the resumption of political life in both Dakar and Paris. Senghor, like everyone else in France, was caught up in the excitement and optimism of liberation. The first political task for France was to write a new constitution for itself and the empire. As Senghor was now well known in those French circles concerned with such problems, he was asked to play a leading role. Robert Delavignette, newly appointed head of the school that trained colonial administrators, invited Senghor to lecture there. Senghor was delighted to accept both offers.

Paris was liberated on August 25, 1944. General Dwight D. Eisenhower, the supreme commander of the Allied forces, generously allowed General Leclerc to lead the first division into the city so that French troops could liberate their own capital. De Gaulle himself soon followed, and was received at the city hall by members of the National Council of the Resistance. For de Gaulle, it was a transcendent moment. He had realized his dream of guiding France through its time of crisis. The next day he led a triumphant parade that began at the Arc de Triomphe and moved amid great popular rejoicing down the Champs Elysées to end at the Cathedral of Notre Dame. There, where French kings had married their queens and Napoleon had held his coronation, the crowd packed the cathedral for a solemn mass. At that moment de Gaulle seemed to personify victory and the restoration of French honor. His attentive listeners were united for a rare, brief moment by their joy in deliverance from the Nazis. De Gaulle now declared that although France had triumphed in battle, "The war continues . . . France must find itself in the first rank of great nations."

Even now, in victory, de Gaulle was preoccupied with the restoration of French greatness, what he repeatedly called the "grandeur of France."[1]

This drive for greatness, always at the center of de Gaulle's thinking, had clear implications for the peoples of the French overseas empire. In the euphoria of liberation, even that most critical of French intellectuals, Simone de Beauvoir, wrote that she felt a happiness that reflected "the magnificent adventure of a world creating itself afresh."[2] The future seemed to hold only promise. The political left and the political right, Frenchman and African, all shared, briefly, a sense that they could find a harmonious resolution of their differences. All it would need was men of good will. Faithful Africa, as Senghor called it, surely would be rewarded for its contribution to this victory and its loyalty to France in the time of peril.

This mood of liberation included a sense of genuine gratitude to the African colonies. After all, the governor of Chad, Félix Eboué, had been the first ranking official to declare for de Gaulle, and his colony had given de Gaulle his first legitimate foothold on French territory. Thousands of Africans had fought and died under French command. African intellectuals in Paris, too, had proved loyal. René Maran had refused to lend his pen to the Nazi cause, even at considerable personal cost. In appreciation for African support, de Gaulle's Committee of National Liberation had called a conference in January 1944 at Brazzaville, the capital of Equatorial Africa. The purpose of the conference was to discuss colonial issues and "to determine on what practical bases it would be possible to found, stage by stage, a French community that included the territories of black Africa."[3] That de Gaulle had taken time out in the middle of the war to consider this issue, an issue that before the war had occupied his attention not at all, is noteworthy in itself. He had gratefully accepted Eboué's loyalty and African support. He also recognized that the whole concept of empire and colonies had been put in question by the war. Britain had already given up its empire in the Far East, and now Winston Churchill was promising India home rule in return for support against Japan. On the other side of the Atlantic, the Americans spoke of the self-determination of nations at the newly formed United Nations. Perhaps most important in de Gaulle's calculations, the French had shown themselves to be weak. They no longer appeared unified or invincible. Africa's support had proved necessary for the very survival of French opposition to the Nazis.

All these considerations led the Committee of National Liberation to take seriously African aspirations for greater respect and autonomy and to organize the Brazzaville conference. Nonetheless the committee did not go so far as to invite African representatives to attend the conference. Indeed, the only black face among the approximately fifty colonial administrators and political leaders who gathered there was that of Eboué himself. Even he attended not as a representative of the vast African population but rather by virtue of his office in the colonial administration. While it would no doubt have been difficult to select representatives of African opinion, no effort was made in that direction. Indeed, there is no evidence that such an idea was even considered. Eboué, old and partly deaf, did manage to read several reports submitted to him by educated Africans living in Brazzaville. He had expressed his own views three years before: "all our efforts must be directed toward the moral and material elevation of the local populations . . . we are a great association whose goal is the improvement of the fate of these populations." And, he continued, we must give up the idea "of remaking native society according to our image and mental habits [and instead] respect its natural institutions."[4] There is considerable irony in Eboué's remarks, by virtue of the very person of this twice-transplanted black man who identified himself so totally with the French point of view that he could speak of "our" policy in Africa. No doubt he glowed when de Gaulle praised him at the Brazzaville conference as a "great Frenchman."[5] Eboué was caught in a familiar and continuing contradiction, the one evident before the war at the congress of scholars and administrators that Senghor had addressed in Paris. France must on the one hand direct and improve, educate and elevate, but at the same time allow the local societies to maintain their basic character. This contradictory resolve was both the strength and the continuing weakness of the French colonizing mission.

The discussions and conclusions of the Brazzaville conference reflected this problem. Both the goodwill of the French and their ambivalence toward the peoples of their empire were much in evidence. On the one hand, de Gaulle opened the conference with the declaration that France was determined "to choose nobly and generously new and practical roads toward the future."[6] René Pleven, de Gaulle's top colonial spokesman at that time, expressed France's desire to find ways by which "the peoples of our empire who shared French sorrows might also be fully associated with our rebirth."[7] What impressed the black Africans most favorably of all was de Gaulle's statement, "we are sure that there will be no progress that is true progress, if those men who live on their native soil do not profit materially and morally from it, and if they cannot raise themselves bit by bit to the level where they will be able, in their own home, to manage their own affairs."[8] What precisely de Gaulle had in mind, or how these changes were to occur, remained conveniently vague. At first glance, de Gaulle seemed to be questioning the long-standing assumption that African and Frenchman must be part of a single polity ruled from Paris. Yet the perpetuation of the empire seemed to be necessary if France was to hold, as de Gaulle insisted it must, its place as one of the world's great nations. Actually de Gaulle himself was preoccupied by other problems. When he stopped in Dakar after the conference, even though he stood on African soil, he did not even mention what victory might mean for the colonies, but chose instead to evoke his beloved France "struggling in sadness, pride, and hope," and ended with a call to the predominantly white crowd to sing the "Marseillaise."[9]

The Brazzaville conference did suggest several specific measures that all Africans supported. Forced labor was to be abolished, more attention given to health and schools (education was to be in French), and a single criminal code applied to all Africans. By these measures the long-standing distinction between citizen and subject would be obliterated with a stroke of the pen. The conferees also agreed that Africans should be encouraged to enter the colonial administration on an equal footing with native Frenchmen, though "the positions of command and direction cannot admit anyone but French citizens." Finally, the delegates resolved that the territories "should move gradually toward administrative decentralization and become legal political entities." This last statement, which would seem to have enormous and far-reaching implications, was buried deep in a document that began with the statement, "The aims of the civilizing labors of France in the colonies exclude all possibilities of development outside of the French imperial system; the eventual formation even in the distant future of self-governments in the colonies must be dismissed."[10]

Here, then, was the old conundrum: acknowledgment of the need for decentralization and participation by Africans in their own affairs, side-by-side with the centuries-old dream of a greater France ruled as one from the center at Paris. Neither at Brazzaville nor at the constitutional conventions that followed the war were the French able to

reconcile their vision of empire and French greatness with their recognition of the need for a self-governing, culturally distinct black
Africa. For the next fifteen years, France and its black African colonies
struggled to find an amicable way to resolve these contradictions.
Senghor found himself squarely in the middle of this struggle. That
it would prove so bitter was not clear at the time of Brazzaville.
Indeed, when Senghor read over the Brazzaville resolutions he wrote
to an acquaintance, "I have just read the conclusions of the conference
at Brazzaville. They are a masterpiece, which will mark the date in
world history. Nonetheless the native in me says to himself: but when
will they be applied?"[11] The native in him may also have noted that
almost precisely one year after the Brazzaville declaration, in December
1944, the ugly side of French attitudes surfaced at Thiaroye, where
some of the very soldiers who had fought for France were shot dead
by their French officers.

By March 1945, the new Minister for the Colonies, Paul Giacobbi,
speaking with the situation in Indochina in mind, suggested that the
former colonies might form "with France and other parts of the
Community, a French Union." Giacobbi further suggested that a
person might be a citizen both of his individual country and of the
French Union. This notion fired Robert Delavignette to envision a
future for the French empire analogous to that of Rome, an empire
in which all free men, regardless of culture and local origin, would
hold a single citizenship.[12]

The first opportunity for action presented itself immediately after
the war. The liberating army quickly joined with representatives of
the home Resistance to establish a provisional government. This government, in turn, called into being a Constituent Assembly. Not that
they were starting from scratch. The Committee of National Liberation had already drawn up a charter, which took the form of a set of
proposals that had the support of the great majority of the resistance
fighters. This program called for universal suffrage (women would for
the first time be given the vote), free education, the nationalization of
some enterprises, and a complex plan of guaranteed social and economic security. It had little to say about the colonies, except that
political, social, and economic rights should be extended to the native
and colonial populations.[13]

The provisional government established a special commission to
decide how the overseas colonies should be represented in the
upcoming Constituent Assembly. The commission took its name from

its chairman, Gaston Monnerville, a man of mixed blood from French Guyana. Impressed by the prominence achieved by this distinguished black man, the black American writer Richard Wright concluded that in France "there were no insuperable barriers to those who declared their allegiance . . . though black and alien, [a man] . . . could become a Frenchman."[14] Monnerville was smart, experienced, and widely respected. Even for him, however, the question of overseas representation was not an easy one.

First, Monnerville might consider the heritage of the past. To the Assembly of the Third Republic, the "old colonies" had sent ten deputies and four senators. Senegal, for example, had had its single deputy intermittently since the French Revolution. What should now be done for the some sixty million souls previously without representation? These peoples, who were half again more numerous than the Frenchmen of the metropole, were scattered over the globe in territories ranging from small islands in the Pacific to the up-country of Central Africa and Southeast Asia. Many of them could not read or write and had no idea where Paris was, let alone what went into the making of a constitution. What about the Frenchmen living in these areas? Should they and the natives vote for a single candidate, or should there be separate voting lists and candidates for the two groups? This last question raised the essential issue: should the vote of a Frenchman and that of a colonial native be equal in value?

It was as a member of the Monnerville Commission that Senghor held his first political post. He and Sourou Migan Apithy, a Dahomean who had also studied in Paris, were appointed to the Monnerville Commission largely because they were on the spot. Senghor was now perhaps the single most respected spokesman for Africa living in Paris. He was a published poet with a book, *Chants d'ombre,* in press, and was sought out by editors for authoritative articles on black Africa and colonial education. He was working on an anthology of black poetry. He had completed a successful stint as a lycée teacher and had just been tapped by Delavignette to teach languages full time at the graduate school for French colonial administrators. (In keeping with the postwar spirit, this school, formerly called the Colonial School, had been renamed the Institute for Higher Study of the Overseas Territories.) It was Delavignette who suggested Senghor for the Monnerville Commission. So hastily were the appointments made that Senghor had to miss the commission's first meeting because it conflicted with his teaching.

The baobab tree.

The outskirts of Kaolack, the largest town in the Serer region of Sine, about 1940.

Mme Hélène Senghor.

Senghor (at far right) and his schoolmates at the Libermann Seminary, 1923.

Senghor and his schoolmates at the secondary school in Dakar, 1927.
Aristide Prat is at the center of the front row.

Senghor and his pupils at the lycée in Tours, 1936–37.

Senghor (front row, second from left) with his fellow prisoners
in a German POW camp, about 1941.

"A warm welcome from Joal to its most illustrious son."
Senghor campaigning, about 1960.

Campaigning in 1960. Senghor is at center right. To his right,
Modibo Keita greets the crowd. Behind them are Lamine Guèye (in the dark suit)
and Mamadou Dia (to his left).

Dakar citizens line up to vote, about 1960.

Senghor (in the light suit) with Falilou Mbacké, grand marabout of the
Mourides (to his left), on an Islamic pilgrimage in 1964.

Senghor with his wife, Colette, and their son,
Philippe-Maguilen, in 1961.

Presidents Senghor and Pompidou during Pompidou's official visit
to Senegal, 1971.

Senghor and Abdou Diouf
at the ceremony transferring
power to Diouf, 1980.

Senghor in retirement.

Dakar today.

Senghor's political debut was not free from opposition. Lamine Guèye has described a heated discussion at a meeting he attended at 184 Boulevard Saint-Germain, the colonial student center. Guèye, who had spent most of the war in Dakar, was now widely recognized as the senior native political figure in Senegal. On his first postwar visit to Paris, he was invited by the students to bring them up to date about what had happened in Senegal during the war. The students urgently questioned him about both political and economic developments in Africa. Guèye tried to persuade them to return home to see for themselves, and assured them that the winds of change had begun to blow in black Africa. Guèye recalls that at this same meeting there was what he called "a family quarrel." Abdoulaye Ly, a young student from Senegal, and Louis Behanzin, a student from Dahomey, attacked the older men from their territories, Senghor and Apithy, for agreeing to serve on the Monnerville Commission. They accused Senghor and Apithy of playing into the hands of the colonial administration, which was pretending to consult representatives of African opinion but in fact had chosen men who would say what the administration wanted and who represented no one but themselves. Ly was particularly abusive toward Senghor.[15] Senghor, in his own defense, pointed out that however cynical the colonial administration might be, it was better to have some African representation on the commission than none at all. He believed that inviting Africans to serve on the commission represented an advance from the French attitude at the time of the Brazzaville Conference, when there had been no effort to include any Africans. Ly and Behanzin did not accept this point of view. They found their elders too moderate and compliant.

Senghor's first political experience also yielded other lessons. The opening proposal presented to the commission by the provisional government as a working paper came as a shock. It suggested a division of the overseas territories according to three types: first, territories such as the Antilles and Algeria, which could be fully assimilated as departments of France; second, territories such as Indochina, Tunisia, and Morocco, which might have the status of associates of France; third, the remaining territories, namely black Africa, where France must continue to pursue a policy of domination. It further proposed that there should be a double college for elections, one for Frenchmen who happened to be residing in a given territory and one for native voters. Each group would vote for its own candidates, with the French proportionately far more heavily represented. Apithy and Senghor

were astonished that the idea that all members of the Union should
hold a single citizenship could be so quickly forgotten. The idea of
the double college, which in effect would make Africans second-class
citizens in their own country, was particularly offensive.[16] The Africans
protested vigorously. The majority of the commission agreed with
them, at least to the extent that there should be a single list of
candidates and that the number of overseas deputies to the National
Assembly should be significantly increased—perhaps to 20 percent of
the total.

In the event, for reasons of its own, the provisional government
decided to ignore the views of the commission majority. It retained a
double-college system in which Frenchmen residing overseas and
native noncitizens would vote for different candidates. It also limited
colonial representation to 64 deputies in an assembly of 586, far short
of the commission's recommendations. Furthermore, in the black
African countries half of the delegates were to be elected by "citizens."
This meant that with the exception of the four communes of Senegal,
where there were African as well as French "citizens," half of the
overseas delegates would be elected by metropolitan Frenchmen who
happened to be living in the colonies. Furthermore, among the native
residents of the colony, suffrage was to be limited to those who held
positions of responsibility or had achieved a certain level of French
education. Only 2.9 percent of the population of Senegal was eligible.
Elsewhere in West Africa between twenty and thirty thousand Europeans would elect four deputies, while eighteen million Africans would
elect six. By comparison, in France itself there was one deputy for
every sixty to ninety thousand voters. The result of the new plan was
that French voters in West Africa were overrepresented, not only
compared to Africans, but compared to Frenchmen living in France
by a factor of three to one.[17]

Even before the commission made its final recommendations, Senghor realized that it did not have the power to determine the method
of overseas representation in the upcoming election. Real power lay
elsewhere. To an extent, at least about the French administration's
intentions, Ly and Behanzin had proved right. Senghor did not even
attend the final session of the commission. Instead, he left for home,
for Senegal. He had received a grant to collect and study Serer and
Wolof poetry in connection with his dissertation on the linguistic
forms of the Senegalese languages. The main part of the thesis for his
Doctorat d'Etat was more than half completed. He hoped to finish it
as a final step toward his grand ambition, to be a professor and member

of the Collège de France.[18] With such plans in mind, Senghor arrived in Senegal early in the summer of 1945.

What struck him at once was the poverty of his countrymen. He soon began to hear tales of the war. At first, they were family stories, such as Hélène's dismay at what she saw as discrimination against loyal citizens of France. Later he heard about the discussion in *Dakar Jeunes* in which he, in absentia, had played a part. He now began to get a sense of what Lamine Guèye had meant when he spoke of new currents astir in Senegal.

He also learned the details about what had happened at Thiaroye. In Dakar, this incident still stung like a fresh wound. For many Senegalese, it had proved a turning point in their attitude toward France. They saw it as proof that Parisian talk about equality and partnership would never be reflected in administrative actions in Dakar. The French could not be trusted.[19]

The elections for the constituent assembly were scheduled to take place that October. Senegal had been allotted two seats according to the two-list system: one for the citizens of the four communes, and one for those subjects of the interior who met the voting requirements. The uncontested choice to run for the citizen seat was Hélène's old schoolmate Lamine Guèye. Guèye was widely respected in the communes. Many Africans felt that he should have had Blaise Diagne's seat when it was vacated by Diagne's death in 1934, and attributed his electoral loss to Galandou Diouf at that time to interference by the colonial administration. The administration had supported Diouf, so the story went, because they feared Guèye as a sophisticated and effective advocate of African interests. At that time, no one could win a local election without the administration's support. Diouf had died in 1941, however, so Guèye no longer faced a strong opposition. Guèye was an intelligent, shrewd veteran of political life in Dakar with a law degree from Paris. It was he who led the outcry over Thiaroye, and who defended in court the Africans accused of having assaulted their French officers. He had also led the Senegalese Socialist party since 1935, a party that had joined with the French Socialist party (SFIO) at the time of the Popular Front and was now the dominant political force in the colony. Now, as in 1936, Guèye's political goal was to see to it that France exhibited "a strict equality in the application of its own laws" and extended citizenship to all Senegalese. He enjoyed an immense personal following among the educated elite of Dakar, who, in turn, rallied their families and clients to his support.[20]

Guèye had been arguing his cause for many years in his party's newspaper, *L'Afrique Occidentale Française* (French West Africa), commonly referred to as *L'AOF*. Now he launched a new group, which he called the Bloc Africain. Its purpose was to unite as many people as possible to agitate for the extension of citizenship to Africans living in the colony. This platform was immensely popular with those Africans who had managed to get an education and now were struggling in the lower ranks of the French administration, as schoolteachers, or as clerks in French businesses. In his newspaper campaign Guèye often referred to Senghor as an example. Senghor was an educated person who in France held a position with pay equal to that of a Frenchman. If he were to come back to Senegal, however, he would receive half the pay of a Frenchman who held the same position. This was patently unfair, a practice typical of the colonial administration and one Guèye hoped to change.[21]

Guèye now decided that he would like Senghor to run for Senegal's second seat to the Constituent Assembly. This seat was designated for the subjects of Senegal and Mauritania. Born a subject himself, Senghor was eminently suited to be the candidate of those few subjects who were eligible to vote. Well educated, eloquent in French, he would be able to hold his own in Assembly debates, no small consideration given the fact that many of the elected representatives from Africa would be making their first trip to Paris. Senghor's detractors later suggested that he was the perfect choice for Guèye because of his total inexperience in politics. Lacking any personal following in the colony, he would have to follow Guèye's lead. Be that as it may, there was opposition to Guèye's choice, both from some of the younger generation of students in Paris, who found Senghor too conservative and would have preferred that Guèye choose one of themselves, and from local politicians in Senegal, who resented Senghor as an outsider who had swooped in to pluck a political plum.[22]

Senghor hesitated. First as aspiring priest, then as teacher, he had had ambitions to shine in the world of mind and spirit, to be his people's trumpet, but he had not thought of himself as a negotiator or a politician. He was close to achieving his youthful goal. He had the respect of his colleagues in Paris, a professional position at the Institute for Higher Study of the Overseas Territories. He was becoming known among French intellectuals of the left, and had close friends in Pompidou and the Cahour family. Was it not enough to bring the cultural contribution of Africa to the attention of the French-speaking world, to teach the future administrators of the colony, and to record for future generations the poetry of the poets of Sine and perhaps even publish their work? Senghor was under no illusion as to the implications of a plunge into politics. It would mean the end, or at least a long deferral, of his dream of becoming a real French professor, a man of letters who served his people with his pen. It would also force hard decisions in his personal life, or so he thought, for he had a close relationship with a Frenchwoman and felt that this was inappropriate for a political representative of black Africa. Blaise Diagne had married a Frenchwoman and served as Senegal's deputy without any apparent feeling of self-contradiction, but the mood of the 1940s was quite different from that of Diagne's time, and Senghor felt it his duty to make his deeds coincide with his words in both his personal and his political life.[23]

Lamine Guèye was a persuasive man. As he had known Hélène Senghor since their schooldays in Saint-Louis and knew René Senghor as well, he did not hesitate to enlist them to convince Sédar Senghor that he had a duty to serve his people in this way. With Hélène and René, who were ambitious for their own children and for their family, he had little difficulty. They had long known that Senghor's talent was out of the ordinary. When Blaise Diagne had been deputy and acting as Senghor's sponsor in Paris, he had often stopped at their house on his visits to Senegal and spoken with them about Senghor. "That one will replace me some day," Diagne had predicted.[24]

Nonetheless Senghor wavered. He believed that he had no true vocation for politics. He felt that he could best serve his people by using his intellectual and literary talents. Yet he had been deeply shocked by the poverty of Senegal when he returned after the war, and he had sensed the atmosphere of expectation that existed throughout the country. He knew that at Thiaroye, by the wartime arrest of René Senghor, and in many other ways, the French did not always act in the best interests of his people. His work on the Monnerville Commission had been disillusioning. The French could not be trusted to carry out their promises. Perhaps Senghor was also drawn by ambition. He had written with enthusiasm about the capacity of a single leader to shape the fate of an entire people. If he could not be one of the pioneers of empire about whom he had read in his schoolbooks, perhaps he could pioneer a new phase in Franco-African relations and shape his people's destiny.

The Senghor family called a council and discussed the issue at some length. They reached a consensus not only on the fact that Senghor had an obligation to accept Guèye's offer but also on the principle that they would pay his expenses and help him in every way they could. As the family was numerous, many of them successful in trade and by now established in a number of different cities—Pierre at Rufisque, René in Joal, Adrien in Thiès—this potential help was considerable. But still Senghor hesitated.

Before he made a final decision, Senghor had to be convinced that the people of the colony would back him. He insisted on Lamine Guèye's assurance that if he agreed to stand for election the political leaders of the colony would rally to his support. Guèye made the rounds and obtained promises of support for Senghor from his own political allies. Senghor, in turn, his reluctance conquered, joined the Socialist party. When the local congress met to select its candidates, there was vigorous debate. Some local politicians continued to oppose Senghor's candidacy, arguing that he had been in France far too long to understand local needs and conditions. But Guèye prevailed. Senghor was declared the candidate of the Bloc African for the second-college seat.

Senghor and Guèye ran on a platform that Guèye summed up in a single sentence: "one sole category of Frenchmen having exactly the same rights in as much as all are subject to the same duties."[25] On October 21, the day of the election, the Bloc's candidates both won easily. Once again, in the autumn of 1945, Senghor set out for Paris, this time with a new charge. His research on languages would have to wait. He had become an official ambassador of his people.

Although most people who knew Senghor at the time agree that he was reluctant to enter political life, it was nonetheless true that he had already given considerable thought to future relations between the African colonies and France. In 1943, even before the Brazzaville conference, he had written an essay entitled "Vues sur l'Afrique noir, ou s'assimiler non être assimilés" (Views on Black Africa, or To Assimilate, Not Be Assimilated), which was published in 1945 in an edited volume, *The Imperial Community*. In this article he makes three key points, familiar from his past work but now placed in a new context. First, Africans must actively assimilate the best of French culture. They should use French techniques to serve their own interests, and so create a relationship totally different from the traditional one. In the past it has been the French who have paced and directed the Africans' assimilation of French ways. Henceforth it must be Africans who put French knowledge to work for African purposes.[26]

Second, the time has come to recognize that Africans have a rich artistic and political culture of their own. Within his own memory, King Koumba Ndofène Diouf had ruled the integrated and balanced society of the Serer. Anyone who might doubt this point, Senghor suggests, need only read the great German ethnographer, Frobenius. African culture, although greatly changed by contact with the French, still preserves its essential character, including features from which the French themselves might well take lessons.

Third, based on these observations, Senghor proposes a political relationship between metropolitan France and its colonies similar to that of capital and province, one much in the spirit of Delavignette's *Soudan-Paris-Bourgogne*. There is no contradiction, he argues, between loyalty to one's province and adherence to a political entity centered in Paris. Indeed it is those without such local roots, Barrès's uprooted, who find themselves adrift in the modern world. Senghor then sketches a set of federal institutions which, he believes, would balance local and central interests. There must be a system of locally elected assemblies, an executive appointed by and answerable to Paris, and an imperial parliament in which both colonies and metropole are represented. He also proposes that metropolitan France support economic development and, above all, education. Not only must vocational and teacher education be expanded, but for the elite, study of French must be supplemented by the study of enthnography and an indigenous language. Maran's *Batouala,* he suggests, should be in the curriculum along with Corneille and Racine. In conclusion, Senghor reassures his French reader, "far from weakening the authority of metropolitan France, it [this system] could only reinforce it because it would be based on the consent of free men."[27] Although he was as yet a political novice, Senghor had a deep reservoir of study and thought on which to draw.

The atmosphere of the Palais Bourbon, where the Constitutional Assembly convened on the afternoon of November 6, 1945, was charged with anticipation. To contemporary observers, it seemed that the spirit of 1789 had been reborn, and that French democracy was once again triumphant. Certainly that noble chamber, home to the fumblings and disappointments of the Third Republic, now housed a new spirit. Fewer than one in five of the new deputies had served in the prewar Assembly. Many had come to prominence in the resistance. Perhaps most striking of all, here and there, dark faces dotted the house, Arabs, Africans, and Hindus from the empire. Amid the hubbub and confusion, even Senghor and his colleague from the Monnerville Commission, Apithy, who knew Paris well, felt a bit bewildered.[28]

The African deputies did not sit together, for tradition required that they sit with the parties with which they were affiliated. For example, Senghor and Lamine Guèye sat with the socialists (SFIO); Houphouet-Boigny from the Ivory Coast with the Union des Républicains et Résistants (URR); and Senghor's old friend Aimé Cesaire with the communists (PCF). Houphouet had persuaded his colleagues that they could have greater impact on policy by seeing to it that there was an African voice in as many parties as possible.

The first business of the Assembly was to choose a new head of government. There could be no other choice than the new symbol of France unified and resurgent, Charles de Gaulle. The Assembly then established a constitutional committee of forty-two members to draft a new constitution for France and its overseas colonies, and turned its attention to passing essential legislation. No sooner had it begun its work, however, than de Gaulle stunned everyone, on January 20, 1946, by resigning his position, announcing that the regime of parties and politicians was reasserting itself and he would have no part in it. De Gaulle's resignation was greeted with dismay in Africa, where he had a real popularity among both the French expatriates and the African population. The unity of the liberation was over.

The constitutional committee had four deputies from overseas constituencies, of whom only one, Paul Valentin, a socialist from Guadeloupe, was not a metropolitan Frenchman. Midway through the project, the socialists replaced Valentin with another overseas deputy, Senghor from Senegal. The SFIO leadership chose Senghor because of his reputation as a poet and an intellectual. When the newly drafted declaration of rights was criticized for its poor grammar and style, the committee turned to Senghor. As one deputy put it, apparently without irony but certainly in high-flown style, "Senghor's grammatical competence and literary virtuosity are highly necessary for the perfecting of this new monument of political literature."[29] It was a happy irony to employ a black Frenchman as official grammarian of its new constitution.

The idealism of the moment, as well as gratitude to the colonies for their support in the war, was expressed by the banning of the word "empire" from the new political vocabulary. One spoke only of the Overseas Territories of France, or the French Union. Such generous impulses were strengthened by the recognition that if France was to continue as a great power in world affairs it needed the strength of its overseas populations. The phrase "a hundred million Frenchmen" had a satisfying ring. At the same time, there was some apprehension lest France, with its population of forty million and its low birth rate, become the colony of its colonies, with their sixty million. A policy of one man, one vote might lead to this absurd result. Partly in acknowledgment of this possibility, however fanciful under the circumstances, the deputies from overseas did not speak out on matters that did not directly concern them.[30]

On matters that did concern them, however, the overseas deputies pushed for their interests. Because the Constituent Assembly had legislative powers as well as a charge to create a new constitution, it was able to pass several laws important to the colonies. It followed up on some of the Brazzaville conference recommendations. One law abolished the *indigénat,* the administrative penal code for the subjects of Africa; another put an end to forced labor throughout the colonies; and a third, the so-called Lamine Guèye Law, ratified the day before the Assembly adjourned, granted citizenship to all the peoples of the French Union—without, to be sure, specifying exactly what "citizenship" entailed.[31] These laws abolished the centuries-old distinction between African citizens and African subjects. The Assembly also made good on another of the promises of Brazzaville by creating a fund for economic and social development, known by its initials as FIDES.

Constitutional articles approved by the constitutional committee were presented one by one to the Assembly for discussion. Article VIII, on the French Union, came up for discussion only toward the end of the Assembly's seven-month session. Though the committee had reached a consensus on the proposed outline for the new French Union, general debate revealed the variety of purposes the newly created Union was designed to serve. Marius Moutet, soon to be Minister for the Overseas Territories, reminded the Assembly: "It is the hour of decision. Either we give satisfaction to the legitimate aspirations of these populations, or we must resign ourselves to seeing them move away. They do not want to be treated as minors any longer, even by a benevolent but authoritarian tutor. They want to be treated as equals."[32] Lamine Guèye took the floor to say that incidents such as those at Thiaroye, then only three months past, reflected attitudes that could not be tolerated.

Senghor, making his first speech before the Assembly, pointed out that France's civilizing mission was an equivocal notion at best if it included the idea that the African was primitive. He criticized the French for offering the colonies a second-class education designed to form good producers and minor functionaries submissive to their masters. Turning to the few Africans present, he summed up his view: "it is your ignorance that creates their grandeur." Though this brought laughter from the house, it was a light touch on a sore spot in the colonial relationship. As long as the colonies were kept dependent and ignorant, France could continue to think of itself as a great nation. There was an alternative, Senghor reminded them, one equally prominent in French tradition: a relationship of equality and fraternity. He called on the French to provide concrete improvements in the overseas territories: more schools, more economic investment, and a more genuine voice for Africans in the running of their own affairs. Words without deeds were not enough. In this, his first speech in the French National Assembly, Senghor showed his characteristic talents: a mastery of French rhetorical technique, a sense of humor, a knowledge of detail, and the ability to appeal to French history and tradition to argue for the African cause.[33]

In this same session, Communist party deputies called for an end to capitalist exploitation of the colonies, the centrist Mouvement Républicain Populaire (MRP) urged France to remain true to its unracist tradition, and more conservative deputies pointed out that beside the United States with its 150 million people and the Soviet Union with its 180 million, France would be doomed to the second rank unless it was united with the vast populations and resources of its overseas colonies. Thus the debate touched on all the major themes of empire, with particular stress on the nationalistic ones. Once again, as in 1870 and 1919, the nationalist argument for empire arose to comfort a France humiliated by military defeat. This was the single debate devoted primarily to colonial issues during the seven months the Constituent Assembly was in session. Clearly these issues were not at the top of France's political agenda.

The draft constitution pleased Senghor and most of the overseas deputies. It created a French Union based on equality and free consent, allowed for African representation in the French National Assembly as well as in a consultative Council of the French Union, and established local territorial assemblies in black Africa. The powers of these local assemblies were to be gradually expanded, as would the size of the African electorate eligible to vote. The draft constitution was presented to French voters for approval by referendum in May. It was voted down, but for reasons having to do with provisions affecting metropolitan France, not the colonies. Frenchmen living overseas voted overwhelmingly against it, however, an omen of things to come.

The defeat of the constitution was a blow to Senghor. In spite of public assurances from Moutet, Minister for the Overseas Territories, that the sections on the French Union would not be changed in any new draft, Senghor and the other overseas deputies grew apprehensive. As it turned out, their fears were justified. The new Constituent Assembly, elected in June 1946, had moved to the right. The euphoria of liberation had been dissipated.[34]

De Gaulle chose this moment to emerge from his seclusion to offer guidance. As far as the French Union was concerned, he agreed that it must be federal in form, but for backward areas, such as black Africa, he suggested that the President of the Republic should rule by decree and executive decision.[35] De Gaulle seemed to have forgotten his debt to black Africa. Of even more immediate and practical concern to the African leaders was the fact that a group of French colonials and right-wing politicians had organized themselves into a powerful political lobby. They convened a congress in Paris on July 30. There they charged the colonies with ingratitude and urged French politicians to keep a tight control on their colonial investments. They further declared that the African deputies represented no one but themselves, and accused them of being separatists, disloyal and hostile to France. They even charged Lamine Guèye and Gaston Monnerville with planning violence.[36] The overseas deputies were stunned. As Monnerville put it, "It was as if many Frenchmen thought that pretty words of thanks for the colonial war effort were enough, and that then they could return to the *status quo ante* . . . it was a stupefying mentality."[37]

Angered by this betrayal, Senghor told an interviewer in August 1946:

> We do not wish any longer to be subjects nor to submit to a regime of occupation . . . while waiting for complete independence, we advocate as a solution federation in the context of the French Union . . . I would like in conclusion to assure the whites of our unshakable will to win our independence and that it would be stupid as well as dangerous for them to wish to make the clock march backwards. We are ready, if necessary as a last resort, to conquer liberty by any means, even violent ones.

These were harsh words for the usually circumspect and gentle Senghor. Until this point, whatever he might have thought privately, he had gone to great pains to couch all of his public statements in terms acceptable to a large part of the French establishment. Apparently Senghor then forgot about this uncharacteristically vehement interview until several years after Senegal's independence, when he was reminded of it by his old friend Mercer Cook. Thereafter he referred to it often and included it in his collected works. The effect was to strengthen his reputation as a politician who had worked for independence from an early time.[38]

In 1946 Senghor was not alone in distrusting the French. In Senegal, too, there was fear of a conservative reaction by the colonial administration. A group of leaders in Saint-Louis sent a telegram to Senghor and Guèye urging them to demand that the wording of the rejected constitution be retained in the new draft or else they would seek complete independence. Young people in Thiès, a city close to Dakar, urged an appeal to the newly formed United Nations unless Africans were given their due rights. Colonial administrators sent reports to Paris that spoke of radical young people clamoring for autonomy and threatening their administration.[39]

The members of the colonial lobby continued to press their point of view: How could the vote of a Paris worker be weighted equally with that of an illiterate Sudanese farmer? They, too, favored federation, but with special laws to reflect the special situation in the colonies. At the very least, the two-college system of elections must be preserved and reinstituted if necessary throughout the territories. To counteract the influence of this newly active colonial lobby, the overseas deputies decided to create a parliamentary alliance to coordinate their activities. Their goal, explained Apithy, the deputy from Dahomey, was to enjoy in their own country the same rights and liberties as the French who lived there, not to sit "on the banks of the Seine, but to make decisions about the affairs of our own country, on the banks of the Congo or the Niger."[40]

The truth of the situation was that most Frenchmen still knew little about their former colonies and had no understanding of the great changes that were taking place there. They had no interest in arguments over what seemed to them to be arcane variations in the constitutional text. This lack of interest strengthened the hand of those few Frenchmen who did care, namely those living in the colonies and those who represented French business interests, who were determined to maintain French control. When in September the Assembly turned to discussion of new provisions for the French Union, no representative of the government even bothered to attend.[41]

The new draft did not honor Moutet's promise that Article VIII would be transferred without change to the new constitution. Instead it closed a loophole that might have allowed the secession of the units of the empire by deleting the statement that the French Union was formed by the free consent of its members. Some felt that this phrase from the earlier draft implied that the colonies could leave the Union at will. The new draft provided that no member of the Union could change its status without a constitutional amendment. As a result, any talk of independence by Africans could be construed as an attack on the constitution. The new draft also set a strict limit on the number of overseas deputies who would be allowed to sit in the National Assembly and reintroduced a two-college system for Africa, thus assuring the white-settler minority of a disproportionate representation. The executive of the colonies, answerable to the Assembly under the earlier scheme, was now to be subject to the president of the Republic, and hence to control by civil servants.

Disappointed and angry at the abandonment of provisions they had thought secure, the African deputies walked out of the Assembly and threatened mass resignation. Only then did government leaders seem to be able to hear their concerns. The result was a few small changes, notably a shift of some of the offending provisions from the status of constitutional articles to that of simple laws. The colonial deputies then reluctantly agreed to support the whole, apprehensive that any delay might lead to yet further retreat. They also recognized that they could expect little from French "goodwill." Senghor commented that but for the vigilance and concerted action of the overseas deputies, things might have gone worse. It took classic political pressure, namely a coordinated threat of resignation, to produce even small results. Among politically active Africans in Senegal, however, more and more voices criticized the deputies for their moderation. At a large demonstration in favor of autonomy for Africa, flowers were laid at the monument to the memory of those killed at Thiaroye. A group of young activists in Thiès, among them Senghor's cousin Adrien Senghor, began to pass around an article attacking Guèye for favoring assimilation when he should be working for independence.[42]

The second draft constitution was overwhelmingly endorsed in a national referendum. So began the Fourth Republic. Its colonial provisions represented a compromise between those who wanted to maintain French domination and those who believed that both justice and necessity required change. Power continued to lie, as it had in the Third Republic, with the fractious National Assembly. On overseas matters, many decisions would continue to be made by the civil service bureaucracy. The much-touted French Union was in fact little more than the old wine of empire poured into freshly labeled new bottles. Overseas representation was still severely limited. Even in the newly created Assembly of the French Union, which had consultative authority only and served as little more than a rubber stamp, electoral laws ensured that few native delegates would be chosen. Nonetheless, the National Assembly did have the power to extend native citizenship and create local self-governing institutions without changing the constitution itself. Such was not to be the case, however. The Jacobin tradition of strong central government prevailed. Most Frenchmen continued to believe that France was generous to its colonies and that France's civilizing mission was of unambiguous benefit to overseas peoples. This they combined with a dim sense that the possession of overseas territories was both the condition and the result of French greatness.[43] Perhaps most important, other issues pressed upon the Assembly and crowded out attention to overseas problems: economic recovery and reorganization in France, inflation, and such political questions as the loyalty of the powerful French Communist party. In actuality, the National Assembly devoted little of its time to colonial issues in the immediate postwar period.

Experience is a great teacher. Struck by their own powerlessness in the face of changing French public opinion, and by the fact that only coordinated action had achieved any success at all, the African members of the parliamentary alliance began to consider forming a truly unified African party. The initiative seems to have come from Lamine Guèye. All agreed that it was a good idea. They held a planning meeting to draw up a manifesto that called upon all African political leaders to gather in Bamako, the capital of the Sudan, to create such a party. The manifesto took care to declare its signers' loyalty to the French Union. It also rejected either assimilation or full autonomy as a realistic goal.

Senghor missed this planning meeting for personal reasons: he was getting married. Just after the war he had met Ginette Eboué, the daughter of the now legendary Félix Eboué, whose sons he had met in a POW camp during the war. Ginette had been born and educated in France. Her mother, like her father, was from French Guyana. It seemed a perfect match: the young up-and-coming deputy from Senegal and the daughter of the most illustrious black hero of empire. The two were married on September 9, 1946, with Lamine and Mme

Guèye serving as witnesses. It was a political event and, Senghor sadly acknowledged later, a marriage of the head and not the heart. A son, Francis, was born in 1947 and a second, Guy Waly, in 1948. Unfortunately love did not follow. Whatever problems the couple had were exacerbated by Mme Eboué, who shared the West Indian's traditional contempt for Africans. She did not hesitate to insult Senghor in front of visitors and continued to think that even the distinguished deputy from Senegal was no proper match for her daughter. The marriage dissolved in the early 1950s.[44]

Personal matters did not prevent Senghor from attending to his political duties for long. In October 1946, a Dakar newspaper announced that he and Lamine Guèye would join other African deputies, Apithy from Dahomey, Fily Dabo Sissoko from the Sudan, and Houphouet-Boigny from the Ivory Coast, at the upcoming Bamako Congress to create a new, all–West Africa political party. When the congress opened nine days later, however, neither Senghor nor Guèye was present, nor were others of their colleagues. The colonial administration and the SFIO had intervened. Both were alarmed by the possibility that black Africans might form a nationalist party that would disrupt the work of the National Assembly. The colonial administration noted that Houphouet-Boigny, with the help of the Communist Party, to which he was then affiliated in the Assembly, had taken charge of the planning for the congress. Fearing that any new party would therefore be dominated by the communists, they put pressure on the socialist African deputies not to go. Marius Moutet, the Overseas Minister and a prominent member of the SFIO, himself spoke with Guèye. For Guèye, who had made his entire career in the SFIO and had a great deal to lose by displeasing its leadership, it was a relatively easy decision. He would not risk defying party discipline to go to Bamako. Senghor had less to lose, but was inexperienced. With new elections coming up in mid-November, Senghor realized that a break with Guèye now would mean the end of his political career, at least for the foreseeable future. The Senegalese electorate was clearly Guèye's to direct. However promising a politician, Senghor was still relatively unknown and totally dependent on his patron. As a result, neither went to Bamako. When asked why he had not gone, Guèye explained that the organizers had misused his name and were so divided among themselves that any congress held under the circumstances could accomplish little. He also reminded those who criticized his subservience to the SFIO leadership that the real enemy was the reactionary colonial lobby.[45] The congress took place as scheduled amid great excitement. Africans were at last beginning to break free from French tutelage.

The Bamako Congress set in motion the first serious attempt by Africans to organize a single political party with local branches thoughout French West Africa. Houphouet-Boigny of the Ivory Coast emerged as the leader of what he called the Rassemblement Démocratique Africaine (RDA). In presenting their basic political objectives, the conferees repeatedly expressed their loyalty to France and the French Republic, going so far as to close the conference by singing the Marseillaise.[46] As the colonial administration had feared, however, the new party chose to affiliate with the French Communist Party. Their own policy was responsible for this outcome, insofar as they had prevented the Africans most opposed to cooperation with the communists from going to Bamako. Many of the subsequent pronouncements of the RDA showed the influence of Marxist rhetoric, but it was a strange Marxism, which denied the existence of classes in Africa or the need for an elite party. Lacking the support of a significant majority of African deputies, however, notably those of Senegal, the RDA failed to achieve its major goal: the creation of a unified party for all French West Africa.

Looking back ten years later, Senghor regretted "the mistake committed by the Senegalese deputies of the time in refusing to go to the Bamako Congress . . . I personally was of a mind to go and did not fail to say so to the leadership of the metropolitan party to which I belonged. But I must modestly make my self-criticism to the end. My mistake was to obey orders that were imposed on me from without." He did not mention at this time that Apithy, the deputy from Dahomey who was also affiliated with the SFIO, had defied party discipline to be at Bamako. But then, Apithy did not hold his position in the shadow of Lamine Guèye. Apithy had held to the course he and Senghor had set when summoned to serve in the Monnerville Commission: without participation there could be no influence; boycott left the field to one's enemies. The RDA leader Houphouet-Boigny, like Senghor, recognized that this had been a turning point: "If Lamine and Senghor had been at Bamako, we would have written another page of history."[47] African leaders later tried repeatedly to form parliamentary alliances and/or a single party across the territories. Each time they failed, victims of clever French maneuvering designed to keep them divided, personal rivalries among themselves, notably between Houphouet and Senghor, and the different specific needs of their constituencies. The result of this failure was to divide the colonies from one another, to further reduce their influence on French colonial policy, and to contribute to what Senghor later called the Balkanization of Africa.

By the beginning of 1948, Senghor was well-known as Lamine Guèye's brilliant apprentice. He had made the decision to seek political leadership of a kind, though he clearly operated in Guèye's shadow. He was still managing to maintain his intellectual interests. His second collection of poems, *Hosties noires,* was in press, and he was finishing a scholarly anthology of black poetry written in French. This included the work of West Indian poets as well as Malagasy and African ones, and Sartre had agreed to write the introduction. Senghor was also part of a successful attempt to find financial support for a new publishing house and its cultural journal, *Présence Africaine,* edited by Alioune Diop, a brilliant Senegalese whom he had met during the war. In the tradition of *La Revue du Monde Noir, Présence Africaine* took up the cause of bringing the work of Africans to the French- and English-speaking worlds. With Senghor's help, Diop was able to convince prominent French intellectuals such as André Gide, Emmanuel Mounier, Albert Camus, and Sartre to serve on its advisory board. Richard Wright was also involved. It was an ambitious undertaking in which French and English versions of the journal were to appear simultaneously.

From 1945 to 1948, Senghor maintained an impressive variety of interests and involvements. He participated in everything of either cultural or political importance that might influence the future of French-speaking West Africa. He had not made a definitive decision, however, about his own future: Was he to be a master of language, to serve his people as their spokesman? Was he to be their ambassador? Intellectual or politician? Or both? He did not want to choose, and so far he had avoided doing so.

9

Master Politician

The year 1948 proved to be a time of decision and new directions for Senghor. Two projects on which he had worked for several years, the *Hosties noires* collection and his literary anthology, were finally completed and published. Both were well-received. The influential French reviewer Pierre Emmanuel found in Senghor's poetry great "elementary images and symbols" that evoked the black continent, images that were those "of a great poet." He also commented that Senghor conveyed the true suffering of the peoples of Africa without giving way to anger. Elsewhere Senghor was praised for his evocative power, which "bathes us mysteriously in the strange charms of his native land." He had the added pleasure of seeing his poems in literary journals alongside the works of such well-known poets as T. S. Eliot, Osip Mandelshtam, Louis Aragon, and Paul Elouard, and Maurice Martin du Gard praised Senghor as a poet, "who sings his race," a poet with strong images and real spirit.[1]

In 1948, also, Senghor lost the second of his parents. His mother, Gnylane Bakhoum Senghor, died early in the year. Her obituary, published in Dakar's Socialist party newspaper, prophesied a glowing future for her son: "You disappeared just at the moment when your long labor was to be rewarded . . . the terrain you chose for your children is favorable for their success . . . Gnylane rest in peace and may the earth of Africa rest lightly upon you—your memory will remain graven in my heart by your children."[2]

Less than nine months later, in October, Senghor made a decision that determined his future. Understandably pleased by his recent literary successes, and finding much frustration in politics, he considered resigning his political posts to devote all of his time to the intellectual life. He knew that he could enjoy the accolades of French political and literary figures by assuming the role of poet, critic, and teacher, and thereby avoid the burdens of the real responsibility that accompanied his political position. By 1948 he had lived almost half of his life in France and felt at least as much at home on the boulevards of Paris as on the sandy streets of his native Joal. Although his fame in France largely rested on poems and essays about Africa, the path of expatriate spokesman was open. Senghor resisted this inviting alternative. He chose instead to step out from Lamine Guèye's shadow, a shadow that no longer provided protection but rather shrouded him in an unacceptable obscurity, and to seek direct political power for himself. It was a decision in which duty, a sense of destiny, and personal ambition all played a part.

Senghor had been drawn more and more deeply into French politics after the war. There he put to use the lessons he had learned at the feet of Blaise Diagne. He understood that fine oratory in the National Assembly and the admiration of French journalists did not necessarily have any effective consequence. He also knew that the real power in French Africa still lay, as it had before the war, with the colonial bureaucracy. The bureaucrats remained while a succession of ministers came and went with the volatile flow of French party politics.

At first Senghor concentrated on the area he knew best, education. Eager to thank Africans for their support during the war, the French government had instructed the Inspector General of Education in Dakar that all Africans who had received the baccalaureate degree between 1939 and 1945 should be offered scholarships to continue their education in France. After a suitable interval, Dakar cabled back that there were no Africans eligible for such support. Informed of what had happened, Senghor and his associates identified candidates, encouraged them to apply, and put pressure on the administration, with the result that several of the promised fellowships were awarded.[3] This experience was similar to that he had had with the constituent assemblies. Whatever the spirit of gratitude to Africa expressed in Paris, it did not necessarily lead to generous acts in the colonies. It was still true, as it been since the beginning of the century, that pressure by an African deputy in Paris was necessary to keep the colonial administration responsive to local needs, and even to the directives of the National Assembly.

Senghor observed, for example, that the administration was using its small budget for expatriot salaries to send French secretaries to Dakar. Senghor urged it to send more teachers instead. He persistently pushed for scholarships for African students, higher salaries for teachers, and the establishment of new schools. Perhaps most important, he began to lobby for administrative reorganization, arguing that education in the colonies should be the responsibility of the National Ministry of Education rather than the Overseas Ministry. If defense was administered from the center, why not education?

Senghor now recognized that educational policies in the colonies could not be evaluated without consideration of their political implications. The rural schools championed by Albert Charton might in themselves be good institutions for the villages, but they were no substitute for a demanding, rigorous education for the most talented. He realized that he had been naive when he had discussed Senegalese education before the war. The colonial administration was promoting the expansion of rural schools as an alternative to improving the urban schools that would create a capable African elite. Colonial administrators knew that well-educated Africans might question their policies, and had been alarmed by the views expressed in *Dakar Jeunes* during the war. Naturally they preferred not to discuss these worries openly. The question for public discussion was framed as the old nineteenth-century question, should Africans be given an education identical (and equal) to that of the French, or should their education be adapted (and watered down) to meet "special African needs"? While Senghor also believed that African children should learn about their own environment, he saw no reason to lower standards in order for them to do so. He knew that the fine talk about adapting education to African needs was a euphemism for preventing African children from getting a rigorous academic training. It was with this in mind that he proposed a law to the National Assembly in August 1947, the so-called Senghor Law. It called for the transfer of responsibility for education in France's overseas territories to the National Ministry of Education. Senghor also began to lobby for the establishment of a university in Dakar, so that more Africans could receive higher education. Among the papers generated on these topics within the Overseas Ministry in Paris was a note from an aide to the Minister reminding him that he alone should decide what was suitable for the colonies, and that this was particularly true "in the matter of education, where there are aspects with a political side."[4]

Senghor followed up his public statements with patient work behind the scenes. He sent numerous letters to ministry officials to show that he had studied issues in detail, understood the difficulty of change, and wanted to work with them, not against them, to find solutions. Here, as in his student correspondence with Charton, he was the model of tact and respect. In his public speeches, Senghor took care always to reaffirm his loyalty to France. On some issues, such as higher pay for teachers and more schools, he made slow progress. On broader issues with administrative and political implications for the overseas bureaucracy, he made none. The Overseas Ministry had no intention of giving up control of African education to narrow specialists "who would not understand," one administrator wrote, "the delicate requirements of the colonial system." One particularly astute administrator recognized that the Senghor Law challenged by implication the very existence of a separate ministry and administration for Overseas France. By analogy it might be argued that all national ministries should simply have overseas specialists.[5]

The issue of administrative reorganization led to bitter infighting within the colonial administration. Several experienced education officials, including both Charton and Capelle, the incumbent Inspector General of Education for French West Africa, supported Senghor's plan. Capelle finally resigned over this issue, saying that he could not improve education in the federation under existing conditions.[6]

The Overseas Ministry fought back. It was determined to retain as much autonomy as possible on all matters concerning its territory. It argued, with some justification, that if responsibility for overseas education were given to the education ministry, it would simply have to develop a cadre of people knowledgeable about overseas situations. The main obstacle to better education overseas, the administrators pointed out, was financial, and reorganization would do little to remedy this situation. Furthermore, it was too late to attempt to achieve assimilation through education. Association was now the only practical goal. Senghor slowly began to realize that the overseas administrators had no intention of giving up control of their territories. A letter of protest signed jointly by Senghor, Mamadou Dia, and other deputies from overseas had no effect. While publicly the civil servants called for more studies, privately they wrote to one another that delay was the best tactic for dealing with these troublesome deputies. Finally one administrator chided another for not offering Senghor more respect. After all, he explained, Senghor was a deputy of the Republic. His note made it abundantly clear that Senghor was important, not because he was an expert on education and the elected representative of Senegal, but because he held a position of authority in France.[7]

While Senghor was busy in Paris playing by French rules and pushing for educational reform, all the while growing more and more conscious of his impotence before the all-powerful and unyielding colonial bureaucracy, the mood in Senegal was rapidly changing. Historians have argued that it was the African students who returned to Senegal from Paris after the war who began to question France's eternal right to rule Senegal. The prevailing idea is that Africans learned in France to think in terms of autonomy and independence. Certainly in Senghor's case this is true. But the groundwork had been laid by discussions in Senegal itself.

It is one of history's ironies that Pierre Boisson, the representative of a Vichy French regime with racist overtones, had given Africans a forum for expressing new and potentially radical ideas, while the Gaullist representatives of Allied victory over fascism and racism quickly suppressed it. The Vichy regime had introduced discriminatory measures, such as segregated railroad cars and special shops in which local Frenchmen had priority when rationed goods were particularly scarce, which angered Africans. It had also encouraged Africans to explore their cultural and historical roots and provided for public discussion in the newspaper *Dakar Jeunes*. To be sure, Boisson's administration had shut the discussion down, but not before the new ideas had been widely shared and debated. When de Gaulle spoke at the Brazzaville conference and offered hope that there might be more autonomy for Africans after the war, his listeners in Dakar began to look forward to more such discussions and more opportunities to shape their own future. They had also noted the words of René Pleven: "the problems of the colonies are no other than the grand and eternal human problems" and his observation that the colonies were fortunate indeed to be able to benefit from "the light of our French genius." The message of the Brazzaville conference was ambiguous.[8]

Many young intellectuals in Dakar found Pleven's assumptions no longer acceptable. They no longer shared the Frenchman's view that French civilization and civilization in general were synonymous. Boisson himself had encouraged them to think otherwise by exploring the distinctive characteristics of their own culture. Furthermore, it was evident that France was not invincible. Africans had seen Frenchman fight Frenchman, and France itself go down to defeat in war. They had heard language at Brazzaville that sounded like promises that they might soon govern their own affairs, as well as language that assumed that nothing had changed. Add to these factors the widely shared sense that Senegal had sacrificed both men and materiel to help France in its hour of need, and the result was an expectation of improvement and change at war's end that approached a sense of entitlement.

There was ample evidence, however, that most colonial administrators in Senegal were blind to this new mood. On March 6, 1945, almost a year after the liberation of Paris and three months after the incidents at Thiaroye, the military tribunal at Dakar sentenced the African "troublemakers" of Thiaroye to ten years in prison. Lamine Guèye, who had defended them in court, marveled that even after several months of reflection the administration could not acknowledge that its own actions and those of its soldiers had contributed to the tragedy. The effort to block scholarships for Africans eligible for them reflected a similar attitude.

Discontent in Senegal was increased by poor economic conditions. Salaries frozen during the war remained frozen in spite of inflation, and in spite of the fact that salaries in metropolitan France had been raised. Secondary school teachers in Dakar, the local intelligentsia, struck for more pay. In December 1946, the elected Council of French West Africa refused to approve the colonial administration's budget. They held out until July, when finally, under pressure from Guèye, they gave in. Guèye had acquiesced to SFIO and administrative pressure. Then, in October 1947, the railroad workers on the Bamako-Niger line went out on strike. This was the first mass strike ever organized by Africans. It grew into a long and bitter struggle. For several months the administration refused even to negotiate with the strikers. At considerable cost and hardship, the Africans held on. The discipline of the strikers and the support given them by the local population gradually earned the begrudging admiration of the administration. One administrator pointed out that the main demand of the railroad workers was that they be given pay and other benefits more equal to those of European workers. He added that although the strikers presented their demands in economic terms, the demands carried racial overtones because certain categories of work were filled mainly by Africans.[9]

Events elsewhere in Africa followed a similar pattern. In 1947, popular demonstrations in Madagascar were put down with force and many people were killed. The response in Paris was to introduce a measure into the National Assembly to withdraw parliamentary immunity from the Malagasy deputies so that they could be arrested for complicity in these events. The SFIO supported the motion. Guèye and Senghor were dismayed. They understood all too well what such an attitude boded for future African leadership. Both voted against the motion, breaking party discipline to do so. Guèye even threatened to resign from the SFIO, so strongly did he feel about the issue.

Even the African deputies themselves did not fully appreciate the rapid evolution of thinking among their constituents. Although Guèye had urged African students in Paris to return home to see for themselves the changes that were taking place in Africa, he himself seemed, as one Frenchman put it, "very Third Republic."[10] Tall, elegant, and well-spoken, Guèye was enjoying his life as a prominent parliamentarian in Paris. He liked gourmet dinners with well-known French politicians. He was loyal to his party, the SFIO, and the party accepted him as the unchallenged leader of French West Africans. He had a well-deserved reputation for courageously defending Africans in colonial courts and demanding that they be given equal rights with Frenchmen. Guèye knew personally all the most important French administrators in Dakar. Many of them owed their positions to his patronage. He was a reliable patron, and his clients in turn gave him the electoral support he needed. It was the old and familiar game that Blaise Diagne had perfected in the first part of the century.

But the African students in Paris, the writers of *Dakar Jeunes,* and the leaders of the railroad strike were no longer satisfied with business as usual. Their attitude toward Guèye's "Third Republic" style is well summarized by the reaction of two of them to a meeting they had with Guèye shortly after the Liberation. André Guillabert and Abdoulaye Ly were students at Montpellier and Toulouse, respectively. They both received telephone calls informing them that Guèye, who had come from Dakar to Paris for his first visit since the end of the war, would like to meet with them. Excited at the prospect of discussing the future with this almost mythical figure, they scraped together the fare for third-class tickets on the night train to Paris. They went to the elegant Hôtel Rondpoint-Champs-Elysées, where Guèye was staying. He received them warmly in his suite and began to regale them with stories about all the ministers and officials he had seen on his visit: he had met with Guy Mollet, Vincent Auriol, and Marius Moutet and had attended receptions at the finest restaurants in Paris. After about fifteen minutes of such talk, Guèye rose, and the next thing the two young men knew they had been ushered out into the

Paris night. Not a word about Africa's future. Guèye seemed, Guillabert later recalled, "a courtesan of the past. He wanted us to go back
to Senegal to go into politics as his clients." The implication was that,
if they did as he wished, they could have a plush life like his. The
students did not really begrudge Guèye his enjoyment of the good
life. What did disturb them was that he should think such a life the
only enticement for an African politician. Eager as they were to play
a part in shaping Senegal's future, they were shocked at Guèye's
cynicism.[11]

Senghor had neither Guèye's experience nor his power. He had not
been part of the political scene before the war, although his early
acquaintance with Blaise Diagne had introduced him to its workings.
He lacked ties forged by mutual interest either to the African elite of
the communes, or to the Europeans and West Indians in Dakar whom
Guèye had rewarded with good jobs, or to Guèye's new clients,
Africans of Senghor's generation such as Alioune Diop and Ousmane
Socé Diop. Furthermore, Senghor's official function was to represent
the former subjects, the men and women born outside the communes,
who had just recently gained the vote. The sight of their poverty had
been an important factor in his decision to enter politics in the first
place. During his campaign, Senghor had stumped the countryside,
going from town to town, to Kaolack, Thiès, and Ziguinchor, and
into remote villages that Guèye had never seen. Dressed not like Guèye
in a Western city suit, but rather in a simple shirt and trousers of
khaki, Senghor soon came to be called the "deputy in khaki," known
for his ability to talk to the people. His curiosity and evident
interest in the life of the village struck all who heard him. As one who
met him then put it, "he informed us and himself at the same time."
Senghor enjoyed going among the people. He believed that in the
villages he would find the world of Negritude intact. "Our people had
not renounced it. They continued to think . . . that the soul of the
Blacks was superior to the mind of the Whites. They continued to
paint, sculpt, sing, and dance in their own style." For him, campaigning was the return of the prodigal son, the rediscovery of a world
he had for many years only imagined. But however romanticized his
vision of the rich cultural life of the traditional village, it did not
totally blind him to its present economic reality.[12]

Lamine Guèye came from a different world, that of the city and the
Afro-French. He had no interest in tedious campaigning, and no need
to seek the support of country dwellers. Once Guèye had taken care

of his friends by seeing to it that they got the important posts they expected, he was delighted to leave to Senghor what seemed to him to be the boring details of local organization.[13] To Senghor fell the task of supervising the selection of candidates for minor posts, notably the local assemblies set up by the new constitution. In the fall of 1946, for example, Guèye returned to Paris, delegating to Senghor the difficult task of putting together the SFIO list of candidates for French West Africa's new elected council. This was the council that subsequently refused to approve the administration's budget. As there were numerous rivalries for these positions, Senghor had a delicate task, one that would make him friends but that also could not fail to make him enemies. The colonial administrators whose job it was to report on political developments marveled privately at his diplomatic skills. As a result of this task and his energetic campaigning, Senghor gradually began to meet many ambitious young men eager to play a part in Senegal's future. They were beginning to organize discussion groups within the SFIO. Many of them had heard about Senghor's prewar speech at the Chamber of Commerce. Some had disagreed with his position at the time, thinking his questioning of assimilation reactionary and self-serving. Now they began to think that he had been right, and that he might be the leader they were looking for. They began to criticize Guèye for his lackluster leadership. A few people seemed to be trying to precipitate a split between the two deputies, and Senghor went out of his way to emphasize their solidarity.[14]

Within the SFIO, both in Paris and in Senegal, there was increasing disagreement on colonial issues. In March 1947 the SFIO newspaper in Dakar, *L'AOF,* which was closely associated with Guèye, announced that it could not publish an article by one of its regular correspondents (the unnamed author was Mamadou Dia), because "it was not truly socialist in its approach." In August the paper carried an acid exchange of insults between two rivals for power in the rich and populous region of Kaolack, Djim Momar Guèye (no relation to Lamine Guèye) and Ibrahima Seydou Ndaw.[15] Lamine Guèye chose to intervene on behalf of the politically weaker of the two, Djim Momar Guèye, and by doing so made an implacable and powerful enemy in Ndaw.

Ibrahima Seydou Ndaw was an individual of extraordinary intelligence and strong personality. One year older than Lamine Guèye, but born a subject, he lacked higher education, and had had neither the opportunity nor inclination to dress and behave in the French manner.

When his rival set out to insult him by calling him "the lawyer in caftan," Ndaw transformed the intended insult into a compliment, a sign that he had remained proudly a man of the people. He chose to dress like them, in the traditional way, rather than to mimic the French. Self-educated in the law, Ndaw used his knowledge to plead eloquently on behalf of the people of Kaolack and the Sine-Saloum.[16] As a result, he had acquired a large and reliable following in the Sine-Saloum, the most heavily populated region of Senegal and the center of the economically important peanut trade.

Battles such as that between Djim Momar Guèye and Ndaw seemed to be local and personal quarrels, but they were often fueled by a more general problem, the fact that all the best jobs were still going to citizens of the former communes. Indeed, Senghor was the only former subject in a top position. Lamine Guèye appeared to be unconcerned about such signs of disagreement within his party, nor did Senghor seem much involved. Nonetheless, colonial administrators began to speculate among themselves that a power struggle between Guèye and Senghor was in the offing. Indeed, one of the more sociologically minded among them pointed out in his political report that some sort of shift in power would be an inevitable result of giving the vote to the former subjects who lived outside the old communes.[17]

In September 1947 the Senegalese branch of the SFIO held its annual conference at Kaolack, the capital of the Sine-Saloum. Until then, any internal party disagreements had been settled within the party executive committee. When occasionally disputes had spilled over into the pages of the party newspapers, as had the quarrel between Djim Momar Guèye and Ibrahima Seydou Ndaw and that between Mamadou Dia and the editors of L'AOF, they had remained at the level of individual problems to be settled within the family. Now, long-simmering resentments came out into the open.

The Kaolack meeting was held at the house of Ibrahima Seydou Ndaw. It attracted all the important local leaders of the SFIO as well as hundreds of supporters newly interested in politics. Paul Bonifay, a European long active in Senegalese politics and then the party's administrative secretary, opened the conference with his political report. When Bonifay's report was complete, Senghor took the floor to object to the fact that it had not been discussed by local party sections before being presented to the conference as a whole. He then launched a blistering attack on the party leadership for what he termed its excessive centralization, nepotism, and habit of clan politics. He objected that there were first- and second-class party delegates, the citizens of the former communes and friends of Lamine Guèye, and all the rest. At the end of this session, the majority of the delegates voted to reject Bonifay's report. Guèye was stunned. He had expected nothing like this from the scholarly Senghor, nor had he had any forewarning of the degree of dissatisfaction within his own party. While he had been worrying himself with parliamentary politics in Paris and dining out with prominent politicians, a whole new generation of party activists had grown up in Senegal. Unprepared as he was, Guèye hesitated even to go to the next session of the conference. A group of delegates went to persuade him, pointing out that it was he, their political mentor, who had taught them the importance of open discussion and honest criticism as an essential part of true democracy. Chastened, but not yet fully aware of the significance of what had happened, Lamine returned to the conference.[18]

The areas of Senghor's support were clear from the vote on Bonifay's report: those who voted against it were the delegates from the small towns and regions of Kaolack, Thiès, Ziguinchor, and the Sine, that is, the former subjects. They made up a new constituency to which Guèye had paid no attention and that owed him nothing. Senghor, in contrast, was well known to these new men, of whom he was the formal representative. He had taken the time to practice the politics of contact, visiting the countryside, talking to people, making friends, and acquiring admirers.

The next day Senghor apologized to Guèye. Indeed there is some evidence that he had not fully appreciated the seriousness of his attack or anticipated the reaction to his speech. As it turned out, he and his supporters were unable to push through his plan for an administrative decentralization of the party, but they did reach an agreement with Guèye on an important issue. Alongside the official SFIO newspaper, *L'AOF,* Senghor was authorized to publish his own newspaper, *La Condition Humaine* (The Human Condition).

From its beginnings, *La Condition Humaine* was clearly Senghor's mouthpiece. Its title reflected his continued sympathy with Catholic philosophy, with its emphasis on culture and the importance of the human personality. The paper focused on education and literature, Senghor's primary interests, and devoted large amounts of space to his articles, speeches, and opinions. Unlike *L'AOF,* it gave relatively little attention to French events that had no bearing on developments in Senegal. It assumed that its readers were primarily interested in Africa and the black world.

Yet *La Condition Humaine* had ambitions to provide more than a cultural education. It suggested that there was a direct connection between such education and political action:

> As more and more Senegalese sit in municipal councils, village commissions, in unions . . . we need more political education . . . a paper of combat and research . . . [to] tell the truth to the international trusts, to the administration, which has a tendency to consider itself an instrument in the service of the metropole, to Europeans, who consider their own interests as coincident with ours, and finally to Africans, who must not sacrifice the general interests of French black Africa to narrow private concerns.[19]

The goal of *La Condition Humaine* was no less than to educate the people of Senegal so that they could better direct their own affairs. Its political purpose was to transform a party that had been created as a coalition of elites and clienteles into a mass party in which individuals would adhere to the party out of personal conviction. It aimed also to cleanse the SFIO.[20]

Senghor stated his position on administrative reform in the second issue: he called for the liberation of Africa in a French setting, and for rapid and progressive autonomy for all French Africa—autonomy, not independence. "And we say that assimilation is an illusion in a world where people have become conscious of their personality and we also affirm that independence is a dream in a world where the interdependence of peoples affirms itself so clearly."[21] Although rhetoric clouded his meaning a bit, Senghor seemed to be suggesting that there was a connection between the fact that African culture had its own intrinsic value and the need for political autonomy for Senegal. As Africans learned more about the first, they would begin to demand the second.

La Condition Humaine kept its readers informed of Senghor's efforts to get new schools and better teachers for the colony, and of his proposal to transfer overall responsibility for education from the Overseas Ministry to the National Ministry of Education. Each issue also carried instructive articles on African culture and a poem, often the work of one of Senghor's friends from his student days. Léon Damas, Etienne Léro, Aimé Césaire, Gilbert Gratiant, Birago Diop, and others were systematically presented for the first time to an African audience. Senghor wrote of a worldwide community of black men who shared the unique and distinctive culture of Negritude, and he presented his readers with examples of its expression. He suggested that self-awareness through poetry and literature was a critical part of the education that would lead to an improvement in the position of Africans, and that West Indian and black American writers could contribute to the African cause.

A second voice spoke with increasing self-confidence and individuality in the pages of *La Condition Humaine,* that of a young teacher, Mamadou Dia. Dia was one of Senghor's earliest and most valued local political supporters. Like Senghor, he had been born in a small town outside the communes and was of mixed ethnic background, in his case Serer and Toucouleur. Unlike the Catholic Senghor, however, Dia had had an austere Muslim upbringing. Born in 1911, five years after Senghor, Dia began his education in a Koranic school and by the time he was ten had memorized much of the Koran. From his pious father and his Muslim teachers, he learned self-discipline, the habit of meditation, and a strong faith. When, by a fortuitous coincidence, the young boy was blessed by a revered Muslim ascetic and founder of one of the great Islamic brotherhoods of Senegal, Ahmadou Bamba Mbacké, Dia's family began to predict for him a great future. Upon entering the school system that the French had established for Africans, Dia did brilliantly, testing first on the important federation-wide exams for entry into the William Ponty teacher training college. Unlike Senghor, Dia did not enter the schools set up for French children, and therefore he had little contact with the French. It was not until he entered Ponty, at the age of seventeen, that he stopped shaving his head in the traditional style. At Ponty he wore European clothes for the first time and learned to eat in the French manner. He did not, however, waver in his strict adherence to Muslim practices, leaving class early if necessary to pray at the proper time. His faithfulness, Dia recalls, earned him the respect of the headmaster himself. During the years he was studying and, later, teaching, Dia always returned in the summer to his village. He remained, therefore, closely in touch with daily life in the countryside.[22]

After graduating from Ponty, Dia decided that he wanted to study for the baccalaureate degree. This was not a path the colonial administrators wanted open to Africans. Senghor's opportunities had been the result of loopholes that had since been closed. Blocked by the administration in the person of that same Charton who had reluctantly supported Senghor's education in France and who thought a system of rural primary schools would provide the education appropriate for Africans, Dia resolved to persevere. After seven years, during which he worked as a secondary school teacher in Saint-Louis and studied at night with the help of a sympathetic Frenchman, Dia won his degree. Like Senghor, Dia was brilliant, proud, and determined.

During the war years, Mamadou Dia was among the young intellectuals, mostly teachers, who objected to discriminatory practices. He organized a friendship society with its own newspaper, but it was broken up by the colonial administration. His articles in *Dakar Jeunes* were among those which most upset the administrators. He believed it was because of these activities that obstacles were put in the way of his further education and that he was later transferred from his teaching position in Saint-Louis to a school in the interior at a small town called Fatick. In Fatick, he quickly earned the confidence of the local population and created a successful agricultural cooperative as well as a respected academic program for his students. He wrote frequently for local newspapers, largely about rural economic conditions and the value of peasant cooperatives. It was from this experience that he wrote the article that *L'AOF* refused to print, giving as the reason that he did not hold proper socialist views.[23]

Dia was still working at Fatick when he first made contact with Senghor. He had long admired Senghor for his speech at the Chamber of Commerce, but had been disappointed when he learned that Senghor was going into politics. Anyone who became a politician, Dia assumed, could not be a man of integrity. He regretted the loss of a "great intellect."[24] Senghor, for his part, read Dia's articles with interest, began to correspond with him, and when they met, quickly recognized Dia's talent. When Dia came to know Senghor and watch him in action, he revised his opinion of Senghor's motivation and political objectives. Senghor generously supported Dia, first in words and then in local politics. But when Senghor proposed Dia as the SFIO candidate for election to the upper house of the French parliament, partly so that Dia could get an eye operation in Paris, he was overruled by the SFIO party committee majority.[25]

Dia's articles in *La Condition Humaine* reflected both his firm character and his deep and abiding concern for the welfare of Senegal's rural population. He took tours through the countryside and reported with compassion and directness on the conditions he found. He explained the need for village dispensaries, wells, and schools, and strongly urged the creation of peasant cooperatives. Dia also mounted stinging attacks on specific SFIO practices and policies, thereby leaving Senghor free to concentrate on issues more suitable for an elder statesman. Dia attacked the politics of personalities and those who ran after medals and honor, providing words but no concrete help for their constituents. Such leaders demanded idolatrous devotion, he wrote, and cared little for the interests of the people.[26]

Dia and Senghor, divided by religion, temperament, and talent, shared a basic honesty and the view that Senegal needed a socialism that would leave room for religious belief. Both were also convinced that the time had come for basic changes in the governance of the colony. And both were ambitious. In their diversity, one Muslim, the other Catholic, one an economist, the other a poet, they complemented and respected each other. Senghor was often in Paris, continuing his representation of Senegal in the National Assembly and lobbying the overseas bureaucracy, growing ever more restless with his membership in the SFIO. Dia remained on the spot, closely in touch with local events, quietly gathering support for his and Senghor's ideas about what Senegal needed.

Relations between Guèye and Senghor, in contrast, were becoming strained, although the wing of the SFIO represented by *La Condition Humaine* continued to consider itself very much a part of the SFIO. Considerable disagreement arose as to how best to settle the continuing strike of the Bamako-Niger railroad workers. Senghor was angered that the colonial administration, backed up by Lamine Guèye and the SFIO, had refused even to talk to the workers' representatives. When the SFIO government in Paris fell and was replaced by a new government dominated by a different political party, Senghor immediately requested an on-the-spot investigation of the colonial bureaucracy's policy.[27] Unlike the government dominated by his own party, the new one was responsive to Senghor's request. Eventually the administration agreed to negotiate, and the strike was finally settled in March 1948.

In June 1948, Lamine and Senghor signed a declaration of unity, further evidence that such unity could no longer be taken for granted by the public and perhaps not by the two men themselves. In July, Guèye's *L'AOF* published a long article acknowledging that there was a need for the reevaluation of black African culture, but warning, without mentioning any names, that race consciousness should not be transformed into a force for political battle: "[you] must not inflame a race without thinking of the whirlwind you may reap."[28] The slap at Senghor was obvious.

Senghor published a letter of resignation from the SFIO that

October. He explained that he could no longer accept the discipline of a party that showed so little interest in the fate of his people. He had watched for three years while the metropolitan parties treated the overseas territories simply as voting machines: "Instead of being ends in ourselves, we have become means in the often sterile game of metropolitan politics."[29] The SFIO had voted against a single college for African elections, which would have given equal weight to the individual votes of Africans and Frenchmen living in the colonies; against equal pensions for French and African veterans; against proportional representation in local elections, which would have created more diversity in the membership of elected councils; and for revoking the parliamentary immunity of the Malagasy deputies. Furthermore, all of his mail, even letters from his wife, was being opened by the colonial administration. With an eye on his electoral constituency in Senegal and the inevitable future conflict with Lamine Guèye, he added that he was resigning not to protest events in faraway Madagascar, as Guèye had threatened to do, but to defend democracy in French West Africa. In Senegal, Senghor continued, the SFIO branch was undemocratic, manipulating appointments and creating and ignoring party statutes at will. Embellishing his direct personal attack on Guèye with professorial flourish, he paraphrased Voltaire's malicious reworking of the Jesuit motto: the local SFIO had become a dictatorial organization devoted "ad majorem Lamini gloriam . . . fortunam que"—that is, to serving the greater glory and personal power of Lamine.[30]

The attitude of the SFIO leadership in Paris further exacerbated Senghor's frustration. When he had appealed to them on the basis of the merits of his case, he had been told that the SFIO would never support him: "It is not a question of socialism or integrity . . . but of power." So long as the SFIO leadership in Paris thought Guèye could deliver the votes in Senegal, he was told, they would support Guèye without further attention to the matter. What Senghor did not not know was that the SFIO leadership was convinced that Guèye had the votes because the local colonial administrators continued to report that Guèye had the overwhelming support of the local population.[31] This was part of an old deal. Colonial administrators supported Guèye and he, one of the few deputies really interested in colonial affairs, supported them. They owed their jobs to Guèye and were eager to keep them, even if it meant misleading the party leadership. Even without this last piece of information, Senghor concluded that never and nowhere did the SFIO leadership consider what was right or wrong, or what was in the best interests of Africa. This was not a party to which he wanted to belong.

Having explained why he could not remain within the SFIO, Senghor turned to the future. He called for a new, democratically organized party with active local sections throughout the land: The Bloc Démocratique Sénégalais (BDS). This new party would work toward the revision of the constitution, whose spirit had been violated by the French National Assembly and the colonial administration. It would struggle against the capitalists by supporting unions and peasant cooperatives in Senegal, and against the SFIO nepotists who put personal interests above those of the country. In a striking image, especially to people for whom loyalty to family and particularly the mother was paramount, he likened Black Africa to an old woman in rags whom the socialist nepotists had starved, humiliated, and prostituted. The BDS would work within the French Union to restore her dignity.[32]

This was no sudden decision for Senghor. He had thought out his break with the respectable French left with characteristic care. In the spring, several months before he published his letter of resignation, he had consulted with Ibrahima Seydou Ndaw, Mamadou Dia, and many others. Part of what he had to decide was whether to recommit himself to the political life as such. Senghor had not sought his place as Lamine Guèye's running mate in 1945, and subsequent experience had removed any illusions he might have had about politics in general, as well as about Lamine Guèye personally. Part of him wished simply to give up politics altogether and live the quiet life of an intellectual. His dream as a student had been to become a professor and a member of the Collège de France. He had proved that he had the ability to achieve success among Paris literary figures. He did not feel a real vocation for politics. He had refused a high-level administrative job as supervisor of education in French West Africa in 1937; he had refused to support a politically oriented West African students' organization in Paris in 1938; he had written about the corruption endemic in the political life. Senghor seems to have been genuinely undecided about his future. Despite the recent birth of his first son and the imminent arrival of another child, family life did not fill the void. He had recently been ill, quite seriously, with malaria. This had given him time to think. He recognized that he had reached a turning point, and that once again he was presented with a choice.[33]

To make this choice, Senghor relied on the painstaking methods that had been ingrained in the dutiful student by French priests and Parisian professors. He set out to gather information, analyze it, and draw his conclusion. He also began to talk and consult. Ibrahima Seydou Ndaw urged him to resist what he called a temptation to give up. Ndaw flattered Senghor, arguing that he and he alone could provide the leadership Senegal needed. It was a challenge presented to Senghor in part by an accident of history, Ndaw said, but one to which he must respond. Senghor countered that he was too weak, Guèye too powerful for a direct confrontation. This was the more true because Guèye was backed by the socialist governor and colonial administration. Ndaw disagreed. He, Ndaw, would deliver the populous Sine-Saloum region for Senghor.[34] No doubt Ndaw was remembering Lamine Guèye's support of his rival some years before, as well as the arrogance of the city dweller toward the subject born and bred in the countryside, which had been a source of irritation throughout his life. He had his own reasons for seeking Guèye's downfall.

Mamadou Dia recalls another of the discussions of this time, one that included his friend Léon Boissier-Palun, a brilliant young lawyer who had gained attention and respect for his defense of African workers' claims at the time of the Bamako-Niger railroad strike. Dia had gone to visit Boissier and discovered him in conversation with Sourou Migan Apithy, who was then the deputy from Dahomey to the French National Assembly. Apithy was passing through Dakar on his way to Paris. Senghor was there, too, packing his bags for the same trip. They were discussing French party politics. Apithy shared Senghor's frustration at having to accept the discipline of metropolitan parties on policies toward the colonies that he opposed. He was planning to try to organize the overseas deputies into a parliamentary alliance distinct from the regular metropolitan parties. Such a parliamentary grouping would welcome the representative of an independent party in Senegal. Senghor, Dia recalls, cautiously suggested they should wait a bit longer before breaking openly with Guèye and the SFIO. Dia pushed for action, as did Ibrahima Seydou Ndaw. Soon, influenced by Apithy's opinion that it was wise to make the break at once, rather than wait for the local SFIO party meeting that might put Senghor in the minority, Senghor finally agreed. Apithy later said that he was quite sure at the time that Senghor had made up his mind well before this conversation, but with characteristic finesse, simply wanted to assure himself of their support. Dia, on the other hand, believed that his was the decisive voice and recalls that Apithy had praised him for his good judgment. Senghor and his friends agreed that the support of Ibrahima Seydou Ndaw was crucial. Once it was assured, Dia was to print up membership cards for the new party to sell. On his next trip to Senegal, just before the local SFIO Congress, Senghor would make the public announcement. Having agreed on this plan, Senghor set off for the airport and flew to Paris.[35]

Senghor's friends in Senegal served him well. They gathered local support, explaining why the new party was necessary and what it stood for. They based their strategy on the knowledge that the Senegalese voters were prepared to support the individual they knew, Dia or Ndaw, not an abstract party or the still relatively unknown Senghor. However much they might desire a more democratic party based on a better educated electorate in the future, for the moment they used their understanding of the local culture and current political climate to build support among the newly enfranchised voters by many means. Ndaw enthusiastically lent his support. Powerful Islamic religious figures received respectful visits from Dia, as did the leaders of the railroad union. The latter, too, were disillusioned by the party of the colonial administration and of Guèye. Out of such disparate groups, a loose alliance was created. The traditional leaders of the countryside were not to be opposed or displaced, but rather enlisted in the cause. Frequent communication kept Senghor well informed and his local supporters' morale high. Thus was the stage set for Senghor's letter of resignation and his public announcement that he would form a new party.[36]

The reasons for Senghor's break with Guèye and the SFIO were many and varied. Certainly Senghor was right that the party's French leadership paid little serious attention to African interests, while continuing to take African voters' support for granted. The SFIO leadership acted on assimilationist assumptions, and never doubted that what served their interests in Paris would be acceptable to Africans as well. Senghor was also right that Lamine Guèye's approach had been formed in an earlier era. Guèye, and his parents before him, were Saint-Louis born, citizen members of an Afro-French community that had worked toward assimilation for more than a hundred years.

Senghor, born little more than fifteen years after Lamine but in a totally different milieu, represented a new generation and a radically different outlook. Though by education and experience more assimilated into French culture than Guèye, Senghor was marked by his country childhood. He had also participated in endless discussions in

Paris with West Indians and black Americans, and later with young African students, about the existence of a distinctive black culture. He questioned both the possibility and the desirability of assimilation for Africans. He also recognized the hypocrisy of the French and how little weight Senegal's needs carried in government circles. Senghor shared the present mood in the colony, the desire for more autonomy and a growing impatience with assimilationist platitudes. The men who had written and read articles in *Dakar Jeunes* no longer thought of their own culture as something to be left behind as quickly as possible, or of their only goal as enjoying the rights of Frenchmen— at the whim of Frenchmen. Senghor shared and indeed had helped shape these views. His ideas about the New Negro and the values of African culture, which were appearing in the pages of *La Condition Humaine,* both echoed and influenced the thoughts and aspirations of the generation now coming of age. Many of Senegal's young intellectuals were, as Mamadou Dia later put it, proponents of Negritude long before they heard the word.[37]

Senghor's more personal motives are necessarily obscure. The role of promising apprentice did not suit him. As a child he had sought his place with the grownups before they saw fit to offer it to him, because, he thought, he had earned it by his hard work and educational achievement. He now felt he had earned his political place, and that place was to be leader. He was recognized as an expert on Senegal and quoted as an authority by Frenchmen such as Robert Delavignette and Paul Alduy in books and in parliamentary debate.[38] His poetry had been reviewed widely and hailed as the authentic voice of Africa. Jean-Paul Sartre, whose prestige was then unrivaled among French intellectuals of the Left, had granted authority to Senghor's ideas about black African culture. Why must he leave the political limelight to Guèye and fight for each and every small reward for his supporters in the "bush"?

There is no doubt that Senghor had developed by this time considerable personal animosity toward Guèye. It is likely that he overestimated Guèye's power and influence, and so exaggerated the extent to which Guèye, and Guèye alone, was responsible for the intransigence of the SFIO and the colonial administration in the face of what to Senghor seemed to be Senegal's obvious needs. The country-bred subject's long-simmering resentment of the privileged citizen and city dweller certainly fueled the anger of Senghor's followers, and perhaps of Senghor himself.[39] More important, however, was Senghor's feeling that he had earned his place as a leading politician. If the older generation would not step down gracefully, he would sweep it aside.

For Senghor, the break was in many ways a great relief—relief from being Guèye's protégé, relief from living in the shadow of an older man, relief from being pressured to support policies he did not believe in, as well as relief at being able to do what he had gone into politics to do, to serve the interests of his people as *he* saw them. He was free to be his own man. This freedom had a price: by reaffirming his commitment to politics, Senghor had to defer the goal of his youth, to be a poet and professor. But at the founding meeting of the BDS, held at a crowded movie theater in central Dakar, Senghor showed no sign of hesitation. He proclaimed that never had he felt "such a sense of accomplishing a sacred duty," or been more at peace with himself. He told his audience that he had at long last freed his conscience and resolved contradictions that had plagued him "for more than a year."[40]

The break with Lamine Guèye was not without cost. It led to personal attacks, insults, and strain among long-time collaborators. Senghor was forced to break with an old friend from the war years, Alioune Diop, who had enjoyed the patronage and encouragement of both Senghor and Guèye. Senghor had enthusiastically supported the creation of Diop's Paris-based journal, *Présence Africaine,* in 1947. Its purpose was Senghor's purpose: "to define African originality and hasten its entrance into the modern world."[41] Senghor had used his contacts with French intellectuals to find funding and support for this venture. He himself served on its editorial board. Now, just a few months later, amid some confusion as to who was responsible for making their quarrel public, Senghor and Diop criticized each other in print for putting personal self-aggrandizement ahead of their common cause. Senghor resigned from the editorial board of *Présence Africaine,* and Diop, in a tone more of sorrow than of anger, publicly questioned Senghor's motives for breaking with Guèye and starting his own party.[42]

For his part, Lamine Guèye chose the high road, acting as if Senghor's resignation from the SFIO and creation of a new political party were matters of little import. His followers, however, mounted personal attacks on "the vain little Negro," "the proud agrégé," "the precious pedant," calling him "a puppet in certain hands" and accusing him of "ingratitude to Lamine Guèye, without whom he would be nothing."[43]

Another friendship foundered on these shoals. Hélène Senghor received a telephone call at her house in Joal from her old school friend Lamine Guèye. She had been serving as the local distributor for *L'AOF,* but was sending huge unopened bundles back to Dakar. Guèye wanted to know the reason for this. What could she answer but the truth, that she would not help a former friend to insult her brother.[44]

Senghor's BDS moved quickly to establish its platform and to organize the promised local sections. It was to be democratic and socialist, against nepotism and the politics of clan, and for the interests of Senegal and West Africa within the French Union. It would respect religion and traditional leaders. It would also act in accord with the principles of scientific socialism.[45] The new party designed its insignia to include a lion on a green background. The lion, as a symbol of courage, loyalty, and strength, held special meaning for Senghor, as it was also the emblem of his father, Diogoye (The Lion) Senghor. Senghor's loyalty to his ancestors was confirmed. He would fight for Senegal under the banner of his father. The color green, too, was a felicitous choice. If for the Christian Senghor green was the color of hope, for the vast majority of Senegalese who were Muslim it symbolized militant faith. For the animists green represented youth and force, and for everyone it suggested new growth after the long dry season that is so often the scourge of Senegal. In explaining the symbolism of the new flag, *La Condition Humaine* acknowledged, "each of us knows that animism continues to well up in us from the depths of past ages like a living spring under the shadows of oriental religions."[46] Right from the beginning, then, Senghor's party understood the power of symbolic expression and made use of a sophisticated blend of traditional and modern appeals to rally support.

From the time that the BDS was founded at the end of 1948 until the federation-wide election of 1951, Senghor and his followers worked constantly to build electoral support. It was not easy, and it took physical as well as moral courage. In 1949, when Senghor first went to Saint-Louis, Guèye's stronghold, there were threats of physical violence. His car was sabotaged. An angry crowd shouted him down. In the streets of the city he was followed and hooted at.[47] It was well known that the colonial governor opposed him, and no one had ever won an election without administration support.

Senghor was not to be intimidated. He patiently stumped the communes and the newly enfranchised countryside in a way no politician, not even he, had done before. Lion and panther were still a danger on country roads. Occasionally a hostile crowd had to be dispersed with gunfire into the air. Senghor did not waver. Traveling by communal taxi and later by jeep, he crossed the country from east to west, from north to south. In his first year of campaigning, by one correspondent's estimate, he traveled ten thousand kilometers and attended some 450 meetings in 45 days.[48] Previously the citizens of the former communes and expatriate Frenchmen had dominated the country's political life; now they were to be challenged by the vast majority, the newly enfranchised former subjects.

There were several keys to electoral support in the countryside. Of these the most important were the leaders of Islam. In Senegal there are a number of powerful Islamic brotherhoods led by marabouts who guarantee to the faithful a place in paradise in the next life in return for absolute obedience in this. Democracy in Senegal transformed some of the methods by which the marabouts exerted their power, but did not diminish its substance. Marabouts could deliver large blocks of votes. Recognizing this fact, Senghor, the Catholic, often accompanied by Mamadou Dia, the Muslim, whose eloquence in Wolof made up for the fact that Senghor spoke it haltingly, carefully made the rounds of the Islamic leaders, promising and delivering coveted favors. Thus Senghor secured the support of the richest and most well-organized of these brotherhoods, the Mourides, as well as the more numerous Tijaniyya. Indeed, so attentive was he to the Islamic brotherhoods at first that his opponents accused him of stirring up Muslim fanaticism in the land.

Soon legends began to develop about the deputy in khaki who would arrive in the village to address villagers gathered under a baobab tree, or to sit in the house of the village headman talking, listening, and asking questions of any who wished to hear him. Even his opponents had to admit that it was Senghor who could talk to the countryside. Stories were told of his modesty, eloquence, and personal courage. One such story told of a visit to a village that Senghor knew to be against him. The village marabout, a Mouride, had been told that the Catholic Senghor was working against the religion of Muhammad. Senghor decided to go to the village to dispel this misunderstanding. One of his entourage was warned that there would be a physical attack on Senghor in the village. Knowing that Senghor would never cancel a visit because of such a rumor, the aide decided not to tell him about the warning lest he worry. The aide himself took precautions by arranging an informal guard. Having arrived in the village and gathered a crowd, Senghor began patiently explaining that he was not against Muslims. To the contrary, he had recently visited the grand marabout of the Mourides, and had received his full support. At that point, a man pushed through the crowd and handed Senghor an envelope, saying, "I am a Mouride, and each time someone speaks praise of my marabout, I must give him money." This was indeed the custom, and Senghor graciously accepted the envelope with money in it. Some minutes later, the man again moved forward from the crowd, walked up close to Senghor, reached into his pocket, and again handed him money, for Senghor had again mentioned the name of the marabout. Senghor's friend had been warned that this was one of the people in the village who might attack Senghor. Rather than risk the man's third approach, two members of the self-appointed guard gradually pushed him back until they had isolated him at the edge of the crowd. Only then did they search him and discover that he was carrying a knife. That night, when Senghor was informed about this small drama, he confessed that he had known about the warning and suspected this man, but had decided that any reaction on his part might enflame the crowd. Senghor had shown no hint of apprehension and had not seemed at all tense. Such calm under pressure added to his supporters' admiration.[49]

For Senghor himself, these campaigns became a triumphant pilgrimage home. In a poem entitled "Messages," he creates an image of himself in dialogue with the village elders under a baobab tree. He recalls that respected men have gathered in that same spot for generations to discuss and resolve questions of importance. He feels the presence of all the traditional trappings of royalty: athletes, horses, and balafong music of praise. His people have recognized his nobility of mind. Toward him now surge honors from the deep wellsprings of the kingdom of childhood and the land of the ancestors. He feels both the weight and the support of the hopes of the young people. He is the "master of sciences and of language" who nourishes his people and who has "imprinted on them the rhythm."[50] He has kept his promise, to be their spokesman and ambassador. His reward surrounds him. Behind this triumph lay his often lonely years of isolation, and his profound belief in the rights and values of his French and African cultures.

The parliamentary elections of 1951 provided the first direct test of strength between Senghor and Guèye. Senegal had the opportunity to elect two deputies to the French National Assembly. In earlier, less inclusive elections in 1948 and 1949, results had been mixed. It had been evident in 1949 that the BDS had a majority of the countryside, but that majority had been more than offset by the SFIO majority in the former communes of Dakar and Saint-Louis. By 1951, however, a new overseas electoral law had tripled the number of people eligible to vote, and the BDS had waged a concerted campaign to get people registered. The balance of the electorate was shifting from the old communes to the countryside.[51]

Senghor had to choose a running mate so as to contest both seats. There was little chance that the BDS could win both positions, if indeed it could win one, so this choice could be made with an eye to attracting votes for the ticket as such. Ever mindful of the sources of Lamine Guèye's support, Senghor settled on Abbas Guèye (no relation), a man outside the BDS inner circle. He was from Dakar, where he had long been active in union affairs and was genuinely popular with the urban workers. He was also supported by a powerful Tijani marabout. He seemed a good choice to attract union and urban voters away from Lamine Guèye and his SFIO running mate, Ousmane Socé Diop. The lines seemed to be drawn: the country versus the town, and within the town, the unions against the notables and intellectuals. For this election, as before, Senghor campaigned systematically throughout the country, carrying the green banner associated by most Senegalese with militant Islam. Thousands of people turned out for large urban rallies.[52]

Senghor spent the evening of the election at Ndaw's house in Kaolack, the capital of Sine-Saloum. The results trickled in, unofficially at first, as friends at different voting places phoned in the tally from their areas. At first Senghor's supporters thought these reports must be wrong, that their workers were exaggerating, but Senghor himself was confident. He and Ndaw and many other supporters stayed up all night, drinking coffee and listening half incredulously to mounting evidence that they were winning, and by a landslide. The official results gave Senghor and his BDS a victory beyond their most optimistic hopes: the BDS had taken both seats. With approximately 314,500 voting, the BDS had over two-thirds of the votes, more than 213,000. A decisive role had been played by the marabouts. SFIO efforts to woo their votes had backfired, and, in contrast to all expectations and partly because of rivalries within the brotherhood, the Grand Marabout of the Mourides had instructed his followers to vote for Senghor.[53]

Lamine Guèye was stunned. His supporters in the local colonial administration were equally shocked. The year of Lamine's sixtieth birthday brought not celebration but defeat. Up until the day of the election, the possibility of his defeat had not even been considered. Now he had no official standing in Paris. Parisians noted with some bewilderment that Africans had rejected their most experienced and respected spokesman.

Late that spring, in March 1952, elections were held for the local territorial assemblies. Once again the BDS showed that it dominated the electorate. By now most of the voters enfranchised by the 1951 electoral law were registered to vote. As a result, the BDS won 41 of 50 seats for Senegal's territorial council, losing only in the cities of Dakar and Saint-Louis. In June, at the opening session of the Grand Council of the French West African Federation, Boissier-Palun, BDS, defeated Lamine Guèye, SFIO, in the election of its chairman.[54] A new era had begun, the era of Senghor.

Between 1948 and 1951, Senghor came into his own as a politician. No longer content to be at the bidding of others, he transformed himself into a political power in his own right. In Mamadou Dia he found his own brilliant apprentice, a man both loyal and capable. They formed a personal alliance based on trust. If Senghor knew how best to present the needs of his people to the French and could also communicate with the simple people of the countryside, Dia had a more detailed appreciation of Senegal's economic and social needs. Dia knew far better than Senghor the individuals and groups with influence in Senegal, and possessed a gift for organization. Each man recognized and appreciated the other's talents. Together they were able to create a political coalition and an electoral strategy in Senegal that proved solid and long-lived.

Even while mastering the arts of politics, Senghor retained his loyalty to old friends and literary interests. Birago Diop, fellow writer and friend from his student days, recalls a visit from Senghor in February 1948, a few months before the break with Lamine Guèye. Senghor had traveled with Guèye, Houphouet-Boigny, and other deputies to Ouagadougou, in what is today Burkina Faso, for an official celebration. Knowing that Birago was working there as a veterinarian, Senghor decided not to stay in the fancy hotel with the other deputies, but to spend the night with his old friend, talking poetry and literature.[55]

In these years, Senghor developed his distinctive political style. He was slow to move, always cultivating the ground carefully first to ensure that a new project would flourish. He was equally cautious in choosing allies, but once chosen, they were supported, praised, and given credit for what they had accomplished. He remembered and sought out old friends. As in his personal life, he sought to reconcile opposites and opponents in politics as well. The person who disagreed was a challenge, not to his power to crush, but to his ability to persuade and win over. Senghor developed an uncanny sense of what people had to have and what they would be willing to accept. He was still a teacher, dealing with sometimes stubborn or unwilling students. Now his class was made up of the people of France and Senegal.

Senghor continued to be a go-between, but had set himself a new purpose. He was still a mediator between French and African, but now he faced the challenge of persuading other Africans to support him. He sought out many different kinds of people, leaders of the Islamic brotherhoods, veterans' groups, trade unions. He pressed for greater coordination and joint action by the African deputies in Paris. Later, in 1957, he even sought out Lamine Guèye and persuaded him to unite his sadly reduced SFIO following with the BDS, arguing that a united front would help in negotiating with the French. By 1957 Guèye posed no real threat to Senghor's sure hold on power, but Senghor felt more comfortable knowing that Guèye was with him and not against him. Any personal grudge Senghor might hold should, and would, be forgotten in service of the greater cause. Furthermore, Senghor's generosity often paid off. When, in 1962, Senghor faced a political crisis, Guèye was there to help him. Even in his student days, Senghor had brought together those who disagreed when he thought they shared a common goal, in the hope that they might come to understand one another. As a politician, he built on this skill. It became his hallmark.

These years before Senegal's independence were important in establishing patterns for the politics that were to follow. The developing political culture of Senegal was greatly influenced by Senghor's personality, which inclined him to persuasion and compromise. It was also influenced by factors beyond Senghor's control, namely his religious and ethnic background. As a Serer when the majority of Senegalese were Wolof, and as a Catholic in a country where the great majority were Muslim, Senghor simply could not rally support with appeals to ethnic or religious affiliation. He had to devise appeals that drew disparate groups together and forge alliances based on other factors. He built on a tradition, established by Blaise Diagne and further developed by Lamine Guèye, that in Senegal ethnic and religious affiliation were not overtly exploited for political purposes. The nation as a whole benefited from this happenstance.

By the early 1950s, Senghor had accepted the fact that Africa had little influence in French political circles. His rising frustration with French politicians and colonial administrators had been focused on Lamine Guèye at first, but he now realized that the cause was not Guèye alone, but rather French attitudes and political structures over which Guèye had little control. However much Africans might try to find ways to work within the system, as they had in creating an independent grouping of African deputies in the French National Assembly, they could not achieve the results they wanted. In the early 1950s, Senghor never used the word independence, but he began to speak frequently of the need for greater African autonomy within the French Union. He mounted a campaign for a revision of the constitution and publicly attacked the hypocrisy of the Frenchman's "civilizing mission," remarking that the white man's burden was proving to be quite a burden on Africa as well. He entreated Africans to take charge of their own future. Africans must "graft the European shoot onto our wild stock." Their goal must be to create the civilization of *métissage* (interweaving), a hybrid that would not be barren, but would grow and bear richer fruit than either Europe or Africa could produce alone. Assimilation could be the foundation for future growth, but only if Africans set the terms on which it took place. "To assimilate, not be assimilated" became Senghor's motto. He offered his own existence as proof that such a goal could be realized. On an individual level, he had joined in one catholic embrace riches drawn from many complementary worlds. Other Africans must do the same. They must take the best of Western European techniques and science and put them to work for African goals.[56]

There is an obvious and striking connection between Senghor's personal development and his political style, as well as between his intellectual views and his political goals. Those who accused Senghor and his poet friends in the 1930s of pretending to talk of poetry and culture while really planning the politics of racism were wrong as to Senghor's original motivation but correct in seeing a direct connection between the two aspects of what was a single career.[57] Senghor never abandoned his conviction that the purpose of politics was to create a setting in which human beings could develop their individual cultures, but his growing sophistication had led him to a conclusion that paralleled that of Kwame Nkrumah, who had coined the memorable political slogan "Seek ye first the political kingdom, and all things else shall be added unto you."[58] Senghor now realized that his vision of a free and self-directing African culture could not be realized without attention to political issues.

These were the considerations that supported Senghor's decision to resolve his political frustrations not by abandoning politics but by moving out from under the shadow of Lamine Guèye. He could continue to be true to his African heritage and yet a respected figure on the French scene. As a modern politician, he could fight confidently under the banner of his father, Diogoye the Lion. His parents were dead. He welcomed his new position as intermediary, and not only, as tradition demanded, between his family and his ancestors, but also between his people and the French.

As he enmeshed himself more and more deeply in the political struggles of his time, Senghor's ideas about African culture, Negritude, and métissage continued to serve as his guide. Their political dimension grew in importance, to a point where they became a rallying cry for his supporters. What had begun as a set of ideas about identity and culture was transformed into a political ideology.

10

Negritude and African Socialism

Senghor's decision to break with Lamine Guèye marked the end of his willingness to accept the traditional rules imposed by Paris on political activity in the colony. Until that time it had been assumed that Africans would join and serve the interests of the metropolitan political parties in return for personal glory and an occasional concession granted if and when the central party leadership deemed it appropriate. The result, as far as Senghor was concerned, had been too many compromises and the danger of sinking unnoticed into the mire of French bureaucracy. Once again he felt the threat of becoming the dutiful black Frenchman so necessary to French imperial interests and national self-esteem. To counter this threat, Senghor once again had a choice. He might simply give up politics. This was an option he considered, to trade power and political importance for the quiet rewards of literature. It seems more than mere coincidence that just before he went public with his decision to break with the SFIO and Lamine Guèye to form a new party he fell ill, as he had in the winter of 1933–1934 when depressed about his academic results and brooding over his identity as a "New Negro." This time it was a tropical disease, malaria. The strains his friends never saw took their toll in other ways.

The ideas Senghor now brought to the political arena, the theories of Negritude and African Socialism, did not spring forth full blown in 1948 like Minerva from the head of Jove. They had developed slowly over time, germinating in a student's isolation, drawing nourishment from his discovery of kindred spirits, and taking shape in his study of contemporary European ethnography and philosophy. When

Senghor was first reaching for a new way of looking at himself, he did not use the word Negritude. He used the black Americans' term New Negro, which he translated directly into French as *Nègre nouveau*. Only later did Césaire coin the new term, Negritude. Senghor grasped this new word as a means to permit and justify a higher level of abstraction. He defined Negritude as the sum total of the qualities possessed by all black men everywhere. As his thinking focused more and more on this concept, he moved away from the realm of fact and individual experience into the realm of abstraction. By the time he had matured as a politician, he had the concept of Negritude ready to serve as the keystone of an ideology, designed to describe a new vision of the black man's place in the world.

Senghor has always credited Césaire with inventing the word Negritude, but the two men developed its significance together. Putting on his scholarly hat, Senghor explained how he and Césaire decided on it. It was an elementary semantic step: they simply transformed the French adjective for black (man), *nègre,* into a noun by adding a suffix, *-itude.* The result was an abstract noun. That is all. For Senghor, it meant "the manner of self-expression of the black character, the black world, black civilization."[1] Césaire used the word somewhat differently. He wrote that "Negritude is simply recognition of the fact of being black, and the acceptance of that fact, of our destiny of black, of our history and our culture."[2] From the first, then, Negritude carried at least two separate meanings. It might refer, as Senghor suggests, to an objective visible reality, namely black culture, style, and character. It might also mean, as Césaire intended, the acceptance by a black individual of the importance of his color and its significance for him in everything he did. In the latter case, Negritude would not be an inevitable aspect of having a black skin, but rather the result of a black individual's conscious choice. For Césaire Negritude was primarily an attitude; for Senghor it was an objective reality.

The first steps in Senghor's thinking about Negritude had been taken by the mid-1930s, before he wrote anything about it or even had the word. He had recognized in Paris that something about him, be it his black skin or his African childhood or both, set him apart now, and apparently forever, from his French schoolmates. He also discovered that, as far as the French were concerned, his difference meant that he was inferior to them. Such a value judgment was simply unacceptable. He was a proud man. The French had to be wrong. He was not inferior. He might be different, but that difference could not mean inferiority. The discovery that there were other black men who thought as he did reassured him that his uneasiness in France was not simply the result of an individual problem or neurotic sensitivity. Other Africans, as well as West Indians and black Americans quite different from himself in culture and upbringing, felt it too. Senghor concluded that, whatever blackness entailed, it was not just a matter for Africans alone but for black men throughout the world.

The first push toward Negritude, then, was the discovery of a common thread in the reaction of many black men to their life in Paris, and of the French to them. It led Senghor to the conclusion that there must be an objective cause for it, some important reason why he had tried, as he put it, to suppress his ancestor, why Du Bois had felt an ever-present sense of twoness, why Césaire also felt uneasy and confused about his true self. Senghor wanted to understand these forces and put his ancestor in a new light. He had to find a way to heal his inner division, to be whole, and to be respected. In that his efforts to deny his African side had taken place in collusion with his kindly French teachers and a whole superstructure of ideas and assumptions embedded in French culture, he had a formidable weight to throw off. He had to rethink his image of himself as a Frenchman who happened to be black. Fortunately, he had a set of "miraculous weapons" granted him by the French themselves: an excellent knowledge of philosophy and history, and a mind well trained by a classical education.

Given the enormity of his task, and the personal success he had already achieved by passing his exams and jumping through the hoops held by his French sponsors, it is small wonder that Senghor experimented cautiously and anxiously with his new persona. He had a great deal to lose if he displeased his French patrons. It is likely that the experience of a happy childhood and a triumphant early career in the French world gave him the confidence and energy to make the attempt. He was content neither to suppress all memory of his childhood past nor to accept permanent second-class citizenship as a discolored Frenchman. A firm sense of his own worth drove him to seek an alternative.

Perhaps the hardest move for him was the one he made with Césaire: to accept the fact that he was black and that this single biological fact influenced all others. He was not and could never be accepted as a full participant in Paris's moveable feast. The reason for his being an outsider was that the French saw him as such. He had a forced choice,

either to accept a life of perpetual striving to be accepted by the
French as an equal, an equality they would never grant, or to join
with other black men to create a new type of black identity. He chose
the second option. He set out to challenge the traditional French
attitude toward Africans and black people in general. This was the
most important decision Senghor ever made. He marked it by
destroying the writings of his youth, and by declaring that he was a
"New Negro." "I accepted myself such as I was . . . I was born again."[3]

Most of what Senghor achieved followed from this decision and
makes sense only in light of it. There were moments when he wavered.
At times, he succumbed to the temptation of being accepted and
rewarded by Europeans he admired in return for playing their game
nicely. His early political success as a dutiful and quiet member of the
SFIO was one example. At other times, it was simply that his energy
flagged. Then he regressed into the role he had played so well as a
young man, that of good cooperative black Frenchman.

If Senghor's most difficult step was to accept himself as a black man
first and foremost, he quickly saw that to declare that he was a New
Negro was not in itself the solution. A new attitude was only a
beginning. Unlike Césaire, Senghor could not accept the French view
that Africans had invented nothing. Scholar that he was, Senghor was
not satisfied simply to argue from his private experience. He wanted
to teach, persuade, and educate. He turned to the work of French and
German ethnographers to find evidence to back up his intuitions and
to make arguments the French establishment would have to listen to.
This was why he traveled up to Paris from Tours to audit courses in
ethnography, spent long evenings reading Frobenius, Delafosse, and
Delavignette, and endlessly discussed their works with Césaire and
other black friends. That is why he was elated when he discovered the
work of European scholars that supported his views. Frobenius's confirmation that there was such a thing as a unified African culture
served Senghor as a counterweight to the view, more common in the
1930s, that there was no civilization in black Africa. It never occurred
to him that he might turn his back totally on what Europe had to
offer.

In the first essays Senghor wrote after achieving his new point of
view, he did not use the term Negritude. At his Dakar lecture in 1937,
for example, he identified himself as Afro-French. This already was a
change from his thinking the day he signed the school register of
Louis-le-grand indicating his nationality as French. Now he saw him-

self as Afro-French or, as he said later in the same speech, a New Negro. Though the reverberations and significance of this term could not have been understood by his African audience, Senghor knew quite well what he had in mind, and with whom he had chosen to ally. He had taken Césaire's subjective step. He had recognized his kinship with black West Indians and Americans and was ready to commit himself publicly to their fellowship.

Two years later, with substantial study of the work of European ethnographers behind him, Senghor began to write in detail about the distinctive qualities of African culture and art. He moved forward from a general declaration that a unique culture existed to an attempt to describe its characteristics. He approached his subject from many different points of view. Some of the information he drew upon derived from his grammatical and linguistic research for his Doctorat d'Etat. He had chosen to work on the linguistic and literary forms of several African languages, with the intention of demonstrating their complexity and sophistication. In this same period, he was also exploring the subjective experience of the black African in his own poetry, and writing essays about Africa for a general audience. The titles of the first three of these essays suggest the direction in which he was moving: "What the Black Man Brings" (1939), "Views of Black Africa, or To Assimilate, Not Be Assimilated" (1943), and "Defense of Black Africa" (1945). From justification and explanation, he was preparing to move toward action. In none of this work did Senghor use the term Negritude. He had spoken of Negritude once long before, in the poem "Portrait" published in 1936, where he referred to his "imperious Negritude," but there was no sign as yet that this word was to be of great future importance.

Senghor now set out to educate the French public. Such was his goal in putting together a section on black African poetry in French for an anthology entitled *The Most Beautiful Writings of the French Union and the Maghreb,* published in 1947. As its title suggests, this collection included writings from all the French colonies. In his section, Senghor wrote a remarkable introduction in which he identified several types of African literature and analyzed their characteristic styles. It was a pioneering attempt to make such a classification.

The next year, 1948, was the key year in the presentation of the concept of Negritude, as it was in Senghor's political career. Senghor's *Anthology of the New Black and Malagasy Poetry in the French Language* was published by the most respected university press in Paris. By including together writers from the West Indies, Madagascar, and French Africa, Senghor was presenting evidence for the unity of the black world. He did not, however, make the argument directly. In short biographical introductions to the work of individual writers, he pointed out that one exemplified the New Negro, or that another had been inspired by his Negritude, but he made no effort to explain what these terms meant. He left the general conclusions to his readers. The anthology had a public success quite beyond that of a similar anthology put together by Léon Damas and published the year before. Perhaps it was read because Senghor had achieved what the black American poet Langston Hughes called the definitive anthology of black poetry. More likely, however, it was read because it included a long introduction by Jean-Paul Sartre, then at the height of his fame.

By agreeing to write an introduction to Senghor's anthology of the new black writing, Sartre granted it immediate importance. His introduction, entitled "Orphée nègre" (Black Orpheus), provided the generalizations so scrupulously avoided by Senghor.[4] It proved important for three reasons. First, it gave to Senghor and his friends the visibility and public importance they had hitherto lacked. Secondly, it provided an authoritative assessment by a respected French contemporary of their work and how it fit into the current intellectual and political scene. And finally, and perhaps most important, it influenced the way Senghor and his friends subsequently thought about themselves. However convinced Senghor may have been of the value of his African heritage, he gained added confidence when he found support for his ideas from French writers he admired, whether it was indirect as in the case of Rimbaud and Barrès, or direct as in the case of Delafosse, Delavignette, Mounier, and now Sartre. That Sartre should support his endeavor was of incalculable importance to him, as well as to his audience.

Sartre devoted little space in "Black Orpheus" to the individual writers whose work Senghor had collected, nor did he show much interest in the poetry for its own sake. He was interested primarily in an abstraction, the notion of Negritude. He wanted to show its connection to what interested him, namely Marx's theory of historical revolution. Sartre wished to enlist the men of Negritude for the French left.

Sartre identifies the current situation of French-speaking blacks as a special case of the general exploitation of man by man that marks the bourgeois epoch. It is a special case because the black man, unlike the white proletarian, cannot understand his place in society simply by considering society's economic structure. He must first recognize that race is the primary factor in his oppression. Consciousness of his Negritude is the black man's first step toward understanding the basic dynamic of his place in capitalist society. Negritude can play for blacks the role that Marxism plays for the proletariat. Negritude will direct black energy toward condemnation of the exploiter and the beginning of revolutionary change. Sartre therefore hails the rise of the idea of Negritude as a first and necessary step toward the black man's participation in the proletarian revolution. But, he continues, Negritude as such is a temporary phenomenon, doomed, as Marx had said in another context, like the owl of Minerva, to take flight at the dawn of the new era. It is a minor thesis in the dialectic. To French bourgeois racism it is an antiracist racism. French racism is but a single strand in the complex web of the interrelated beliefs that make up bourgeois ideology. Come the revolution, French bourgeois ideology and racism will disappear simultaneously. With the disappearance of French racism, its antithesis, Negritude, will also disappear. In the new society, race will have no meaning.

In an odd and unexpected way, then, Sartre, who begins his essay as the champion of the blacks, ends by denying their basic premise. He discounts any possibility that there may be a positive content to Negritude. He never even considers that black African culture may possess elements of enduring value, or have a destiny apart from that of France. Rather, he supports the contrary idea, namely that any black contribution can only be a minor one, a small contribution to the onward progress of France and the international revolution.

In spite of the fact that Sartre was interested in Negritude mainly because it provided him with a new opportunity and a somewhat fresh perspective from which to push his views about revolution, his definition of Negritude influenced the way the word was later used. He pointed out the variety of its meanings and some of its inherent contradictions.

Negritude, according to Sartre, is "a certain quality common to the thought and conduct of blacks."[5] Sartre thus assumes that the black man's conduct and thought are two faces of a single phenomenon. The black man can find Negritude in either of two ways, by looking within, at his own personality, or by looking without, at African civilization. Either method will lead him to a single reality. On this point, Sartre agreed with Senghor. To it, however, Sartre adds a bit of

Marx. Marx argued that a man's thoughts were the direct result of his economic and social activity. Existence, as Marx put it, determines consciousness. Therefore Negritude and African reality must be a perfect fit. This explains why Negritude can be discovered by the African poet who delves within as well as by the ethnographer. The poet can play the role of the Evangelist who announces the good news: Negritude will be born again. But here Sartre finds a contradiction. The black poet, Sartre points out quite correctly, becomes self-conscious and anxious to articulate his Negritude only when he comes into contact with white Europe. It is only after he has ceased to live unreflectively and totally within the world of objective Negritude that he feels the need to express his subjective Negritude. This is the irony of his history. The black poet writes an Orphic poetry—hence the Black Orpheus of Sartre's title—because he must first desert his native land before he returns to it by descending into himself. For the black diaspora, it is only by reentering Africa and coming into contact with the objective world of Negritude that subjective Negritude can be reawakened.

The language and structure of Sartre's arguments are those of Hegel and Marx with the obligatory pairing of objective and subjective, existence and consciousness. But Sartre does identify clearly a basic contradiction in the development of Negritude, namely that its poets are men who have left Africa behind them. The René Maran whom Senghor hailed as one of the first writers of Negritude was born in Martinique and educated in France. He was able to be a poet of Negritude, according to Senghor's brief comments in the anthology, because he was of distant African parentage and had also lived in Africa, "which gave him consciousness of it."[6] Senghor seems here to be suggesting that the characteristic black style of expatriate black writers can shine forth only if they renew themselves by contact with Mother Africa. But Senghor himself had the contrary experience. He found that he could write the poetry of Africa only when in Europe, that is, only when he could put distance between himself and the culture that inspired him. Sartre did not reflect further on the irony that the milieu that created Negritude was that of exiles far from home, or that the expression of Negritude was most dear to those no longer part of the black African world. He did see, however, that Negritude was a reaction, a reaction to confrontation with Europe or, as he put it, an antithesis to the European thesis, an anti-racist racism.

Sartre provided both a definition of Negritude and a theory about its function and future. He believed that Negritude would enable black men to participate in the coming revolution when all oppressed people would join hands to overthrow the bourgeoisie. At the moment of revolution, according to Sartre, Negritude would renounce its pride of color and sacrifice itself to the proletarian cause. It would then disappear into the universal culture of the future.

Whatever difficulty Senghor may have had in accepting Sartre's view of the inevitable eclipse of Negritude, he could but rejoice in the fact that Sartre took his work seriously and provided a wide audience for the writers of Negritude. Thereafter there were readers, and publishers, for black poetry and essays.

Many of the basic notions that Senghor now developed in connection with the concept of Negritude had been present in his thinking for some time: the belief that there were qualities common to black men throughout the world, that the work of all black artists shared a characteristic style, and that Africa possessed a rich culture qualitatively different from that of Europe. What Sartre added was confirmation of the value of a particular word, Negritude, as a shorthand term for an extended theory of group identity. Senghor continued to speak of the New Negro and the Negro-African for some time even after 1948. He also continued to emphasize the importance to his thinking of a concrete group of particular individuals. Only gradually, with time, were the earlier concepts abandoned in favor of the greater abstraction, Negritude.

Ten years later, at the end of the 1950s, Senghor was using the word Negritude as a synonym for black African sensibility and culture. As his explanation of its etymology indicates, Negritude is nothing more than a word, a noun constructed out of the adjective for black. Blackness or racial origin is at its root. To this extent, Sartre was right. Negritude was an anti-racist racism, at least at first.

Senghor has acknowledged that Sartre was right to emphasize that Negritude was born in opposition to white racism. As Senghor began to identify the distinctive qualities of Negro Africa, he did so by noting its differences from white Europe. Disclaimers and occasional reminders that all human qualities might be found, albeit in different mixes, among all peoples were lost in Senghor's constant emphasis on this contrast. By the time he had developed the dichotomy in its final form, most of Senghor's specific research lay far behind him. His ambition then was to make of Negritude a concept that might take its place among the great principles of his day, grand principles such as humanism and socialism. He wanted a concept to serve both abstract and concrete purposes simultaneously. Or, to put it another way, he tried to create an abstraction that would be accepted as an accurate description of something that existed in the real world. To some, it seemed he had fallen into the trap he had vowed to avoid, the belief that words in themselves can conjur something into existence.

Given this dynamic at the foundation of Senghor's theory of Negritude, he had to develop a theory of white European culture, or what might be called "Blanchitude"—a term too ugly for him ever to have used—to serve as its foil. Senghor expounded on two sets of characteristics, one said to be characteristically African and another, its opposite, said to be peculiarly white European. The result was the creation of models of two cultures that were not independent of each other but curiously linked by a law of opposites. Senghor's critics have enjoyed pointing out that he betrayed his debt to Western thought at the very moment he claimed to be breaking free from it, bound as he was to defining self strictly in terms of other. They have also enumerated his borrowings of an idea from this or that European critic of contemporary European society. The most important influence of Western thought and culture on Senghor, however, or perhaps it should be called a constraint rather than a positive influence, was that he felt compelled to argue for Africa's total difference. He seemed unable to argue that the culture and sensibility of African and European were alike in some ways and different in others. To this extent, he accepted the racist premise that race was the root cause of basic differences among peoples. What he did not accept was the Europeans' judgment of value. He rejected the idea that these differences were those of inferior and superior, inescapably separating inferior black from superior white.

Two papers Senghor wrote in the 1950s for presentation at the First and Second Congresses of Black Writers and Artists set out publicly his theory of Negro-African aesthetics and civilization in its mature form. The first paper, delivered in 1956, focuses on the Negro-African aesthetic and sensibility. The second, presented in 1959, focuses on the civilization that black Africans have created. Together with other writings completed by the end of the 1950s, these papers provide the essential content of Senghor's theory of Negritude.[7] Only in the last of them, however, did Senghor present his thinking as an exposition on Negritude, using the word as a shorthand way of referring to a whole constellation of ideas that were now, for him, self-evident.

Senghor begins his 1956 paper with what he considers the beginning, the "physiopsychology of the Negro-African." His awkward term "physiopsychology" suggests that in his view the physiological and psychological are inseparable. The unique way the Negro-African perceives the world is the ultimate source of his distinctive culture. On its difference from the European physiopsychology, Senghor cites Joseph Arthur Comte de Gobineau, the French diplomat and man of letters, "Emotion is Negro as Reason is Greek," and Count Keyserling, who remarked on the great emotional warmth of the black. Senghor then elaborates on the significance of these emotional qualities in the language of contemporary psychology. It is emotion and empathy, the qualities that black Africans have in abundance, that provide the human energy to create societies and understand the world. Emotion integrates consciousness. It connects man to man, observer to observed. Analytical reason can identify and describe. It can separate and reconstruct, but it cannot connect. Emotion and intuition lead to a connection between observer and observed and so to an understanding more complete than, and therefore superior to, that possible through analytical reasoning. In support of this assertion, Senghor elsewhere cites another authority, Albert Einstein, who wrote that "the mystical emotion" is the true source of knowledge and of art. According to Senghor, the African perceives the outside world with all of his senses simultaneously. He approaches each object gently, anxious not to harm it, eager to comprehend it whole, for he assumes that he shares with it and all else in the world certain essential qualities. What interests the African is less the superficial appearance of an object than its inner meaning, less its external sign than its sense. And the sense is not its use in a material way, but its moral and mystical significance. The black man goes beyond and behind daylight reality to the essence beneath. To this extent, he might seem to share the aesthetic of the modernist poet or the Surrealist in his rejection of the importance of the superficial appearance. Unlike the European Surrealist, however, who downplays the importance of external appearance because he thinks that all experience is subjective, the African minimizes the importance of external appearance because he knows that it is only the surface manifestation of an underlying reality. That underlying reality, not his own mind, is the focus of his interest. Knowledge of material objects is simply a means to understand the essence and order of the world. That order is the only important reality, and has an existence quite apart from any of its individual manifestations, including himself.[8]

Senghor sees a direct connection between this way of perceiving the world, what he calls the physiopsychology of the African, and the characteristic black African world view. Africans believe there is a single life force that manifests itself in a wide variety of ways. Its enhancement is the highest good. Without it, nothing can exist. Everything visible in the world, rising from the grain of sand, through animals, to man, to his ancestors, and finally to God, is connected to it and dependent on it. All are part of a single whole. The life force itself, however, can appear only in and through these various forms of being and so is dependent on them in turn. Therefore the black African is careful to harm nothing and no one unnecessarily. Indeed, his duty is to enhance all forms of life and through them to strengthen the life force upon which he also depends. The African goal is to live in harmony with all being.

Far different, Senghor argues, is the approach and world view of the white European. The European relies almost exclusively on one way of knowing, analytical reason. He focuses his analytical eye on a world he assumes to be full of objects totally alien to himself and with which he has no inner connection. Whereas the black African relies on emotion and intuition to tie himself to a world of which he believes himself an inextricable part, that white European uses reason to separate himself from it. He analyzes objects by breaking them up into their constituent parts in order to see each part in isolation. To understand something, Senghor explains, the European sets himself apart from the world, and sets each bit of the world apart from every other bit. He then dissects the object "in an unpitying analysis." Reason has no sympathy. The European understands the world bit by bit, part by part. According to Senghor, such an approach has isolated Europeans from nature and led them to see it as alien. For them, nature is interesting or valuable only if it can be made useful to man. This European attitude toward the world has existed since long before the scientific revolution of the twentieth century. For two thousand years, the Middle Ages excepted, the Western European "has mutilated Man, opposing reason to imagination, discursive to intuitive knowledge, science to art." He has tried to use nature and to possess it. And in possessing, he kills. The black African considers this attitude toward nature a foolish arrogance. Senghor refers to the words of a wise old man of his country: "The Whites are cannibals. They do not respect life." They call what they do the humanization or domestication of nature, "but they do not realize, those Whites, that life is not to be domesticated, and especially not God who is the source of all life and in whom all life resides. It is life that humanizes, not death. I am afraid all this will turn out badly. The Whites in their destructive madness will end up bringing us misfortune."[9]

The African's way of knowing and his view of the world are articulated in his religious beliefs and practices. Because the African perceives that all objects in the natural world share a common essence, he feels linked to all being, animate and inanimate, as well as to his now dead ancestors. All are presences to him that must be respected. These perceptions make him an animist. His animist belief commands that he preserve this communion of living and dead, spirit and flesh, man, God, and nature. He must treat all things with charity to preserve all life in the biosphere and the connections between past, present, and future life.

The same physiopsychology and the metaphysic connected with it determine the quality and style of African art, music, and poetry. Here Senghor draws on his own recent research. In the Negro-African arts and poetry, rhythm rules, tying the parts together. It is not the mechanical rhythm of the machine but the varied rhythm of the seasons, of life. Rhythm is as central to African poetry and sculpture as it is to African music. The methods of African poetry are also revealing. Rarely does the poet explain or describe the appearance of an object in detail. He works by means of symbol. Water is evoked, for example, not because of its color or form, but because it signifies purity and life. An elephant is named to evoke his force; the spider to evoke his prudence. African poetry uses sound, assonance, alliteration, repetition, and above all rhythm. The poet uses these techniques to open up a pathway from the listener to an underlying reality. He never creates art for its own sake alone, but always to enhance his capabilities and those of his audience to connect themselves to the vitality that sustains the world.[10] Such are the characteristics of the black African, his world view, and his art.

In a paper delivered at the Second Congress of Black Writers and Artists in 1959, Senghor developed his theory of the connection between this distinctive African sensibility and the organization of African society. Here he corrected his terminology of three years before, rejecting the word physiopsychology in favor of the word psychology because, he said, physiopsychology suggests a biological factor that, however important, is poorly understood.[11] While continuing to refer to the contrast between black African and white European sensibilities, Senghor now analyzes the societies that have resulted from these differences. He begins by emphasizing the importance of the geographical milieu, the physical and economic setting in which black Africans live. It is important, Senghor argues, to understand that the black soul, or the psychology of the Negro-African, has been formed under the influence of a tropical climate and in an agricultural and pastoral milieu. To those who may object to this seemingly Marxist approach, he replies that even the Jesuits have accepted the positive contributions of Marx, particularly since the discovery of Marx's early manuscripts, which emphasize his humanist goals.

African society rests on the family, an extended group made up of all the descendants, living and dead, of a common ancestor. This group may consider an animal or a tree as one of its members, an illustration of the fact that the African does not consider himself qualitatively different from these other forms of life. This is the meaning of the totemism that European observers have misunderstood and labeled evidence of primitive thinking. The head of the family, its oldest living member, provides a link between the living and dead members of the family. The family head also serves as mediator among the living, as priest, judge, and administrator. Yet never is he free to act in an arbitrary manner. The family is a democratic community in which all decisions are made by a council of elders, which meets to discuss important matters and to consider the wishes of the ancestors. A high value is placed on hearing all views and reaching a consensus acceptable to everyone.

The family is not the only group to which an individual belongs. He is a member of an age group, whose members are educated together when they are young and remain together for mutual help as they grow older. He may also take part in a craft group or in a male society, just as his sister may be in a women's society. Throughout his life, then, the African has membership in a number of different groups and, through them, a definite place in his world.

The importance of the group to the individual, as well as the African's relationship to the natural world, is reflected in the fact that African society has no provision for the individual ownership of land. Instead it has a system of ownership best called family ownership, which exists as a right to the use of land. The founder of the family gains this right by making an agreement with the spirit of a particular place. This spirit retains what might be likened to the right of eminent domain. The family must remain on good terms with this spirit if the land is to prove fruitful and productive. It is the duty of the family head to see to it that these good relations prevail. Hence the obligation of Diogoye Senghor, for example, to sacrifice cattle to the family ancestor to ensure the good fortune of all Senghors. If the land is not productive or the family does not prosper, the family may decide that the head is not doing this job well and must be replaced. The head is also responsible for allotting parcels of land to individual family members for their use. The individual works the land and has a right to what it bears. Relying here on information provided by Maurice Delafosse, Senghor points out that in Negro-African society only work conveys the right of individual ownership. There is private ownership in a harvest, or in a wooden bowl made by its owner, but never in the land itself.

In these ways, collective organizations enfold the individual in Africa. Yet he is not crushed. What the African knows, Senghor points out, is that the realization of human personality lies less in the search for singularity than in the development of his potential through participation in a community. In a collective setting, Senghor adds, in terms reminiscent of Marx, even work itself is not alienated. In black Africa, working the land "permits the accord of man and the universe . . . [man] is liberated by work."[12] Such is the world of Negritude.

Senghor's idyllic picture of Africa contrasts sharply with his image of the West. The European sensibility, with its dependence on analytical reasoning and its manipulative approach to the material world, has created a society that is damaging to man. As Senghor sees it, the European has analyzed and sought to master the physical world. By focusing all his energies on this task, he has achieved a remarkable scientific technology and enhanced his physical well-being. But there has been a great cost. His conception of what is real and important has directed his energy away from seeking to understand the ultimate reality that binds the world together. Instead of trying to understand and live in harmony with nature, he has ruthlessly bent nature to serve his immediate needs. Similarly, he has sought to escape human community rather than to create it, because he sees community participation as a possible limit on his individual freedom, rather than as a necessity for his personal fulfillment. For the European, freedom is the right to be left alone. He therefore sets up barriers to defend himself from the claims of others. He sharpens conflicts rather than trying to harmonize individual views to maintain the group. The price of this European freedom is solitude and isolation. The European's hard-won freedom impoverishes him by preventing the personal growth that is made possible only by close relationships with other people and membership in a community. It limits his opportunity to develop his emotional, spiritual, and artistic capacities. For illustration of these differences between European and African, Senghor turns to art. In Europe, it is the unique piece that is admired, not the beautiful or profound one that may, or may not, be like other pieces. The European believes that the individual becomes an individual only by asserting his uniqueness. The African, in contrast, believes that what is most profoundly human about him is what he shares with others. He does not put up his guard against his fellows, but participates with them in a common effort to realize their total human potential.

It is important to remember that in his discussion of the characteristics of African and European societies Senghor is seeking a foil to set off the virtues of Africa. He emphasizes only what divides. As he does so, he must operate at such a level of abstraction that it is hard to recall that a laborious study of concrete material preceded his arrival at these idealized models. It is also important to keep in mind that Senghor speaks from the perspective of the colonized African. There is no more vivid example of depersonalization and disregard for anything other than a man's economic value than Africa's experience of slavery, racial discrimination, and economic and political domination. In the back of his mind Senghor always remembers, in the words of his own poem, that Western guns destroyed African empires, Western axes cut down African forests, and Western intellectuals tried to wipe out African barbarism, preaching that their civilization and Civilization as such were identical.

By the time he had completed his description of the black African sensibility and society, Senghor had developed abstract models of two types of society. On one side he places the black African, who has used all his senses, intuitive reason, and empathy to understand the world and to create communities that nurture the development of human personality. The African values the emotional and spiritual aspects of life that bind him to the community, and seeks through poetry and art to enhance them. On the other side he places the white European, who searches restlessly for material power and individual autonomy. The European seeks to develop his individual distinctiveness, and to escape from community and any obligation it might impose on him. His society is bound together only by formal law, regulation, and force, and has become a society in which each person jostles the other in his struggle for a private material success. The Europeans have created a civilization of great technical and material power, but it has been bought at the price of an emotional and spiritual impoverishment. They have also, in their arrogance, begun to threaten the very nature and survival of life.

On the white European side, then, Senghor places rationalism on both the epistemologic and social level, materialism, and egoistic individualism. On the black African side, he places intuitive reason, empathy, and a concern for the whole, for spiritual values and the creation of a nourishing community. These sets of qualities cluster in a familiar way, a way easily recognized by the reader of European sociologists ranging from Marx to Tönnies, Durkheim, and Weber. The European sociologists, however, were not contrasting black and white. They were interested in differences between preindustrial and industrial societies or, in Marx's case, capitalism and the world of communism. Marx, for example, called capitalist many of those developments Senghor called typically European. Marx identified the tendency to treat people as things and to reduce human relationships to those of cash value as characteristic of capitalism. He described one class, the bourgeoisie, as motivated only by a rapacious desire for material riches. When Marx described, very briefly, the society he believed would exist after the revolution, he described a society in which a man would be free to develop his many-sided personality, no longer tied to a single stifling occupation, a society in which, as in Senghor's Africa, men could enjoy all aspects of life in cooperation with one another.

Max Weber, writing at the turn of the century, also saw Europe as a society characterized increasingly by rationalization and intellectualization, and, above all, by what he regretfully called the disenchantment of the world. Like Senghor, he felt the human pain and loss suffered in the new society and feared its future consequences: "Not summer's bloom lies ahead of us, but rather a polar night of icy darkness." Weber's view of Europe's future, articulated in the early 1900s, had much in common with Senghor's view of Europe's present in the 1950s. Weber foresaw a world in which the human heart would be imprisoned in an iron cage; Senghor wrote of a New York in which life had become rusted like steel and hard cash bought artificial hearts.[13]

Emile Durkheim expressed himself less poetically than Weber, but was no less conscious of an enormous change in the organization in European society. He, too, believed that the new industrial society would be qualitatively different from the preindustrial society of the past. He argued that the division of labor that made industrialization possible destroyed the shared experience that had been the foundation of earlier forms of community. Specializations and fragmentation were the inevitable consequences of the more efficient workplace. Another European sociologist, Ferdinand Tönnies, also tried to capture the essential differences between preindustrial and industrial society. Like Senghor, he developed two models as polar opposites. He called *Gemeinschaft* a society in which people satisfied their economic, social, and emotional needs in a single community bound together by emotional and family ties. He contrasted it with *Gesellschaft*, a society in which individuals joined a variety of specialized groups, each of which was designed to serve specific, limited interests. In the latter men are bound together not by emotional or moral ties but by rational calculations of self-interest.[14]

The similarities between these observations and those of Senghor are startling. The great difference, of course, is that Marx, Weber, Durkheim, and Tönnies all thought that they were describing different stages in the development of a single culture, while Senghor thought he had identified essential differences between two distinctive cultures. Senghor traced the distinctively Western outlook back in time, back past the beginnings of industrialization to Rome. For him, one set of qualities had always characterized the white European, even before the industrial period. The other set was basic to a totally different culture, that of Negritude.

These parallels suggest several conclusions. First of all, they are a reminder of Senghor's special perspective. He looked at industrial France as an outsider from a preindustrial society. From his point of view, the two, French and industrial, were inextricably intertwined just as capitalism and industrialization had been for Marx. Neither Senghor nor Marx wished to consider that the benefits of industrialization they sought might carry with them the social consequences they deplored. Senghor also viewed a rich and economically powerful society from the standpoint of a poor one, one it had colonized, exploited, and mistreated. This special perspective predisposed him to contrast African and French in ways that confused what was distinctively African with what seems to characterize many preindustrial societies. The thinking of many non-Western nationalists, the Russian Slavophiles of the nineteenth century, for example, or Gandhi in the early twentieth, also fits into this pattern. Fortunately for the simplicity of his ideas about Africa's future, Senghor did not see this possible flaw in his analysis. He did not even consider that the spirit of European culture and of industrial civilization might be one and the same, or at least have much overlap. Therefore he was able to argue that Africa could preserve and develop the characteristics of Negritude even as it moved forward to industrialize.

If Senghor looked at France from the perspective of an outsider, he also looked at Europe with the eye of the insider schooled in the French intellectual tradition. His criticisms of Europe for excessive materialism, individualism, and a tendency to carry rationality to a life-denying extreme found many echoes in a long tradition of Western self-criticism. Senghor had discovered this vein in the poetry of Rimbaud and Baudelaire, who questioned whether reason could ever lead to understanding. He had found it in the novels of Barrès, who contrasted the rich realities of blood, soil, and tradition with the lifeless abstractions of Parisian intellectuals who mistook the arguments of reason for the voice of truth. And he had found it even in the movies of revolt against industrial conformism, ranging from René Clair's *A Nous la Liberté* to Charlie Chaplin's portrayals of the trials and tribulations of the little tramp crushed by an impersonal world. He had found it again among his French contemporaries of the interwar period, who attacked French materialism and the dehumanization and conformity of modern industrial life, in a particularly congenial form among such Catholic thinkers as Paul Claudel, Jacques Maritain, and Emmanuel Mounier with his theory of personalism and sensitivity to the spiritual poverty of French life, and in a far less congenial form among fascist supporters of the Vichy government. And finally, in his reading of the remarkable Jesuit philosopher Teilhard de Chardin, Senghor had found the promise that the world was evolving toward a point where man would be restored in his totality and love would harmonize all human differences. The positive goals of these Catholic thinkers and their determination to find ways to restore the primacy of the human personality and community fit well with Senghor's vision of the values to be found in African societies.

It is worth noting that Senghor was always selective in what he chose to attack in the West. He never attacked Christianity. He might well have extended his contrasts of sensibility and society to include a comparison of animist and Christian belief. The Christian Bible's statement that in the beginning God gave man dominion over all the earth and the power and right to name all living creatures would have fit perfectly with Senghor's general argument that European culture from its beginnings encouraged man to seek mastery of nature. Yet Senghor did not choose this example to support his point of view. In his youth he had been a devout believer, and although as a young man he had briefly doubted his faith, he had long since returned to it. He continued to find much in contemporary Catholicism of enduring value, and he appreciated the encouragement given him by Mounier and the group of Catholic thinkers who had created the review *Esprit*. In Teilhard de Chardin, he found a sophisticated philosophy that supported and influenced his ideas about Negritude and its future. When Senghor criticized the West, he was always influenced by his own purposes and sensibility.

By taking advantage of Western self-criticism, Senghor found a way to unite his double perspective, his view from within French culture and his view from without. This explains the peculiar triumph he felt whenever he could point out that many Europeans had come to think as he did about the shortcomings of their own culture, that the Catholic left was attacking excessive rationalism and materialism, that European artists and musicians were learning from black artists, or that modernist poets were seeking to emulate techniques that black poets had discovered long ago. He reported triumphantly:

> We now find the European Whites themselves—artists, philosophers, even scientists—going to the school of participant reason. We are witnessing a true revolution in European epistemology . . . The new method and hence the new theory of knowledge arose out of the latest scientific discoveries: relativity, wave mechanics, quantum mechanics, non-Euclidian geometrics. And out of new philosophical theories: phenomenology, existentialism, Teilhardism. It was a response to the need to outgrow the scientific positivism of the nineteenth century and even dialectical materialism . . . Nowadays . . . we find discontinuity and indeterminism at the bottom of every-thing, of the mind as well as the real.[15]

The deep satisfaction Senghor took in Europeans' rejection of old-fashioned positivism reflects his continuous need to find authoritative support for the wisdom of what he had identified as the Negro-African approach. His education had made him too much a part of the European intellectual tradition to reject it whole. He needed to remain within it even as he attacked it. When he could find European support for his African point of view, the focus of his double perspective was sharp.

Because of Senghor's thorough knowledge of Western thought and the ease with which he participated in the intellectual debates of his day, it would be possible to identify European sources for his every idea, to find, as some have done, curious parallels to Fascism and the social criticism of the 1930s, debts to Sartre and particularly to the *Esprit* group and the Catholic philosophers Mounier and Maritain, borrowings from ethnographers and poets—in short, to show that Senghor's every thought was unoriginal and derived from European sources. Up to a point this would be an interesting exercise, as much for his similarity to thinkers he did not read as for borrowings from those he did. It would show clearly that Senghor was a man of his time and place. But as Sir Isaiah Berlin has said, ideas do not beget ideas as butterflies beget butterflies; ideas grow, take shape, and gain importance in response to the lives and needs of real people. What is important about Senghor's thinking about Negritude is not that it was derivative in its particulars—one can say the same thing of the work of all influential thinkers, Marx being a prime example—but that Senghor put common ideas together in a new way and marked them with his own stamp. What is important to understand is not that he borrowed, but why he chose to borrow what he did. Even more important is to understand why it was that the particular pattern of ideas he created carried with it the power to influence so many others.

It is evident that Senghor opened himself most fully only to those Western ideas that suited his purposes. Whether it was an ethnographer whose work provided information about the uniqueness and achievements of African civilization, a poet or novelist who proclaimed the importance of intuition and an emotional grasp of reality, or a contemporary religious thinker, scientist, or social critic who saw in European development distortion that needed correction, all those whose work influenced Senghor did so in large part because their ideas suited his purpose. They aided him in his search for an identity of which he could be proud, the search for the holy grail of Negritude. They helped him to crystallize his ideas about ways in which Africa and Europe differed from one another. They encouraged him to see

where European culture was flawed and incomplete, and fed his conviction that Africa possessed something of value. There was system in
what Senghor chose to borrow. Often it was a matter of the conver-
gence of ideas, of European self-criticism with his own observation.
He took from Europe what Césaire had called the "miraculous arms"
of its own rich tradition, and used them to fight against Europe's
assumption of total supremacy.

During the same time that Senghor was developing his understanding of the distinctive qualities of African culture, he was well
aware that Africa itself was changing. He knew from his own experience that it was no longer possible to speak of a pure African culture,
if indeed that had ever been possible. African culture had long been
a mixture of Berber and black African, of Islam, Christian, and animist,
of French and African, and now, increasingly, of the traditional peasant
and the urban industrial worker.[16] In 1937 at Dakar, he had spoken
of his own reality and that of his country as Afro-French. Indeed he
had stated then that for the African there was no question of whether
or not to assimilate. That question was ill-conceived. It was rather a
question of whether or not the African would assimilate French influence actively, as an animal transforms the food it eats into the tissue
that it needs to grow in its own form, or whether the African would
allow himself to be passively absorbed into French culture.[17] Any
creative civilization, he argued, had to take nourishment from without.
No culture or race that tried to exclude all others could flourish.
Synthesis, or as Senghor called it *métissage* (interweaving or cross
breeding), not separation, was the path to individual and social development.

This view was strengthened by Senghor's experience of the war.
The harsh lesson of the Nazis was that racial pride and cultural exclusion led to horror and death. The lesson of the Greeks, freshly understood during long nights of captivity, was that it is the cross-fertiliza-
tion of peoples and cultures that provides the most fertile soil for the
flowering of a people and its culture. Senghor suggested a strategy
for African society that closely matched his personal experience.
Inward looking was at least as important as outward looking in Senghor's discovery of the possibilities of métissage. He had recognized,
mastered, and become proud of himself as a blend of numerous influences: his mixed ethnic background, Peul and Serer, his mixed religious heritage, Catholic and animist, and his mixed culture, African
and French. From these diverse elements, he had managed to create

an integrated personality. African society must now do the same. The social goal was no more nor less than the personal goal multiplied by many individuals.

As he developed this idea, Senghor grew in his conviction that the assimilation of certain aspects of European culture into the African way of life was a necessity for Africa's further progress. This in no way challenged his more basic notion of the importance and value of black African culture. Indeed, in order to carry through an active and creative assimilation, he argued, Africans would have to understand their past clearly and investigate its significance. "The old Africa is dying," Senghor wrote. "Customs and languages are being transformed with incredible rapidity." It was important to record it before it is too late. But admiration and respect for the past, he was sure, must not tempt Africans to try to withdraw from participation in the modern world: It was not a question of resuscitating the past, or of living in the Negro-African museum, but rather of making sure that in transforming the African milieu Africans remained true to the best tradition of the past.[18]

In spite of the evident problems of such a solution, particularly in light of the basic opposition Senghor saw between the principles of African and European societies, Senghor never seemed to doubt that some kind of reconciliation or equilibrium could be found. The African's ability to create an equilibrium of man and nature was one of his traditional strengths. Senghor's own conviction that reconciliation must be possible was strengthened by his belief in the God of Catholicism, the producer of human community and the guarantor of harmony and peace in the universe. It also reflected his own temperament. Senghor had long seen rupture as defeat, harmony and cooperation as victory. But perhaps most important of all, on the personal level, he had no choice. He was the two, African and French, traditional and modern. His poetry had made it clear: he could not choose.

These superficially contradictory ideas, that Negritude must be preserved and developed, and that the only way for a civilization to grow and develop is by taking nourishment from other peoples and cultures, found their own reconciliation in an all-encompassing theory that Senghor began to articulate in the late 1950s. He spelled out his theory in some detail in a long article on the thought of the Jesuit scientist and philosopher Pierre Teilhard de Chardin. Drawing on the work of Teilhard, and through him on Hegel, Senghor argued that the assimilation of certain aspects of European culture into the African way of life is but one example of a general process that must take place on a worldwide scale if there is to be human progress. In the future, there must and will be a moment of epiphany, a world-historical moment, in which all cultures will present themselves at a "rendez-vous de donner et recevoir," a grand moment of give-and-take in which each culture selects what it most needs from the others, and in which each is thereby enriched. Some of man's achievements will be discarded as no longer useful or as harmful, while others will become strengthened and more widespread. Just as Africa will benefit from an infusion of the inquisitive spirit and a higher development of analytical reason, so Western Europe, now locked in a dehumanizing worship of machines and material wealth, will benefit from the African contribution of its greater emotional and spiritual development, vitality, and understanding of the interconnectedness of all life in the universe. In the past, Senghor continues, each people developed in isolation and cultivated only certain human qualities while neglecting others. Therefore each realized only a part of its total human potential. The range of human possibility, now developed to a high degree but isolated in separate civilizations, must be merged to form one, panhuman civilization. Then man will be able to develop his personality free from all limiting contingencies. He will inherit the wealth of all previous history, and the result will be a qualitative leap forward for mankind as a whole. This is the desirable goal for the twentieth century, and one made possible for the first time by national development, technological advances such as those in communications, and the spread of international contacts.[19] This is Senghor's dream, what he, like Teilhard, calls the creation of the civilization of the universal.

At this point in Senghor's thinking, Negritude reappears as an important idea: Negritude is Africa's contribution to the coming universal civilization. The rendezvous of giving and taking must be a meeting of equals, and this is possible only if each culture has something to contribute. Therefore it becomes the duty of Africans to study and cultivate what is uniquely theirs, not for their own benefit and self-respect alone, but to perfect their contribution to the universal civilization, "so that we answer 'present' at the rebirth of the world / as the leavening needed for the white flour. / For who would teach rhythm to the dead world of machines and cannons? / Who would loose a cry of joy to wake the dead and the orphans to see the dawn?"[20] Hence the emphasis in the pages of *La Condition Humaine* on literature, philosophy, and the writings of West Indian and black Americans as well as Africans. The spiritual wisdom and vitality of Negritude will prove of far greater importance to Europe than Africa's raw materials ever were. Africans will benefit equally from Western Europe's contribution. They will utilize European technology and scientific achievements. They need the European leavening—Senghor uses the same word to indicate the effect of each upon the other—of energy and inventiveness. The intuitive reason of Africans and the discursive reason of Europeans are not exclusive but complementary. Together they make up a "reason which is a more complete reason, which alone will permit us an integral grasp of the world."[21]

Senghor expressed this idea both in essays and in poetry. It is set out clearly in a poem inspired by his visit to New York as a delegate to the United Nations General Assembly in 1950:

New York! At first your beauty confused me and your great long-
    legged golden girls
I was so timid at first under your blue metallic eyes, your frosty smile
So timid
. . . . .
No child's laughter blossoms, his hand in my fresh hand
No mother's breast. Legs in nylon. Legs and breasts with no sweat
    and no smell.
No tender word for mouths are lipless. Hard cash buys artificial
    hearts.
. . . . .
New York! I say to New York, let the black blood flow into your
    blood
Cleaning the rust from your steel articulations, like an oil of life
Giving your bridges the curve of the hills, the liana's suppleness.
See, the ancient times come again, unity is rediscovered the
    reconciliation of the Lion the Bull and the Tree
The idea is linked to the act the ear to the heart the sign to the
    sense.[22]

The idea that Africa would bring new life to Europe, and Europe make possible the development of Africa, became increasingly important to Senghor as he devoted himself to politics.

In 1959, in an important policy statement to young political activists in Senegal, Senghor defined his political goal as the creation of an African socialism.[23] African socialism was to be the political and social analog of métissage. The ideal society was to be African, in that it would remain true to the culture of Negritude, and socialist, in that it was to borrow the most advanced technological and organizational forms from the West. It was up to the African to choose the most useful discoveries of Western technology and culture, adapt them, and introduce them into a Senegalese context. That Western forms might be incompatible with African ones, or that the import of Western technology and forms of organization might set in motion changes that would shake African society to its foundations, does not seem to have troubled Senghor at this time. But since the society of Senghor's Negritude shared many of the characteristics Western scholars have identified as those of a preindustrial society, an outsider could not but observe that such a solution would not be easy, and that at the very least it would require careful planning to counter those trends hostile to the preservation and development of the culture of Negritude.

Senghor was careful to distinguish his African socialism from Marxist socialism as preached in Europe. Like most French intellectuals who came of age in the thirties, Senghor could not be indifferent to Marx. He had rejected many of Marx's most basic ideas when he first read him in the thirties. At that time Senghor was far more interested in poetry, African ethnography, and personal issues than in economics or social theory. Certainly the formulation of Negritude owed nothing to Marx. Indeed, Senghor castigated as deserters of Negritude those Africans who espoused Marxism. Senghor objected to Marx because of his determinism and contempt for spiritual values. He saw him as the example of Western thought at its most sterile extreme: "discursive reason pushed to its farthest limits . . . lost . . . in a materialism without warmth, in blind determinism."[24] If Marx was right and the march of history inevitable and irreversible, there could be no purpose in human life or value in any human ideal. The very notion of purpose would be meaningless. Senghor rejected this possibility and the reasoning on which it was based.

Nevertheless, when Senghor read Marx's early manuscripts after the war, in the deputies' library of the Palais Bourbon, he admired them very much, so much so that he wrote an article arguing that Marx was a humanist and attacking those who equated Marxism with Soviet communism. Elsewhere, defining the humanist as one who wishes to make man more truly human, "by making him participate in everything that can enrich him in nature and history," and relying heavily on Marx's "The German Ideology," Senghor argued that Marx was first and foremost a humanist who sought the enrichment of man and his liberation from material necessity. To support this interpretation, he quoted a passage from *Das Kapital:* "What from the very first distinguishes the most incompetent architect from the best of the bees, is that the architect has built a cell in his head before he constructs it in wax. The labor process ends in the creation of something which, when the process began, already existed in an ideal form . . . he realizes his own purpose." Senghor judged this passage one of the most profound and beautiful Marx ever wrote, because it presented man as an essentially purposive being, acting with consciousness and liberty.[25]

Senghor also admired Marx as a sociologist who had illuminated the ways in which concrete economic and historical circumstances shape and limit man's being. Marx had, he thought, correctly analyzed the dynamic of nineteenth-century European capitalism, but in the twentieth century the European working classes were no longer the most oppressed and exploited group in society. Exploitation of class by class had been replaced by a global system in which nation oppressed nation. The "have-not" nations were the twentieth-century proletarians.[26] Thus Senghor rejected much of the usual Marxist tradition and certainly socialism as practiced in the Soviet Union. He rejected Soviet communism as a model because the Soviets had forgotten that human dignity and freedom were the goals of socialism. He also rejected the inevitability of class struggle in all societies, steadily maintaining that classes in the Marxist sense had never existed in West Africa and never would in Senegal. Rather, he placed his African socialism in a context larger than that of Marx alone, one that included the socialisms of Fourier, Proudhon, and Saint-Simon, and that retained its ethical and voluntarist emphasis.

For Senghor, African socialism is both a goal and a process. As a goal, it is a society in which the human personality can reach its potential, a world, described briefly by Marx, in "The German Ideology," where the individual is able "to do one thing today and another tomorrow, to hunt in the morning, fish in the afternoon, rear cattle in the evening, criticize after dinner, just as I have a mind." He will no longer be constrained by economic necessity but will be free to develop his many-sided potential. Senghor found the same goal in the *plus-être* of Teilhard de Chardin, a situation not just of well-being but of greater being, the realization of all the potential of the human mind and heart.[27]

As a process, African socialism combines the best and most advanced of Western ideas, those of socialism, with the best of African tradition.

It is socialist in technique in that it utilizes advanced Western technology and scientific methods of planning. It is African in spirit in that these techniques will be adapted to African realities and subordinated to African goals. Modern socialism will prove compatible with African tradition because Africa is a traditionally communitarian society and in Africa, Senghor cannot resist adding for the benefit of his European audience, "we had already achieved socialism before the coming of the European."[28] For Senghor, African socialism is both means and end, both goal and technique.

Senghor had now the outlines for a political ideology, useful both to rally people to his support and as a general guide for his own decisions. He had a theory of the African's human nature, a preliminary analysis of what was wrong with contemporary African society, namely the denial of the value of their own culture by Africans eager to imitate the French, and a visionary goal, African socialism. Problems confronting Senegal in 1959 might be attributed to the stifling of Negritude by French domination. The goal for the future was an African socialism that would develop and build on the culture of Negritude using the most advanced technology and "socialist" techniques of Europe. The plan of action was not yet clearly articulated, but gradually even the cautious Senghor had begun to talk of the need for autonomy, a political arena in which Africans could develop the culture of Negritude. In the future Senegal would continue to borrow from France and other European countries what was assumed to be culture-free technology, but would put it to use to serve African purposes. By this technique of using the best that each society had to offer, Senegal would be able to create a setting in which Africans could develop their full human potential. The concepts of Negritude and African socialism thus became guides and justifications for future political action. In 1956 Senghor made this connection clear: "We wish then to liberate ourselves politically precisely in order to express our Negritude, that is to say, our real black values."[29]

The origins of Senghor's political ideology lay in his personal experience, first articulated in poetry written for himself and the very small black community in Paris, but with an eye also on the French who sought to deny him equality and dignity. It was a fact of history that other educated Africans were subject to the same social and psychological forces that shaped his life. Their number was significantly greater in the generation that followed him than in his own. Young men in Senegal had begun to develop their own ideas during and after the war. They found that Senghor's poetry and essays answered many of their questions, clarified their confusions, and provided a new vision of themselves and their future. Senghor's skill with words and symbols enabled him to express this vision with power and appeal.

What had begun for Senghor as a complicated personal and intellectual quest was transformed into a matter of great public interest. He and his ideas were thrust forward to provide leadership for others. The words Negritude and African socialism became shorthand ways to refer to complicated ideas that had grown out of much thinking and studying but which Senghor no longer took the time to justify or explain. They resonated deeply with African desires for independence, dignity, and a prosperous future. Negritude and African socialism now served as the cornerstones of a political ideology, a set of ideas that influenced large numbers of people to identify themselves in a new way, to look at the world from a slightly different point of view, and soon, to want to act on their own to change their world. Out of Senghor's rejection of the place prepared for him by the French and his confused search for an alternative had been born a political ideology that helped propel Senegal onward to independence.

11

Toward Independence

Senghor matured rapidly as a politician in the 1950s. During the early and middle parts of the decade, he continued to believe that the key to political solutions for Africa had to be found in Paris despite the fact that black West Africa was certainly not at the top of the French agenda. On the contrary, the French were preoccupied with a series of other challenges to the Fourth Republic, challenges the republic failed to meet effectively. A series of weak governments proved incapable of any decisive action. Senghor's frustration with inaction in West Africa, inaction he blamed on Lamine Guèye, was more properly attributable to the French system as such. During Senghor's first term as deputy, from December 1946 until the summer of 1951, eleven ministries served an average of less than six months each. In the second session, between August 1951 and January 1956, the record was no better. The result was a vacuum of leadership not only in colonial policy but in all policy. Describing this era, de Gaulle wrote, "the multiplicity of viewpoints which is peculiar to our people . . . would once again reduce the State to being no more than a stage for the confrontation of amorphous ideologies, sectional rivalries, semblances of domestic and external action without continuity or consequence." De Gaulle had little patience with the bickering of political parties when important issues were at stake. As it was, the government could not and did not act forcefully to meet any of its challenges. Its failure to resolve internal problems was matched by its even greater ineffectiveness overseas. Senghor observed that the Fourth Republic seemed to be "always behind by one reform."[1] The French refer to this period as one of immobility.

For Senghor it proved to be a period of enormous frustration. Having established a secure electoral base in Senegal and found capable men whom he could trust to back him, he was ready to work within the French system to get what he wanted: greater autonomy and improved economic conditions for the people of West Africa. His most ringing speeches, both in the French National Assembly and in the countryside of Senegal, called for social and economic betterment, and invariably declared his unshakable loyalty to France.

The Paris government did provide some financial support during this period. The Investment Fund for the Economic and Social Development of the Overseas Territories (FIDES), established in 1946, provided some capital for development projects. It is estimated that, between 1946 and 1958, 70 percent of the public investment in French Africa was contributed from the metropolitan budget, with the rest originating in the individual territories themselves. FIDES funds supported housing in Dakar as well as roads and bridges. A second fund, designated for rural development, financed a large number of small projects. Too often, however, projects were lavish, poorly planned, and of doubtful economic value. As is customary with aid from rich countries to poor ones, there were strings attached: the funds were required to be spent to buy French products, and many projects seemed designed to serve particular French business interests rather than those of the poorest segment of the African population. One result of this relationship was that French and West African economic integration increased significantly during the late 1940s and the 1950s.[2]

There was measurable progress in education. In 1955 about 10 percent of Senegal's school-age children were in school. By 1960 the number had risen to 17 percent. Higher education was made available in Dakar at the newly founded Institute of Higher Studies, later to become the University of Dakar, although of some seven hundred students enrolled at the University, more than 50 percent were of French origin.[3]

Nonetheless the African deputies who sat in the National Assembly accomplished little in comparison to what they wanted and their constituencies expected. By the early 1950s they realized that neither the French public nor the French elected deputies knew or cared very much about black Africa. The great majority of Frenchmen thought of what they now called the Overseas Territories, if they thought of them at all, as a reflection of French greatness. They had no interest in how the peoples of these territories might view themselves or France. As a result, the African deputies saw, they would get little support either from the French deputies or from French public opinion. They would have to develop political ties to the majority coalition in the Assembly and use political pressure to influence exec- utive decisions—in short, to play the French political game along with other special-interest groups.[4] Most key decisions would be made, as they always had been made, by the bureaucracy at the rue Oudinot in Paris. There the strings continued to be pulled by French companies with overseas interests. Although the Ministry for the Colonies had been renamed the Ministry for Overseas France, the same men sat at the same desks and wrote their discussion notes on paper left over from the old days, paper that carried the letterhead of the Ministry for the Colonies.[5]

It was at this point that the true implications of Senghor's failure to join Houphouet-Boigny at the Bamako Congress in the autumn of 1946 began to be clear. Not only had the Africans failed to create a territory-wide political party that might put its combined pressure on the French government, but the split begun there between Houphouet and Senghor had widened and grown. So long as Houphouet's party, the Rassemblement Démocratique Africain (RDA), remained closely tied to the French communists, Senghor felt that alliance was impos- sible. In November 1950, after the RDA broke with the communists, and again in 1951, Senghor and Houphouet held discussions to see if they could form a coordinating group in the French National Assembly, but the talks led nowhere. Personal rivalries, pressures from subordinates, and the manipulations of the French combined to keep the two men apart. French parties vied for their support, and the two appeared increasingly to be rivals and opponents rather than fellow workers for a common cause.

Failing to accomplish unity by means of a personal alliance, Senghor and Houphouet each tried to establish his own interterritorial party. In this, Senghor was even less successful than Houphouet, as local leaders proved jealous of their independence and different situations required different approaches. The best Senghor could achieve was a loose alliance of some of the African deputies in a parliamentary grouping called the Independents from Overseas (IOM), while Hou- phouet's allies developed branches of the RDA throughout the West African territories.

The National Assembly's ministerial governments in the meantime, ever in search of adherents to their fragile and ephemeral majorities, rewarded individual deputies for their support and exacerbated the divisions among the Africans. Senghor, for example, was a member of the French delegations to the consultative assembly of the Council of Europe in Strasbourg and to UNESCO. In October 1950 the French nominated him for the United Nations Trusteeship Council. Africans were particularly useful in explaining French colonial policy to international organizations. Keeping ever in mind his long-term plans for Africa, Senghor hoped that French participation in international groupings might help create attitudes conducive to a more flexible approach to its overseas territories. If the French government could accept limits on its power for the sake of European cooperation, he reasoned, perhaps it would also accept a federated arrangement with Africa. He began to envision a grand confederation of Europe and Africa, "Eurafrique," which would unite a federated West Africa with a federated Europe, an arrangement that would, he maintained, unite complementary cultures and economies to the advantage of all concerned.[6] Senghor now used political words, such as federation, confederation, and Eurafrique, to set forth in a political context what was for him a simple and familiar idea, that of integration and the creation of unity out of diversity, or métissage.

Despite all their talk and political maneuverings in Paris, the African deputies had virtually no effect on French policy. What broke the logjam of immobility was not the work of the well-mannered African deputies but events overseas. After the bombing of Haiphong harbor in 1946, the war in Indochina became a bleeding sore. Then there were "the events" in Madagascar, in which many people were killed. In January 1952, anti-French riots broke out in Tunisia. That March there were similar riots in Tangiers. The sultan of Morocco was forced into exile. In May 1954, French forces in Indochina surrendered to the Vietnamese nationalists at Dien Bien Phu. The next day, discussions began in Geneva that led to the ill-fated division of Indochina into two nations, North and South Vietnam. Ho Chi Minh now ruled an independent north. In November of that same year, insurrection in Algeria finally transformed the "colonial question" into a top priority for thousands of Frenchmen. Algeria, unlike the other overseas territories, was home to over one million French settlers, the so-called *pieds noirs,* or those with black feet, who had put down their roots in that North African soil. The beginning of the Algerian War opened French ears so that they were at last able to hear the serious and insistent voices clamoring from overseas for a new relationship with France.

Senghor found himself in the thick of France's last-ditch attempts to salvage its special ties with North Africa. Appointed in 1955 as a secretary of state in the second cabinet of Edgar Faure, he was among those asked to study the problem of the overseas territories. Once again he found himself in the familiar role of go-between, the person who understood both the French and their adversaries and who sought to find grounds for reconciliation. He participated discreetly in the talks with the Tunisian leader Habib Bourguiba that led to internal autonomy for Tunisia and allowed Bourguiba's return to his country from exile. Parallel discussions with Moroccan leaders led to the return to Morocco of the exiled sultan and the proclamation of Moroccan independence. Senghor's most important contribution to these agreements may well have been his private advice to the prime minister, Edgar Faure. He cautioned Faure not to give the Tunisians the impression that the French considered internal autonomy an end in itself rather than a step toward independence. Bourguiba was a moderate nationalist, Senghor explained, "a man of the West, a mixed cultural product of the Mediterranean," in short, a man like himself, with whom the French could do business, and like himself, Senghor may have been thinking, determined on independence. Senghor urged Faure to work with the present, moderate, nationalist leaders, and to develop an approach toward Morocco and Tunisia that would represent a first step toward a new federal framework.[7] Senghor now called for confederation, the creation of a vast association of separate and equal entities, some of which might be individual states, others of which might be federations, such as the federation of French West Africa.

The situation in Algeria offered no such quick solution. As Pierre Mendès-France, negotiator of the Geneva Accords that enabled the French withdrawal from Indochina and advocate of the negotiated settlements in Tunisia and Morocco, put it, in Algeria it was quite different, it was a question of "the integrity of the national territory." The departments of Algeria, he told the National Assembly in November 1954, "are a part of the French Republic. They have been French for a long time in an irrevocable way." Unlike Tunisia, Algeria was part of France. Therefore, French soldiers stationed in Algeria fought, not to keep alien peoples under French control, but for transplanted French families, French farms, and many profitable French businesses. An underlying belief that the struggle was linked to the Cold War competition between East and West added another dimension. The result was division among Frenchmen at home, as well as among the people of Algeria. Some agreed with François Mitterrand, who exhorted his fellow Frenchmen to remember that "from Flanders to the Congo, there is one law, one sole nation, one sole parliament. It is the constitution and it is our will." It seemed that with each defeat, the rhetoric of French nationalism grew more strident.[8]

This sort of rhetoric fell on fertile soil. There was great popular support for a French Algeria, largely because of the French population settled there but also for more symbolic reasons. The military, humiliated by its recent defeat in Indochina, was determined to show its mettle. Prominent men from both right and left, ranging from Gaullists such as Jacques Soustelle, who was himself from a *pied noir* family, to the Archbishop of Toulouse, to Senghor's old friends Pompidou and Delavignette, joined an organization established to fight for a French Algeria. Even Paul Rivet, an ethnologist and a former teacher of Senghor's known for his sensitivity to cultural differences, predicted dire consequences if France were to grant independence to all who asked for it. Native populations, he wrote, "would fall into disorder and anarchy and, as a result, be subjected to the dictatorship of one man or a minority. All of the history of the last fifty years provides evidence of this troubling and cruel truth. Independent, they will remain ignorant of true liberty." Additional worries continued to preoccupy the French. "The drama is not only that of Algeria; it is that of decadence . . . To abandon Algeria is to condemn France to decadence." While such men were organizing and talking, young Frenchmen were dying in Algeria and terrorists were planting bombs in cafés in Algeria and, increasingly, in Paris. Disturbing stories of the hideous torture of suspected Algerian terrorists by French soldiers and police began to filter back to Paris. The situation was growing increasingly ugly.[9]

Senghor found himself in a difficult position. He and the other African deputies knew that the Algerian war strengthened their hand. At the same time they were still hoping to be rewarded by a France grateful for their loyal support in her time of trial. They feared that if they opposed government policy in Algeria the government might retaliate by refusing to grant them concessions in West Africa. As a result of this thinking, not one of the West African deputies opposed the French government's request for emergency powers to prosecute the Algerian war. They also sided with the government when it asked for special war credits.[10] They hoped they would be rewarded with a bargain to their advantage in West Africa.

The situation for the African deputies was further complicated by pressures from their constituencies at home. After his first triumph over Lamine Guèye, Senghor had called together the Senegalese students in Paris, only to find among them bitter opposition to his parliamentary alliance with the moderate African deputies to form a group of overseas deputies, the IOM. By the time of the Algerian war, members of this younger generation were beginning to return to Senegal. They were impatient with the meager concessions granted to leaders who did not make demands but waited meekly for crumbs from the imperial table, as some of the more Marxist among them put it. Senghor realized there was nothing he could do to stop the growing radicalization of the young, both in Paris and at home. Should France fail to bend, he realized, there was danger of violence, even in Senegal. In 1954 he told the National Assembly, "French Africa is on the move under governments of immobilism . . . over the long term, this can only lead to catastrophe." In the same speech, ever the diplomat, he assured his colleagues of the goodwill of French Africa and urged them to honor their promises to support economic and political democracy in Africa.[11]

Parliamentary elections early in 1956 elected a new National Assembly, but did little to improve the government's decisiveness. In his Senegalese campaign, Senghor once again stumped the countryside, mixing the traditional with the modern to appeal to his people. Rallies often began with dances led by women of Senghor's party, the BDS, wearing the symbolic green of their party. A griot, the traditional historian and praise-sayer, would sing the virtues of the candidates before introducing them. Then Senghor, or the chief speaker, would address the crowd through a megaphone.[12] Senghor was now immensely popular. Once when he visited a village shortly after a new road had gone in, a traveling companion saw that "the peasants of the village threw themselves on their knees along the new road, touching the road with their heads and lips; then, getting up, they came to kiss Senghor's hand and touch the cloth of his suit. Senghor for them was already an idol."[13] Few Senegalese villagers could have understood fully the implications of what Senghor had to say. Nonetheless they recognized him as a master of language, a man of learning and wisdom, and a person worthy of their trust. They followed him gladly.

In the course of the 1956 electoral campaign, Senghor began to elaborate a full political doctrine, both an explanation of Senegal's situation and a plan of action. He called now for autonomy, but he did not yet use the word independence. Autonomy would grant West Africans the right to manage "our own affairs by means of sovereign local assemblies." There must be no more "blind submission to ideas imposed from Paris and above all to *ukases* from abroad." His use of the Russian word *ukas* (command) was intended to reassure his French friends that he shared their opposition to Soviet influence and to communism and was himself no radical. With such a platform, and with the great organizational strength of the BDS behind him, Senghor and his new running mate, Mamadou Dia, swept the country with a landslide victory.[14]

In West Africa as a whole, however, Senghor's allies lost ground to the adherents of Houphouet's RDA in the elections of 1956. As a result, Houphouet, not Senghor, led the largest West African party in the new National Assembly. Houphouet now became the African most favored by potential prime ministers trying to put together majority coalitions. Senghor, on the other hand, was spared the dilemma of deciding whether or not to participate in French governments that prosecuted the war in Algeria. The result of this new balance of forces was that Houphouet, not Senghor, now had the stronger voice in shaping the French response to the increasing pressures from overseas.

Teetering back and forth between resistance and concession to the Algerian nationalists, the new French government finally realized that comparable movements for autonomy elsewhere could not be ignored forever. It seemed finally to realize the wisdom of the nineteenth-century poet Lamartine, whom the overseas deputies quoted to make their point: "The dangerous liberties are the liberties that the people tear out for themselves, not the ones they are given." Some Frenchmen were beginning to share this view. The Overseas Minister, Gaston Defferre, argued that the government must "not give the impression that France will undertake reforms only when the blood begins to flow." Leaning on the advice of Houphouet, Defferre proposed to the National Assembly the *loi cadre,* or outline law, to establish a new political framework for West Africa. Far greater autonomy was to be offered the West African states.[15]

The loi cadre provided for the devolution of power not to the West African federation but to the individual territories. Such a development would radically change the configuration of West Africa. At

present, the governor general of the federation had executive responsibility for all eight territories and was advised by a council of elected
representatives from each of them. The federal government sat in
Dakar. Should the federation be dissolved, the relative importance of
Dakar would certainly diminish, and Houphouet's relatively prosperous Ivory Coast would no longer have to contribute to a federal
budget that disproportionately benefited the poorer territories. This
was one of Houphouet's considerations in supporting the proposed
law.

From Senghor's point of view, this new law, like all of his experience
with France, had both its light and its dark sides. It did provide
considerably more power to the local territorial assemblies. It would
also create a single electorate throughout French Africa and, most
important, local executives. By not providing for an executive at the
federal level, however, it would mean the end of the federation and
the Balkanization of Africa into small, weak states.

Senghor naturally wanted to maintain the importance of Dakar, and
he also suspected the motivation of the French. Implementation of
the loi cadre would give Africans the autonomy for which they cla-
mored and, at the same time, divide them from one another. It was a
classic example of the time-honored policy of divide and rule. A strong
federation might have had real bargaining power. Small, weak individual territories would not. When Senghor put forth his objections
to the proposed law in the National Assembly, he did so to an empty
chamber, the emptiness not of boycott but of indifference. The French
deputies did not consider this question one of great importance. The
loi cadre was approved as proposed and put into effect.[16]

In the midst of these negotiations, Senghor made an important
personal decision. On one level it reflected his confidence, and on all
levels it had powerful long-term personal and symbolic implications.
Senghor's marriage to Ginette Eboué had been the perfect political
marriage, but far more important, it had satisfied his vow to make his
deeds coincide with his words. Many educated African men of his
generation married Frenchwomen, in part because they knew few
educated African or West Indian women. Senghor believed he could
not do so without compromising his position. After his marriage to
Ginette Eboué dissolved, however, he fell in love with Colette Hubert,
a Frenchwoman who had been serving as his secretary. They were
married in 1957 and had one son, whom they named Philippe-
Maguilen, Philippe "the honored one."

By the mid-1950s Senghor was fully committed to his political career. Yet this was not an all-consuming passion; he remained true to his other vocation, that of poet. From the midst of the pressures and turmoil of his public life, he would withdraw from time to time to concentrate on his poetry. From it he continued to draw energy and perspective. In 1949 he published a slender collection of lyric love poems, *Chants pour Naett* (Songs for Naett), and in 1956 a second collection, *Ethiopiques,* in which he returned with new authority to many of the themes he had treated before. He again wrote of the beloved, of Africa, and of the unbreakable bonds that tied him to his native land. He also treated the apparent conflict between a commitment to poetry and to politics, and mused over the attractions and limitations of worldly success.

The poet of *Ethiopiques* is in more control of his life than was the poet of *Chants d'ombre* and *Hosties noires.* He has achieved a balance that takes into account both his mixed heritage and his personal experience. He knows that he has become the man he wanted to become. Now he no longer considers a future role, but has begun to live one he has chosen for himself. He has been recognized and honored by his people. He is the master of sciences and of the word. He has the jaw of the lion and the smile of the sage. He is "the prince of north and south, the rising sun and the setting sun . . . the beat of the tom-tom and the strength of future Africa." The poet exults in his calling as the one who sings the charms of the absent one, the beloved woman, Africa. From his exile in a European world rigid with the frost of a winter night, he continues to yearn for the absent one, recalling her every detail. She is the green of spring, the gold of the savanna. Like flour, she nourishes, and like the wind, she cures. Her eyelids are of fur and rose laurel petals. It is she who will endure. The singing of her beauty and timelessness is the poet's contentment. It is in this collection and in this context that Senghor's poem "New York" appears. It too is a poem of confidence, the poet secure in the knowledge of the value of what Africa can bring to the ossified society and steel rigidities of New York: the oil of life. Africa will be the yeast to its flour, the beat of a drum, the rhythm of life. Africa will make it possible once again to unite the idea "to the act, the ear to the heart and the sign to the sense." There is no doubt any longer in the poet's mind that he and Africa have much to offer the world.[17]

A cycle of other poems in *Ethiopiques,* "Epîtres à la princesse" (Letters to the Princess), takes up the theme of the relationship of Africa and Europe, black and white, from a different point of view. The situation is no longer that of *Chants d'ombre* and *Hosties noires* when the poet felt himself condemned to struggle with a relationship that had been thrust upon him. Now it appears that it is the poet who has taken the initiative. It is he who chooses to make a relationship with a white woman, and through her with white Europe, rather than being forced to endure the white world that has intruded on Africa. These poems are dedicated to the Marquise de Betteville, the mother of Colette Hubert. Just as the black woman whose beauty Senghor sang in earlier poems fused with his image of Africa, now the white woman and her European world are treated as one. Through love for her, he can find love for those who fought his people, ruined his ancestors' shrine, and despoiled his birthplace. He can forgive those responsible for "that other exile even harder on my heart, the tearing of self from self, from the tongue of my mother, the mind of the ancestor, and the tam-tam [rhythm] of my soul."[18] Through love, a divided world can be healed. His integrity demands that he embrace his double heritage.

Senghor closes this collection with a series of songs that evoke affectionate images of Europe and Africa, the Ave Maria of Joal and the cool stones of the Portuguese fort, the voice of the ancestors and that of the loyal wet nurse. All mingle together in a warm and comforting memory of childhood. The poet makes explicit the connections and confusions of his inner landscape, identifications that both inform his poetry and create his sense of completeness. He always confuses, he writes, "childhood and Eden," as he mixes death and life, a sweet bridge unites them. The ancestors are present and alive, and they provide comfort and strength. He confuses, he continues, the present and the past.[19] It is enough to name the places, the sounds, and the colors of childhood to conjure himself into Eden and the experience of safety and wholeness.

But there is now another division to be healed, that between the calling of poet and that of politician. This is the subject of a dramatic poem for several voices that also appears in *Ethiopiques*. It takes the form of a dialogue between the Zulu warrior Chaka and persistent questioners. Chaka is tempted by white voices, much as Christ in the wilderness was tempted by the Devil. The poem has been highly criticized because the historical Chaka was a bloodthirsty warrior-tyrant, responsible for the deaths of thousands of Africans and whites in wars waged in Southern Africa in the first part of the nineteenth century, whereas Senghor's Chaka is a man who has sacrificed himself, body and spirit, for his people. Regardless of this discrepancy, or any failings of the poem as play or poetry, Chaka's meditations on the costs and value of his calling allow Senghor to treat questions that he must have had to consider as his public life consumed more and more of his energies. Other poems written for this collection exalt both roles, poet and public leader, suggesting that there is no need to choose between them and that neither exacts a great human cost. "Chaka" expresses the situation entirely differently.

Senghor's Chaka sacrifices everything to his obligation to lead his people. He first kills Nolivé, the woman he loves. A questioner, identified only as a white voice, accuses him of murdering in her his conscience, the person who might have restrained his bloodthirsty search for power. Chaka answers that he had to kill Nolivé because he feared that his love for her would make him weak and vulnerable. He must be strong. He cannot afford this soft side. The greatest evil is not, he continues, the destruction of life, as the white voice tells him. The greatest evil would be to be weak in the service of his people. Chaka accuses the white of advancing the self-serving morality of the strong. The white voice has an interest in persuading him to embrace a morality that will benefit white power. Chaka's duty is to sacrifice his personal love in order to meet the requirements of leadership and fulfill his duty to his beloved people.

The white voice now tempts Chaka with flattery, identifying him as a great poet who must develop and honor his poetic gift. That, too, Chaka has had to sacrifice. He has no time for poetry. As another great poet of revolution, the Russian Vladimir Mayakovsky, put it, the revolutionary poet must step on the throat of his own song. He must use any talent he has for the great cause of his time. He must harden himself. Poetic sensitivities are a luxury. Chaka declares that he will break the false peace of oppression to make the war of liberation. He must give himself over to killing out of love for his black people. He must become a mind, not a heart, and a man of action rather than of reflection.

The white voice finally accuses Chaka of glorying in his power; Chaka answers quietly that this power has been his Calvary. With each death, he has suffered. He has had to shatter his own dream of all men as brothers. Only death will release him from this suffering. He struggled for a long time to deny his vocation as a leader, because he felt more comfortable as a poet and feared the consequences of becoming a man of action. Finally, reluctantly, he gave in to the call of duty. He knows that only in death can he again find union within himself and with his loved one. Then he can become what he had always wanted to be, "the one who accompanies . . . the baton that beats the drum," the drum that "brings forth the light of the new world."[20]

By the time he wrote this poem, Senghor had begun to understand the price demanded by the life of action. He had experienced the pressure on the politician to be hard, to ignore the promptings of his heart in order to listen to the dictates of his mind. He also knew the temptations of power. Whether it be painful breaks with friends forced on him by a vision of what his people needed, as in his split with Lamine Guèye and Alioune Diop, or silence on matters of conscience in the hope of securing some important future good, as in his votes on Algeria, the politician in Senghor knew that he could not always listen only to his heart and conscience. He also recognized, in the abstract at least, the seduction of flatterers and the temptations of power.

The writing of "Chaka" gave Senghor the opportunity to meditate upon such pressures and such choices, and to think about where they might lead. Chaka had to sacrifice what he loved most for the sake of his people. He also acted in ways contrary to white morality. Senghor was not Chaka. He was not yet ready to renounce his calling as a poet. He still wished to serve his people as their voice. Nevertheless he shows in this poem that he was fully conscious of the moral and personal risks of the life he had chosen.

By 1956, the year *Ethiopiques* appeared, Senghor also saw clearly the connections between his thinking on personal and cultural issues and a particular political agenda. Though he had liked to think that he might keep these two aspects of his thinking separate, it was becoming increasingly clear that this was impossible. The inevitable connection between culture and politics was illustrated at the First Congress of Black Writers and Artists, held in Paris in September 1956. The conference represented the fulfillment of a dream long-held by Senghor and many of his West Indian and Senegalese friends. It brought together black writers and artists from all over the world to discuss their common interests.

The congress was organized by Alioune and Christiane Diop of

Présence Africaine. They invited to Paris sixty prominent black writers and artists from the English- and French-speaking worlds, from Haiti and the French Antilles, from the British West Indies and the United States, and from Africa. These ranged from Senghor's old friends Césaire and the American Mercer Cook to the talented British West Indian writer George Lamming, black American writers such as Richard Wright, and the West Indian–born psychiatrist Frantz Fanon. The very existence of such a gathering seemed to confirm the basic premise of Negritude, namely that all black people had much in common. Its importance was underlined by the fact that the meeting was held at the Sorbonne, the center of French humanistic learning. Its stated purpose was to discuss the past and future of black culture. Indeed Senghor and the Diops were anxious to avoid the political questions that were on everyone's mind.

In this public forum of artists and writers Senghor put forth his thinking about the black sensibility and its culture. Senghor spoke now as a recognized authority and man of substance. He was no longer an unimportant lycée teacher writing poems or essays for the small world of Paris intellectuals, but a public figure, putting his ideas about culture and Negritude squarely in the public domain.

Senghor set out his conception of the Negro-African aesthetic and sensibility in a carefully prepared speech that explored the dichotomy between the black African and white European manners of approaching experience and the reflection of this dichotomy in art and culture. This was the setting in which he explored the "physiopsychology" of the Negro-African. It was a clear statement of his concept of Negritude. So great was Senghor's prestige among French-speaking blacks, and so well-known his general position, that this formal exposition of his views brought only their praise. Its effect on the English-speaking participants, however, was quite unexpected. In the two-hour session set aside to discuss Senghor's paper, it became clear that a great gulf divided the French-speakers from their English-speaking counterparts. While Senghor reached for lofty, characteristically French abstraction, the English-speakers were trying to develop a more concrete and practical approach. Each group revealed the extent to which it had been influenced by the language and culture of its respective colonization. As one delegate put it, language is not simply a matter of words but a way of thinking. While the French-speakers showed their mastery of theory and the influence of French existentialism and Marxism, the English-speakers focused on practical questions of what to do next. Richard Wright articulated their differences:

> I was stupefied with admiration with what Leopold Senghor said here today . . . It was a brilliant speech and a revelation to me—a brilliance poured out in impeccable, limpid French, about the mentality and sensibility of the African;—a poetic world, rich, dynamic, moving, tactile, rhythmic. Yet, as I admired it, a sense of uneasiness developed in me . . . This is not hostility; this is not criticism. I am asking a question of *brothers*. I wonder where do I, an American Negro, conditioned by the harsh industrial, abstract force of the Western world . . . where do I stand in relation to that culture? If I were of another colour or another race, I would say "All this is very exotic, but it is not directly related to me" and I could let it go at that. *I can not* . . . I am black and he is black; I am an American and he is French, and so there you are. And yet there is a schism in our relationship, not political but profoundly human. Everything I have ever written and said has been in defense of the culture that Leopold Senghor describes . . . and yet, if I try to fit myself into that society, I feel uncomfortable.[21]

The conferees stumbled over two truths, one identified by Wright and the other by Senghor and Césaire. Wright felt that he was American and Senghor French. Yet Senghor and Césaire knew that if any one of them went out of the conference hall and strolled down a Paris street he would be immediately identified as a black man by any Frenchman he passed. It is this eye of the other, the same eye that captured Du Bois some fifty years earlier, that continued to make the Negro identity inescapably important. This remains true, Césaire and others argued, even if a black man himself does not think of himself first and foremost as a black person. However different black men may be from each other by language, culture, and point of view, the sense of self as black above all is thrust upon every black person by the European world. "He carries this definition with him like a limb."[22]

The delegates were able to agree that their situation needed to be changed. How to do this, however, was a matter on which there were basic disagreements. Richard Wright suggested, somewhat tentatively, that there might be some connection between the values of the culture Senghor described and the ease with which Europeans had dominated Africa, that perhaps African culture acted as an aid to the European guns. He questioned the value of that culture in relationship to the future. "I do not condemn it. But how can we use it?" Perhaps there were powerful Western values, Wright continued, that Africa must latch onto in order to destroy the foul relationship developed by colonization. Perhaps the only way to cast off Western domination was to use the secular, rational approach learned from the West to create a modern, industrial Africa. His own tough-souled pragmatism, the product of his American upbringing, suggested this course.[23]

Frantz Fanon, a West Indian psychiatrist then working in Algeria, put the same idea a bit differently. Treating the black man as exotic and different is one of the ways, he said, that white men have diminished him. Such racist attitudes, which encourage black men to accept their own inferiority, help to legitimate domination and economic exploitation by whites.[24] By implication, Fanon seemed to be saying that Senghor's Negritude was a variation on this dangerous theme.

Césaire chose to emphasize a different part of the agenda for the future. He shared Wright's view that black men must develop a modern outlook. What he hoped for was an integrated culture that would blend the traditional values of the past with selected aspects of modern and secular culture. What had seemed to be contradictions must be transcended to create something entirely new, a culture that would have integrity and be felt as "ours." And, he added firmly, all culture to flourish needs a cadre and structure. A political and social regime that suppresses the self-determination of a people kills at the same time the creative power of that people. The only way a people can create an integrated culture, one that does not perpetuate the inner divisions from which black people currently suffer, is for them to be able to take the initiative. It is not, therefore, compatible with colonization.[25]

Later in the conference, Senghor burst out, "We wish then to liberate ourselves politically in order to express our Negritude, that is, our true black values." He had been talking culture and psychology but thinking politics, and he was already thinking of the next steps. When the political question is resolved, Senghor continued, "there will be another problem, that of choice among the civilizations with which we come into contact. We will have to see what we will take from Western civilization and what we will keep from the Negro-African civilization."[26] Senghor still did not doubt that such a reconciliation was possible. He had managed it on a personal level; it must therefore also be possible on a cultural and social level. This was for him a matter of faith. For him, the personal, cultural, and political formed a series of interconnected challenges amenable to parallel solutions. From his point of view, the individual personality and society as a whole operated according to the same rules. What was possible for one must be possible for the many. This assumption later proved to be the source of many of his miscalculations.

The discussion at this congress about the nature of blackness and the role of traditional African culture foreshadowed much of the criticism Senghor's ideas would receive in the future. Was the sense of unity that black men felt simply the creation of the eye of the other, the result of Europeans' racist attitudes? Was it simply a racist reaction to a racist challenge and therefore, as Sartre had argued, a transitory phenomenon doomed to pass with the revolution, with the end of colonization, or even, less dramatically, if Europeans' attitudes changed? Alternatively, might Negritude be a new racism, based on the assumption that the physiology of black men set them apart from all others? How else could Senghor support the claim that black men, regardless of their cultural environment, shared a characteristic style? Senghor himself did not want to accept this logical step, that Negritude was an innate attribute of biology or race and therefore a racist concept. In fact, the word itself was semantically focused on color, and Senghor's use of it therefore unavoidably carried racist overtones, whatever his disclaimers. Regardless of the reason why this word had been chosen, and regardless of why an "antiracist racism" might be understandable in the Paris of the 1930s and 1940s, its origins marked both term and concept. Senghor himself acknowledged that there was an element of antiracist racism in Negritude as he had first understood it, but that Nazi racism and "the catastrophes it engendered were soon to bring us to our senses. Such hatred, such violence, ah! above all, such weeping and such shedding of blood produced a feeling of revulsion."[27] There is every reason to believe that Senghor did indeed leave racism behind him. His own behavior certainly shows no sign of racism against whites. Nonetheless, the word he had chosen as his battle cry, Negritude, was not so easily purged of its early meaning. Only much later, after Senegal gained its independence, did Senghor implicitly accept the fact that the racist implications of the word Negritude were too strong for him to want to continue to use it as a political slogan. Without renouncing the concept of Negritude, Senghor began to use another term, *Africanité,* to denote the values and culture of the African world. This word focused attention on a common geographical location and a shared history as the source of a common culture, rather than on the race of the people who had created it.

The racism implicit in the concept of Negritude was not what most disturbed the black intellectuals gathered in Paris in 1956, however. They challenged Senghor on other grounds. American and West Indian participants questioned whether the unity attributed to black people by white racism really was more important than the evident diversity of black cultures. Others questioned whether the culture of Negritude, which Senghor claimed to be characteristic of traditional Africa, still existed and, if it did, how it could survive the industrial transformation. If the reality of Senegal was already a mixture of French and African cultural elements, then just as surely the "kingdom of childhood" must be disappearing. Senghor refuted these arguments. He believed that the preservation of the essential features of black African culture was compatible with self-government and economic development. He went further. He believed that the strengthening of the unique aspects of African culture was a precondition of any truly independent development. For him, political independence was simply a way to create the conditions for the flowering of African culture. This was the program he summed up later with a call for African socialism.

Events proved Senghor's ideas to be politically effective in helping rally Africans to fight for their independence. In the 1960s and 1970s, however, after Senegal gained its independence, Senghor's talk about Negritude and the cultural characteristics and abstract virtues of pre-industrial, traditional African culture began to seem far removed from the daily needs of the people of Senegal. The criticisms leveled at Senghor in 1956 at the First Congress of Black Writers and Artists were ones Senghor never succeeded in putting fully to rest. What had made sense to him personally, and as an artist and a thinker, did not make the transition to political ideology as effectively as he had hoped.

However loudly the organizers of this conference on black culture may have protested their innocence of political motives, the French thought otherwise. How could they not? While the conferees were meeting in September 1956, the press was full of stories from North Africa—of protests in Tunisia against military intervention by French troops, of a new statute for Algeria, and of terrorist ambushes of French soldiers. It was impossible not to set *Présence Africaine*'s cultural congress against this background of turbulence in the colonies. Though Césaire admitted to a friend that he had not planned to call for an end to colonization but had been carried away by the excitement of the moment, and though Senghor had carefully avoided the word independence in his prepared comments, there was now little doubt of the connection between assertions of Negritude, with its call for cultural revival, and movements toward political liberation. As the French weekly *Figaro Littéraire* put it, this strange congress in theory examined black poetry, music, dance, and art "which have inspired the respect, late but uncontestable, of contemporary Western artists," but in fact it "became a political meeting of the most aggressive kind." Senghor and his student friends had begun their exploration of the black experience and culture for personal reasons, but now their concerns and conclusions had taken on serious political implications. "What is most astonishing," the *Figaro* correspondent continued with splendid parochialism, "is that the serene impartial Sorbonne . . . would open itself to such a meeting."[28] There was little question that Senghor's personal views and political responsibilities now pointed him in a single direction. He was ready to work for political liberation and African unity.

Given that the *loi cadre* of 1956 encouraged the separation of African states one from another, while rewarding them with promises of more autonomy, Senghor saw two arenas for immediate action, one in the former federation and the other within Senegal. He set out first to establish political alliances across West African territorial boundaries to serve as a countervailing force to the pressures for its Balkanization into small separate states. Once again he attempted to create a federation-wide party, and once again he tried to form an alliance with Houphouet's RDA. But again these efforts failed, for many of the same reasons as before.

Senghor also set out to promote local unity in Senegal in order to strengthen his hand in any upcoming negotiations with the French. He sensed a groundswell for action among the young. He himself had finally grown impatient with French stalling and with what now appeared to him as a cynical effort to divide West Africans in order to weaken them. Early in the summer of 1956, Senghor invited delegations from the four main Senegalese parties to a conference to discuss the creation of a single party.[29] First the young intellectuals to his left were persuaded to join him in a party with a new name, the Bloc Populaire Sénégalais. In return, their leaders were granted prominent places on the party bureau. The new party's newspaper, which replaced *La Condition Humaine,* was called *L'Unité.* The new party's name was a conscious echo of the Bloc Africain created by Lamine Guèye after the war. In the spring of 1958, Senghor managed to persuade Guèye's socialist party to join him, again changing the name of the party to create the Union Progressiste Sénégalaise (UPS). In his willingness to rename his party and to speak of fusion rather than absorption in spite of the fact that the new party looked much like his own party of old, Senghor demonstrated his characteristic sensitivity to his colleagues' pride and the importance of symbolic concessions. In the generosity with which he rewarded his former opponents by giving them important posts, he displayed a behavior that was both his strength and his weakness. He was determined to bring people together, even if it meant deferring a substantive goal. He was also able to forgo immediate personal recognition in order to serve his long range purpose. The UPS gradually brought into its fold all politically active Senegalese except for a few tiny splinter parties. That did not mean that all its members shared a single view by any means, but on the broad issue of unified action to gain greater autonomy from France, the party could act as one.

Senghor himself was growing more militant. At a party meeting early in 1957 he declared, "I urge you to consider yourselves henceforth as in a state of legal resistance," explaining that resistance to oppression was the most sacred duty of democracy. He was not alone in his impatience. Modibo Keita, leader of the RDA from the Sudan, declared at the RDA meeting in September, "We are at the hour of choice. Africa has chosen. France hesitates. Time is passing. The chances of building the Franco-African community diminish each day. Events are moving faster than the intellectual conversion of certain French politicians." In France, Senghor still tried to avoid the word independence, speaking instead of the need for Frenchmen to recognize the distinctive character of the African nations and to join with them in a "confederation."[30]

By now, many Frenchmen at long last had realized there was a need for action. Some had begun to think that the colonies cost France more than they were worth; others that France had no choice but to accept independence or prepare for violence. A few still searched hopefully for evidence of African loyalty. The review that reported on African business, *Marchés Coloniaux* (Colonial Markets), which had deleted the word colonial from its title and was now called *Marchés Tropicaux du Monde* (Tropical Markets of the World), cited the American politician Adlai Stevenson—"I have never heard a black African speak ill of France"—to suggest there was no need to worry and went on to imply that the relationship between France and Africa retained its traditional harmony.[31]

On May 13, 1958, the French army in Algeria staged a revolt against the parliamentary government. For a moment it looked as if there might be a coup d'état in France itself. The Fourth Republic collapsed. General de Gaulle was recalled to power. Once again it was time to make a new constitution.

De Gaulle's first pronouncements about the overseas territories were characteristically vague. He saw the French Union as "a vast and free community . . . a great political, economic, and cultural ensemble that fits modern conditions of life and progress." He carefully avoided anything specific about what he had in mind for its future and, above all, the word independence. But the West Africans had grown tired of such vague promises. At a West African political congress held that summer at Cotonou, even Senghor was willing to speak of independence, though he qualified his remarks by saying that true independence "is a victory gained not so much over others as over ourselves." The congress unanimously adopted the slogan of immediate independence and resolved to take all necessary measures to mobilize the African masses behind this policy. They were determined to wait no longer.[32]

What the new constitution would offer Africa was yet to be decided. De Gaulle asked Senghor, Guèye, and Houphouet to serve on a committee to make recommendations about the status of West Africa. Senghor, trying to reconcile his commitment to independence with his dream of a federated West Africa, cast about for the proper formula, getting no further than his old proposal for a confederation. Nonetheless the first draft of the new constitution ignored these recommendations and avoided mention of the possibility of the eventual independence of member states. The Africans were outraged. At this point, de Gaulle intervened to insist that the constitutional framework should include a provision for "autonomous states." Senghor later attributed de Gaulle's flexibility on this point to the advice of one of his chief advisors, Senghor's old friend Georges Pompidou. Senghor had sent Pompidou a long handwritten letter explaining how important it was that the constitution include the principle of self-determination for member states.[33]

The final version of the new constitution did give member states the opportunity to decide whether or not to be members of the French community. Overall, however, Senghor was gravely disappointed: there was no mention of the possibility of federated states adhering to the community as a group, and there was only one way for the Africans to express their opinion about the constitution. There was to be a referendum, in which they could vote yes to unity with France and break up the old federation forever, or they could vote no, thereby refusing to ratify the constitution and opting for immediate independence by default. When Senghor asked de Gaulle what would be the consequences of a "no" vote, the general answered, "that territory would have seceded and would be from then on considered foreign. France will know how to draw all the consequences of that choice."[34] It sounded like a threat.

De Gaulle then set out on a tour of the black African territories to gather support for a "yes" vote. It began with tumultuous welcomes, first at Tananarive (Antananarivo), where he promised that members of the community would be autonomous states, and then at Brazzaville, where he gave an emotional speech in a stadium named for his old comrade-in-arms Félix Eboué and ended dramatically, "I have spoken. You have heard me." Such it was also in the Ivory Coast and in Guinea. In Guinea, however, although big, well-orchestrated crowds turned out for de Gaulle, the men lining the street on one side, the women on the other, the Guinean leader, Sekou Touré, struck a discordant note. He seemed to be speaking not so much to his eminent guest as to the Guinean crowd. After a long discourse to the effect that there could be no true development and no true dignity without liberty, Touré declared, "we prefer poverty in liberty to riches in slavery." The crowd cheered. Touré ended his speech by expressing his hope that liberty would be possible within the French Union. De Gaulle was visibly distressed. There, for the first time, he seemed seriously to consider that a territory might vote no and so reject what, from his point of view, were the obvious benefits of remaining in the French orbit. He concluded his speech by saying that he would always keep a warm memory of their beautiful city, "if I should not see you again."[35]

De Gaulle's entry into Dakar, the last city on his tour, further jolted his confidence. Despite the best efforts of those locally in charge to see to it that de Gaulle received traditional Senegalese hospitality, there were placards along his route that read "Immediate independence," "Down with de Gaulle," and, even more rudely, "Get out of here" (*Va t'en*). Neither Senghor nor Dia was on hand to greet him. Dia had suddenly found it necessary to leave for medical treatment in Switzerland, and Senghor had been called to Normandy "on urgent family business." De Gaulle could not fail to get the message: neither wanted to face him. The route of his motorcade was quickly changed so that he would not drive through the center of the city, lest the unruly crowd upset or even attack him. When he finally reached Dakar's central square, de Gaulle addressed a crowd from which the police had tried in vain to evict the young militants. Valdiodio Ndiaye, the Minister of the Interior, standing in for Senghor and Dia, spoke of Senegal's desire for friendship based on a recognition of the right to independence, but was noncommittal on whether he and his party were supporting a "yes" vote. In reply de Gaulle spoke for a brief four minutes. He offered the crowd a choice: "If on September 28 (the day set for the referendum), you want independence, take it."[36] It was now up to the Senegalese.

In the aftermath of de Gaulle's visit, Senghor, as he so often did, found himself squarely in the middle. Young militants in Senegal were pushing for immediate and total independence. In late August they organized a pilgrimage to Thiaroye, "to honor the memory of the black soldiers massacred in 1944 by General de Gaulle." More than one thousand people took part in this demonstration, which ended in violence. The Cotonou congress, a bare two months before, had declared for independence. Senghor had endorsed this position. But he now had second thoughts. Not least of the pressures on him were those of the colonial administration and French business interests, which threatened to call in all outstanding loans. There was also the conservative countryside to consider, for the marabouts were quite satisfied with the status quo. They opposed any sharp break with France, and they were a main source of Senghor's electoral support. Lamine Guèye, who still commanded a considerable following in Saint-Louis and Dakar, was also firmly against a radical break with France. He clung to the idea of working with the French in a spirit of equality.[37]

Mamadou Dia, Senghor's second in command, went to Guinea to discuss the situation with Sekou Touré. He returned from this visit inclined to join Touré in a "no" vote. Senghor, too, was tempted. Indeed, their pointed failure to receive de Gaulle in Dakar indicated that at the very least they had not decided what to do.[38]

The UPS held several tense meetings early in September. At one meeting, shortly after de Gaulle's visit, the militant "no" wing of the party played a tape recording of Senghor's speech at Cotonou, in which he had called for independence. By now, however, Senghor had been persuaded that a "no" vote would be too costly. He reached into his verbal reserves and drew out an argument for "yes" that he hoped would not contradict his Cotonou statement too directly and would still prove acceptable to everyone. "Yes," he said, was a yes to independence in association with France, and yes to African unity. As so often before, his eloquence and authority carried the day. When it became clear that the party majority would support a "yes" vote, the leaders of the left, Amadou Moctar Mbow, Assane Seck, and Abdoulaye Ly, resigned from the UPS to form their own party. The fabric of party unity that Senghor had so carefully woven unraveled at the first test.

On September 28, 1958, the day of the referendum, the Senegalese followed Senghor and overwhelmingly voted yes. By a vote of 870,362 to 21,907, they voted to remain within the French Union. Of all the French African states, only Touré's Guinea had the temerity to vote no. And they paid for it. The French pulled out immediately, taking their records, their moneys, and even their medicines with them. French policemen smashed furniture and broke windows in their quarters. The French did not suffer lightly what they saw as ingratitude.[39]

As yet it was not fully clear what a "yes" vote meant. De Gaulle himself had muddied the waters by saying that France had no intention of giving up its creative work in Africa, but would pursue it under new conditions in keeping with the evolution of its peoples. Defense and foreign affairs, he suggested, should continue to be the concern of the community as a whole. Senghor's statement about what he had voted for was equally vague. What did independence in association with France really mean? How was this to be compatible with African unity?

Senghor, finally convinced that political independence was necessary and inevitable, focused on what seemed to him to be the most pressing future need: the avoidance of the Balkanization of West Africa. Without federation, he felt sure, the tiny states of West Africa would be doomed to poverty and perpetual dependence on others, probably France. He was not alone in this view. He had a great deal of support, particularly from the younger generation of political leaders now just beginning to make their opinions known. They shared Senghor's concern about the viability of independent African states. Houphouet refused to budge, however, even though several leaders of his party supported the idea of federation and split with him on this issue. When the federal council of the former AOF met at Dakar after the referendum, it dutifully voted itself out of existence. It then immediately reconstituted itself as a constitutional assembly to work out a plan for a West African federation. In sessions marked by a mood of cooperation and goodwill, it quickly established a constitution with a strong federal executive and provisions to encourage entry of new members. Delegations from Dahomey, Upper Volta, Senegal, and French Sudan supported it. Senghor, with characteristic tact, suggested that the new federation be called Mali, thus conjuring up the historic empire centered in Sudan led by a distant ancestor of Sudan's present leader, Modibo Keita.

Nonetheless, opposition to the proposed federation soon manifested itself. There proved to be some truth to the idea that the French wanted to keep Africa divided into small units, each of which would therefore be dependent on France. To many Frenchmen, the word federation seemed synonymous with secession from the French community. The fact that the renegade Guinea had recently declared its intention to federate with Ghana, an English colony, merely reinforced the idea that those who sought African federation were disloyal to France. Such doubts were further reinforced by Houphouet-Boigny. He believed that federation would work to the disadvantage of the Ivory Coast, and, having demonstrated his loyalty to France at the time of the Algerian revolt and being the most recent black African member of a French government, he had the ear of the administration. Both in Upper Volta, where the government hesitated to oppose Houphouet for economic reasons, and in Dahomey, local considerations led to a decision not to join the new federation. Only Senegal and Sudan remained firm.

On September 22, 1959, the Mali Federation made a formal request to the French government that it be recognized as an independent nation. It was the first such request under the new constitution. De Gaulle, ever in search of the dramatic occasion, informed the petitioners that he would deliver the answer of France in person. He flew to Dakar in December. As if to make amends for their hostile reception the year before, large Dakar crowds bathed the general in a warm welcome.

Everyone knew that it was a historic moment. Senghor prepared his speech with exceeding care and invited some old friends from his Paris days to be present. He saw the connection between their late-night talks on the Left Bank and today's triumph. The federal assembly of Mali met in a packed hall. Senghor spoke first. He began by saying that the new federation sought independence with no wish to make hostile claims or to submit grievances. He praised de Gaulle's farsightedness, evoking first the de Gaulle of the Resistance, and then the de Gaulle of the Brazzaville conference, and finally the man who in Algeria was able to say to a hostile crowd, "I have understood you." You have understood, Senghor continued, that we seek independence, but not in isolation. In conclusion, Senghor repeated the words of the disciples to Christ on the road to Emmaus: "abide with us, for it is toward evening and the day is spent." Then, in a quiet voice to a silent hall, he repeated the phrase in Latin, "Mane nobiscum quoniam advesperascit."[40] Senghor's intellectual elegance was never more evident than on this day. As a good Catholic, however, Senghor must also have remembered that Christ did not stay with the disciples as they begged him to do, but, having assured himself of their faith and given them proof of his continuing spiritual presence, disappeared to leave them to build his church in their own way (Luke 24:15–31).

De Gaulle answered with equal style. First thanking Senghor for his kind words, he declared that the moment had come to speak directly the unvarnished truth. He hesitated. He, like Senghor, had a fine sense of drama. The hall again fell silent. Senghor, knowing the surprises of which de Gaulle was capable, had a moment of anguish remembering that Guinea had had its independence, but had paid dearly for it. De Gaulle might have decided that independence and friendship with France were incompatible according to his grand vision. De Gaulle continued. France was prepared to grant Mali a status that "I prefer to call national sovereignty rather than independence." It was to be a sovereignty with the "support, help, and agreement of France . . . you can count on France." Even now de Gaulle could not be completely clear. Nonetheless Senghor had what he wanted, independence in friendship with France. It also seemed he had achieved another of his goals, albeit in modified form, namely the beginning of a federated West Africa, independent but linked by ties of history and goodwill to France.[41]

The strength of the new federation remained to be tested.[42] Between de Gaulle's visit to Dakar in December and the formal declaration of Mali's independence in June, there were already signs of discord. The Senegalese were eager to maintain close economic ties with France, far more so than their radical Sudanese neighbors. The Sudanese leader, Modibo Keita, assumed that the goal of the federation was to create a unified, centralized state, whereas the Senegalese wanted a decentralized, looser arrangement more in keeping with their long democratic tradition. Perhaps the greatest difficulty of all lay in choosing who would hold the top post in the new federation. Stormy meetings in the spring reached an apparent compromise, although later no one could agree on what that compromise had been, and the minutes of the meeting mysteriously disappeared. Nonetheless, at the ceremony marking the formal independence of Mali, Keita went out of his way to endorse the Senegalese position that political independence could not be fully realized without economic development, and Senghor spoke warmly of the brilliance of the Sudanese leaders. On the day of independence, the two men appeared together with Mamadou Dia and Lamine Guèye to lay the cornerstone of a new grand mosque in Dakar, as if thereby to consecrate the new state. Keita became the president of the federation, Senghor president of the National Assembly, and Mamadou Dia prime minister and minister of defense. While Keita and Senghor devoted themselves to the politics of the situation, Dia turned his formidable energies to the problem of economic development. Guèye, who had been born in the Sudan and was courted by Keita and his supporters, remained in the background.

It was soon apparent that Senghor had been overly optimistic about the viability of the new federation. So numerous were its problems and misunderstandings that it seems unclear in retrospect how the two nations had ever expected to work together. The optimism of its founders quickly dissipated. The differences in the political styles and goals of its leaders were too great. Keita was Marxist by belief and authoritarian by temperament, while Senghor, the devoutly Christian humanist, put great store by flexibility and compromise and supported the idea of a decentralized federation. These differences were exacerbated by the varied cultural traditions and recent historical experiences of the population at large. Senegal had a long history of representative government and experience with the give and take of politics. Sudan had none. Furthermore, Keita showed extraordinary obtuseness by meddling in Senghor's home territory. At a meeting of the UPS, to which he had been invited by Senghor, Keita openly criticized his host, to the delight of the more radical members of Senghor's party. Not only did he criticize Senghor and Dia publicly, he tried to forge his own ties with the Islamic marabouts in Senegal. The federation limped along for a bare six months. In early August, when Senghor was in France for his annual summer vacation, Dia and a colleague flew to Paris to warn him that Keita was pushing for a unitary state with himself in charge. The Senegalese must move first, they argued.

Senghor decided that the federation was not worth the price of granting all power to Keita. He returned immediately to Dakar. Quietly he and Dia informed the regional governors that there was danger of a Sudanese takeover. Next they ordered the party activists to bring loyal men into Dakar, peasants from the villages. Keita, for his part, declared a state of emergency, fired Dia as Minister of Defense, and gave orders to the Sudanese commander of the federal armed forces to prepare to move on Dakar. Worries about a possible coup had proved correct. Each man feared the other. These fears led to the moves that made their fear reality. Fortunately for Senghor, the largely Senegalese troops refused to obey their Sudanese commander and, under the command of a French colonel, had him arrested instead. With that, the outcome was assured. Keita and his close associates were arrested and sent by sealed train back to Mali. A loyal French military officer had proved a key player in this outcome favorable to Senghor.

One month later, Senegal promulgated a new constitution for itself as a separate, independent state. Senghor was elected president of independent Senegal in January 1961.

Independence brought with it the collapse of Senghor's dream of African federation. He had achieved independence in friendship with France, but the conditions he thought necessary for Africa's future economic and political development had escaped him. Faced with a choice between the maintenance of the Mali Federation and his own political power, he had chosen to take Senegal out of the federation. Now he had secure control of his own country, Senegal. The next challenge was to find the way to its future development.

12

President Senghor

When Senghor became president of independent Senegal, his political career virtually fused with the history of his country. Political, economic, and cultural policies all bore his stamp. To this day, many of those policies remain controversial, and their long-run implications are still to be fully understood. But, to the surprise of almost everyone, the gentle poet and parliamentarian turned out to have impressive political skills and an iron will that enabled him to maintain power and political stability in Senegal for twenty difficult years.

Senghor's political style as president remained consistent with the one he had developed while working for independence, and with the intellectual and personal style he had developed many years before. From the French, he had learned to speak publicly of broad idealistic goals, while at the same time dealing shrewdly in the back room according to principles akin to what Americans call logrolling. From his Serer and African roots, he seemed to retain the sense that social equilibrium rather than total subjugation of troublesome groups was the proper goal for a ruler, and that he must gain the support of all groups in the society, not simply a powerful majority. He was able to listen well and to compromise when necessary, all the while preserving a keen sense of other people's motives and a firm determination to reach his most important long-term goals. Again and again he worked out terms of collaboration with leaders of opposition groups so that they were willing to join his government rather than work against it. He seemed able to forgive their transgressions but took care not to forget them, for underneath this apparent flexibility he retained the stubborn determination of the peasant from Sine and the drive that had propelled him from Djilor to Ngazobil, to Dakar, and finally to Paris. To this drive he added a sure instinct for when to stand firm and when to yield, and an extraordinary ability to wait patiently for the right moment at which to make his move. A sense of the long term, no doubt reinforced by his study of the past and his philosophical nature, allowed him to keep setbacks in perspective and to accept the slow pace of progress toward his goals. These characteristics made it possible for him to weather many challenges to his power, particularly in the early years of his presidency. One of the first and most significant challenges occurred in December 1962. It put him to a severe test, and it illustrated both the strengths and the weaknesses of his political approach.

Mamadou Dia and Senghor had long enjoyed an extraordinary partnership in which each seemed content to trust the other and to divide responsibility. After the creation of the BDS, Senghor spent most of his time in Paris representing Senegal in the National Assembly, while Dia organized and nurtured their political support at home. Later, when the *loi cadre* began to create some political autonomy in West Africa, it seemed only natural that Senghor should put Dia's name forward to head the newly created territorial administration. Dia concentrated on local problems while Senghor continued to focus on Senegal's relations with France and desperately tried to preserve something of the old West African federation. While there were occasional signs that Dia saw things somewhat differently from Senghor—he was rather more tempted than Senghor to say no to de Gaulle in 1958, for example—the two were always able to make their peace in a spirit of respect and mutual trust.

The arrangements for the Mali Federation perpetuated their familiar division of labor. Dia was to continue to have day-to-day responsibility for Senegal's affairs, while Senghor would consider more general questions of overall policy for the federation. When the federation fell apart and Senegal became independent, the new constitution created institutions similar to those of the French Fourth Republic. The position of president of the Republic, with ultimate responsibility and power, went to Senghor, while that of president of the Council of Ministers, charged with the day-to-day administration of the government, went to Dia. As such, Dia was head of the government and responsible to the National Assembly rather than directly to Senghor. He seemed content to remain second to Senghor. Indeed, he urged

Senghor to create a presidential system in which he, Dia, as first minister, would be directly responsible to Senghor, the president of the Republic. Senghor disagreed, preferring a greater division of power.[1]

The existing arrangement was to Senghor's liking, for he could be first in the country, its representative abroad and ultimate authority, but at the same time be free from the cares of daily administration. Senghor readily acknowledged that Dia was the administrative and economic expert at home, while he himself concentrated on general policies for Senegal's future. He preferred the role of clan elder, respected philosopher, and senior statesman. He was thoroughly enjoying his prestige in Europe. There he was greeted as the living embodiment of the Greek humanist ideal. Indeed, de Gaulle himself praised Senghor by calling him poet and writer as well as chief of state.[2] The persona that Senghor had so carefully nurtured was a public success.

Senghor continued to write poetry that was acclaimed in France. His collection *Nocturnes,* published in 1961, contained a revised version of his earlier *Chants pour Naett,* now tactfully reworked out of deference to his wife, Colette Hubert, to eliminate all suggestion that the loved one was a black woman. It also included several new poems, which he called elegies. For this book Senghor won a prize for the best poetry collection in French published by a foreigner. A review in the respected *Figaro Littéraire* called him "one of our greatest living writers."[3]

The elegies of *Nocturnes* take up what is a new theme for Senghor. In earlier poems he had expressed his personal feelings about Africa and France, and had consciously used his poetry as a means to explore the experience of a French-speaking African and present it to a European audience. This was particularly evident in *Hosties noires,* which revealed Senghor at his most militant and politically engaged. Having now chosen to act more directly in the political world, Senghor returned in his poetry to more personal concerns. He seemed to recognize that his writing of poetry was more than a method of communicating with others, that the act of writing poetry was in itself a healing experience for him. The poet nurtured the politician. Each time Senghor began to write, he withdrew into himself. He was able then to tap into the emotional sources of his life, Eden-Childhood-Africa, from which he drew vitality. The enormous self-discipline he demanded of himself in his public and personal life could there give way to the glorification of emotion. The mind of Chaka could temporarily be supplanted by the heart of Negritude.

In "Elégie de minuit" (Elegy of Midnight), the poet traces the creative process and its significance. The poet is showered with honors. The world praises him, but within he experiences "a Sahara, an immense emptiness without life." Sleepless again as he had been when a student in Paris, he finds no solace in his books, "which look at me from the depths of their eyes." Neither the music of love nor the rhythm of poetry can drive away his despair. He lives a hell. The poet prays to God for help. He prays to be reborn in the kingdom of childhood. He will be patient, as he has always had a peasant patience, and await the dawn. He will await the sleep that nourishes the poet, that has nourished the poets of his people, Marône the poetess and Kotye Barma the sage.[4]

Other elegies evoke the more conscious tension between the social role that engulfs the political man and the deeper poetic self. The poet fears that without his poetic vocation he would become nothing but a political person, a creature totally defined by his public acts, and so pulled down by the determinisms of the external world. "The proper characteristic of man," Senghor wrote elsewhere, "is to snatch himself above the earth, to rise above his roots and blossom in the sun, to escape in an act of freedom his natural determinations."[5] To achieve this leap required the energy that Senghor drew from his roots. It also required a place on which to stand, an Archimedean point protected from the world's demands. The act of writing poetry renewed Senghor in both a moral and a psychological sense. It provided an essential foundation for the maintenance of the equilibrium and balance he so highly prized. It also helped him maintain his perspective on the political world in which he had chosen to live.

While Senghor continued to write poetry and play the role of elder statesman, Dia threw himself fully into the tasks of economic development. Central to their shared view of African socialism was the policy of *animation rurale,* according to which peasant cooperatives would be created in the countryside. Carefully selected, trained peasant *animateurs* would be put in place to encourage local people to take initiative in their own communities. To aid him in implementing this policy, Dia relied upon young French technical assistants, largely of a leftist bent, a growing number of young Senegalese technocrats, and the peasant animateurs themselves. Dia paid little attention to politics as such. Indeed, until February 1962 he held no important post in the ruling party but concentrated all of his energy on his administrative and economic tasks. Here there were many signs of accomplishment. In 1960-61 about one-quarter of the peanut crop was marketed by the new cooperatives, by 1961-62 the figure was approaching one-half, and the target for 1962-63 was 75 percent of the total crop.[6] In the summer of 1962 the government created a new state bank for the sole purpose of lending to these cooperatives. To many observers it seemed that Dia was bent on eliminating private enterprise in agriculture.

By this time Dia had become a formidable figure, intelligent, determined, and hard working, a devout Muslim for whom his faith was an added source of strength. He spent long hours in his office buried in statistics, reports, and general administrative work. By his talent, hard work, and obvious devotion to the people, Dia inspired his co-workers to do likewise. Totally honest himself, he expected the same of others. One French consultant, an economics professor at the Collège de France, characterized him as "a man of exceptional rank, quality, and energy. A specialist on economic matters, perhaps the only person in an African state to have interested himself to such a degree in these problems . . . he is a person of calm, purity."[7] But Dia was also a man with little tolerance for compromise, whose determined and effective actions began to alienate both French and Senegalese businessmen, threaten the marabouts, and even anger the radical Left. Furthermore, Dia made little effort to placate these groups. He had no time for the endless rounds of meetings with petitioners and politicians with which he might well have filled his days, nor, unfortunately, did he take the time to keep close watch on his colleagues who might be less honest than he.

It is quite understandable that Dia and his policies would have disturbed many sections of Senegalese society, both the new Senegalese bourgeoisie and the big French companies who rightly saw in the creation of the cooperatives a threat to their control of the peanut trade. Politicians opposed Dia's proposals that would forbid politicians from engaging in private business; the French muttered against his socialist economics and his proposal that the French vacate their military base, and wondered what he had discussed during a recent visit to the Soviet Union. Many people felt threatened by Dia's recurrent austerity and anticorruption campaigns. The marabouts, too, saw danger in Dia's policies. That the marabouts should fear Dia, the Muslim, rather than Senghor, the Catholic, may at first seem odd. In

fact, Dia appeared dangerous on two counts. The wealth of the marabouts, particularly the powerful Mourides, derived from their control
of the peanut fields worked by their devoted followers. The spread of
secular peanut cooperatives would create a direct challenge to their
chief source of economic power. What further challenged them was
the fact that Mamadou Dia, as a devout and educated Muslim, was
committed to a dynamic vision of his faith in which a revitalized Islam
would be compatible with modern forms of social organization. He
proposed the teaching of Arabic in state schools and the creation of
an institute of Islamic studies.[8] Such an agenda threatened the power
of the traditional marabouts in a way that Senghor, as a Catholic,
never could.

Senghor, in contrast, was widely perceived as a man of compromise.
He was gracious, affable, and well known in the top circles of Senegalese society as well as to the representatives of the French companies.
He had acceded to many French demands at the time of independence,
according to which there were special guarantees for French investors,
a French military base in Senegal, and provisions for French advisors
close to the presidency. His door was always open to visitors, both
because he enjoyed them and understood the political value of such
contacts and also because, unlike Mamadou Dia, he was not weighed
down by the detailed work of governing Senegal. Because of these
conversations and his greater political experience, Senghor was far
more aware than Dia of the growing opposition to their economic
programs. To many, Dia seemed a dangerous, ideologically motivated
technocrat, a man with a vision of a modern, equitable Senegal to be
sure, but a man in a hurry. Senghor seemed far more sophisticated,
able to see many sides of all issues, and most important, a man of
moderation and French culture. He was a person with whom one
could talk. Like Blaise Diagne and Lamine Guèye before him, he had
learned from experience the complexity of politics. Perhaps to Dia it
seemed that Senghor was too much at home with the French and too
willing to compromise, precisely what Senghor had once thought of
Diagne and Guèye. Senghor's African socialism left plenty of room
for foreign economic activity. But to the extent that the two men
shared a single vision of Senegal's future, their differences in style and
approach helped make them an effective pair. Those frightened by
Dia's innovations were reassured by Senghor's calm, sensible manner,
while those eager for change felt they had found their champion in
Dia.

Senghor's respect for Dia was evident in many of his postindependence speeches where he spoke warmly of Dia's accomplishments. In 1960 Senghor sent Dia to represent Senegal at the United Nations, where he addressed the General Assembly, and when Senghor himself went the next year he reminded the Assembly of the speech of his "brilliant colleague."[9] Both at home and abroad, Senghor was more than willing to give credit to his hard-working, competent colleague.

Nevertheless, after independence the situation was not quite as it had been before. Senghor no longer had a French audience and the arena of the French National Assembly in which to demonstrate his oratorical and political skills. In October 1960 he moved his principal residence from Paris to Dakar. Naturally he then began to follow local events more closely, with the inevitable result that he began to have more opinions about them. The politicians and the Dakar elite now saw him as a possible ally against what they considered Dia's excessive zeal for rural cooperatives and other new policies that threatened their interests. Dia, meanwhile, had become accustomed to running the government of Senegal with a relatively free hand and understood the policy of African socialism in his own way. The time had now come when rhetoric about Negritude and African socialism had to be supplemented by concrete policy and specific actions. Dia saw the problem clearly: "Practically everywhere one sees vigorously socialist resolutions voted by the parties in power" but these resolutions had little impact "at the level of daily responsibilities."[10] Perhaps this observation was intended as a criticism of Senghor. In any event, Dia suggested that he himself would see to it that there was some connection between socialist rhetoric and practical policy.

The political situation in Senegal at this time was far more fluid than the existence of an entrenched ruling party would suggest. Lamine Guèye, who before independence had fused his socialist party with Senghor's BDS to form the Union Progressiste Sénégalaise (UPS), now held the post of President of the National Assembly. Other former opponents, too, had been persuaded to join the UPS in return for government posts. Such unity had been relatively easy to manage in the context of the move toward independence, and fit with Senghor's well-known preference for bringing the opposition into the fold. As a result, the UPS housed within itself all the major conflicts of Senegalese society. Local struggles for power took place within the party rather than between members of the party and nonmembers. It was therefore not surprising that in February 1962, when the UPS held a conference in Thiès, some party members looked to Dia to support them in local quarrels with men more closely associated with Senghor.[11] In those disputes which involved a person active in Dia's administration or in animation rurale, Dia naturally felt under some pressure to help. If Dia stepped in, however, it was all too easy to cast disagreements of local origin as a contest between him and Senghor.

Each August, like the top French administrators before him, Senghor went to spend his annual vacation in France. While Senghor was away, in the summer of 1962, Dia and one of his ministers, Joseph Mbaye, made tours of the countryside to survey economic progress and to talk with some of the most important marabouts. When Senghor returned from his long vacation, members of his entourage, rivals and enemies of Dia, reported that Dia had taken these tours to build up his personal support among the animateurs and to discredit Senghor with the marabouts. Rumors of trouble between Dia and Senghor began to circulate in Dakar, encouraged and embellished by those opposed to Dia's policies and to Dia personally. In October, at a UPS meeting, Dia went out of his way to dispel them, saying, "There can never be a serious difference between my friend of seventeen years, my companion in struggle . . . my brother and me."[12] Nonetheless, in November there was a cabinet reshuffling, which Dia at first tried to resist. One of the issues was the corruption of some of his ministers. The result was a compromise, in which a few of Dia's close collaborators lost their posts but the strongest of them remained in the government. Dia himself, already Minister of Defense, added internal security to his responsibilities and also retained his position as president of the Council of Ministers. Dia then went off to the island of Gorée for a four-day vacation. He was utterly exhausted by his heavy workload and the tension generated by the political infighting that swirled around him.

There is considerable confusion about the events that followed, as well as about the intentions of the people involved.[13] To some, it seemed that Dia had attempted a coup d'état. Others believed that Senghor had been misled by French intelligence and Dia's enemies into thinking that he was planning a coup when he was not. Yet others thought that Senghor had provoked a crisis in order to eliminate Dia. All agreed that many people had intrigued to drive a wedge between the two men. Whatever the true origins of the dispute, once the battle was joined, Dia acted in ways that lent credence to the idea that he wanted to push Senghor aside and take power for himself.

The crisis was triggered by the decision of Théophile James, a deputy said to be a creature of private business interests, to introduce into the National Assembly a vote of censure against Dia's new government. It was early in December, about four weeks after the cabinet reshuffling. The motion was aimed primarily at forcing the government to end the state of emergency that had been in effect since the breakup of the Mali Federation. Many deputies felt that Dia had extended the state of emergency in order to avoid consulting them on important matters. Such may well have been the case. Dia's view of what was needed was not compatible with that of many Assembly delegates, all of whom had been elected before independence in a totally different political context. The delegates were particularly annoyed that Dia's new government demanded that they should not engage in business ventures. Dia, for his part, knew that lengthy parliamentary discussions would slow him down, perhaps even force compromise in the economic policies central to his plan. Therefore he simply bypassed the Assembly and ruled by decree, as he could legally under the terms of the still-existing state of emergency.

No one, at least no one in the foreign press, took the motion for censure very seriously at first. The president of the Assembly, Lamine Guèye, was out of town.[14] There was a big international colloquium on socialism and economic development taking place in Dakar at the time, designed in part to show off recent accomplishments. Senghor gave the opening speech, Dia the closing one. Here, as elsewhere, there was whispering in the hall about trouble, and word spread that it was significant that neither Senghor nor Dia had listened to the other's presentation. Meanwhile, Théophile James kept on collecting signatures for his petition.

The Assembly met the morning after Lamine Guèye returned, on December 14. It was about two-thirds full and faced a routine agenda. James chose that moment to introduce his motion to censure Dia's government. By law, it had to be voted on within two days. Upon hearing about this, Dia called a meeting of the Council of Ministers for the next morning. Clearly angered by the effrontery of the politician-delegates, he argued that the existence of the state of emergency meant that such a motion was illegal. In the heated discussion that followed, no decision could be reached.[15]

The political bureau of the UPS then convened. It was split about evenly between supporters and opponents of Dia. No one wanted to cast the issue as one of support of or opposition to Dia, however, so the discussion focused instead on the relative power and position of party and state: was the National Assembly free to censure or dismiss a man endorsed by the party's political bureau, or not? According to the letter of the constitution, it was. Yet the reality of power was such that the party in fact determined who held all important positions, including that of head of government. Dia reasoned, understandably if not constitutionally, that only the party's political bureau could remove him from his position. Furthermore, he argued, the Assembly no longer represented the mood of the country, as it had been elected in 1959, before independence. Heated discussion did not lead to consensus. According to one account, the majority of the UPS political bureau condemned the motion of censure and agreed that the National Assembly should delay voting on it until the council of the party had a chance to meet. Presumably Senghor supported this decision, but neither he nor Guèye made a public statement. It was finally agreed that the decision should be left to the national council of the party at a meeting scheduled for later in the week. Many observers thought that at such a meeting Dia would receive majority support.[16]

Events then quickly followed one after the other. The National Assembly decided to ignore the challenge to its authority and to meet the next morning to vote the motion of censure. As soon as he learned of this effort to circumvent the party's authority, Dia, according to his memoirs, went to Senghor. Rather than addressing the matter at hand, however, Senghor began to discourse on the difficulties inherent in Senegal's present form of government and the need to create a strong presidential regime. Senghor further proposed that Dia take the position of president and offered to take second place. Dia recalls that he was astonished, and refused, because for him Senghor had always been the leader and should remain so. Furthermore, he reminded Senghor that he, Dia, had recently proposed the creation of a presidential regime, with Senghor as president, and that Senghor had said then that the form of government was not an issue. Now Senghor simply said that he had changed his mind. It was then, according to Dia, that he realized that the break between them was complete, and he accused Senghor of masterminding the motion of censure.[17]

During the night, Dia called out the territorial guard. In the morning, when the delegates arrived at the Assembly building, it was surrounded by a cordon of guard troops. They made no effort to prevent the delegates from entering, however, and indeed when

Lamine Guèye arrived he joked with reporters and seemed totally at ease. First Dia and then Senghor entered the building. Newspapermen noticed that Senghor tried to begin a conversation with Dia in the halls, but that Dia seemed very angry and the two talked only a few moments. Dia left. Senghor left. At this point, the territorial guard entered the building and forced the delegates to leave, thereby preventing them from taking their vote to censure Dia. Yet such was the peaceful and unthreatening atmosphere, one reporter noted, that "the gardeners calmly continued to water the lawns in front of the Assembly building."[18] Dia later said that his only goal was to prevent the deputies from voting and so violating their earlier agreement to wait until after the party meeting. Guèye spread word that the delegates should come to his house later in the day to take their vote.

Senghor in the meantime had issued an order to the army unit of parachutists in Rufisque to come to Dakar to guard the palace. Their commander refused to carry out the order unless, as the constitution required, it was also signed by Dia as Minister of Defense. He therefore took the order to Dia, who ripped it up, only to issue an identical order under his own name. Senghor's will was done, but Dia saw to it that it was done in a constitutional manner. The parachutists came into the city and took positions at the palace and the administrative building. Later Dia said that he thought at this point that Senghor had violated the constitution by issuing a direct military order and was planning a coup. Senghor then issued a second order, declaring a state of emergency and assuming the powers of commander-in-chief of the army. The general of the army, now thoroughly confused and unwilling to choose between his two masters, Dia as Minister of Defense and Senghor as emergency commander-in-chief, decided to resign. Senghor appointed a successor, Jean-Alfred Diallo, a man clearly loyal to him.[19]

That same day, early in the evening, forty-eight members of the eighty-delegate National Assembly met at the house of Lamine Guèye. Guèye had previously consulted with Senghor. There, in the presence of journalists as well as party militants, and after several eloquent speeches about the rights and obligations of minorities and majorities, the constitution, and the liberty of Senegal, those present, a majority of the delegates, decided to ignore the decision of the UPS political bureau to settle the matter at its upcoming meeting, and voted unanimously in favor of the motion of censure. Worth noting is the fact that a sizable minority, thirty-two of the eighty Assembly members, either chose not to attend or, according to Dia's account, were not informed of the meeting.[20] In the meantime, telephone lines to the palace had been cut. One of Senghor's aides managed to smuggle a cassette into the radio station to announce the result of the vote. When its transmission began, however, it was cut off.

At 9 P.M. Dia, who had been unable to leave the administrative building all day because parachutists had surrounded that building as well as Senghor's residence, sent a coded message ordering the republican guard at Thiès to come to the capital. The nature of the order he gave is obscure: was it "to take the palace" or, as Dia later said, "to protect it"—and if to protect it, from whom? In any event, the message was decoded by French intelligence, which alerted Senghor. He quickly ordered a truck blockade to be set up across the road from Thiès to Dakar so Dia's troops could not enter the city. The guard unit could easily have forced this makeshift blockade. Not wanting to use force, however, the guards began to chat with their friends who were manning the blockade. In such a small country, all the officers knew one another, and no one wanted to press the issue. Senghor then managed to broadcast an appeal to the nation from a hastily assembled transmitter in Rufisque.

It was now clear that the military forces could, if they chose, play the decisive role. They were reluctant to do so. It was also apparent to all that French troops, stationed near Dakar and now on alert, were loyal to Senghor. The general of the Senegalese army had decided to resign rather than to act in a constitutionally murky situation. Senghor had had to replace him with a junior officer more loyal to himself. The heads of the various forces that had been called up, the parachutists and the territorial and republican guards, decided to go as a group to speak with each of the three top politicians, Guèye, Senghor, and Dia. They went first to Guèye. Should they, the military, take power? Guèye argued against it, citing the constitution and Senegal's long and peaceful political tradition. The military men also went to the palace. Senghor, who had retired for the night, went down to greet them in pajamas and dressing gown with, he recalls, his constitution in his hand. He went alone with them into the library, wondering whether they had come to arrest him. When the military men explained their purpose, he talked to them at great length, arguing against a takeover and explaining that the constitution gave him, the president, the right to command them at a time when the Republic was threatened. His views made a strong impression. Then the military men went to Dia. Dia says that he agreed to seek a political compromise and thought the matter was settled.[21] According to other accounts, when Dia saw the officers he thought that the republican guard had made it to Dakar, and that the military men had come to offer him their loyalty. When they explained their actual mission he began to berate them, "and went on at great length in bitter words." This emotional outburst apparently convinced the military commanders that Senghor was the better fit to rule.[22] Dia seemed to have cracked under pressure. Many later attributed his behavior to exhaustion after many months of grueling work and political strain. Once again, the self-mastery that Senghor had learned long ago from his Catholic teachers at Ngazobil served him well.

The various military men—parachutists and territorial and republican guard—then simply went back to their quarters. Dia left the administrative building and went home thinking that the details of a compromise were to be worked out later. Senghor was forming a provisional government, however, and its first act was to put Dia and several of his followers under house arrest.

It remains unclear even in retrospect who acted first and with what motives. The official version, consistent with that of the French reporters on the spot, who were known to favor Senghor, is that Senghor sought until the very last minute to find a compromise with Dia. According to this view, Dia had been planning a coup, used force to prevent the National Assembly from exercising its constitutional right to censure the government, and refused to recognize that he was in the minority in the party political bureau. Confronted with this violation of the constitution, Senghor had no choice but to invoke his emergency powers under the constitution, take command of the armed forces, and arrest Dia.[23]

The evidence presented at Dia's trial, which took place about six months later, was less clear-cut. Senghor, it turned out, had ordered the army division of parachutists into Dakar before, not after, the delegates of the National Assembly were forcibly dispersed. It also seemed odd that Dia would have rewritten and confirmed Senghor's order to the parachutists if he had been planning a coup. At the trial it also appeared likely that Dia's government had had the support of the majority of the party political bureau, if not of the National Assembly. It was also alleged that many of the deputies in the Assembly had been bought off, perhaps by the French, perhaps by others. At the very least, the trial called into question the idea that Dia had been carefully planning a coup d'état against Senghor. To this day, Dia denies that this was his intention.

Many continue to believe that the confrontation was maneuvered by the forces of reaction, local and French, determined to divide the two men and put an end to Dia's assault on entrenched interests. One of Senghor's aides of that time has since written that he himself masterminded the motion of censure, and that only after he and James had begun to collect signatures did Senghor discover what he had done. At that point, according to this account, Senghor let the drama play itself out. Such a story would tend to confirm the idea that supporters manipulated the two men into their confrontation.[24] Others maintain that Senghor knowingly brought on the crisis to chasten his rival, anticipating a last-minute compromise. Yet others maintain the reverse, that it was Dia who knowingly precipitated a crisis, expecting Senghor to yield when he realized that most party leaders opposed him.[25] Whatever the motivation of the chief actors, it is clear that many people had an interest in splitting the two men, and that Dia showed a singular lack of political judgment as the crisis developed.

Most observers at the trial expected that Dia and his supporters would be let off lightly, such was the lack of hard evidence against them. Dia gained sympathy by the dignity and directness with which he presented his testimony, the loyalty to him of his fellow defendants, and the high praise for his character from Frenchmen who knew him well. But the trial did not turn out as expected. Dia was sentenced to life imprisonment. In the event, he served twelve years in the little village of Kedougou in eastern Senegal. His supporters, too, received long terms. Although the procedure followed the letter of the Senegalese law, the members of the high court were the same individuals whose business dealings Dia had criticized and who, as deputies in the National Assembly, had voted to censure him. Several French correspondents concluded that although the trial had been procedurally correct and the defense given every opportunity to present its evidence, the harsh sentencing revealed that it had really been a political trial.[26] Indeed, if the affair is judged solely by its result, it is clear that Senghor eliminated his main political opponents in a single thrust.

Reading accounts of the trial published in France, however, Senghor grew furious. It was the first time he had been attacked by members of the French intellectual establishment. He defended himself in print, arguing that these French intellectuals had no understanding of the true situation in Senegal and had preserved their colonial presumption that if in Africa things were not as in France, Africans had fallen short.[27]

The details of the Dia crisis are important because they foreshadowed much that was to come. These events proved a turning point, as well as the first real test of Senghor's political style and toughness. They also revealed several unusual and enduring characteristics of Senegalese politics—unusual, that is, for Africa.

The crisis had held the potential for a military coup and bloodshed, but in fact not a single person was killed. Indeed, it unfolded within an extraordinarily friendly atmosphere. The gardener continued watering the lawn in front of the National Assembly building; Senghor's parachutists surrounding the administrative building shared plates of rice and swapped talk with Dia's supporters who were inside the building; Senegalese troops on either side of a road blockade refused to use force against their friends and relatives. The main concern of both military and civilian leaders was to avoid bloodshed and find a peaceful, political solution, in what they proudly call "the Senegalese way." Considering how crises in other African countries have been solved since their independence, it is highly significant that the military did not attempt to seize power for itself. The constitution did prevail. Long years of experience with representative institutions and law in the communes of Senegal had resulted in a legalistic political tradition with real local roots. Guèye, Senghor, Dia, the military leaders, and other lesser figures believed that laws and parliamentary institutions were not to be lightly set aside.

There was no overt foreign intervention, either, although the French hovered in the background. Their intelligence service helped Senghor, and a French advisor established what proved to be a crucial emergency telephone link out of the palace so that Senghor could rally his forces. Perhaps French intelligence did mislead Senghor at the beginning about Dia's intentions, or Dia about Senghor's. Certainly French business interests lobbied against Dia. Most important of all, the presence in the country of French troops known to be loyal to Senghor had a profound effect on all concerned. Nonetheless, it remained primarily a Senegalese quarrel solved by local people according to their own rules.

Senghor's personal and political style proved its value. As problems with Dia developed, he acted with characteristic caution. He did not let himself appear to be directly embroiled in the quarrel. It was the

National Assembly that provoked a showdown. To be sure, if he had come out publicly against the Assembly's taking a vote, he might have prevented it. He did not. Patiently he allowed the situation to ripen. When he did decide finally to act, whether or not it was on the basis of a false understanding of Dia's intentions, he did so calmly and firmly. He kept his composure and used his mastery of words and the constitution to persuade those who might have wavered, notably the military men, over to his side. His practice of making friends of former rivals also proved its use, for Lamine Guèye was a key supporter at the critical moment. Finally, at Dia's trial, Senghor saw to it that legal procedures were followed. Given the verdict, and the sense both in Senegal and in France that the sentences were unduly severe, it was not a glorious moment. Seeing no alternative, Senghor had the courage to act and to offend. Perhaps his anger at his French critics drew its force from the fact that he found it so hard to offend some of the French in order to please the others, or from his dismay at what had happened. He must have regretted losing a man as able as Mamadou Dia and one with whom he had collaborated so successfully for many years. For once he had not managed to find a compromise acceptable to all concerned. It was his first important political challenge, and he met it decisively and successfully. Many of his friends were surprised to find that he possessed the necessary toughness.

That the Senegalese government came through these events without violence and without totally disregarding its own laws and constitution was a tribute to the civility of all involved. To that extent, the outcome of the December events was a victory for the country as a whole. Yet it was also a tragic outcome in that it cost Senegal one of its most capable and outstanding leaders, one it could ill afford to lose. Senghor and Dia had been a remarkable team. It seems likely that both had wanted to find a compromise, but that they were pressured by their supporters not to yield until each found himself in a position from which he could not withdraw without losing face. Many years later, after his release from a long detention, Dia could still speak of Senghor with real enthusiasm for their early collaboration. He still took pride in the confidence and respect Senghor had had for him in the early days, and he still was stunned by his trial and the severity of his sentence. Such an attitude seems odd in a man who supposedly planned a coup to rid himself of a hated rival. Senghor's aides, meanwhile, continued to refer to the attempted coup d'état as if Dia's ill will were beyond question, and only after almost twenty years did

Senghor acknowledge publicly that Dia had some good qualities.[28] What the "evil advisors" interpretation fails to take into account is that Dia and Senghor were both men of strong personality and great ability. They also had strikingly different political styles with conflicting views on means if not ends. While it seems that others precipitated the break, it is difficult to imagine how they could have worked together over the long term.

Once Dia was gone, Senghor stood alone. He no longer had someone to his left who would take the initiative in making the changes necessary for rural change and economic development. So long as Dia was in power, he could push the policies that caused opposition, while Senghor could present himself as moderate and understanding. Senghor could explain and make amends for his stubborn colleague, while at the same time supporting his basic policies. Now it was Senghor who would have to take the initiative and responsibility for new policies. Animation rurale was quickly abandoned, not because it was a failure but probably because it showed signs of being too successful. It is impossible to be sure that even Dia and Senghor working together could have pushed this policy through against the opposition of both the Muslim brotherhoods and the French commercial interests. What is sure is that its failure marked the end of real agricultural reform. The Mourides had been essential to all Senghor's political victories. The French were expected to provide the investment Senghor believed necessary to Senegal's future economic prosperity. Alone, Senghor dared not risk challenging either group.

After this political crisis had been resolved, Senghor went before the nation with bad news: the economic plan had fallen behind. With this announcement, he effectively discredited Dia's economic management. He also criticized the party, calling for its revitalization as a source of popular support for government policy, and presumably for him. Finally, Senghor took special pains to reaffirm Senegal's foreign policy, noting specifically that "in our relations with France, there are no clouds." The French business weekly reported this phrase with obvious satisfaction, making it clear in its account of the "Dakar events" that everything had turned out for the best.[29]

Having learned a number of political lessons, Senghor introduced a revised constitution that established a strong presidential system. His rhetoric began to suggest a new authoritarianism and an impatience with politicking. He now spoke of his ruling party with references to Lenin, arguing that "our party must be the consciousness of the masses . . . It must not only echo . . . [popular aspirations but be] their scientific expression as well."[30] All this must be in keeping with the principles of Negritude, of course, but even in the traditions of Negritude Senghor now found the basis for a unitary approach. Negro-African philosophy and democracy, he explained, were based on the concept of personality rather than on that of the individual as in Europe. African democracy was not the rule of the minority by the majority, but required consensus. Senghor likened his role to that of the elder and teacher, who explains and persuades until this consensus is achieved. It was therefore possible for him as president to "personify the nation" as did the European monarch or African ruler in former times.[31] Elsewhere he suggested the army as a model for the future: "composed of all strata of the nation, removed from the battles of clan and politician . . . [it] exists only to serve . . . the national will. Our army presents to us the image of the new nation."[32] Senghor's new notion of himself as the personification of the nation, a nation yet to be built, one that would be based on a will to live together in the future rather than on the ethnic and linguistic ties of the past, had another source as well: de Gaulle's vision of himself as the guardian of France. Like de Gaulle, Senghor was growing increasingly impatient with political bickering, which, in his view, served no useful purpose. Rather than wait for the villagers to learn how to organize their own cooperatives effectively, for example, the government would appoint administrators to do it for them. "Faith," Senghor told Dakar medical students in 1963, "is not enough in the twentieth century to move mountains. We live in a century of science and technology."[33]

Dangerous as such language might sound to a world sensitive to the rhetoric of "scientific" socialism and Marxist-Leninist one-party regimes, in fact neither Senghor's party nor his government had the potential for dictatorial rule or even for pushing through policies opposed by entrenched interests. Senghor himself had a real aversion to violence. He and his early followers had tried to create a party that would educate and mobilize the people directly, but had failed, settling instead for what in Senegal is called clan politics, a politics of brokered interests and alliances between the party and traditional elites such as the marabouts and the notables of country towns. This arrangement shared some of the characteristics of the urban political machines that flourished in the cities of the United States in the early and middle years of this century. Votes were traded for material benefits by middlemen, who organized people for political purposes and provided them small favors in return, and who took for themselves enough to make it worth their efforts. While from one perspective such a system might be called corrupt, from another it was a relatively efficient way to keep peace in the countryside, mobilize votes for the government, and allow resources from the center to be distributed to local constituents. Neither ideological appeals nor force proved necessary to mobilize support for Senghor's regime.[34]

Senghor continued to draw his chief political support from the Muslim brotherhoods, especially the powerful and economically dynamic Mourides. Rather than challenging their power, as Dia had threatened to do, Senghor found that he, like the French colonial authorities before him, had to provide the marabouts with special favors, such as large loans and strategically placed development projects. Occasionally these loans supported productive economic ventures, but more often they disappeared in lavish living and display. Senghor dared not attack or deny the marabouts lest they withdraw their political support. For the present, they were a force for stability; in the future they might be won over to a new point of view or weakened by the development of the modern sector, but in the meantime they served a necessary function. The representatives of the central government in the countryside, who were usually also the local representatives of Senghor's party, honored an unwritten agreement that the government would not challenge the marabouts' power. Western education, for example, made relatively little headway in the central territories of the Mourides, not only because the education budget was not large enough to support schools throughout the country but also because the Mourides preferred to limit the education of the faithful to their Koranic schools, which taught students to obey their Islamic leaders. Under such conditions, large areas of the country remained impervious to central government authority; there the government could rule only with the consent and help of the marabouts. The villagers grew to depend on the marabouts as their link to both God and state.[35] This situation endured with little change throughout the twenty years Senghor was president.

Recognizing that he was strong with respect to any potential political opposition at the center, but weak with respect to carrying out any policy that threatened entrenched interests in the countryside, Senghor was forced to accept this balance. To quiet his opponents among the urban intellectuals, he offered positions in the government and material inducements. Gradually all significant political opposition succumbed to Senghor's talent for persuasion, but the cost was a huge and wasteful bureaucracy that gobbled up approximately half of the state's budget. Top Senegalese bureaucrats demanded and received the perquisites of their French predecessors such as cars and long vacations, while they also honored the demands of their own culture by trying to find jobs for their large extended families. The benefit of Senghor's approach was a relatively peaceful climate in which French economic experts could do their planning and Senegalese students could develop their skills eventually to replace them.

Senghor now had to face the legacy of the manner in which Senegal had achieved its independence. He had worked in the French style, providing eloquent ideals for the people and negotiating behind the scenes with the elites. He had negotiated with de Gaulle, his advisors with de Gaulle's advisors. He had not developed a highly structured, disciplined political party. He had neither mobilized the Senegalese population with an angry anti-French ideology nor broken the power of the local elites, notably the religious leaders. He had offered no scapegoat for Senegal's problems. To the contrary, he had warned that political independence was only a first step and that future success would demand hard work. As he believed French help would be crucial for future economic development, he had agreed at independence to consult with the French before taking any important foreign policy decisions, to coordinate defense, to continue to tie Senegal's currency to the French franc, and to guarantee to French firms and French citizens rights equal to those enjoyed by Senegalese. Many French officials stayed on in an advisory capacity, as did teachers at both the university and secondary school levels, in order to maintain "French standards." Senghor even invited French advisors whom he had known in Paris into his inner circle. The French population of Dakar actually grew after independence.[36]

Far from deploring this situation, Senghor defended it. To nationalize French or other foreign companies, he argued, would be to "kill the goose that laid the golden egg." So long as these companies provided jobs and training, paid their taxes, and reinvested some of their profits, their continued presence and prosperity could only benefit Senegal. He would not, he repeated often, Africanize at a discount—that is, put unqualified Africans into jobs being done well by Frenchmen. Only when there were competently trained African cadres to replace them should the French be asked to leave.[37] The result for the time being seemed to be a division of labor whereby the French ran the economy and the Senegalese the government.

Senghor was simply continuing the strategy of his long and highly successful political career. Nor was it evident, according to currently prevailing theories of economic development, that he had much alternative. He shared the common assumption of the time that Western technology and economic theory were culturally neutral and possessed a magic key to painless economic development. According to this economic science, the road to prosperity for all developing countries lay through state initiative and planning, economic specialization, and industrialization. The world was to form one single market in which each country would do what it did best, and all would prosper. Joining this world market was the sole way to improve the material well-being of the poor in all countries.[38] These views of international economic specialization and open trade were developed in Europe and the United States, precisely those countries which, along with Japan, were best suited to compete successfully under such conditions.

Senghor faithfully followed the directives of his French advisors. They maintained that future development was impossible without an efficient, and expensive, infrastructure to support new industries. This had to be the top priority and required large infusions of capital, capital that Senghor believed would have to come from France. These same French advisors were needed to see to it that the capital was used wisely—which usually meant that French companies were contracted to do the work. They also advised Senegal to encourage the development of its sole export crop, the groundnut. Only gradually did it become clear that Senegal's dependence on this single crop, along with its undependable weather, left the country extraordinarily vulnerable to changing world prices and to international competition. North American peanut growers, for example, with more capital-intensive means of production and sophisticated access to world markets, were formidable competitors who made no allowances for Senegal's fragile economic situation.

At first, Senghor worried less about the presence of French influence than about its possible loss. The French government, for its part, was motivated by two not always compatible goals. It felt an obligation to assume some responsibility for its former colonies. It also wanted to maintain a privileged place in the political, cultural, and economic life of the new states. The French hoped to substitute influence for domination. A few voices were raised in France against such close ties, arguing that France was spending too much money on its former colonies and gaining little in return. France should direct its aid "to Garonne, not Gabon," that is, it should meet the needs of its own poor rather than seek influence abroad. Such were the views of the Cartierists, so named for Raymond Cartier, who wrote a series of articles in *Paris-Match* in 1964. They believed the government's idealistic rhetoric about aid and shared Senghor's assumption that French capital investment benefited Senegal more than it did the French.

A French commission charged to assess ten years of independence in Senegal concluded that the situation was far more complicated than the Cartierists believed. Under the umbrella of French aid to Africa, individual French firms made large profits in Senegal in the early 1960s. Much of it was repatriated to France, while French technical advisors not only lived well at Senegal's expense but saw to it that French interests were served. The desire to help, which was genuine, and the desire to maintain influence, which was equally genuine, were not always compatible. Both became entangled with the determination of French companies to make their profits. There was one well-documented case, for example, in which American plans to build a fertilizer plant in Senegal were thwarted because the new plant would have competed with French importers. In other cases, French firms employed far fewer Senegalese than promised and automated their factories in order to reduce wage bills. Though the French spoke in public about France's duties to humanity, and though many French advisors worked in good faith, individual firms continued to act in their own economic interests.[39]

The economic record of the first decade of independence was mixed at best. Schools and medical facilities were built, and the country seemed stable politically, but the government remained heavily dependent on French assistance and investment. The GNP grew gradually, averaging between 2 and 2.5 percent per year. Senegal's population also grew by at least 2.2 percent per year, evidence of improved medical care and adequate nutrition; thus economic growth and population growth were about the same, so that per capita income grew little if at all. Exports did not increase, and there were few new jobs in the modern economy for increasing numbers of school graduates.[40] By 1970 even this modest economic growth was slowing. A series of drought years drastically reduced the peanut crop, still Senegal's major source of foreign exchange. Convinced as he was that Senegal's economic problems would yield to technology and modern planning, Senghor was slow to see poor performance as a reason to rethink his entire strategy.

Senghor continued to be an active proponent of France's continued role overseas. He now introduced a new concept that paralleled many of his old ones, that of Francophonie. Playing on de Gaulle's fear of the eclipse of France as a major power and horror of creeping Frang-lais, Senghor joined Habib Bourguiba to call for an active grouping of French-speaking nations to exchange cultural and technical assis-tance. Such a grouping would, in Senghor's view, provide France with its grandeur and Senegal with needed practical help. This idea appealed particularly to the French Canadians, who were seeing support in their cultural and political struggles against English speakers at home. But the French were understandably reluctant to endorse this plan on a grand scale, knowing that they would be expected to donate a large portion of its financial support.

After considerable delay, representatives of twenty-six Francophone nations finally met in Niamey in 1968 to set up an agency for cultural and technological cooperation. As things turned out, the organization of Francophonie limped along with a very small budget. That it existed at all was a triumph and illustration of Senghor's technique and the desire of France to maintain itself as a world presence. Senghor, believing in the practical and symbolic advantages of cooperation between France and Africa, was able to find the words to appeal to both African and French, as well as the patience to push the idea stubbornly for many years. Only much later, in 1986, did this idea finally lead to the first meeting of Francophone government leaders in Paris. It was hosted by François Mitterrand, then president of France, a man who had vigorously spoken out in the 1950s in favor of keeping Algeria French and of maintaining the colonies as an integral part of France. In 1986 he reiterated the importance to France and French culture of the former empire. Canada, in keeping with what many Africans had in mind, pledged $10 million in medical aid to the Francophone developing countries.[41]

In 1966 Senghor presided over a great triumph for Senegal: the Third World Festival of Negro Arts, held in Dakar. The first such conference had been held in 1956 at the Sorbonne, the center of French scholarship, the second in 1959 in Rome, the capital of Chris-tian Europe. Now, in 1966, it was possible to hold a World Festival of Negro Arts in Dakar, on independent African soil. It was both a practical and a symbolic triumph.

The purpose of the conference, as Senghor told the audience rather grandly on opening night, was "the defense and illustration of Negri-tude . . . the elaboration of a new humanism, which this time will include all of humanity on the whole of our plant earth." For three weeks some ten thousand visitors representing thirty-seven nations, as well as hundreds of individual artists, poets, musicians, and writers, enjoyed an array of conferences, plays, films, theatrical productions, and exhibitions of all kinds. Over one hundred fifty films were entered in a juried film competition. Aimé Césaire, Léon Damas, and Alioune Diop were there, as was an impressive American delegation that included Duke Ellington and Langston Hughes as well as the black American sociologist St. Clair Drake. Senghor's old friend and translator Mercer Cook was then the American ambassador to Senegal. The DePauw Gospel Choir sang in Dakar Cathedral. Haile Selassie made a state visit. Even the Soviet Union sent a representative in the person of the popular poet Yevgeny Yevtushenko, who, in this exotic climate, enjoyed a long and pleasant talk with Langston Hughes.[42]

Although there were inevitably grumbles around the edges of such a vast gathering, such as mutterings that black American radicals had been denied entrance and that English-speaking and Francophone participants had little in common and that therefore the basic premise of Negritude was invalid, the festival was a tremendous triumph for Senghor personally and for Senegal.[43] For those who participated, it was a confirmation of the power and creativity of black artists. André Malraux, then the French Minister of Culture, took this opportunity to lavish praise on Senghor, saying that "For the first time a statesman takes into his fragile hands the destiny of a continent" and proclaims its coming of age. Senghor reminded those Senegalese who complained about the expense of the festival that riches lie not only in the ground, but in artists and poets: "We ought not to regret the financial sacrifices the festival has cost us, because it is a matter of culture and, to repeat once again, culture is at the beginning and end of development."[44]

Césaire summed up what the festival meant to him and Senghor on a more personal note: "One might say that everything we said together and looked for together has been crowned by the festival. It is remarkable for a man to realize his dream. In my opinion, it is a great political act, and in it resides the essential idea of his rule. I say, 'hats off!'"[45]

These were heady years for Senghor. They brought prizes for his poetry in France, official visits to Presidents Kennedy and Johnson in the United States, honorary degrees from American, Brazilian, and French universities, and election to the French Academy of Moral and Political Sciences, where he was invited to fill the vacancy created by the death of Konrad Adenauer. At Senghor's induction ceremony in 1969, Giscard d'Estaing praised his wisdom and moderation in charting the future of his people, while Jacques Chaban-Delmas, descendant of one of the great Bordeaux commercial families that had done business in West Africa for more than a hundred years, hailed him as a man famous in all the universe who owed his accomplishment "not to intrigues and false appearances, but all to himself."[46] It seemed as if by some sleight of hand Senghor had become the perfect black Frenchman, playing the role he had yearned to play as a child but had rejected as a young man. His support of Negritude and independence had not destroyed but attracted French respect.

During these years, Senghor spent much of his time away from Senegal continuing to proclaim his idealistic goals and reiterating the importance of Negritude: "Only the recovery of our identity will lead to the recovery of our wealth, that is to say, our power of emotion, imagination, and expression," and elsewhere, "cultural liberation is the *sine qua non* of political liberation." He continued to believe that if the mystique of development could be introduced into the heads and hearts of Senegalese the game would be won.[47] He stressed the need for education, appealing to the young to study and serve the state, to the bureaucracy to curb corruption, to unions and salary earners to remember that they were privileged and prosperous compared to their compatriots in the villages, and to all Senegalese to develop the qualities of Negritude and work toward African socialism. He appealed to the French by means of his talk about Francophonie, and negotiated quietly for aid and technical advice.

By focusing on culture and Negritude rather than on terms of trade, proclaiming that African humanism was compatible with private enterprise, and promising not to Africanize at a discount, Senghor became a great favorite with France. But, too busy to reevaluate the abstract views developed many years before, he seemed to be losing touch with his own constituency. Although Negritude had proved a valuable idea for intellectuals trying to establish their self-respect in a European milieu and had justified the movement for independence, it was primarily a cultural concept, not a political one. It was not particularly useful in promoting loyalty to a new nation-state. Senghor tried to fill the gap by distinguishing between political and cultural homelands, but such ideas were cumbersome, hardly suited to generate much popular enthusiasm. The idea of Negritude, which, if it had political implications, suggested a single common interest, bore little relationship to a new and complex reality in which French advisors and importers, small French, Lebanese, and African tradesmen, the Islamic brotherhoods, the notables of the towns, and even the burgeoning ranks of government employees all had interests and positions of their own.

The failure of Senghor's ideas of Negritude to galvanize public support for his policies was evident, and was confirmed by several studies undertaken in the mid-1960s. When a group of middle-level functionaries in Senegal were asked whether they understood the concept of Negritude, only about half answered in the affirmative. Those answering yes said that Negritude referred to African art and culture and respect for the African heritage. They did not associate it with any particular political policy or with their own state. Another survey discovered that of 679 villagers in the southern Senegalese province of the Casamance, 599 had never heard the word Negritude.[48]

The concept of African socialism, unlike that of Negritude, had seemed to suggest a specific political and social policy to be followed after independence. In actuality, however, it proved sufficiently flexible and abstract to encompass almost any policy. By African socialism Senghor meant the use of advanced European-style technology by Africans who respected their own traditional culture. This idea was too vague to provide much guidance for making specific decisions, such as resolving conflicts between local and foreign enterprises or the urban and rural elites. Senghor continued to use the phrase, believing that scientific planning and the use of advanced technology would lead to economic development without arousing significant political or social opposition. But the idea of African socialism never really took root among the people. The same survey of Senegalese functionaries found that most of them had some ideas associated with the phrase "the African way to socialism," but when asked to define it, they spoke of social justice and sharing the land equally, rather than of technology or economic planning. Their wholehearted support for Senghor clearly did not grow out of a detailed understanding of his ideas.

To those concerned about their daily bread, and particularly to the leaders of the towns who felt they did not get the power and respect they deserved, Senghor's continued emphasis on the arts and culture and an African socialism that seemed in reality to favor French business sounded increasingly hollow. His continued references to Negritude and African socialism seemed to be a mystification, an effort to divert attention from real conflicts of interest rather than to clarify or resolve them. That he now used the word Africanité instead of Negritude, in order to avoid the charge of racism and attach his ideas more closely to Africa, made little difference. In March of 1967, when he was celebrating a Muslim holiday at the great mosque of Dakar, Senghor was attacked by a man with a knife. Fortunately he was not hurt. It turned out that the would-be assassin had been conspiring with former supporters of Mamadou Dia. In the spring of 1968, in echo of the student strikes in Paris, students in Dakar organized a protest. It seemed likely that the unions would join them, but the government managed to prevent what might have been a fatal alliance. The support that proved decisive in this crisis, ironically in the light of Senghor's modernizing rhetoric, was the chief Mouride marabout, who sent several thousand of the faithful into Dakar armed with machetes to demonstrate in front of the presidential palace in support of Senghor. The police used tear gas on the students, and although both the Senegalese army and the French garrison were put on alert, it proved unnecessary to use regular troops. Once again, Senghor demonstrated that he could remain calm and move quickly and firmly in time of crisis.[49]

Deep-seated problems were not so easily resolved. In 1971, when Senghor's old friend Georges Pompidou visited Dakar in his new capacity as president of France, demonstrators armed with Molotov cocktails were arrested and charged with plotting to assassinate him. In 1972 and again in the spring of 1973, students took to the streets demanding better stipends, an end to corruption, the rejection of neocolonialism, and the expulsion of the French from high positions. This time Senghor had to call out the troops. He then launched a diatribe, claiming that the students were influenced by communists and "teleguided" from France. A month later a student leader who had been arrested in connection with the violence during Pompidou's visit died in prison under suspicious circumstances. The public blamed the Interior Minister, Jean Collin, and assumed, perhaps correctly, that Senghor was remote from the details of the affair. Collin was a Frenchman who had married one of Senghor's nieces and taken Senegalese citizenship. He was hard-working and competent but ruthless and widely disliked. He bore the brunt of the criticism against the government's most unpopular acts.

By the early 1970s the mood in Senegal was ugly. It was true, as

Senghor argued, that students were privileged with respect to the rest of the population and that they were asking for funds and jobs that simply were not there. But it was also true that French technical advisors were making large salaries and living very well at the expense of the Senegalese government, that French books were still being used in schools, that French companies were still making substantial profits on the export trade, that the government was making large "loans" to the Mourides in return for their political support, and finally that the bureaucracy, swollen with those who were willing to support Senghor in return for a share in the good things of life, was full of people who supplemented their salaries with the fruits of graft and corruption. The poet-statesman, who repeated his paeans to Negritude and African socialism and basked in French praise, behaved as if nothing was amiss in his own country. He seemed to have lost his desire to talk directly to his people and his ability to understand their needs. He did not even try. Perhaps it was his age—he was almost seventy. Perhaps it was simply that his accomplishments were those of an era that had passed, and that new times called for new approaches he could not muster.

Intellectuals began to call Senghor "the little Nazi" to draw attention to his rigid authoritarian ways. Now he rarely ventured into the countryside other than to visit his clients and supporters, the Mouride marabouts. At a time when many African leaders appeared proudly in flowing traditional robes, Senghor always wore well-tailored French suits. The deputy in khaki who had settled under the baobab tree to listen and talk with the village elders had disappeared. In his place now sat a distant and powerful figure who appeared to have little interest in the sufferings of his people.[50] Even French literary critics who reviewed his poetry in French journals bemoaned the contradiction between his appealing poetic persona and his authoritarian politics at home. Instead of addressing specific problems, Senghor retreated into a cloud of rhetoric. Between him and the people of Senegal stood the iron fist of a minister whose foreign birth was an insult and a challenge to a young African generation anxious for power themselves. Actually Collin's presence was a testimony to Senghor's political shrewdness: the Frenchman, like the slave armies of the Serer kings, could never develop an independent power base from which to challenge his patron.

It seemed now that Senghor's inability to break with the French and his political habit of making peace with the opposition by offering them good jobs had served him well personally and kept the peace, but only at the price of such great corruption and economic stagnation that his basic authority was being undermined. Senghor weathered the storm by standing firm and using a show of force. By the early 1970s, however, his image as the politician willing to talk with everyone had been shattered. Visitors to Senegal at this time commented that Senghor seemed frail and overwhelmed by recent events. Rumors spread that he was ill and would soon resign.[51] Few of his ministers appeared capable or trustworthy. More and more of the burden of decision fell on Senghor personally.

But the stubborn peasant surprised his critics. In April of 1969 Senghor created a new organization, the Club for the Nation and Development, to serve as a forum for discussion by young Senegalese technocrats. It offered an opportunity for legitimate criticism of the regime and the consideration of new ideas. In February 1970 he presented for ratification a new constitution to prepare for his succession. The post of prime minister was reinstated and, after some jockeying among his associates, Senghor chose for the position a relatively unknown thirty-five-year-old technocrat without significant political experience, Abdou Diouf. There were other signs that Senghor had at last heard the message and had consolidated his power in order to make needed changes. In a cabinet reshuffling in 1973, twelve of twenty ministers were replaced with younger men, all under forty-three.[52] Senegal's new generation of technocrats was coming of age.

In foreign policy, too, there were signs of change. Senghor had long favored a close relationship with France, but by the early 1970s he had begun to reassess its real value to Senegal. The creation of the European Economic Community was a further complicating factor. In 1970, Senegal joined the Organization of African Unity (OAU) majority in condemning France for selling arms to South Africa, and began to put increased pressure on French companies operating in Senegal to hire Senegalese for local management positions. To his criticism of French communists and trade unions for interfering in Senegal's internal affairs, he added a bitter observation about growing racism in France.[53]

This cooling toward France was accompanied by new initiatives in Africa. Although Senghor had foreseen some of the consequences of Balkanization in West Africa and had tried to prevent the breakup of the federation, after independence relations with his African neighbors had taken second place to attempts to get aid from France. Senghor and Abdou Diouf now tried to breathe new life into old ideas about African cooperation. To them it was increasingly evident that Africans must rely more heavily on their own efforts and not expect to be saved by outside aid. Senegal joined Mali and Mauritania to form an organization for the development of the Senegal River. Senegal's efforts to group Francophone states in West Africa continued, not only with an eye to enticing French aid but also in the spirit of creating a counterbalance to the great weight of English-speaking Nigeria in a West African union of the future. Now virtually all leaders in West Africa recognized that cooperation among states was to everyone's benefit, although progress was slow because each also jealously guarded his independence.[54] Whether linguistic ties inherited from the colonial era, precolonial ethnic affiliations, or larger regional groupings would prove to be the basis for future collaboration was not yet clear, but it was evident that many problems, such as desertification, population growth, and migration, as well as the lack of large domestic markets for industrial economies of scale, required common effort for solution. Senghor's world view allowed easy adaptation to this idea: first would come loose federations among different regions and linguistic groups, then, as a second step, a real organization of African unity. Negritude could serve as its cultural foundation. While still not ready to give up his greater vision of Europe and Africa combined for mutual advantage, Senghor, or at least Senegal, began to focus more realistically on smaller designs.

The new emphases abroad had their analogy in economic policies at home. Confronted with a drastic deterioration in the terms of trade for its export crop, groundnuts, as well as hunger in the land as a result of mismanagement, corruption, and terrible drought, the government began to focus on diversifying the economy. This disenchantment with the monocrop economy paralleled a similar shift in Western experts' understanding of economic development. Fishing, phosphates, and tourism were promoted as new sources of foreign exchange, while the peasants were encouraged to grow more food for local markets. The latter change took place even without the government's initiative, as food was scarce in the countryside. In 1970, the marabouts, whose job it was to bless the seeds at sowing time, refused to bless the groundnut seeds and blessed only the food crops, millet and sorgum.[55] Senghor continued to travel and keep Senegal visible in international and cultural gatherings, while Abdou Diouf quietly put his economic measures into effect. At last Senghor had found a competent associate to replace Dia, whom he had lost more than ten years before.

Early in the spring of 1976, the year of his seventieth birthday, Senghor again proposed constitutional changes that were ratified by the National Assembly. Senghor's critics shook their heads over a new provision that allowed the president to stand for election as many times as he pleased. According to the previous constitution Senghor would have had to step down in 1983, three years before his eightieth birthday. Now he could maintain power indefinitely. This new constitution gave the president the right to retire in favor of his prime minister, should he have a mind to do so, thus granting him the right to pick his successor.

The new laws also legalized three political parties, the ruling party, one to its right, and one to its left. In explaining this arrangement, Senghor argued that the proliferation of too many small parties would threaten political stability, but that the existence of choice was essential for African socialism. He cast himself in the role of paterfamilias and professor, patiently teaching his family what was best for them. Two new political parties were duly registered: to the left of the ruling party the Marxist Party of African Independence (PAI), and to its right the Senegalese Democratic Party (PDS). The ruling party, the UPS, was formally disbanded and rechristened the Socialist Party (PS). It held the safe middle ground that should attract the majority for years to come. The few political prisoners, including Mamadou Dia, were released. New unions were also legalized and restrictions on the press reduced.

Senegal's political life was immediately enlivened. Publications proliferated. Celebrating his seventieth birthday the next fall, Senghor quoted the Latin canticle to an interviewer: "Now I can say 'nunc dimittis servum tuum, Dominee'—let now your servant depart, Lord, since my dearest wish has been accomplished. Give to my black people pride in their own values; at the same time let them realize their weaknesses."[56]

Senghor's final political wish was to commit Senegal firmly to representative democracy. He also wanted to reestablish his position as a democratic socialist. With the quickening of political life and a relatively free press, criticism of the government came out into the open. Each of the opposition parties had its own newspaper, as did the newly liberated Mamadou Dia. There were other new publications devoted to humor, young people, and sport. Some published articles in Arabic and in Wolof, the most widely spoken African language in Senegal. Several newspapers quickly took up criticism of "old Leo" or "Leo the lion," as they called him, in what may have seemed to Senghor an ironic echo of his identification with Diogoye the lion. He had made the lion the emblem of the BDS, and later of Senegal itself, even instituting the Order of the Lion as the highest honor Senegal could bestow. What had been a serious matter for him was simply a joke to a younger generation.

These same newspapers had a more serious side. They pointed out problems in government policy, ranging from obstructionist tactics toward a Japanese auto manufacturer who wanted to enter the Senegalese market but would have competed with an established French company, to personal attacks on Senghor for taking money from the public purse to buy French property. In the latter case, Senghor took the newspaper to court and, confronted with evidence that contradicted its story, the newspaper retracted it. That incident in itself provided evidence of an honest effort on Senghor's part to encourage a free and responsible press. One of the papers that had been most critical of Senghor cautioned its readers, "Senghor is objectively our only ally in the government. He really wants a free press." There was some truth in this observation. Shortly thereafter a deputy of Senegal's National Assembly attacked Senghor's experiment with democracy for allowing "enemies of the regime to bring in false ideas . . . Senghor is making a mistake; we need order for progress."[57]

In the first elections under the new constitutional system, which were held on February 26, 1978, the ruling PS won the overwhelming majority of the votes cast, more than 80 percent, with the PDS receiving about 265,000 votes and the Marxist PAI just over 3,000. The effect on the National Assembly was that the PS held 82 seats, the PDS 18, and the PAI none. Only about 43 percent of those eligible chose to vote, however, a sharp contrast with the turnouts of earlier years when well over 90 percent of those eligible had gone to the polls and voted for Senghor. Enthusiasm for Senghor was clearly on the wane. Rumors again spread that he was in poor health and would resign. To Diouf he gave increasing responsibility and visibility, calling the new government the Diouf government and giving Diouf the job of presiding over weekly cabinet meetings. Senghor announced that he would fill out his term, but when journalists questioned him about his real intentions he answered with a Serer proverb: "The stalking hunter does not cough."[58]

Senghor's experiment with democracy coincided, unfortunately, with a turn for the worse in the economy. Senegal, like all poor African countries dependent on the export of raw materials for foreign exchange, suffered greatly in the late 1970s from a deterioration in the terms of trade. Oil prices rose dramatically, as did commercial interest rates. Drought reduced both the groundnut yield and that of food crops. Between 1977 and 1978 the exchange earned by the groundnut crop fell by two-thirds, both because the crop was smaller and because of a drop in its price. Between 1978 and 1979 the price of groundnuts fell a further 25 percent, while the average price of what Senegal had to import, which now included food, grew by 15 percent. In 1946 one pound of groundnuts had bought one pound of rice. By 1976 it took three pounds of groundnuts to buy that same pound of rice. Senegal's foreign debt ballooned in size, more than doubling between 1976 and 1980.[59] Looking to the north, the Senegalese saw the borders of the Sahel desert advancing. The peasants not only had nothing to sell; they began to starve. The situation was exacerbated by a geometric population growth, from 3.15 million in 1962 to 5.86 million in 1981. Senegal gratefully accepted emergency aid. In 1980, for the first time, Senegal saw no way to balance its budget. Senghor sent Abdou Diouf to Paris to ask President Giscard d'Estaing for help. It was the first time Senegal had asked for a direct loan to meet current expenses. To most people's surprise, Giscard agreed, thus rewarding Senegal for its faithfulness to France and its perfect record on debt repayment. No doubt Giscard was also looking to a future when Diouf, not Senghor, would be in charge.[60]

On December 31, 1980, at the end of a rather lackluster speech, Senghor quietly announced his decision to resign in favor of Abdou Diouf. To him it was a relief, as it was to many of his compatriots. Some said that they heard Diouf's inaugural speech, pleasantly free from the high-flown and increasing stale Senghorian rhetoric about culture and Negritude, with tears in their eyes. However much admiration and support Senghor had had in 1939, 1945, 1948, and even 1960, it had been dissipated by 1980. Before his resignation, Senghor had prepared the population for a hard struggle ahead. Now people looked to Diouf, the technocrat, to lead it.

Once again, Senghor had proved to be a pioneer. He was the first African leader to give up power voluntarily. Some now say he had lost his ability to deal with Senegal's problems and had no choice, but other African leaders had not accepted their loss of popularity and effectiveness. Senghor had the wisdom to see and the grace to act.

It has been suggested that Senghor's political methods were those of "the prince," an African leader who keeps the peace by receiving notables and wisely adjudicating disputes, ruling by virtue of the authority of his person without the support of legitimate institutions, and without attempting to alter the social and economic structure of his country.[61] Such a characterization of Senghor is only partially correct and is certainly incomplete. It captures neither the complexity of Senegal's political life in the era of Senghor nor the special conditions that made this distinctive political culture possible.

When Senegal became independent in 1960, it had a long tradition of electoral politics. For more than one hundred and fifty years, the African citizens of Senegal's communes had elected local representatives and participated in the rule of their towns. They were accustomed to forming alliances, following individuals, creating political parties, publishing their views, and abiding by electoral outcomes. However alien French law and constitutional forms might be to those of traditional Africa, the French and Africans of Senegal had created a framework within which urban Senegalese had acquired considerable experience in the use of French political institutions. Senghor himself was a master of this system, with abundant experience in both France and Senegal. Although African citizens were few in number before World War II, they had created a strong tradition of representative government that was distinctly theirs. They brought this with them to postindependence politics.

The character and the role of the Islamic brotherhoods also influenced what was possible and not possible in independent Senegal. The family and village remained the primary units of Senegalese society, but beyond them the brotherhoods provided the organization within which many rural Senegalese lived their lives. The brotherhoods, like Senegalese society in general, showed great tolerance for ethnic and class differences in accepting members, but jealously guarded the economic and social control of their villages. Within the brotherhoods, the laws of Islam and the marabouts ruled supreme.

Senghor could also draw on a third political and social tradition, that of the Serer of Sine. He understood politics as the art of satisfying the demands of many different groups and finding a balance among them. His conception of the political leader was of a person who may provide both philosophical and spiritual leadership, but whose primary task is to listen and find consensus. This is not the kind of leader who forces others to do his will. It was and is the kind of leader expected and admired by most Senegalese, for the traditions of the Serer and other large ethnic groups in Senegal are similar. It was because he adhered to these principles that people in Senegal respected and approved of Senghor.[62] Senghor may well have acted as "the prince," but it was a prince whose style of dealing with his constituencies was supported by local expectations and experience.

These three traditions helped establish the framework within which Senghor added his piece to Senegal's developing political culture. Senghor consciously used his personal authority to strengthen the legitimacy of Senegal's new political institutions. He set out to construct an authoritative legal and constitutional system on the Western model that would ensure popular confidence in government. He worked to create a modern state, where jobs would be allotted on the basis of merit and constitutional and secular laws would regulate the relations of the government to its citizens and the relations of citizens to one another. In most ways these laws were in keeping with the spirit of popular expectations for government. While it is true that the constitution was often amended, it is equally important to note that Senghor chose to amend the constitution rather than to ignore or abolish it. He tried to avoid the use of force, and used his personal prestige not to violate laws but to add to their authority. Thus Senghor's technique for achieving and maintaining political consensus drew heavily on his personal power and skill, but included the use and strengthening of political and legal institutions, which he hoped would gain legitimacy in their own right.

Unlike the so-called prince, Senghor did have a strategy for change. A major goal of his education policy was to create a corps of Senegalese technocrats. They were to replace his French advisors and administer scientifically based development plans that would shift the economic and social balance of the country gradually from the traditional to the modern sector, undermining the power of the marabouts in the process. The effect was to be a peaceful revolution. In fact, however, administrators such as Diouf did not remain isolated from politics, nor develop an ethic of honest public service. Industrialization did not occur, and the power of the marabouts remained unbroken. Senghor did have a plan for change; it simply did not work.

Senghor presided over his country in ways drawn from his own experience, trying to preserve a balance between the values and methods of the two worlds that had made him what he was. Independence in friendship with France was his great triumph. But in politics the refusal to choose can prove to be a kind of choice. Senghor's critics have argued that by cooperating with the French, relying on foreign capital investment administered by the state, and trying to develop an export economy, Senghor stifled local initiative and condemned his people to prolonged dependence on the former colonial power.[63] From this perspective, Senghor's decision in 1962 to oust Mamadou Dia, and to pull back from creating peasant cooperatives, was the fatal moment at which he chose the French, abandoned the countryside, and betrayed his earlier, and correct, conviction that agricultural reform must take priority in any development program. In 1962, however, nothing had seemed so clear-cut. Hindsight is both clear and oddly blind, for it overlooks the context of emotions and misapprehensions with which decisions are invariably made. Senghor did make an important choice, but he felt it as a forced choice. He heeded the prevailing economic wisdom of the early 1960s, namely that the state would have to invest capital in the economic infrastructure and take the initiative if economic development was to be successful. He believed that by preserving his own power and the goodwill of the French he was enlarging the opportunities for Senegal.

Had Senghor resigned the presidency at the height of his enormous popularity in 1960 or 1962, he might have been remembered as a great poet who inspired and led his people to independence. Had he resigned in the turbulent times of the early 1970s, as many of his friends urged him to do, he might well have been seen as a great poet and independence leader who was seduced by power, and whose willful blindness to reality rendered him at best incompetent, and at worst a vain old lion, hungry for personal honors. Thinking perhaps of his place in history, Senghor managed a last burst of political creativity in his final years as president, and accomplished what no one expected of him, a revitalization of democracy in Senegal.

Senghor's immediate legacy was recognized by Amnesty International in 1981, when Senegal was cited as among the countries with the world's best records on human rights. In 1983, Abdou Diouf was overwhelmingly reelected in a multiparty election that was preceded by a lively press campaign. Now Diouf held power in his own right. Commenting on his country's unusually democratic and open political life, Diouf expressed a belief that matched Senghor's: the fact that a country was poor was no excuse for trampling on human rights.[64]

From the standpoint of economics, however, Senghor's record was far less impressive. Diouf had inherited a difficult challenge. Unfavorable terms of trade continued to plague the economy. French interests continued to dominate the import-export trade, one place where profits could still be made, and French companies continued to expatriate their profits. Senegal's foreign debt mounted at a dizzying rate. By 1982 debt repayment equaled 23 percent of the value of exports and was projected to reach 50 percent by the end of the decade. Under pressure from the International Monetary Fund and the World Bank, the government created an economic and financial adjustment program for 1985–1992. It reduced protection for local industries and cut government spending, thereby adding to unemployment. Repayment of interest to international lenders had to take priority over social services. Health expenditure as a percentage of the overall budget fell, for example, from 9 percent in 1970–71 to 5.8 percent in 1985. Nonetheless, the population continued to grow rapidly. By the late 1980s, about half of the population was under the age of sixteen.[65] Young people found few jobs and faced a grim future.

As the Diouf regime neared the end of its first decade in power, its attempts at administrative decentralization and the reduction of bureaucratic interference in the rural economy were praised by its lenders, as were stringency measures designed to enable Senegal to repay its loans. The economy experienced modest growth. But the government's efforts were sorely compromised by old habits and ministerial jealousies, as well as by widespread corruption and greed. In Dakar, rich and poor alike told stories about government officials who had diverted public funds to private use, granted contracts to friends and relatives, or extracted "loans" from Senegalese banks that they had no intention of repaying. The peasants continued to work for little reward, contributing their labor not to create the capital necessary for investment and new jobs but rather, it seemed, to pay off debts and support the relatively luxurious lifestyle of Diouf and his entourage. Noticing, for example, that rice was imported from Indochina rather than grown in the Casamance or Senegal River regions of their own country, people did not accept the explanation that this was a rational policy but wondered instead who was making a profit. Although government corruption and mismanagement may not have been significantly greater than in many other countries, in a small, poor country such as Senegal they were highly visible and therefore the more dispiriting to those who were expected to make sacrifices today for the common good of tomorrow. Rather than accepting the government's reasons for cutting back on social services, people felt that the government had deserted the poor and the unemployed in their hour of need. Economic problems were threatening to undermine the political balance so carefully created by Senghor. Confidence in the morality and competence of the government, which had surged when Diouf came into power, gave way to cynicism.

In 1988 elections were held as scheduled and, true to the tradition established by Senghor and Diouf, numerous parties competed for votes. Before the results were announced, however, the government declared a state of emergency and arrested Abdoulaye Wade, the leader of the main opposition party, whom it accused of fomenting violence. The Diouf regime then announced the electoral victory of its own party. Young people took to the streets of Dakar, convinced that fraud had prevailed over justice. The police and the civil guard were called out.[66] Wade's arrest was a precedent that troubled many Senegalese. Mamadou Dia, now old and partially blind, made a moving appeal to the government to respect Senegal's democratic traditions. Now Senghor was criticized, not because he had stayed so long, but because he had insisted on choosing his successor and had made such a poor choice.

As they turn to face this political, economic, and moral crisis, Senegalese do not refer to Senghor's grand ideological concepts. After a decade without him, Senegalese do not talk of Negritude or African socialism. Those who are looking for new principles on which to found their personal and collective morality are turning either to traditional African culture, as indeed Senghor urged them to do, or to Islam.[67] The rural population and many of the urban poor look to the marabouts for social guidance and spiritual security. They may hold the key to Senegal's future, for the great revolutions of our time have been brought to the cities by the countryside. Evolution has usually depended on city folk, who, like Senghor, have tried to borrow and learn from others while preserving ties to their own past. In the schools of Senegal, children continue to steep themselves in the French language and culture and to learn about the possibilities of modern science and technology. They, too, have a stake in Senegal's future, and it is on them that Senghor rested his hopes.

It is still difficult to assess Senghor's record, and to separate those areas in which he merits credit or blame because he chose wisely or foolishly from those areas in which he was the creature of forces beyond his control. He did not succeed in creating an Afro-French culture or the Eurafrican partnership that he had envisioned as a young man. He did not accomplish an economic miracle and create in Senegal the paradise of which many Africans dreamed in the 1960s. But there have been few economic miracles in independent Africa, and none in countries with as few natural resources as Senegal. In the 1970s and early 1980s, many Senegalese openly blamed Senghor for the nation's problems, forgetting that their ability to express their views freely and safely was a rare gift in Africa. For them the idea of Negritude seemed irrelevant, for they had forgotten the time when everything African had been scorned by Africa's own elites and Senegal had been ruled from Paris.

Today views of Senghor are changing. Many Senegalese have begun to look back nostalgically at the time when he was president, praising him as a great poet and a man of idealism and personal honesty. They remember that he had a talent for talking with simple people and are proud of the respect he earned from the Europeans. The delicate balance of political and economic interests that he created preserved them from the violence and ethnic strife that have been the scourge of many of their African neighbors.

Senghor established a set of political institutions which he built carefully by drawing on the resources of Senegal's political culture and on his own gifts for understanding people, distinguishing the important from the trivial, and finding workable compromises. He understood that if he relied on force to settle disputes today, he would lose his power to rule peacefully tomorrow. This practice of negotiation and compromise supported the institutions he valued: multiparty elections, the rule of law, and a relatively free press. Together they make up Senghor's political legacy to his country. It is now up to the people and government of Senegal to decide whether or not these institutions will be preserved through a period of economic hardship.

13

Emeritus

W hen Senghor relinquished power at the end of 1980, his life and that of his country again diverged. Even in retirement, however, Senghor did not choose to follow an easy course. He continued to seek the statesman's role, eager to play a part in conciliatory efforts around the world, and to encourage regional groupings in Africa as steps toward African, Eurafrican, and eventually worldwide cooperation. Particularly dear to him now was his status as democratic socialist, and the part he could play as a moving force in the Interafrican Socialist Organization.[1] There were additional rewards of age, including, perhaps most important to him, election in 1984 to that most admired of all French institutions, the Académie Française. Henceforward he would be one of the "immortals." He was welcomed into the academy by Edgar Faure, in whose cabinet he had served in 1955. Recognizing the duality of Senghor's career, Faure addressed him thus: "You are among those who think that poets, because they are visionaries, are qualified to lead the destinies of peoples during periods of change, when the movement of history is so rapid that one can only keep up with it by preceding it."[2]

In 1985 Senghor enjoyed the recognition, unusual for a living writer, of having the venerable Bibliothèque Nationale in Paris mount a large exhibition in his honor. He supported the idea on the condition that the exhibition emphasize his intellectual and literary work rather than his political career.

During these retirement years, Senghor gradually disengaged himself more and more completely from Senegal's political and economic struggles. He returned to the preoccupations of his youth, to poetry and philosophy. He enjoyed working on the committees of the Académie Française, spending much of his time in Paris or at his wife's family home in Normandy. At least twice each year, in May and November, he returned for extended stays in Dakar. There he was sometimes seen shopping in the main Dakar market, and people told tales of his conversations with the market women that showed that he had not lost his gift for talking to the simple people of Senegal.

His most visible public activity was devoted to the Senghor Foundation, which he had established to support education and promote African culture. The goals of the foundation, according to its statement of purpose, are to safeguard and enrich the Negro-African heritage and contribute to international understanding by supporting researchers, promoting scientific and cultural work by Africans, and collecting and diffusing works on the African oral tradition.[3] From its headquarters in Dakar, where it maintains a small library and staff, it has sponsored conferences, awarded grants, and established prizes for outstanding work by African authors. The foundation represents Senghor's continued effort to further a cause for which he worked throughout his long career. Over the work of this foundation, as he once did over the politics of Senegal, Senghor exercised tight control.

In 1988 Senghor published a book entitled *Ce que je crois* (What I Believe).[4] In it he distills his many years of thinking about French and African history. In essence the book repeats and embellishes ideas that Senghor developed in the 1930s. It documents the antiquity of life in Africa, the contributions of ancient African culture to other civilizations, the particular gifts of the French, and the extraordinary importance of what Senghor calls the revolution of 1889, that moment in French history when artists and philosophers recognized the shortcomings of their own rationalistic tradition and began to turn to other cultures for inspiration. He ends his book with some observations about the United States, as a land in which people of varied biological and cultural heritages have come together to build a creative and powerful state. The book confirms the remarkable consistency of Senghor's thinking and his preoccupation with a few broad general ideas. It also reveals Senghor's strengths and weaknesses, his love of research, philosophy, and words, his enjoyment of and skill in abstract discussion, his didacticism, and also an all-too-human tendency to extract and emphasize only those facts which support his views. Most characteristic of all, *Ce que je crois* expresses Senghor's grand and generous dream of bringing people and cultures together in mutual respect in order to build the civilization of the universal.

In his personal life, these same years were hard. Senghor suffered two bitter blows. The first was the death, apparently by suicide, of his brilliant, academically minded son, Guy, in Paris. This was the boy born during the political campaign of 1948, the child of Senghor and Ginette Eboué, who carried the name of Senghor's beloved Uncle Waly. Though Guy was raised by his mother and estranged from his father, his death removed any hope Senghor might have had that father and son might one day be reconciled. The second and even more devastating blow was an automobile accident in 1982 that killed Senghor's youngest son, Philippe-Maguilen Senghor. Philippe was the only son of Senghor and Colette Hubert, a handsome and gifted young man, seemingly the perfect blend of black and white, and the apple of his father's eye. He was also very popular in Senegal. His funeral brought an outpouring of thousands of mourners in Dakar. Since then a number of medical clinics have been named in his memory.

In a moving poem about Philippe's death, which he dedicated to his wife, Senghor enters into a dialogue with God: "for our autumn of decline, he was the spring / . . . Brutally you wrenched him from us, as the thief a treasure on the high road." The poet traces the phases of his grief. At first he denied the reality of death. He could not believe the news. A just God would not have allowed such a thing. Now he asks God's pardon for this momentary refusal of His justice. He believes that his son is yet another sacrifice demanded of him by God for Senegal. Nonetheless it is a struggle for the poet to offer this sacrifice without protest. Were not three hundred years of colonial domination enough? Was not his life's work sufficient? "We have given everything to this country, to this our continent / Days and nights and vigilance, fatigue, pain, and combat among the assembled nations." How could God demand still more, the poet seems to be saying. God tried Abraham by demanding that his son, Isaac, be sacrificed, but took mercy on an old man. Senghor's Isaac has not been spared. God has also tested the mother, whom the poet describes as "crucified" by her loss. The poet does not give way to anger, nor will he give up his faith. He accepts that "the labyrinth of Your designs is impenetrable." Until this moment, the thread of faith had protected him from the Minotaur. Now, close to the end of his own life, he can no longer see his way clear through the maze of God's designs. The poet's mind tells him that he has no choice but to accept what has happened, "that Your will be accomplished." But he will not pretend that he under-stand's God's purpose. At the funeral, the poet hears his son's name on the lips of mourners who have come to pay him homage from throughout the land. They repeat his name, Philippe-Maguilen, as they have repeated those of his ancestors, for all Africa knows that the dead endure only if the living chant their names. The poet takes comfort in the incantations of Africa. He also hears a child's clear voice singing an old Afro-American spiritual, "Steal away, steal away, steal away to Jesus." As he concludes this anguished and very beautiful poem, the poet seeks solace in a harmonious blend of Christian and African chants, where mingle now, as they had in his childhood, the harmonies of Christianity and traditional Africa. Now neither alone, nor even both together, can fully obliterate the pain of loss.[5]

Philippe's death removed the personal heir who might have served as the visible and symbolic evidence of Senghor's love for France. Neither in public nor in private life did Senghor succeed in passing on the heritage of assimilation as he had planned. It is as if Senghor himself were so completely a transitional figure as to be a hybrid, incapable of producing a viable heir. He had faced problems and found solutions that did not seem important to those who came after him. He had met the challenge of forging a new type of link to the West, only to discover that it, like France's civilizing mission, was fatally flawed. Two such different peoples could not find a way to build a common future.

Early in life, Senghor had the sense that he had been singled out to play a great role. He saw this role not as a European might have seen it, as a right to individual success, but rather as one inseparably linked to that of the group into which he was born. He felt himself called to a duty he could not escape, first to God, and then to his people. He began as the intellectual who would understand and speak for his toiling black people. Then he became their ambassador to the assembled nations, and finally, their president. This vocation was synonymous with the person Senghor had become. He seemed to sense this, for he once wrote that he had awakened from a dream in panic. He had dreamed that he had become white. The panic derived, he wrote, from the knowledge that if he were white there would be no reason for his suffering. He could no longer be the leader of his black people. Under such circumstances, he would have no choice but suicide. Questioned further why this dream had held such terror for him, he answered more prosaically that if he were white, he would have no defense against his pride.[6] Whatever the deepest sources of this dream, it suggests that Senghor realized that his role as spokesman and go-between was indistinguishable from the person he had become. He had successfully created himself as the prototype of his own ideal, the French Negro able to incorporate the best of the two cultures that had formed him, nourished him, and granted him their praise. His very being offered proof of the creativity that might result from Africa's encounter with the West.

There is a mythic quality to Senghor's life and vision. This is true in part because Senghor was a conscious mythmaker. As a poet, he drew on his personal feelings and dreams and reworked them to express the more general experience of his people. He wanted to create life-enhancing images and myths. Once, to counter the criticism that Africans live by archetypal images, he pointed out that the peoples of Europe and the United States also live by archetypal images, "for what are Free Enterprise, The American Way of Life, Democracy, and Communism, but myths around which hundreds of millions of men and women organize their lives? Negritude itself is a myth . . . a living, dynamic one." Senghor saw his as the highest possible calling, that of mythmaker, and identified himself proudly as a "master of languages" and of the word.[7]

At another level, Senghor's life story itself has the makings of myth. It becomes the legend of the boy born poor in a distant place, who shows early signs of precociousness to those in his immediate, small world, and who moves steadily and surely toward the center of historical importance. He was the boy from the bush who won all the prizes from the whites. Then, coming of age in dramatic fashion, he offered the world a fresh vision. Senghor offered to those who were black and French the possibility of becoming New Negroes, French Negroes rather than the black Frenchmen that others expected them to be. Standing on that ground, he moved forward to tilt with the dragon, the French and their arrogant view of Africans. This hero defeated the dragon, not so much through trickery or strength as through determination and intelligence, generosity and forgiveness, using the miraculous tools of education and culture that he had acquired from the French themselves. Once he had his victory, he and the French were reconciled. The hero then moved on to preside over a new kingdom. Up to this point, Senghor's life follows the archetypal plot of the literary odyssey or legend. When Senghor told his own story, he occasionally omitted, consciously or not, those details which did not fit with this tale of gradual but continuous ascent to victory.

The distinction between this uplifting myth and the reality of Senghor's life is that this king-president could not simply live happily ever after. He was a real philosopher and president, responsible for a real kingdom, with a real history and real problems. Senghor did not flinch. Knowing, as he must have done, that his myth would be irreparably tarnished, he threw himself into the fray to try to bend history to fit his dream of France and Africa working together. To criticize him for not succeeding fully is to forget that he did accomplish much.

The year before he resigned as president of Senegal, Senghor acknowledged that he did not expect to live to see the Senegal he had dreamed of, a Senegal he unselfconsciously called the promised land. He knew that the reconciliation of Negritude and modernity would not be accomplished in Senegal in his lifetime. "In the morning when I awake," he wrote, "I feel all the world that weighs on me . . . [but] when I open the window and see the sun rising over Gorée, over the island of slavery, I say to myself, all the same, since the end of the slave trade, we have made progress."[8]

Senghor has called his life's work the poetry of action. Had he not been involved in politics, he believes, his poetry might have been more abundant, but it would have lacked the dimension added by his worldly experience. Had he not been a poet, the politician might have lost his sense of direction and become the creature of worldly pressures and everyday demands. As it was, each facet of his talent added to the brilliance of the other. Both served a single purpose: his wish "to create a new world . . . a new philosophy, a new literature . . . a new society." Whatever Senghor's humility before God and his simplicity toward men, his ambition was great. Just as he refused to choose between his talents as poet and politician, sensing that each added depth to the other, so, too, he refused to choose between his two homelands, France and Africa. He knew their strengths and weaknesses, their darkness and their light, and he loved them both. His life was dedicated to bringing the best of each to the other.[9] Was it not a task worthy of a great heart?

A Note on Sources

Information about Senghor's politics is readily available. His poetry has been published in both French and English in multiple editions. What is elusive is information about his childhood and his later formative years, that important time between his arrival in Paris as a student in 1928 and his first published article in 1935. This is the period during which Senghor transformed himself from a passive creature of others' intentions into an actor on his own behalf. During these years, he rethought and reformed his identity as a black man in European society. This change set the stage for his later power and influence. There are three main sources of information about this period. They are, in order of their increasing reliability, the later reminiscences of Senghor and his friends, poetry written by Senghor then or shortly thereafter, and Senghor's correspondence written at the time.

Memory must always be approached with some skepticism. Cautioning the biographer setting out on an interview, Valdimir Nabokov warns, "Beware the most honest broker. Remember that what you are told is really three-fold: shaped by the teller, reshaped by the listener, concealed from both by the . . . man of the tale." In Senghor's case, his own and others' memoirs about his childhood and student days are sparse, except for fond but impersonal recollections of his student years at Lycée Louis-le-grand in Paris. His friends have been willing to be interviewed and have told numerous anecdotes, but in light of Senghor's later prominence, it is possible that an anticipatory glow recasts their recollections of his early achievements. It would be natural for them to read back into these early years the success and assurance that they knew him later to possess. In such case, memory is subject to error or rearrangement, not because of a conscious effort to distort the past, but because of the selective nature of memory itself. What Senghor chooses to remember and make public is even more strongly influenced by such pressures and by a natural desire to present himself as the perfect example of a man both black and French who blends the best of both into a single personality. Nonetheless, to the extent that a number of different individuals' recollections confirm one another or recall behavior rather than feelings or attitude, they are useful to the biographer. Such recollections are often the only source for the important period of childhood and early youth, the time before anyone had thought to record the activities of the child who was to become an important man. Although the sources for Senghor's childhood are few and largely dependent on such memories, when Senghor himself read the first two chapters of this book, he confirmed with some surprise that they had captured the essence of his family situation and the world in which he grew up.

Senghor's poetry is a rich contemporary source for his feelings and experience, but cannot be assumed to be an unguarded reflection of his innermost mood or thought. Senghor is a poet, not a clinician. His poetry expresses what mattered to him and what he wished to share with others transposed into art. There is also the evidence of the many published essays, which set out Senghor's cultural and political views. They bear an interesting genetic resemblance to what is expressed in his poetry but are clearly distinct from it. These two sources for understanding Senghor's early adulthood are supplemented by his correspondence with colonial administrators in Dakar. This correspondence reveals how precariously he walked the line between success and failure, and how skillfully he presented different faces to his friends and to his sponsors. Unfortunately the letters he wrote home to Hélène Senghor have been lost, put, she said, into a drawer where they were eaten by insects and crumbled with time.

Finally, there is the large public record of what Senghor actually did. Here, too, much remains obscure. Lack of archival access is a significant drawback in writing about a still-living figure. And yet, as I think about my most valuable sources for learning about Senghor and his times, I realize that many of the people whom I interviewed for this book have since died. Each of them was, as the Africans like to say, a living library. I have had the great pleasure of consulting this library, and a small part of it is preserved here.

Notes

Several African states have changed their names since independence: the Upper Volta to Burkina Faso, Dahomey to Bénin, and the French Sudan to Mali. I have generally referred to these countries by the name in use at the time of the events that are being discussed.

1. Childhood

1. The general information for Senghor's early childhood is drawn from my interviews with members of his family: his aunt Hélène Senghor (Mme René Senghor); his older sister Dior Senghor; and various of his nieces, nephews, and cousins—Lat Senghor, Pierre Senghor, Katrine Senghor, Blaise Senghor, and Marie-Thérèse Basse. These interviews were conducted in Dakar, Kaolack, and Joal, Senegal, in June 1973 and March 1976. Interviews with Senghor himself in Burlington, Vermont, in June 1971 and in Dakar in June 1973 and March 1976 supplemented them.

2. Senghor, "Elégie des eaux," *Nocturnes,* in Senghor, *Poèmes* (Paris: Le Seuil, 1984), p. 208. Unless otherwise noted, all translations from the French are my own. Quotations from Senghor's poetry appear by permission of Georges Borchardt, Inc.

3. Senghor's sister Dior insists that her mother was Serer (interview, Kaolack, June 16, 1973). Senghor himself has simply registered the fact that there is some doubt about his ethnicity in that his mother's name was Peul, his father's Malinké. The fact that his mother's brother was a shepherd, a common Peul occupation, is not decisive, for the Serer combined the occupations of shepherd and cultivator. If Sédar's maternal grandfather was, as is said, the headman of a Serer village, it seems unlikely that Sédar's mother was 100 percent Peul. Others have suggested that Senghor's mother's name, Bakhoum, is a griot name, making it unlikely that her father was the head of a village. This confusion underlines the complexity of ethnic identification in an area of considerable mobility and intermarriage where there was no enmity between central and peripheral groups.

4. L'Abbé P.-D. Boilat, *Esquisses sénégalaises* (Paris: P. Bertrand, 1853), pp. 107–112. The Abbé Boilat was a Creole born in Saint-Louis and educated in France.

5. Ibid., p. 113.

6. "Journal de la Mission de Joal de 1900 à 1931," ms. cited in Michèle

Dorsemaine, Alfred Fierro, and Josette Masson, eds., *Léopold Sédar Senghor* (Paris: Bibliothèque Nationale, 1978), p. 8. This is the catalog of a large exposition at the Bibliothèque Nationale in Paris that gathered together much previously unpublished information about Senghor.

7. Malik Guèye, School Report, 1908, cited in Denise Bouche, *L'enseignement dans les territoires français de l'Afrique occidentale de 1817 à 1920,* 2 vols. (Lille: Atelier Reproduction des Theses, 1975), II, 634.

8. Senghor, "Eléments constitutifs d'une civilisation d'inspiration Négro-africaine," in Senghor, *Liberté 1: Négritude et humanisme* (Paris: Le Seuil, 1964), p. 268.

9. The information about the Serer is drawn from Pathé Diagne, "La monarchie sérère, XIV–XIX siècles," in his *Pouvoir politique traditionelle en Afrique occidentale* (Paris: Présence Africaine, 1967), pp. 56–94; "Djilor," *Dakar Jeunes,* no. 28 (July 16, 1942); and James Shank, "The Serer," manuscript, ca. 1970.

10. "Djilor," *Dakar Jeunes.*

11. Senghor, "Que m'accompagnent kôras et balafong," *Chants d'ombre,* in *Poèmes,* pp. 31–32. For confirmation of a chronological sort for this memory, see "Djilor," *Dakar Jeunes.*

12. Senghor, "A l'appel de la race de Saba," *Hosties noires,* in *Poèmes,* pp. 57–58. The English translation is from Senghor, *Selected Poems,* trans. John Reed and Clive Wake (New York: Atheneum, 1969), pp. 29–30.

13. "Que m'accompagnent kôras et balafong," *Poèmes,* pp. 36–37. Translation by Reed and Wake in *Selected Poems,* p. 18.

14. Senghor, "Commes les lamantins vont boire à la source," in *Liberté 1,* p. 221.

15. Interview with Dior Senghor, June 16, 1973.

16. Senghor, *La poésie de l'action: Conversations avec Mohamed Aziza* (Paris: Stock, 1980), p. 48.

17. Marthe Ponet-Bordeaux, *Mgr. Hyacinthe Jalabert: Une vie de missionaire* (Paris: Beauchesne, 1924), pp. 19, 123–128. Senghor cites Libermann's motto in "Ce que l'homme noir apporte," *Liberté 1,* p. 23. Information about life at Ngazobil is from *Journal de Ngasobil,* no. 2 (1892–1934), Archives générales, Congrégation du Saint-Esprit, Chevilly-la-rue, France, and from the author's interview with Mother Gonzague Valot, Dakar, March 25, 1976. She was a nun at Ngazobil when Senghor was a student there. In 1976, she was ninety-four years old.

18. Ponet-Bordeaux, *Jalabert,* p. 127.

19. Ibid., p. 125.

20. Senghor, *La poésie de l'action,* p. 49; James Bruce-Benoît, "Témoignage," in *Hommage à Léopold Sédar Senghor, homme de culture* (Paris: Présence Africaine, 1976), p. 219.

21. Raymond Leslie Buell, *The Native Problem in Africa,* 2 vols. (New York: Macmillan, 1928), II, 57; Hardy is cited on p. 59.

22. Interview with Mother Gonzague Valot, March 25, 1976.

23. Jean Rous, *Léopold Sédar Senghor* (Paris: Didier, 1967), pp. 15–16. Rous was a political collaborator of Senghor's.

24. Ernest Milcent and Monique Sordet, *Léopold Sédar Senghor et la naissance de l'Afrique moderne* (Paris: Seghers, 1969), pp. 21, 26.

25. Ibid., p. 22.

26. Interviews with Hélène Senghor, Joal, June 17, 1973, and March 17, 1976. Her story is based on these interviews and interviews with other members of her family. Van Vollenhoven was indeed in Saint-Louis as acting governor of the colony in the years of her brevet, 1907–1908. *Annexes, International Council on Archives, Guide to the Sources of the History of Africa,* vol. 3, no. 1 (Zug, Switzerland: Interdocumentation Co., 1971), p. 899. See also Lamine Guèye, *Itinéraire africaine* (Paris: Présence Africaine, 1966), p. 14.

27. G. Wesley Johnson, *The Emergence of Black Politics in Senegal* (Stanford: Stanford University Press, 1971), chs. 1 and 2.

28. Interview with Hélène Senghor, June 17, 1973. Bouche, *L'enseignement,* I, 417–418, 422–423.

29. The information on Guèye is from Babacar Ndiaye and Matar Diouf, *Vie et oeuvre de Lamine Guèye, 1891–1968: catalogue de l'exposition des archives* (Dakar, 1987).

30. There is some controversy about this date. Milcent and Sordet, *Senghor,* p. 27, and Rous, *Senghor,* p. 16, give 1922 as the date Senghor entered Libermann Seminary. The records of the Congrégation du Saint-Esprit indicate that the seminary was opened in 1923. See letter of Father Lalouse to Le Hunsec, Sept. 29, 1923, dossier 267-A, Archives Générales, and Dorsemaine et al., *Senghor,* p. xii.

31. Archives Nationales du Sénégal (ANS) 2G 37/3, Dakar. Lalouse's speech was published in *Annales Apostoliques,* cited by Milcent and Sordet, *Senghor,* pp. 27–28.

32. Rous, *Senghor,* p. 16.

33. Interviews with Senghor, June 8, 1973, and March 9, 1976.

34. Interviews with Hélène Senghor.

35. Interview with Senghor, March 9, 1976; Milcent and Sordet, *Senghor,* p. 29; Senghor, *La poésie de l'action,* pp. 47–55.

36. Interview with Senghor, March 9, 1976.

37. Milcent and Sordet, *Senghor,* p. 27; Senghor, *La poésie de l'action,* p. 51.

2. The French

1. Rapport politique, 1927, Archives Nationales du Sénégal (ANS) 2G 27/18; Ernest Milcent and Monique Sordet, *Léopold Sédar Senghor et la naissance de l'Afrique moderne* (Paris: Seghers, 1969), pp. 27–28.

2. Robert Delavignette, *Freedom and Authority in French West Africa* (London: Oxford University Press, 1950), p. 139.

3. Philip Curtin, *Economic Change in Precolonial Africa* (Madison: University of Wisconsin Press, 1975), pp. 286–290.

4. G. Wesley Johnson, *The Emergence of Black Politics in Senegal* (Stanford: Stanford University Press, 1971), p. 20. This is the chief source used for the early

history of Senegal and the development of its political institutions. See also Curtin, *Economic Change*, pp. 112–121.

5. Curtin, *Economic Change*, pp. 188, 162, 192, 326, 328–334.

6. Raymond Betts, *Assimilation and Association in French Colonial Theory: 1890–1914* (New York: Columbia University Press, 1961), p. 8.

7. Jules Michelet, *Introduction à l'histoire universelle* (Paris, 1834), pp. 78–79.

8. Senghor, *Libertè 1: Négritude et humanisme* (Paris: Le Seuil, 1964), p. 98.

9. *Très humbles doléances et remonstrances des habitans (sic) du Sénégal aux citoyens français tenant les états généraux*, April 15, 1789, Saint-Louis, mimeo in the possession of M. and Mme Rocques, Paris, p. 2.

10. Johnson, *Emergence of Black Politics*, pp. 24–25.

11. *Très humbles doléances*, p. 12; Johnson, *Emergence of Black Politics*, p. 24.

12. Raoul Girardet, *L'idée coloniale en France: 1871–1962* (Paris: La Table Ronde, 197?), pp. 10–23; Winifred Baumgart, *Imperialism: The Idea and Reality of British ι. French Colonial Expansion, 1880–1914* (London: Oxford, 1982), pp. 56–58, 71, 118. See also the more impressionistic account of Mort Rosenblum, *Mission to Civilize: The French Way* (San Diego: Harcourt Brace Jovanovich, 1986), chs. 1 and 2.

13. Emile Zola, *Fécondité* (Paris, 1899), excerpted in Georges Hardy, ed., *Les colonies françaises: L'Afrique occidentale française* (Paris: Renouard, 1937), pp. 149–150.

14. André Demaison, "Faidherbe" (Paris, 1932), cited in Hardy, *Les colonies*, pp. 152–154.

15. Sékéné Mody Cissoko and Djibril Dione, *Histoire de l'Afrique* (Paris: Présence Africaine, 1972), pp. 124–128.

16. Michael Crowder, *Senegal* (London: Methuen, 1963), pp. 16–17.

17. Faidherbe cited in Betts, *Assimilation and Association*, p. 112; William B. Cohen, *Rulers of Empire: The French Colonial Service in Africa* (Stanford: Stanford University Press, 1971), pp. 10–12.

18. Delavignette, *Freedom and Authority*, pp. 112–113.

19. Crowder, *Senegal*, pp. 25–27.

20. Johnson, *Emergence of Black Politics*, pp. 42–45, 22; Crowder, *Senegal*, pp. 17–24.

21. Johnson, *Emergence of Black Politics*, p. 46.

22. Recounted to Bakory Traoré by his grandfather. Interview with Bakory Traoré, Dakar, March 15, 1976. On the tradition of the deputy, Johnson, *Emergence of Black Politics*, pp. 48–54.

23. G. Wesley Johnson, "Commémoration du centenaire de la naissance de Blaise Diagne," *Notes Africaines*, no. 135 (July 1972), pp. 57–95, esp. pp. 73–77, 84.

24. Ibid., pp. 74–75.

25. *L'Action Sénégalaise*, June 11, 1932, cited in Donal Cruise O'Brien, *Saints and Politicians: Essays in the Organization of a Senegalese Peasant Society* (London: Cambridge University Press, 1975), pp. 166–170. Johnson, *Emergence of Black Politics*, pp. 205–219.

26. ANS 2G 37/3; Cruise O'Brien, *Saints and Politicians,* p. 170.

27. School Inspector's Report, cited in Eugen Weber, *Peasants into Frenchmen: The Modernization of Rural France, 1870–1914* (Stanford: Stanford University Press, 1976), p. 4.

28. John Stuart Mill, *On Liberty* (1859; New York: Appleton-Century-Crofts, 1947), p. 10.

29. L'Abbé P.-D. Boilat, *Esquisses sénégalaises* (Paris: P. Bertrand, 1853), pp. xiii, 467, 474–475.

30. *Grand dictionnaire universel du XIX siècle* (Paris: Pierre Larousse, 1874), pp. 903–904.

31. From the Larousse illustrated dictionary, edition of 1905, cited in James Spady, "Negritude, PanBaNegritude, and the Diopian Philosophy of African History," *Current Bibliography of African Affairs* 5, no. 1 (Jan. 1972), p. 15.

32. Cited in Betts, *Assimilation and Association,* p. 15.

33. Ibid., p. 68.

34. Girardet, *L'idée coloniale,* p. 157.

35. Raymond Leslie Buell, *The Native Problem in Africa,* 2 vols. (New York: Macmillan, 1928), II, 86–87.

36. Cited in ibid., II, 87.

37. Harmand cited in Betts, *Assimilation and Association,* p. 122. For a general discussion of the new "science" of society that justified the new policy, see Betts, ch. 4.

38. Camille Guy, "Discours," Prize Day, July 10, 1902, cited in Denise Bouche, *L'enseignement dans les territoires français de l'Afrique occidentale de 1817 à 1920,* 2 vols. (Lille: Atelier Reproduction des Theses, 1975), II, 568. William Ponty, opening statement to the Governing Council, June 20, 1910, cited in Bouche, II, 568–569. Van Vollenhoven cited in Cohen, *Rulers of Empire,* p. 114.

39. Bouche, *L'enseignement,* I, 421–422; II, 475–490.

40. Ibid., II, 504.

41. A. Mairot, "Rapport sur les écoles," Jan. 1, 1906, cited in Prosser Gifford and Timothy Weiskel, "African Education in a Colonial Context: French and British Styles," in *France and Britain in Africa,* ed. Prosser Gifford and William Roger Louis (New Haven: Yale University Press, 1971), p. 677.

42. *Moussa et Gi-gla: Histoire de deux petits noirs:* all quotations are cited in Buell, *The Native Problem,* II, 62–63.

43. Buell, *The Native Problem,* II, 61.

44. Louis Guillabert, speech to the general council, June 5, 1905, cited in Bouche, *L'enseignement,* II, 507; ibid., II, 604; Lamine Guèye, *Itinéraire africaine* (Paris: Présence Africaine, 1966), pp. 14–15.

45. Georges Hardy, "Bulletin de l'enseignement de L'AOF," Feb. 1916, cited in Gifford and Weiskel, "African Education," p. 691.

46. Article 12 of 1903 Ordinance on Education in A.O.F., cited in ibid., p. 691.

47. Bouche, *L'enseignement,* II, 857.

48. Letters of Father Lalouse to Msgr. Le Hunsec, March 24, 1927, and Nov.

20, 1927, Archives Spiritaines, 262-A, Congrégation du Saint-Esprit, Chevilly-la-rue, France.

49. Interview with Dr. Linhard, Dakar, March 12, 1976. Dr. Linhard was in Senghor's class at the lycée.

50. James Bruce-Benoît, "Témoignage," in *Hommage à Léopold Sédar Senghor, homme de culture* (Paris: Présence Africaine, 1976), pp. 219–220, 223.

51. Senghor, "De la liberté de l'âme ou éloge du métissage," *Liberté 1*, p. 99.

52. Hardy cited in Buell, *The Native Problem*, II, 59. Cheikh Hamidou Kane, *Ambiguous Adventure,* trans. Katherine Woods (New York: Walker, 1963), pp. 150–151.

53. Mme Daniel, address at the prize day of the Cours Secondaire de Dakar, July 7, 1928, typescript in the possession of Dr. Linhard, Dakar.

54. Interview with Dr. Linhard, March 12, 1976; interview with Abdoulaye Ly, March 22, 1976. Ly graduated from the lycée several years after Senghor.

55. Interview with Pierre Senghor, Dakar, June 14, 1973.

56. Letters of Father Lalouse to Msgr. Le Hunsec, March 24, 1927, and Nov. 20, 1927.

57. Interview with Dr. Linhard, March 12, 1976.

58. Interview with Senghor, Dakar, March 6, 1976.

59. Interviews with Marie-Thérèse Basse and Blaise Senghor, Dakar and Joal, March 17, 19, 1976.

60. ANS 0 931/176.

3. Paris

1. "Paris," in Senghor, *Liberté 1: Négritude et humanisme* (Paris: Le Seuil, 1964), p. 312.

2. Ernest Hemingway, *A Moveable Feast* (New York: Scribner, 1964); Janet Flanner, *Paris Was Yesterday: Articles from the New Yorker, 1925–1939* (New York: Viking, 1972).

3. Flanner, *Paris Was Yesterday,* pp. viii–xx.

4. Nancy Cunard, ed., *Negro* (1934), abridged and reedited by Hugh Ford (New York: F. Ungar, 1970).

5. Ibid., pp. xi–xxvii.

6. James Spiegler, "Aspects of Nationalist Thought among French-Speaking West Africans, 1921–1939" (D. Phil. diss., Oxford University, 1968), p. 55; René Violaines, "Mon ami René Maran," in *Hommage à René Maran* (Paris: Présence Africaine, 1965), pp. 15–89. The *Othello* story is from interview with Louis Achille, Lyon, Jan. 21, 1989.

7. Paul Guth, *Mémoires d'un naïf* (Paris, 1953), pp. 187–191.

8. Senghor, "Lycée Louis-le-grand, haut lieu de culture française," *Liberté 1,* pp. 403–406; enrollment book for 1928, Archives Louis-le-grand, Paris.

9. *Louis-le-grand 1563–1963, études, souvenirs, documents* (Paris, 1963), pp. 9–12.

10. For life at Louis-le-grand at this time, see Senghor, "Louis-le-grand," *Liberté 1,* pp. 403–406; Paul Guth, "La khâgne du lycée Louis-le-grand au temps

des années folles," pp. 259–269; and Jose Lupin, "La prison des esprits libres," pp. 251–256, in *Louis-le-grand 1563–1963;* interview with Jean Valdeyron, Paris, June 21, 1975.

11. Lupin, "La prison," p. 252; interview with Valdeyron, June 21, 1975.

12. Lupin, "La prison," p. 255.

13. Senghor, "Lycée Louis-le-grand," *Liberté 1,* pp. 403–404; teachers' record books, 1929, 1930, Archives Louis-le-grand.

14. Interviews with Senghor, Dakar, March 6 and 25, 1976; Senghor, "Lycée Louis-le-grand," in *Liberté 1,* p. 405.

15. Interviews with Valdeyron, June 21, 1975, René Brouillet, Paris, June 19, 1975, and Robert Verdier, Paris, June 13, 1975. All three were at Lycée Louis-le-grand with Senghor.

16. Senghor, "Pierre Teilhard de Chardin et la politique africaine," *Cahiers Pierre Teilhard de Chardin,* vol. 3 (Paris: Le Seuil, 1962), p. 18.

17. Interviews with Brouillet, June 19, 1975, and Verdier, June 13, 1975.

18. G. Wesley Johnson, "Commémoration du centenaire de la naissance de Blaise Diagne," *Notes Africaines,* no. 135 (July 1972), p. 61.

19. W. E. B. Du Bois, "The Negro Mind Reaches Out," in Alain Locke, ed., *The New Negro* (New York: A. and C. Boni, 1925), p. 399; Blaise Diagne, letter to Marcus Garvey, cited in Raymond Leslie Buell, *The Native Problem In Africa,* 2 vols. (New York: Macmillan, 1928), II, 81.

20. Johnson, "Commémoration du centenaire," p. 61.

21. Senghor, "Lycée Louis-le-grand," *Liberté 1,* p. 404; interview with Senghor, March 6, 1976.

22. Senghor in interview cited by Merry Bromberger, *Le destin secret de Georges Pompidou* (Paris: Fayard, 1965), pp. 50, 51.

23. Senghor, "Lycée Louis-le-grand," *Liberté 1,* p. 405.

24. Letter of Georges Pompidou to Senghor, June 16, 1969, in Michèle Dorsemaine, Alfred Fierro, and Josette Mason, eds., *Léopold Sédar Senghor* (Paris: Bibliothèque Nationale, 1978), p. 32.

25. Bromberger, *Le destin secret,* p. 51; Senghor, "Lycée Louis-le-grand," *Liberté 1,* p. 405.

26. Maurice Barrès, *Les déracinés* (Paris: Plon, 1922); Ernest Milcent and Monique Sordet, *Léopold Sédar Senghor et la naissance de l'Afrique moderne* (Paris: Seghers, 1969), p. 36. Jacques Louis Hymans, *Léopold Sédar Senghor: An Intellectual Biography* (Edinburgh: Edinburgh University Press, 1971), was the first to track down many of the intellectual influences on Senghor.

27. Senghor, comment in broadcast of Roger Stéphane, "Portrait-souvenir de Maurice Barrès," Paris, June 22, 1962, cited in Milcent and Sordet, *Senghor,* pp. 36–37. See also Senghor's letter to Jacques Louis Hymans, 1963, in Hymans, *Senghor,* p. 264.

28. Robert Schilling, "Pour Léopold Sédar Senghor," quoted in Dorsemaine et al., eds., *Senghor,* p. 30; Archives Lycée Louis-le-grand, Paris. The student record book at Lycée Louis-le-grand indicates that Cresson taught Senghor philosophy in 1930–1931, his last year at the school.

29. Information on Rimbaud is from Arthur Rimbaud, *Une saison en enfer;*

Les illuminations; A Season in Hell; The Illuminations, trans. Enid Rhodes Peschel (New York: Oxford University Press, 1973), pp. 3–33.

30. Ibid., pp. 52–53.

31. Ibid., pp. 54–55.

32. Ibid., pp. 168–169.

33. Henri Baudet, *Paradise on Earth: Some Thoughts on European Images of Non-European Man* (New Haven: Yale University Press, 1965), pp. 10–11, 29–35.

34. Peschel, in Rimbaud, *Une saison en enfer,* p. 21.

35. Senghor, "Teilhard de Chardin," p. 19.

36. Senghor, letter to Jacques Louis Hymans, in Hymans, *Senghor,* pp. 263–264; Sénghor, "La parole chez Paul Claudel et chez les Négro-africains," in Senghor, *Liberté 3: Négritude et civilisation de l'universel* (Paris: Le Seuil, 1977), pp. 348–386.

37. Interview with Verdier, June 13, 1975; Bromberger, *Le destin secret,* p. 61.

38. Charles Baudelaire, "A une Malabaraise," *Flowers of Evil,* Centenary Bilingual Ed., ed. Marthiel and Jackson Mathews (Norfolk, Conn.: New Directions, 1955), pp. 418–419.

39. Baudelaire, "La chevelure," ibid., pp. 259–261.

40. "Joal," Senghor, *Poèmes* (Paris: Le Seuil, 1984), pp. 15–16.

41. "Femme noire," *Poèmes,* p. 16. Translation from Senghor, *Selected Poems,* trans. John Reed and Clive Wake (New York: Atheneum, 1969), p. 6.

42. Cited in Solomon Alhadef Rhodes, *The Cult of Beauty in Charles Baudelaire* (New York: Institute of French Studies, Columbia University Press, 1929), pp. 2–3.

43. Margaret Gilman, *Baudelaire the Critic* (New York: Columbia University Press, 1943), pp. 189–190, 164.

44. Senghor, "Francité et Négritude," *Liberté 3,* p. 19; "Fonction et signification du premier festival mondial des arts nègres," *Liberté 3,* p. 59; Senghor, *Ce que je crois* (Paris: Grasset, 1988), pp. 209–216.

45. Teachers' comment books, 1930–31, Archives Lycée Louis-le-grand. Interview with Senghor, March 6, 1976.

46. Robert Delavignette, *Exposition coloniale internationale de Paris: Afrique occidentale française* (Paris: Société d'Editions Géographiques, Maritimes et Coloniales, 1931).

47. Guth, "La khâgne du lycée Louis-le-grand," p. 263.

48. Roger Martin du Gard, *The Thibauds,* trans. Gilbert Stuart (New York: Viking, 1939), pp. 451, 453–454.

49. Marius Ary Leblond, ed., *Anthologie coloniale, morceaux choisis d'écrivains* (Paris: I. Peyronnet, 1929), pp. 15–17.

50. Raoul Girardet, *L'idée coloniale en France: 1871–1962* (Paris: La Table Ronde, 1972), pp. 124–125.

51. Duplessis-Kergomand, "Discours," July 12, 1931; Académie de Paris, *Distribution solonnelle des prix* (Cahors, 1931), pp. 19–21. Archives Lycée Louis-le-grand.

52. Senghor, "Lycée Louis-le-grand," *Liberté 1,* pp. 405–406; "Paris," *Liberté*

1, p. 313; "Prière de paix," *Poèmes*, p. 95 (this poem is dedicated to Georges and Claude Pompidou and signed "Paris, 1945"); "Chants pour signare," *Poèmes*, p. 173.

4. The Milieu of Negritude

1. Archives Nationales du Sénégal (ANS) O 931/176.

2. Aimé Césaire, "Nous acceuillons l'Afrique réétablie dans son droit et dans sa dignité," *Le Soleil* (March 4, 1976); Mbwill Ngal, *Aimé Césaire: Un homme à la recherche d'une patrie* (Dakar and Abidjan: Les Nouvelles Editions Africaines, 1975), p. 42.

3. Michèle Dorsemaine, Alfred Fierro, and Josette Masson, eds., *Léopold Sédar Senghor* (Paris: Bibliothèque Nationale, 1978), p. 52.

4. Interview with Léon Damas, Washingon, D.C., Jan. 6, 1973; Ngal, *Césaire,* pp. 42–44. Lilyan Kesteloot, *Les écrivains noirs de langue française* (Brussels: Editions de l'Institut de Sociologie de l'Université Libre de Bruxelles, 1963), is the pioneering work on this milieu in this period.

5. Interview with Damas, Jan. 6, 1973; interview with Mercer Cook, Washington, D.C., March 2, 1979.

6. John Paynter, *Fifty Years After* (New York: Margent Press, 1940), pp. 62–66. Information about the Achilles and the Nardals is also drawn from interview with Louis Achille, Lyon, Jan. 21, 1989.

7. *La Revue du Monde Noir*, no. 1 (Nov. 1931), pp. 1–2. Rpt. as *La Revue du Monde Noir (The Review of the Black World)*, nos. 1–6 (Nendeln, Liechtenstein: Kraus Reprint, 1971).

8. Ngal, *Césaire,* pp. 46–67.

9. Interview with Cook, March 2, 1979; Mercer A. Cook, "Some Literary Contacts: African, West Indian and Afro-American" in Lloyd W. Brown, ed., *The Black Writer* (Los Angeles: Hennessey and Ingalls, 1973), pp. 119–140; interview with Lat Senghor, Dakar, June 6, 1973. Lat Senghor indicated that his cousin Sédar was reciting poetry by the American poets on his visit home in 1932; sure evidence for his knowledge of the New Negro movement in the United States is available only for somewhat later, 1934.

10. Nathan Huggins, *The Harlem Renaissance* (New York: Oxford University Press, 1971), pp. 7–11.

11. Alain Locke, ed., *The New Negro* (New York: A. and C. Boni, 1925), pp. 3–16. Huggins, in *The Harlem Renaissance,* stresses many of the same factors.

12. Mercer Cook, ed., *Le noir: Morceaux choisis de vingt-neuf français célèbres* (New York: American Book Co., 1934). Evidence of growing American interest in French-speaking black people is suggested by the fact that Cook's book was reviewed in *The Crisis* in 1935: Guichard B. Paris, "French Textbooks and the Negro," *The Crisis* 12 (Nov. 1935): 344–345.

13. A note of Sept. 10, 1937, summarizes the statement of purpose of *La Revue du Monde Noir:* ANS 17G 58/17.

14. A. G. Perier, "La poésie ethnique," *La Revue du Monde Noir*, no. 6 (April 1932), p. 46.

15. Paulette Nardal, "Eveil de la conscience de race," *La Revue du Monde Noir*, no. 6, pp. 25–31.

16. Césaire cited in Ngal, *Césaire*, p. 64; "Paris," Senghor, *Liberté l: Négritude et humanisme* (Paris: Le Seuil, 1964), p. 313; Senghor, "Pierre Teilhard de Chardin et la politique africaine," *Cahiers Pierre Teilhard de Chardin*, vol. 3 (Paris: Le Seuil, 1962), p. 18.

17. Frantz Fanon, *Black Skin, White Masks*, trans. Charles Lam Markmann (New York: Grove Press, 1967), pp. 147–153.

18. Cook, "Some Literary Contacts," p. 122.

19. Birago Diop, *La plume raboutée*, vol. 1 (Paris: Présence Africaine; Dakar: Les Nouvelles Editions Africaines, 1978), p. 79.

20. On *Légitime Défense* see Kesteloot, *Les écrivains noirs*, pp. 29–82.

21. Ernest Milcent and Monique Sordet, *Léopold Sédar Senghor et la naissance de l'Afrique moderne* (Paris: Seghers, 1969), p. 52; Archives de la Ministère de la France d'Outre-mer, SLOTFOM 111/119.

22. Interview with Cook, March 2, 1979. Cook's views are confirmed by private communications from Brian Weinstein, biographer of Félix Eboué, and Armand Guibert, Paris, June 11, 1975.

23. Diop, *La plume raboutée*, 1, 77–79.

24. Claude McKay, *Banjo* (New York: Harpers, 1929), p. 320. On the influence of this book on black students in Paris see Léonard Sainville, "Témoignage" in *Hommage à Léopold Sédar Senghor, homme de culture* (Paris: Présence Africaine, 1976), p. 130.

25. Senghor, "L'apport de la poésie nègre au demi-siècle," *Liberté 1*, p. 133.

26. Sainville, "Témoignage," pp. 128–134. See also Césaire, "Nous acceuillons l'Afrique," and Ngal, *Césaire*, p. 261.

27. Letters of Blaise Daigne, July, Nov., and Dec., 1931, ANS 17G 470/126; letter of Senghor to the inspector general of education, Oct. 10, 1931, ANS O 931/176.

28. Senghor, letters of March 15 and April 15, 1932, ANS O 931/176.

29. Senghor, letter of July 20, 1932, ANS O 931/176.

30. Interview with Lat Senghor, June 6, 1973.

31. Senghor, letter to the inspector general of education, Oct. 21, 1932, ANS O 931/176.

32. Senghor, letter to the inspector general of education, Dec. 25, 1933, ANS O 931/176.

33. Interview with Senghor, March 6, 1976; Sainville, "Témoignage," pp. 130–131. Damas also emphasized that this period forged Senghor's character. Interview with Damas, Jan. 6, 1973.

34. Senghor, letter to the governor general, Aug. 2, 1934; letter from Senghor's professor of Greek and Latin, July 22, 1934; letter about Senghor by his supervisor, July 18, 1934. There are also letters by Bayet and others. ANS O 931/176.

35. Senghor, letters to the inspector general of education, Sept. 15, 1934, and the governor general, Oct. 12, 1934, ANS O 931/176.

36. Interview with Louis Achille, Jan. 21, 1989.

37. Senghor, letters to the inspector general of education, Oct. 19, 1934, Dec. 2, 1934, Aug. 17, 1935, ANS O 931/176; police report, ANS 21G 141/108.

38. Senghor, *La poésie de l'action: Conversations avec Mohamed Aziza* (Paris: Stock, 1980), pp. 59–60; interviews with Senghor, Burlington, Vt., June 13–14, 1971.

39. Césaire cited in Ngal, *Césaire,* pp. 60–61. Ngal reports that Césaire and Damas both remember there being several issues of *L'Etudiant Noir,* but only one issue has been found. Archives de la Ministère de la France d'Outre-mer, SLOTFOM V/21.

40. Interview with Damas, Jan. 6, 1973; Kesteloot, *Les écrivains noirs,* ch. 7. Unfortunately Kesteloot had access neither to *La Revue du Monde Noir* nor to *L'Etudiant Noir.* In their absence, she relied heavily on the testimony of Damas. As a result, she tended to underestimate the continuity between some of the ideas expressed in *L'Etudiant Noir* and those which had preceded them, and to over-estimate the importance of *Légitime Défense.*

41. For the views of black intellectuals in Paris in the 1920s and 1930s, see James Spiegler, "Aspects of Nationalist Thought among French-Speaking West Africans, 1921–1939" (D.Phil. diss., Oxford University, 1968). See also J. Ayo Langley, *Pan-Africanism and Nationalism in West Africa, 1900–1945: A Study in Ideology and Social Classes* (Oxford: Clarendon Press, 1973). Parallels between the thinking of the earlier generation and those of the Negritude generation are striking, particularly for the writings of Garan Kouyaté, Tovalou Houénou, and Emile Faure. In an interview in March 1975 in Dakar, Senghor said he had never heard of these men. However, there is evidence that men Senghor knew and worked with did have direct contact with members of this earlier generation. One of the early journals, *Cri des Nègres,* announced the first meeting of the West African student group of which Senghor was president. Archives de la Ministère de la France d'Outre-mer, SLOTFOM V/21; SLOTFOM 111/119. With only one exception, police reports of this period do not mention Senghor or his young student friends, those of the Negritude group. There is no sure evidence that Senghor inherited the results of the older generation's work other than indirectly. On *L'Etudiant Noir* itself, see Dorsemaine et al., eds., *Senghor,* p. 48.

42. Aimé Césaire, "Nègrerie—jeunesse noire et assimilation," *L'Etudiant Noir* (March 1935), p. 2, cited in Dorsemaine et al., eds., *Senghor,* p. 48.

43. Gilbert Gratiant, "Mulâtres . . . pour le bien et le mal," *L'Etudiant Noir,* cited in Dorsemaine et al., eds., *Senghor,* p. 50.

44. The general biographical information on Maran is from articles by Senghor and René Violaines, in *Hommage à René Maran* (Paris: Présence Africaine, 1965), pp. 9–13, 15–41.

45. René Maran, *Batouala* (Paris: Albin Michel, 1921), p. 9–18; Maran, letter to Violaines, Nov. 5, 1922, cited by Violaines in *Hommage à René Maran,* pp. 18–19; ibid., p. 40.

46. Maran, letters to Violaines, Feb. 23, 1931, Aug. 3, 1947, Nov. 1, 1947, cited by Violaines, ibid., pp. 28, 32–33.

47. Senghor, "L'humanisme et nous: René Maran," *L'Etudiant Noir,* exposition at the French Library, Boston, Nov. 1980.

48. Maran, inscription in book, his *La maison du bonheur* (Paris, 1909), given to Senghor; cited in Dorsemaine et al., eds., *Senghor,* p. 48.

49. Senghor, "René Maran: précurseur de la négritude" (1963), *Liberté 1,* p. 407 (emphasis in the original).

50. Senghor, letter to the governor general, Oct. 18, 1935, ANS O 931/176.

5. Coming of Age

1. "Le Sénégal, le latin et les humanités classiques," in Senghor, *Liberté 3: Négritude et civilisation de l'universel* (Paris: Le Seuil, 1977), pp. 414–415.

2. Ibid.; Senghor, letter to the governor general, Dec. 5, 1935, ANS O 931/176; interview with M. and Mme Marcel Baumlin, Paris, June 25, 1975. The Baumlins were teachers at Tours and friends of Senghor's during his time there. They are the main source for anecdotes about him during this period.

3. Interview with M. and Mme Baumlin, June 25, 1975; interview with Louis Achille, Lyon, Jan. 21, 1989.

4. "Que m'accompagnent kôras et balafong," in Senghor, *Poèmes* (Paris: Le Seuil, 1984), p. 31. Translation from Senghor, *Selected Poems,* trans. John Reed and Clive Wake (New York: Atheneum, 1969), p. 14.

5. "Le portrait," *Poèmes,* pp. 219–220.

6. Inspector general of education, report to the governor general of French West Africa, Dec. 11, 1935, ANS O 931/176.

7. Louise Delafosse, *Maurice Delafosse, le Berrichon conquis par l'Afrique* (Paris: Société Français d'Histoire d'Outre-mer, 1976); for relations with Blaise Diagne, esp. pp. 310–314.

8. Maurice Delafosse, *Les nègres* (Paris: Rieder, 1927). See also L. Delafosse, *Maurice Delafosse,* pp. 392, 372; Raymond Leslie Buell, *The Native Problem in Africa,* 2 vols. (New York: Macmillan, 1928), II, 89.

9. "Ce que l'homme noir apporte," in Senghor, *Liberté 1: Négritude et humanisme* (Paris: Le Seuil, 1964), p. 26. See also his postface in L. Delafosse, *Maurice Delafosse,* pp. 401–403.

10. Senghor, "The Lessons of Leo Frobenius," in *Leo Frobenius: An Anthology,* ed. Eike Haberland (Wiesbaden: F. Steiner, 1973), p. vii; rpt. in Senghor, *Liberté 3,* p. 398.

11. Eike Haberland, "Editor's Postscript," in *Frobenius,* pp. 223–230.

12. Leo Frobenius, "The Nature of Culture," in Haberland, ed., *Frobenius,* p. 21.

13. Robert Delavignette, *Soudan-Paris-Bourgogne* (Paris: Grasset, 1935), p. 25; Raoul Girardet, *L'idée coloniale en France: 1871–1962* (Paris: La Table Ronde, 1972), pp. 175–190.

14. Emmanuel Mounier, "Refaire la Renaissance," *Esprit,* no. 1 (Oct. 1932), pp. 5–51, esp. pp. 31–41.

15. Senghor, letter to Maurice Martin du Gard, Dec. 4, 1943, in Michèle Dorsemaine, Alfred Fierro, and Josette Masson, eds., *Léopold Sédar Senghor* (Paris: Bibliothèque Nationale, 1978), pp. 83–84.

16. Senghor, "L'apport de la poésie nègre au demi-siècle," *Liberté 1,* p. 136; Mbwill Ngal, *Aimé Césaire: Un homme à la recherche d'une patrie* (Dakar and Abidjan: Nouvelles Editions Africaines, 1975), pp. 261, 62–63.

17. Léon Damas, *Poètes d'expression français* (Paris: Le Seuil, 1947), pp. 244–245; Senghor, ed., *Anthologie de la nouvelle poésie nègre et malgache de langue française* (Paris: Presses Universitaires de France, 1948, 1969), pp. 179–180; Senghor, "Flavien Ranaivo," *Liberté 1,* p. 183.

18. Senghor, "Le message de Goethe aux nègres-nouveaux," *Liberté 1,* p. 83.

19. Senghor, "L'apport de la poésie nègre," p. 133; "Flavien Ranaivo," p. 183.

20. Interview with Senghor, Dakar, March 6, 1976.

21. Aimé Césaire, *Cahier d'un retour au pays natal* (Paris: Présence Africaine, 1968), pp. 10, 30–31, 68, 106–108. On the psychological dimension of Césaire's poetics, A. James Arnold, *Modernism and Negritude: The Poetry and Poetics of Aimé Césaire* (Cambridge, Mass.: Harvard University Press, 1981), pp. 261–263.

22. Senghor, "Pierre Teilhard de Chardin et la politique africaine," *Cahiers Pierre Teilhard de Chardin,* vol. 3 (Paris: Le Seuil, 1962), p. 17.

23. Senghor, "Le message de Goethe," pp. 83–84; "De la liberté de l'âme ou éloge du métissage," *Liberté 1,* p. 99.

24. "Nuit de Sine," *Poèmes,* p. 14. Translation by Reed and Wake, *Selected Poems,* p. 5.

25. "Femme noire," *Poèmes,* pp. 16–17. Translation by Reed and Wake, *Selected Poems,* p. 6.

26. "Joal," *Poèmes,* pp. 15–16.

27. Senghor, "Comme les lamantins vont boire à la source," *Liberté 1,* p. 221; "Que m'accompagnent kôras et balafong," *Poèmes,* p. 28; "Ethiopiques," *Poèmes,* p. 140.

28. "Epîtres à la princesse," *Poèmes,* p. 138.

29. William E. B. Du Bois, *The Souls of Black Folk* (Greenwich, Conn.: Fawcett, 1961), pp. 16–17. For information about Du Bois, Francis L. Broderick, *W. E. B. Du Bois* (Stanford: Stanford University Press, 1969), esp. ch. 1. Many of the most articulate of the New Negroes were likewise black Americans of unusually good education and high status; see Martin Kilson, "Politics and Identity among Black Intellectuals," *Dissent* (Summer 1981), pp. 339–349.

30. The Larousse definition of "nègre" is cited by James Spady, "Negritude, PanBaNegritude, and the Diopian Philosophy of African History," *Current Bibliography of African Affairs* 5, no. 1 (Jan. 1972): 15.

31. "Jardin de France," *Poèmes,* p. 223. Translation from Ellen Conroy Kennedy, ed., *The Negritude Poets* (New York: Viking, 1975), pp. 129–130.

32. Senghor, "Teilhard de Chardin," pp. 17–18.

33. "Totem," *Poèmes,* p. 24; "Chants pour Signare," *Poèmes,* p. 189.

34. "A l'appel de la race de Saba," *Poèmes*, p. 59; Senghor, interview with Jacques Louis Hymans, Dakar, Aug. 1, 1960, in Hymans, *Léopold Sédar Senghor* (Edinburgh: Edinburgh University Press, 1971), p. 72.

35. Senghor cited in Papa Guèye Ndiaye, *Ethiopiques: Edition critique et commentée* (Dakar and Abidjan: Nouvelles Editions Africaines, 1974), cited in Dorsemaine et al., eds., *Senghor*, p. 83.

36. "In Memoriam," *Poèmes*, p. 10; "Le message," *Poèmes*, pp. 18–20.

37. "Neige sur Paris," *Poèmes*, p. 22.

38. "Prière aux masques," *Poèmes*, pp. 23–24.

39. "Ndéssé ou 'Blues'," *Poèmes*, p. 25; "A la mort," *Poèmes*, pp. 25–26.

40. Senghor, letter to Maurice Martin du Gard, Dec. 4, 1943, p. 84; "Que m'accompagnent kôras et balafong," *Poèmes*, pp. 28–37.

41. "Le retour de l'enfant prodigue," *Poèmes*, pp. 47–52.

42. Senghor, letter to René Maran, June 6, 1945, in Dorsemaine et al., eds., *Senghor*, p. 84.

43. Senghor, letter to A. Badiou, Feb. 20, 1957, cited in Hymans, *Senghor*, p. 80.

44. Letter to René Maran, June 6, 1945.

45. Letter to Maurice Martin du Gard, Dec. 4, 1943.

46. Erik Erikson, *Young Man Luther* (New York: Norton, 1962), pp. 14–15.

47. Senghor, "Teilhard de Chardin," pp. 18–19; interview with Senghor, Burlington, Vt., June 13, 1971; Hymans, *Senghor*, p. 72; ANS 21G 142/108.

48. Marc Sankalé, "L'aîné du Quartier Latin ou déjà la passion de la culture," in *Hommage à Léopold Sédar Senghor, homme de culture* (Paris: Présence Africaine, 1976), pp. 189–194.

49. Senghor, "L'Afrique s'interroge: Subir ou choisir," *Liberté 1*, p. 92.

50. Senghor, interview with Armand Guibert, in Guibert, *Léopold Sédar Senghor: L'homme et l'oeuvre* (Paris: Présence Africaine, 1962), pp. 143–144.

6. Spokesman

1. Senghor, letters to the inspector general of education, March 12, 1936, and to the governor general, Jan. 11, 1937, and March 12, 1936, Archives Nationales du Sénégal (ANS) 17G 470/126.

2. Nicole Bernard-Duquênet, *Le Sénégal et le Front populaire* (Paris: L'Harmattan, 1985), pp. 83–88.

3. ANS C 193/95.

4. Interview with Lat Senghor, Dakar, June 6, 1973.

5. James Bruce-Benoît, "Témoignage," in *Hommage à Léopold Sédar Senghor, homme de culture* (Paris: Présence Africaine, 1976), p. 224.

6. "Avec M. Léopold Sédar Senghor," *Paris-Dakar* (Sept. 3, 1937); the interview continues in the Sept. 4 issue, p. 1. Jacques Louis Hymans, *Léopold Sédar Senghor* (Edinburgh: Edinburgh University Press, 1971), p. 94, argues that Senghor was already thinking of a future political career. His evidence is that Senghor used a word, *rassemblement*, that is often used to refer to a political grouping. I

think it unlikely that Senghor had such thoughts at this time. It is worth noting that the colonial administration's police records for this time mention Ousmane Socé Diop's political ambitions but make no mention of Senghor. ANS 21G 141/108.

7. ANS 17G 470/125.

8. *Paris-Dakar* (Sept. 6, 1937), p. 5.

9. Ibid. (Sept. 7 and 8, 1937). Senghor's talk, "Le problème culturel en AOF," was first printed in *Paris-Dakar* (Sept. 6–8, 1937). A more accessible but somewhat cut version is in Senghor, *Liberté 1: Négritude et humanisme* (Paris: Le Seuil, 1964), pp. 11–21. References in the text are to the latter version.

10. Interview with Senghor, Dakar, March 6, 1976.

11. ANS 17G 470/126.

12. Marcel de Coppet in *Education Africaine*, no. 98, (Oct.–Dec. 1937), pp. 210–213.

13. Interviews with André Guillabert, Paris, June 25, 1975, and with Cissé Dia, Dakar, March 12, 1976.

14. Exposition Internationale de Paris, *Congrès international de l'évolution culturelle des peuples coloniaux, Septembre 26–28, 1937: Rapports et compte rendu* (Paris, 1938). List of participants, pp. 21–25. See also pp. 13–20.

15. Comte da Costa-Lobo, "L'éducation dans les territoires d'outre-mer du Portugal," *Congrès internationale*, pp. 194–205. For order of speeches, ibid., p. 8.

16. Senghor, "La résistance de la bourgeoisie sénégalaise à l'école rurale populaire," *Congrès internationale*, pp. 40–44.

17. See papers by Charles Béart, Fily Dabo Sissoko, and Paul Ledreux, *Congrès internationale*, pp. 108–115, 116–120, 211–214.

18. Cited by Denis Blanche, "Préface," ibid., pp. 18–19.

19. Ibid., pp. 10–11.

20. Archives de la Ministère de la France d'Outre-mer, SLOTFOM C/119.

21. Note of Léopold Sédar Senghor, professor at the Lycée Descartes, Tours, to M. de Coppet, typescript, stamped "received, March 2, 1938," ANS O 614/31, pp. 1, 8–9, 13, 19–20, 22.

22. Senghor, interview, 1966, cited in Ellen Conroy Kennedy, ed., *The Negritude Poets* (New York: Viking, 1975), p. 122.

23. Senghor, letter to de Coppet, Sept. 24, 1937, ANS 17G 470/126.

7. The War Years

1. Interview with Senghor, Burlington, Vt., June 13, 1971.

2. Senghor, *La poésie de l'action: Conversations avec Mohamed Aziza* (Paris: Stock, 1980), pp. 82–84.

3. Robert Aron, *The Vichy Regime: 1940–1944* (New York: Macmillan, 1958), p. 12.

4. Robert O. Paxton, *Vichy France: Old Guard and New Order, 1940–1944*

(New York: Knopf, 1972), pp. 3–50. This is the source for most general statements here about Vichy France.

5. Jean Touchard, "L'esprit des années 30: Une tentative de renouvellement de la pensée politique française," in *Colloques cahiers de civilisation: Tendances politiques dans la vie française depuis 1789,* ed. Guy Michaud (Paris, Hachette, 1960), pp. 89–118.

6. Martin Wolfe, "French Interwar Stagnation Revisited," in Charles K. Warner, ed., *From the Ancien Regime to the Popular Front* (New York: Columbia University Press, 1969), pp. 159–180.

7. Touchard, "L'esprit des années 30," pp. 91–93, 98–102, 107–110; Emmanuel Mounier, "Refaire la Renaissance," *Esprit,* no. 1 (Oct. 1932), pp. 5–51.

8. Paxton, *Vichy France,* pp. 146–153.

9. *Hosties noires,* in Senghor, *Poèmes* (Paris: Le Seuil, 1984), pp. 55–96.

10. Senghor, letter to Denise Carrier, Jan. 15, 1945, in Michèle Dorsemaine, Alfred Fierro, and Josette Masson, eds., *Léopold Sédar Senghor* (Paris: Bibliothèque Nationale, 1978), p. 91.

11. "Prière des Tirailleurs sénégalais," *Poèmes,* p. 71.

12. "Au gouverneur Eboué, *Poèmes,* p. 74.

13. "A l'appel de la race de Saba," *Poèmes,* p. 61.

14. "Désespoir d'un voluntaire libre," *Poèmes,* pp. 66–68.

15. Cheikh Faty Fall, "L'opinion publique dakaroise, 1940–1944" (M.A. thesis, Faculty of Letters and Human Sciences, University of Dakar, 1973); "Tyaroye," *Poèmes,* pp. 90–91.

16. "Taga de Mbaye Dyôb," *Poèmes,* pp. 79–80.

17. "Ndessé," *Poèmes,* pp. 81–82; "Chant de printemps" and "Aux soldats négro-américains," *Poèmes,* pp. 85–90.

18. "Prière de paix," *Poèmes,* pp. 92–95.

19. *La poésie de l'action,* p. 184; Senghor, "Pierre Teilhard de Chardin et la politique africaine," Cahiers Pierre Teilhard de Chardin, vol. 3 (Paris: Le Seuil, 1962), pp. 17–21: Senghor, "Le message de Goethe aux nègres-nouveaux," *Liberté 1: Négritude et humanisme* (Paris: Le Seuil, 1964), pp. 83–86.

20. Senghor, interview in *Dakar-Matin* (April 25, 1961), cited in Jacques Louis Hymans, *Léopold Sédar Senghor: An Intellectual Biography* (Edinburgh: Edinburgh University Press, 1971), p. 110.

21. "Le message de Goethe," pp. 83, 86.

22. Ibid., pp. 85–86; *La poésie de l'action,* pp. 84–85.

23. "Vues sur l'Afrique noir ou assimiler non être assimilés," *Liberté 1,* pp. 39–69.

24. *La poésie de l'action,* p. 84.

25. Simone de Beauvoir, *The Prime of Life,* trans. Peter Green (Cleveland: World Publications, 1962), chs. 7, 8.

26. Interview with Claude Pompidou, Paris, Dec. 7, 1984.

27. Marc Sankalé, "L'aîné du Quartier Latin, ou déjà la passion de la culture,"

in *Hommage à Léopold Sédar Senghor, homme de culture* (Paris: Présence Africaine, 1976), pp. 193–194.

28. Interview with Sourou Migan Apithy, Paris, Nov. 20, 1985.

29. Anonymous, *L'Etudiant de la France d'Outre-mer: Chronique des Foyers,* no. 1 (July 1943), p. 1.

30. Senghor, *L'étudiant de la France d'Outre-mer,* no. 8 (March–April 1944), pp. 24–25.

31. Sankalé, "L'aîné du Quartier Latin," p. 193.

32. *Paris-Dakar* (Oct. 15, 1939), cited in Faty Fall, "L'opinion publique dakaroise, 1940–1944," pp. 18–22. On the press in Africa during the war, see also Arlette Fontaine, "La presse au Sénégal: 1939–1960" (Doctorat du 3e cycle, University of Dakar, June 1967).

33. The main source for information about Boisson and the Vichy regime in Senegal is Daniel Chenêt, *Qui a sauvé l'Afrique?* (Paris: Elan, 1949), pp. 18–23, 37–40.

34. From essays by A. Camara and Abdel-el-Kadar Fall, ANS O 31/31.

35. *Dakar Jeunes* (March 12, 1942; Jan. 8, 1942). One of the first to point out the importance of *Dakar Jeunes* was Michael Crowder in *Senegal: A Study of French Assimilation Policy* (London: Methuen, 1967), pp. 41–42.

36. Pierre Boisson, circular to governors of the federation, June 26, 1941, cited in Chenêt, *Qui a sauvé l'Afrique,* pp. 20–21. On Boisson, see also Maurice Martin du Gard, *Chronique de Vichy: 1940–1944* (Paris: Flammarion, 1948), pp. 280–282. Senghor, letter of Oct. 18, 1935, ANS O 931/176.

37. Fara Sow, *Dakar Jeunes* (March 5, 1942).

38. Ousmane Socé Diop, "L'évolution culturelle de l'AOF," *Dakar Jeunes* (Jan. 29, 1942), p. 2.

39. D. Diawara, *Dakar Jeunes* (April 23, 1942), and Ouezzin Coulibaly, ibid. (June 11, 1942).

40. Joseph Baye, *Dakar Jeunes* (March 26, 1942); Mamadou Dia, "De la vie spirituelle en AOF," ibid. (March 12, 1942).

41. Fara Sow, *Dakar Jeunes* (March 5, 1942).

42. Dia, "Littérature et préjugés," *Dakar Jeunes* (May 14, 1942); Charles Béart, ibid. (June 18, 1942).

43. Letters of the police chief of the first section, Saint-Louis, Feb. 16, 1942, and of the director of political affairs, Berthet, May 13, 1942, to the director of the bureau of information, ANS O 31/31. Georges Manue, *Dakar Jeunes* (May 19, 1942). Several administrators argued that there were no grounds for stopping the discussion, and also defended the Africans who were trying to organize to defend their professional interests. They felt it was a mistake to consider such efforts subversive. Unsigned note of May 21, 1942, to the director of political affairs, and letter from Biènes to the governor general of French West Africa, March 13, 1942, ANS O 31/31.

44. Notes from the inspector general of education to the head of the information service, June 25, 1942, ANS O 31/31.

45. Faty Fall, "L'opinion publique dakaroise, 1940–1944"; Lamine Guèye, *Itinéraire africaine* (Paris: Présence Africaine, 1966), pp. 110–114. Crowder, *Senegal*, p. 40, disputes that Africans were more harshly treated than French.

46. Letter of H. Deschamps to the governor general of French West Africa, Sept. 9, 1943, ANS O 31/31.

47. Interview with Hélène Senghor, Joal, March 17, 1976.

8. Brilliant Apprentice

1. Alexander Werth, *France, 1940–1955* (New York: Holt, 1956), pp. 218–219.

2. Simone de Beauvoir, *The Prime of Life*, trans. Peter Green (Cleveland: World Publications, 1962), p. 473.

3. Edward Mortimer, *France and the Africans, 1944–1960* (London: Faber, 1969), p. 28.

4. Félix Eboué, cited in Michel Devèze, *La France d'Outre-mer: 1938–1947* (Paris: Hachette, 1948), pp. 178–179.

5. Dorothy Shipley White, *Black Africa and De Gaulle* (University Park: Pennsylvania State University Press, 1979), p. 116.

6. Cited by William B. Cohen, *Rulers of Empire: The French Colonial Service in Africa* (Stanford: Stanford University Press, 1979), p. 166.

7. Ruth Schachter Morgenthau, *Political Parties in French-Speaking West Africa* (London: Oxford University Press, 1964), p. 38.

8. Cited by Lamine Guèye, *Itinéraire africaine* (Paris: Présence Africaine, 1966), p. 118.

9. *Afrique en Guerre* (Jan. 27, 1944); White, *Black Africa*, pp. 126–127; Cohen, *Rulers of Empire*, pp. 165–170.

10. Cohen, *Rulers of Empire*, p. 169; Morgenthau, *Political Parties*, pp. 39, 58.

11. Senghor, letter to Raymond Postal, cited in Ernest Milcent and Monique Sordet, *Léopold Sédar Senghor et la naissance de l'Afrique moderne* (Paris: Seghers, 1969), p. 78.

12. Devèze, *La France d'Outre-mer*, p. 210; Mortimer, *France and the Africans*, p. 55; Robert Delavignette, "L'Union française," *Esprit*, no. 112 (July 1, 1945), pp. 214–236. Delavignette's article is dedicated to Senghor. Senghor's article in the same issue of *Esprit*, "Défense de l'Afrique noir," is dedicated to the memory of the Tirailleurs Sénégalais who had died for France.

13. Werth, *France*, pp. 222–223.

14. Constance Webb, *Richard Wright* (New York: Putnam, 1968), pp. 289–290.

15. Guèye, *Itinéraire*, pp. 129–130; Milcent and Sordet, *Senghor*, p. 84; interview with Sourou Migan Apithy, Paris, Nov. 20, 1985.

16. Interview with Apithy, Nov. 20, 1985.

17. Morgenthau, *Political Parties*, p. 40; Jean Suret-Canale, *Afrique noire: De la colonisation aux indépendances, 1945–1960*, vol. 1 (Paris: Editions Sociales, 1972), p. 30.

18. Milcent and Sordet, *Senghor,* pp. 85–86; Senghor, letter to Mercer Cook, read by Cook in interview, Washington, D.C., March 2, 1979.

19. Interview with Edouard Basse, Dakar, March 20, 1976.

20. Bakory Traoré, "Evolution des partis politiques au Sénégal depuis 1941," in *Forces politiques en Afrique noire,* ed. Traoré, Mamadou Lô, and Jean-Louis Alibert (Paris: Presses Universitaires de France, 1966), pp. 14–16; Guèye cited, p. 23.

21. Ibid., pp. 20–21.

22. Interview with André Guillabert, Paris, June 25, 1975; interview with Abdoulaye Ly, Dakar, March 22, 1976.

23. Interviews with Senghor, Burlington, Vt., June 13–14, 1971; interviews with Blaise Senghor and Marie-Thérèse Basse, Dakar, June 17, 1973. For the atmosphere of the time, see the address of Louis Achille to an interracial conference in 1949, cited in Frantz Fanon, *Black Skin, White Masks,* trans. Charles Lam Markmann (New York: Grove Press, 1967), p. 71. Earlier the police had noted that Senghor disapproved of mixed marriages, ANS 2G 41/108.

24. Interview with Hélène Senghor, Joal, June 17, 1973.

25. Traoré, "Evolution des partis," p. 24.

26. "Vues sur l'Afrique noir, ou s'assimiler non être assimilés," in Senghor, *Liberté 1: Negritude et humanisme* (Paris: Le Seuil, 1964), pp. 39–69.

27. Ibid., pp. 60, 66.

28. Gordon Wright, *The Reshaping of French Democracy* (New York: Reynal and Hitchcock, 1948), pp. 99–107; Apithy cited in Milcent and Sordet, *Senghor,* p. 89.

29. Wright, *Reshaping of French Democracy,* p. 118.

30. Ibid.

31. Guèye, *Itinéraire,* pp. 144–145.

32. Moutet's speech of March 22, 1946, cited in Suret-Canale, *Afrique noire,* vol. 1, p. 37.

33. Senghor's speech of March 21, 1946, in Senghor, *Liberté 2: Nation et voie africaine du socialisme* (Paris: Le Seuil, 1971), pp. 9–16.

34. Wright, *Reshaping of French Democracy,* pp. 190–192.

35. Ibid., pp. 194–198; Morgenthau, *Political Parties,* p 86.

36. *Marchés Coloniaux,* July, Aug., Sept. 1946, cited in Gaston Monnerville, *Témoignage* (Paris: Plon, 1975), p. 389; Guèye, *Itinéraire,* pp. 158–159; Suret-Canale, *Afrique noire,* pp. 46–53.

37. Monnerville, *Témoignage,* p. 388.

38. Senghor, *Gavroche* (Paris), no. 102 (Aug. 8, 1946), rpt. in *Liberté 2,* pp. 17–18; interview with Mercer Cook, March 2, 1979.

39. Political report, Aug. and Sept. 1946, ANS 2G 46/124.

40. Suret-Canale, *Afrique noire,* p. 47. Apithy cited in Ernest Milcent, *L'AOF entre en scène* (Paris: Témoignage Chrétien, 1958), p. 36.

41. Paul-Henri Siriex, *Félix Houphouet-Boigny, l'homme de la paix* (Paris, Dakar, and Abidjan: Seghers and Nouvelles Editions Africaines, 1975), p 77.

42. Senghor, "Les négro-africains et l'Union française," *Revue Politique et Par-*

lementaire (June 1947), pp. 205–208; Monnerville, *Témoignage,* pp. 392–393; Guèye, *Itinéraire,* p. 165; political reports to the high commissioner, June and Sept. 1946, ANS 2G 46/126. For a general view of the role of African deputies, see Philippe Guillemin, "Les élus d'Afrique noire à l'Assemblée Nationale sous la Quatrième République," *Revue Française de Science Politique* 8, no. 4 (Dec. 1958), pp. 861–871.

43. Raoul Girardet, *L'idée coloniale en France: 1871–1962* (Paris: La Table Ronde, 1972), p. 201.

44. Interview with Senghor, June 13, 1971; interview with Mercer Cook, March 2, 1979; personal communications from Brian Weinstein, Nov. 2, 1974, and Armand Guibert, June 11, 1975; interview with Louis Achille, Lyon, Jan. 21, 1989.

45. Milcent, *L'AOF,* pp. 36–39; ANS 2G 46/124; Milcent and Sordet, *Senghor,* pp. 98–99.

46. Milcent, *L'AOF,* p. 40.

47. "Discours d'ouverture," Congrès constitutif convention africaine, Dakar, Jan. 11–13, 1957, cited in Traoré et al., eds., *Forces politiques,* p. 35; interview with Apithy, Nov. 20, 1985; Houphouet, 1952, cited in Traoré, p. 35.

9. Master Politician

1. Pierre Emmanuel, *Temps Present* (March 8, 1945). J. Authier, *Nouvelles Littéraires* (Sept. 1948). *Hosties noires* was also reviewed favorably in *Cahiers du Sud* 28, no. 292 (2nd semester 1948), pp. 553–554. *Poésie,* vol. 45 (Paris: Seghers, Jan. 1945). Maurice Martin du Gard, *Chronique de Vichy: 1940–1944* (Paris: Flammarion, 1948), p. 428.

Senghor's publisher, Le Seuil, 27 rue Jacob, Paris 75006, has an archive of reviews of his poetry. There is also an abundant critical literature. Two recent assessments that are readily available in English are Abiola Irele's introduction in *Selected Poems of Léopold Sédar Senghor* ed. Abiola Irele (London: Cambridge University Press, 1977), and Janice Spleth, *Léopold Sédar Senghor* (Boston: G. K. Hall, Twayne, 1985). Among English translations, particularly recommended is *Léopold Sédar Senghor: Selected Poems/Poésies Choisies,* a bilingual text with English translations and an introduction by Craig Williamson (London: Rex Collings, 1976).

2. *L'Afrique Occidentale Française (L'AOF)* (Feb. 6, 1948).

3. James Bruce-Benoît, "Témoignage," in *Hommage à Léopold Sédar Senghor, homme de culture* (Paris: Présence Africaine, 1976), pp. 225–226.

4. Senghor, *Condition Humaine* (Feb. 11 and 25, 1948); note of May 1949, Ministère de l'Education, Mission des Archives (MEMA), Paris, F17 bis 3273.

5. Senghor, Letters, MEMA F17 bis 3273; note to minister of Overseas France, Sept. 19, 1947, and note of director of political affairs, MEMA, F17 bis 3298.

6. Albert Charton, letter of June 4, 1948, and Capelle, letter of Dec. 4, 1950, MEMA, F17 bis 3298.

7. Correspondence and administrators' notes, MEMA, F17 bis 3274, 3298; letter to minister of Overseas France, May 7, 1949, and administrator's note, MEMA, F17 bis 3273.

8. Pleven's speech at Brazzaville rpt. in *Afrique en Guerre* (Feb. 24, 1944), p. 1.

9. Political report, 1947, ANS 2G 47/133.

10. Interview with Robert Verdier, Paris, June 23, 1975.

11. Interview with André Guillabert, Paris, June 25, 1975.

12. Interviews with Ségan Ndiaye, March 14, 1976, Cissé Dia, March 12, 1976, and Mamadou Dia, March 25, 1976, Dakar; Senghor, "Pierre Teilhard de Chardin et la politique africaine," *Cahiers Pierre Teilhard de Chardin* (Paris: Le Seuil, 1962), p. 18.

13. Interview with Guillabert, June 25, 1975.

14. Political reports, Oct. 1946, ANS 2G 46/124, and Jan. 1947, ANS 2G 46/126.

15. *L'AOF* (March 7 and Aug. 15, 1947).

16. Interview with Majib Ndaw, Dakar, March 4, 1976; Bakory Traoré, "Evolution des partis politiques au Sénégal depuis 1946," in *Forces politiques en Afrique noire*, ed. Bakory Traoré, Mamadou Lô, and Jean-Louis Alibert (Paris: Presses Universitaires de France, 1966), pp. 46–47.

17. ANS 2G 46/124.

18. *L'AOF* (Oct. 3, 1947). Interviews with Ségan Ndiaye, March 14, 1976, Cissé Dia, March 12, 1976, and Mamadou Dia, March 25, 1976.

19. *Condition Humaine,* no. 1 (Feb. 11, 1948).

20. Interview with Mamadou Dia, March 25, 1976.

21. *Condition Humaine,* no. 2 (Feb. 26, 1948).

22. The information on Dia's childhood is from his memoirs, Mamadou Dia, *Mémoires d'un militant du tiers-monde* (Paris: Publisud, 1985), pp. 1–23.

23. Ibid., pp. 34–37.

24. Interview with Mamadou Dia, March 25, 1976.

25. Interview with Guillabert, June 25, 1975.

26. *Condition Humaine,* no. 1 (Feb. 11, 1948), and no. 2 (Feb. 25, 1948).

27. Political report, 1947, ANS 2G 47/133.

28. Fofana Abdoulaye, *L'AOF* (July 29, 1948).

29. Senghor, letter to Guy Mollet, *Condition Humaine,* no. 14 (Oct. 5, 1948). Robert Verdier, an SFIO leader of the time, confirmed Senghor's assessment in an interview, Paris, June 13, 1975.

30. *Condition Humaine,* nos. 14 and 15 (Oct. 5 and 19, 1948).

31. *Condition Humaine,* no. 14. Political reports for 1946–1948, ANS 2G 46/126, 2G 47/133, 2G 48/131.

32. *Condition Humaine,* no. 15.

33. Interviews with Guillabert, June 25, 1975, Verdier, June 23, 1975, and

Majib Ndaw, March 4, 1976. On refusing to support the students' organization, Archives de la Ministère de la France d'Outre-mer, SLOTFOM III/119. Senghor, *La poésie de l'action: Conversations avec Mohamed Aziza* (Paris: Stock, 1980), pp. 105–107, 137. *Condition Humaine,* no. 15, ibid., no. 8 (May 26, 1948).

34. Interview with Majib Ndaw, March 4, 1976; interview with Guillabert, June 25, 1975.

35. Interview with Sourou Migan Apithy, Paris, Nov. 20, 1985; interview with Mamadou Dia, March 25, 1976.

36. Interviews with Mamadou Dia, Cissé Dia, and Majib Ndaw, 1976; interview with Apithy, 1985; interview with Bakory Traoré, Dakar, March 15, 1976.

37. Dia, *Mémoires,* pp. 35–37.

38. Paul Alduy, *L'Union française: Mission de la France* (Paris: Fasquelle, 1948), p. 125; Robert Delavignette, *Service africaine* (Paris: Gallimard, 1946), pp. 236, 254.

39. Alioune Diop, *L'AOF,* no. 2260 (Oct. 28, 1948); Pathé Diagne, private communication, June 30, 1985.

40. *Condition Humaine,* no. 15.

41. Alioune Diop, "Niam n'goura ou les raisons d'être de *Présence Africaine,*" *Présence Africaine,* no. 1, (Oct.–Nov. 1947), p. 7.

42. *L'AOF* (Oct. 28, 1948). *Condition Humaine* had until then praised Diop and advertised *Présence Africaine,* notably in issues of Feb. 11, March 10, and Nov. 16, 1948. Senghor expressed doubt that Diop had really written the open letter published in *L'AOF* on Oct. 28.

43. *L'AOF* (Sept. 30, Oct. 21, Oct. 28, Dec. 23, Nov. 4, 1948).

44. Interview with Hélène Senghor, Joal, March 17, 1976.

45. *Condition Humaine,* no. 15.

46. Ibid., no. 18 (Nov. 30, 1948).

47. Traoré, "Evolution des partis," p. 46.

48. Ernest Milcent and Monique Sordet, *Léopold Sédar Senghor et la naissance de l'Afrique moderne* (Paris: Seghers, 1969), p. 124. The best general account of the politics of this period remains Ruth Schachter Morgenthau, *Political Parties in French-Speaking West Africa* (London: Oxford University Press, 1964), pp. 139–153. On the 1951 campaign, Traoré, "Evolution des partis," pp. 46–51; Kenneth Robinson, "Senegal," in *Five Elections in Africa,* ed. W. J. M. Mackenzie and Kenneth Robinson (Oxford: Clarendon Press, 1960), pp. 281–390.

49. Interview with Cissé Dia, March 12, 1976.

50. "Messages", from "Ethiopiques" in Senghor, *Poèmes* (Paris: Le Seuil, 1984), p. 107.

51. Morgenthau, *Political Parties,* p. 152.

52. Ibid., pp. 145–153; political reports of the governor of Senegal, 1951, ANS 2G 51/144.

53. Political reports, 1951, ANS 2G 51/144; interview with Cissé Dia, March 12, 1976; Milcent and Sordet, *Senghor,* p. 126.

54. Ernest Milcent, *L'AOF entre en scène* (Paris: Témoignage Chrétien, 1958), p. 73.

55. Interview with Birago Diop, Dakar, March 1976.

56. On the French political context that frustrated African deputies, Philippe Guillemin, "Les élus d'Afrique noire à l'Assemblée Nationale sous la Quatrième République," *Revue Française de Science Politique* 8, no. 4 (Dec. 1958), pp. 861–877; Janet G. Vaillant, "African Deputies in Paris: The Political Role of Léopold Senghor in the Fourth Republic," in *Double Impact: France and Africa in the Age of Imperialism*, ed. G. Wesley Johnson (Westport, Conn.: Greenwood Press, 1985), pp. 141–152. Senghor, "L'Afrique s'interroge: subir ou choisir?" *Présence Africaine*, nos. 8–9 (March 1950), rpt. in *Liberté 1: Négritude et humanisme* (Paris: Le Seuil, 1964), p. 91.

57. Manuel Sauvage, *Annales coloniales,* cited by Mamadou Dia, *Condition Humaine* (Sept. 13, 1949).

58. Cited in Rupert Emerson, *From Empire to Nation: The Rise to Self-Assertion of Asian and African Peoples* (Boston: Beacon Press, 1960), p. 83. This extraordinary book remains a source of insight into the process of decolonization.

10. Negritude and African Socialism

1. "Problématique de la négritude," in Senghor, *Liberté 3: Négritude et civilisation de l'universel* (Paris: Le Seuil, 1977), pp. 269–270. There is a large secondary literature on Senghor's theory of Negritude that includes scholarly assessments and critical attacks of both a literary and political kind. Among them are, on the scholarly side, Louis-Vincent Thomas, "Panorama de la Négritude," *Langues et Littératures* (Dakar) 14 (1965): 45–101; Sylvia Washington Bâ, *The Concept of Negritude in the Poetry of Léopold Sédar Senghor* (Princeton: Princeton University Press, 1973); Irving Leonard Markovitz, *Léopold Sédar Senghor and the Politics of Negritude* (New York: Atheneum, 1969). Representative of more critical attacks are Marcien Towa, *L. S. Senghor, négritude ou servitude* (Yaoundé: Editions CLE, 1971), and Stanislas Adotevi, *Négritude et Négrologues* (Paris: Union Générale d'Editions, 1972). Early support by an African scholar for the idea of the unity and antiquity of African civilization was provided by Cheikh Anta Diop, *Nations nègres et cultures* (Paris: Présence Africaine, 1955).

2. Césaire, cited in Senghor, "Problématique de la Négritude," p. 270.

3. Senghor, letter to Maurice Martin du Gard, in Michèle Dorsemaine, Alfred Fierro, and Josette Masson, eds., *Léopold Sédar Senghor* (Paris: Bibliothèque Nationale, 1978), pp. 83–84.

4. Jean-Paul Sartre, "Orphée nègre," in Senghor, ed., *Anthologie de la nouvelle poésie nègre et malgache de langue française* (Paris: Presses Universitaires de France, 1948, 1969), pp. ix–xliv.

5. Ibid., p. xv.

6. Senghor, "L'Afrique noire," in Mohamed el Kholti, Léopold Cédar (sic) Senghor, Pierre Do Dinh, A. Rakoto Ratsimananga, and E. Ralajmihiatra, eds., *Les plus beaux écrits de l'Union française et du Maghreb* (Paris: Colombe, 1947), p. 247.

7. The following discussion of Senghor's theory is based on articles reprinted

in his *Liberté 1: Négritude et humanisme* (Paris: Le Seuil, 1964): "Ce que l'homme noire apporte" (1939); "L'esthétique négro-africaine" (1956); "Eléments constitutifs d'une civilisation d'inspiration négro-africaine" (1959). Other works by Senghor consulted: "De la négritude: Psychologie du négro-africaine," *Diogène*, no. 37, Jan.–March 1962, pp. 3–16; *On African Socialism*, trans. and ed. Mercer Cook (New York: Praeger, 1964), and "Negritude and African Socialism," *St. Antony's Papers*, vol. 15 (London: Chatto and Windus, 1963), pp. 9–22.

8. "Ce que l'homme noir apporte," *Liberté 1*, p. 24; and "Eléments constitutifs," ibid., p. 264.

9. "Eléments constitutifs," pp. 258–259; "Laye Camara et Lamine Diakhaté, ou l'art n'est pas d'un parti," *Liberté 1*, p. 157; "De la négritude," pp. 4–5.

10. "L'esthétique négro-africaine," *Liberté 1*, pp. 202–217.

11. "Eléments constitutifs," pp. 256–257.

12. Ibid., pp. 275–276; *On African Socialism*, pp. 93–94.

13. Max Weber, "Politics as a Vocation," in H. H. Gerth and C. Wright Mills, eds. and trans., *From Max Weber: Essays in Sociology* (New York: Oxford University Press, 1958), p. 128; Weber, "Science as a Vocation," ibid., p. 155; Weber, *The Protestant Ethic* (New York: Scribners, 1958), pp. 180–183; Senghor, "A New York," *Poèmes* (Paris: Le Seuil, 1984), p. 116.

14. Emile Durkheim, *The Division of Labor in Society*, trans. George Simpson (Glencoe, Ill.: Free Press, 1964). On Tönnies, Thomas Burton Bottomore, *Sociology: A Guide to Problems and Literature* (London: Allen and Unwin, 1962), pp. 93, 113–114; Janet G. Vaillant, "Dilemmas for Anti-Western Patriotism: Slavophilism and Negritude," *Journal of Modern African Studies* 12, no. 3 (1974): 377–393.

15. Senghor, "De la négritude," p. 9.

16. Senghor, "Le problème de la culture," *Liberté 1*, p. 96.

17. This passage about the value of assimilation is deleted from the version of the article that Senghor reprinted in his collected works of 1963. The result is to make the 1937 version sound more militant. For the omitted passage see Senghor, "L'université dans l'empire," in Jean Dumont, ed., *Essais et études universitaires: Lettres 1* (Paris, 1945), p. 47.

18. Senghor, "Vues sur l'Afrique noire ou assimiler non être assimilés," *Liberté 1*, pp. 60–69; "Negritude and African Socialism."

19. *On African Socialism*, pp. 134–154; Senghor, "Pierre Teilhard de Chardin et la politique africaine," *Cahiers Pierre Teilhard de Chardin*, no. 3 (Paris: Le Seuil, 1962), pp. 15–65; Pierre Teilhard de Chardin, *The Phenomenology of Man* (New York: Harper, 1961).

20. "Prière aux masques," *Poèmes*, pp. 23–24.

21. Senghor, "L'université de Dakar," *Liberté 1*, p. 296.

22. "A New York," *Poèmes*, pp. 115–117. The English translation is from Senghor, *Selected Poems*, trans. John Reed and Clive Wake (New York: Atheneum, 1969), pp. 78–79.

23. Senghor, "Nationhood: Report on the Doctrine and Program of the Party of African Federation," and "The African Road to Socialism: An Attempt at a Definition," in *On African Socialism*, pp. 7–65, 67–165.

24. "Teilhard de Chardin," p. 22; Senghor, "Les données du problème," *Développement et socialisme, colloque sur les politiques de développement et les diverses voies africaines vers le socialisme, Dakar, décembre 3–8, 1962* (Paris: Presénce Africaine, 1963), pp. 11–17.

25. Senghor, "Marxisme et humanisme," *La Revue Socialiste,* n.s. 19 (March 1948), pp. 201–216; Senghor, "Socialism Is a Humanism," in Erich Fromm, ed., *Socialist Humanism* (Garden City, N.Y.: Doubleday Anchor, 1965), pp. 53–67; "Teilhard de Chardin," pp. 22, 25; *On African Socialism,* pp. 29–34 (quotation from Marx, p. 34).

26. *On African Socialism,* pp. 132–133.

27. Karl Marx, "The German Ideology," in Robert C. Tucker, ed., *The Marx-Engels Reader,* 2nd ed. (New York: Norton, 1978), p. 160; "Teilhard de Chardin," pp. 61–62.

28. *On African Socialism,* p. 49; "Les données du problème," pp. 14–15.

29. Senghor, "Débats," *Présence Africaine,* n.s., no. 8–12 (June–Nov. 1956), p. 215.

11. Toward Independence

1. Charles de Gaulle, *Memoirs of Hope, Renewal and Endeavor,* trans. Terence Kilmartin (New York: Simon and Schuster, 1971), pp. 5–6; Senghor, "Pour une solution fédéraliste," *La Nef* (June 1955), rpt. in *Liberté 2: Nation et voie africaine du socialisme* (Paris: Le Seuil, 1971), p. 158.

2. Joseph-Roger de Benoist, *L'AOF de la conférence de Brazzaville (1944) à l'indépendance (1960)* (Dakar: Nouvelles Editions Africaines, 1982), pp. 137–140; Jean Suret-Canale, *Afrique noire: De la colonisation aux indépendences, 1945–1960,* vol. 1 (Paris: Editions Sociales, 1972), pp. 103–111, 117–119.

3. Benoist, *L'AOF,* pp. 142–148; *Education Africaine,* no. 31, pp. 23–24; Olivier Le Brun, "Education and Class Conflict," in Rita Cruise O'Brien, ed., *The Political Economy of Underdevelopment: Dependence in Senegal* (Beverly Hills, Calif.: Sage, 1979), p. 185.

4. Philippe Guillemin, "Les élus d'Afrique noire à l'Assemblée Nationale sous la Quatrième République," *Revue Française de Science Politique* 8, no. 4 (Dec. 1958), pp. 861–877.

5. Ministère de l'Education, Mission des Archives (MEMA), Paris, F17 bis 3298, F17 bis 3273.

6. Senghor, "Place de l'Afrique dans l'Europe unie," Assemblée Nationale, July 9, 1949, *Liberté 2,* pp. 60–65; "L'Eurafrique, unité économique de l'avenir," Assemblée Nationale, Jan. 17, 1952, ibid., pp. 90–94; "L'Afrique et l'Europe: Deux mondes complémentaires," *Marchés Coloniaux* (May 14, 1955), ibid., pp. 148–157.

7. Jean Rous, *Léopold Sédar Senghor* (Paris: Didier, 1967), pp. 29–30.

8. Mendès-France and Mitterrand cited in Raoul Girardet, *L'idée coloniale en France: 1871–1962* (Paris: La Table Ronde, 1972), pp. 202, 238.

9. Rivet and Jacques Soustelle cited in ibid., pp. 264–265, 249–250.

10. Ruth Schachter Morgenthau, *Political Parties in French-Speaking West Africa* (London: Oxford University Press, 1964), p. 82.

11. Kenneth Robinson, "Senegal," in *Five Elections in Africa,* ed. W. J. M. Mackenzie and Kenneth Robinson (Oxford: Clarendon Press, 1960), pp. 322–323. Senghor, Assemblée Nationale, June 17, 1954, *Liberté 2,* pp. 146, 142–147.

12. Robinson, "Senegal," p. 378.

13. Christine Garnier and Philippe Ermont, *Le Sénégal: Porte de l'Afrique* (Paris: Hachette, 1962), p. 130.

14. Robinson, "Senegal," pp. 381–382; Bakory Traoré, "Evolution des partis politiques au Sénégal depuis 1946," in *Forces politiques en Afrique noire,* ed. Bakory Traoré, Mamadou Lô, and Jean-Louis Alibert (Paris: Presses Universitaires de France, 1966), p. 64. This is an excellent source for Senegalese party politics during this period.

15. Lamartine cited in Paul Alduy, *L'Union française: Mission de la France* (Paris: Fasquelle, 1948), p. 91. Defferre cited in Paul-Henri Siriex, *Félix Houphouet-Boigny, l'homme de la paix* (Paris, Dakar, and Abidjan: Seghers and Nouvelles Editions Africaines, 1975), p. 147.

16. Senghor, *Condition Humaine* (April 14, 1956); Siriex, *Houphouet-Boigny,* p. 155.

17. "Messages," from *Ethiopiques,* in Senghor, *Poèmes* (Paris: Le Seuil, 1984), p. 107; "Le Kaya Magan," *Poèmes,* pp. 104–105; "L'absente," *Poèmes,* pp. 110–114; "A New York," *Poèmes,* pp. 115–117.

18. "Epîtres à la princesse," *Poèmes,* p. 138.

19. *Poèmes,* pp. 148–154.

20. "Chaka," *Poèmes,* pp. 118–133; quotation, p. 132.

21. Richard Wright, "Intervention," Sept. 19, 1956, *Présence Africaine,* n.s. 8–10 (June–Nov. 1956), p. 67.

22. Aimé Césaire, "Intervention," ibid., p. 374; George Lamming, "The Negro Writer and His Worlds," ibid., p. 321.

23. Ibid., p. 68; Richard Wright, "Tradition and Industrialization," ibid., pp. 347–360.

24. Frantz Fanon, "Racisme et culture," ibid., pp. 125–126.

25. Aimé Césaire, "Culture et colonisation," ibid., pp. 200–202, 194.

26. Ibid., pp. 215, 216–217.

27. Senghor, "Negritude and African Socialism," *St. Antony's Papers,* vol. 15 (London: Chatto and Windus, 1963), p. 12.

28. *Le Monde* (Sept. 19, 21, 22, 1956); *L'Humanité* (Sept. 20, 24, 1956); interview with Mercer Cook, Washington, D.C., Oct. 22, 1984. *Figaro Littéraire* (Sept. 29, 1956), p. 3.

29. Traoré et al., eds., *Forces politiques,* pp. 66–67.

30. *Le Monde* (Feb. 26, 1957), cited in Ernest Milcent and Monique Sordet, *Léopold Sédar Senghor et la naissance de l'Afrique moderne* (Paris: Seghers, 1969), p. 152. Keita cited in Siriex, *Houphouet-Boigny,* pp. 165–166. Senghor, interview in *Le Monde* (Sept. 4, 1957), cited in Traoré et al., eds., *Forces politiques,* p. 72.

31. André Blanchet, *L'itinéraire des partis africains depuis Bamako* (Paris: Plon, 1958), p. 110.

32. William J. Foltz, *From French West Africa to the Mali Federation* (New Haven: Yale University Press, 1965), p. 88. Information on the general political events of this period is drawn from this book. The opening speech at Cotonou, July 25, 1958, is cited on p. 90.

33. Senghor, *La poésie de l'action: Conversations avec Mohamed Aziza* (Paris: Stock, 1980), pp. 119–120.

34. De Gaulle in debate of constitutional committee, Aug. 6, 1958, cited in Jean Lacouture, *Cinq hommes et la France* (Paris: Le Seuil, 1961), p. 347.

35. Ibid., pp. 347, 350–352. Brazzaville speech cited in Gil Dugué, *Vers les États Unis d'Afrique* (Dakar: Lettres Africaines, 1960), p. 111. Dugué's account of de Gaulle's visit to Conakry supports those of Lacouture and Milcent.

36. Ernest Milcent, *Au carrefour les options africaines: Le Sénégal* (Paris: Centurion, 1965), pp. 55–57. Rous, *Senghor,* pp. 35–36; Dugué, *Vers les États Unis,* p. 116.

37. Benoist, *L'AOF,* pp. 152, 427; Foltz, *From French West Africa,* p. 93.

38. Rous, *Senghor,* pp. 35–36.

39. Ibid., p. 37. Lacouture, *Cinq hommes,* pp. 357–358, 364–365.

40. Rous, *Senghor,* pp. 39–40.

41. Ibid., p. 40.

42. On the breakup of the Mali Federation, Milcent, *Au carrefour,* pp. 62–73; Foltz, *From French West Africa,* chs. 7–10. On Guèye's position, Magatte Lô, *Sénégal: L'heure du choix* (Paris: L'Harmattan, 1985), p. 32.

12. President Senghor

1. Senghor, *La poésie de l'action: Conversations avec Mohamed Aziza* (Paris: Stock, 1980), p. 168.

2. Christine Garnier and Philippe Ermont, *Le Sénégal: Porte de l'Afrique* (Paris: Hachette, 1962), p. 131.

3. *Figaro Littéraire* (April 15, 1961), p. 12.

4. "Elégie de minuit," in Senghor, *Poèmes* (Paris: Le Seuil, 1984), pp. 198–200.

5. Senghor, *On African Socialism,* trans. and ed. Mercer Cook (New York: Praeger, 1964), p. 12.

6. Paul Thibaud, "Dia, Senghor et le socialisme africain," *Esprit* 32, no. 320 (Sept. 1963), pp. 341–343.

7. François Perroux, *Le Figaro* (May 10, 1963).

8. Mamadou Dia, *Mémoires d'un militant du tiers-monde* (Paris: Publisud, 1985), p. 132.

9. Senghor, "Indépendance et voie africaine du socialisme," *Liberté 4: Socialisme et planification* (Paris: Le Seuil, 1983), pp. 11, 12, 19.

10. Ernest Milcent, *Au carrefour des options africaines: Le Sénégal* (Paris: Centurion, 1965), pp. 76–77, 158–160. Mamadou Dia, *Nations africaines et solidarité mondiale,* 2nd ed. (Paris: Presses Universitaires de France, 1963), p. 168.

11. Philippe Decraene, "Le coup de force de Dakar," *Communauté France-*

Eurafrique 137 (Dec. 1982), pp. 20–21; interview with Bakory Traoré, Dakar, March 15, 1976.

12. Mamadou Dia, cited in *Afrique Nouvelle,* Nov. 1, 1962.

13. This account is based largely on the writings of two correspondents who were in Senegal at the time, Ernest Milcent and Philippe Decraene: Milcent, *Au carrefour,* pp. 74–98; Decraene, "Le coup de force de Dakar," pp. 20–21; Decraene, "Réflexions sur les recents événements du Sénégal," *Académie des sciences d'outre-mer, comptes rendus mensuels des séances,* vol. 23 (Feb. 1 and 15, 1963), pp. 53–63. Also consulted: Jean Rous, *Léopold Sédar Senghor* (Paris: Didier, 1967), pp. 54–57; Rous, *Chronique de la décolonisation* (Paris: Présence Africaine, 1965), pp. 266–272; Thibaud, "Dia, Senghor"; *Afrique Nouvelle* (Dec. 21–27, 1962, and Dec. 28–Jan. 3, 1962); Dia, *Mémoires; Magatte Lô, *Sénégal: L'heure du choix* (Paris: L'Harmattan, 1985); interviews with Traoré, March 15, 1976, and Michel Aurillac, Paris, Jan. 19, 1989. All of these written accounts, with the exception of those by Dia and Thibaud, are by men known to be sympathetic with Senghor.

14. Milcent, *Au carrefour,* pp. 83–85.

15. Ibid., pp. 85–89.

16. Thibaud, "Dia, Senghor," p. 335; interview with Traoré.

17. Dia, *Mémoires,* pp. 148–150. The accounts of Thibaud, "Dia, Senghor," p. 335, and Lô, *Sénégal,* pp. 53–61, support Dia's view, although Lô credits himself rather than Senghor with having initiated and carried out this plan.

18. Milcent, *Au carrefour,* p. 92.

19. Dia, *Mémoires,* pp. 150–152. Dia offers as proof of his good intentions the fact that he did not countermand Senghor's unconstitutional order to the parachutists but reissued it under his own name. By omitting mention of the state of emergency, Dia argues that Senghor, not he, violated the constitution. Michel Aurillac, a French lawyer present in the palace that long day and evening, has pointed out that there was no explicit provision in the constitution for its suspension in time of emergency, but that such a right is "generally understood" in French law, and that since the Senegalese constitution was based on principles of French law, such an understanding applied. This and other documents of the evening were typed by Mme Senghor, as there was no access to the palace and no one else was available to type them. Interview with Aurillac, Jan. 19, 1989.

20. Dia, *Mémoires,* p. 148; Milcent, *Au carrefour,* p. 94.

21. Dia, *Mémoires,* pp. 152–153.

22. Milcent, *Au carrefour,* pp. 97–98. Dia, of course, describes the scene differently.

23. Such is the view presented by Milcent and Decraene. For the official view, see Présidence de la République du Sénégal, *L'Esprit et nous: Sur les événements du 17 décembre 1962* (Dakar, ca. 1963).

24. Lô, *Sénégal,* pp. 53–61.

25. The notion that neither man wished to break with the other and that they were manipulated into their confrontation by their supporters is widely believed by Senegalese informants. Many also argue that the politicians who supported Dia against Senghor, of whom the most active was Valdiodio Ndiaye, took

advantage of Dia's poor political sense and manipulated him into a position from which he could not retreat.

26. *Le Monde* (May 10, 1963); *Le Figaro* (May 11, 1963); *France Observatoire* (May 9, 1963); Thibaud, "Dia Senghor"; Dia, *Mémoires,* pp. 148–153, 167, 180–188, 200–201.

27. Présidence de la Republique, *L'Esprit et nous,* pp. 11–12.

28. Interview with Dia, Dakar, March 25, 1976; Dia, *Mémoires,* pp. 177, 180. Senghor made his statement in an interview broadcast over Dakar radio in late January 1989. See also Senghor, *La poésie de l'action,* p. 169.

29. *Marchés Tropicaux et Méditerranées* (Dec. 22, 1962).

30. Senghor, *On African Socialism,* p. 159. See also Irving Leonard Markovitz, *Léopold Sédar Senghor and the Politics of Negritude* (New York: Atheneum, 1969), pp. 63, 147, 195–196, 204, 221.

31. Senghor cited in Markovitz, p. 204; Senghor, letter to Mercer Cook, May 16, 1963, cited in Cook's introduction to Senghor, *On African Socialism,* p. vi; François Zuccarelli, "L'évolution récente de la vie politique au Sénégal," *Revue Française de la Politique Africaine,* no. 27 (July 27, 1976), pp. 85–97.

32. Senghor, "Message au peuple sénégalais," April 3, 1963, typescript, Archives Nationales du Sénégal (ANS), Dossier Senghor.

33. "Allocution du Président Senghor au collège médical," 1963, typescript, ANS, Dossier Senghor.

34. See the definition and discussion of the political machine in Edward C. Banfield and James Q. Wilson, *City Politics* (Cambridge, Mass.: Harvard University Press, 1963), esp. ch. 9. Senghor's basic political methods and policies are well described in Markovitz, *Senghor,* chs. 6–8. Added detail is provided by Edward J. Schumacher, *Politics, Bureaucracy and Rural Development in Senegal* (Berkeley: University of California, 1975). The point to be emphasized is that clan politics and the trading of favors, or "corruption," are not unique to Senegal.

35. There is a large literature on the Islamic brotherhoods in Senegal. See Lucy C. Behrman, *Muslim Brotherhoods and Politics in Senegal* (Cambridge, Mass.: Harvard University Press, 1970); Donal Cruise O'Brien, *Saints and Politicians: Essays in the Organization of a Senegalese Peasant Society* (London: Cambridge University Press, 1975), esp. ch. 2 and p. 74; Moriba Magassouba, *L'Islam au Sénégal: Demain les mollahs?* (Paris: Karthala, 1985); Christian Coulon, *Le marabout et le prince: Islam et pouvoir au Sénégal* (Paris: Pedone, 1981).

36. Jean Rous and Michel Aurillac, for example, both served as Senghor's personal advisors after independence. Rita Cruise O'Brien, *White Society in Black Africa: The French in Senegal* (London: Faber, 1972).

37. Senghor, *On African Socialism,* pp. 58–59, 80, 94–95.

38. Ibid., pp. 154–165; Markovitz, *Senghor,* chs. 6–8, provides ample evidence of this view.

39. Teresa Hayter, "French Aid to Africa: Its Scope and Achievements," *International Affairs* (London) 41, no. 2 (April 1965), pp. 237–238; Albert Bourgi, *La politique française de coopération en Afrique: Le cas du Sénégal* (Paris: Librairie Générale de Droit et Jurisprudence; Dakar: Nouvelles Editions Africaines, 1979),

pp. 20–23; Rita Cruise O'Brien, ed., *The Political Economy of Underdevelopment: Dependence in Senegal* (Beverly Hills, Calif.: Sage, 1979), esp. chs. 3–7.

40. Samir Amin, *L'Afrique de l'ouest bloquée* (Paris: Minuit, 1971), ch. 1, esp. pp. 44–46.

41. Jean-Claude Luc, "Les chances de l'agence de coopération culturelle et technique des pays francophones," *Revue Française d'Etudes Politiques Africaines,* no. 57 (Sept. 1970), pp. 62–81; "How to Organize Francophonie," *Africa Report* 13, no. 6 (June 1968), pp. 12–15; "Pursuing a Dream at a Gallic Summit," *Maclean's: Canada's Weekly News Magazine* (Feb. 24, 1986), pp. 22–28.

42. Newell Flather, "Impressions of the Dakar Festival," *Africa Report* 11, no. 5 (May 1966), pp. 57–60. *Le Monde* (April 4, 1966); interview with Mercer Cook, Washington, D.C., Nov. 6, 1984.

43. Interview with Cook; Hoyt W. Fuller, *Journey to Africa* (Chicago: Third World Press, 1972), pp. 92–93.

44. Malraux's actual phrase was even grander: "l'avènement de l'Esprit" (Rous, *Senghor,* pp. 78, 80–81). This phrase has religious overtones, especially if "Esprit" is capitalized, and might be translated "advent of the (holy) spirit," or "of mind writ large."

45. Césaire, interview with *L'Unité Africaine,* cited by Rous, *Senghor,* p. 80; Senghor, "Le rêve s'est réalisé," *Nouvelles Littéraires* (June 16, 1966).

46. Institut de France, Académie des Sciences Morales et Politiques, "Installation de Léopold Sédar Senghor," typescript, Le Seuil Archive, Paris.

47. Senghor cited in *West Africa* (London), no. 2641 (Jan. 13, 1968), p. 35; Senghor, *On African Socialism,* pp. 58–59; Senghor, "Le Sénégal en marche," *Les Cahiers Africains* 5 (1961).

48. François Zuccarelli, *Un parti politique africain: l'UPS* (Paris: Pichon and Durand-Auzias, 1970), pp. 233–235.

49. *Le Monde* (June 8, 11, 15, 1968); Pierre Biarnès, *L'Afrique aux africains* (Paris: Colin, 1980), pp. 126–132; Colin Legum and John Drysdale, eds., *Africa Contemporary Record, 1968–1969* (London: Africa Research Ltd., 1969), pp. 578–580. The latter is a general reference for events during this and subsequent years.

50. Gerti Hesseling, *Histoire politique du Sénégal* (Paris: Karthala, 1985), p. 257–272.

51. C. I. Sulzberger, *New York Times* (Oct. 27, 1967); Biarnès, *L'Afrique,* p. 130; private communications, Dakar, 1973; interview with Mercer Cook, Washington, D.C., March 2, 1979.

52. Jean-Pierre Ndiaye, *Monde noir et destin politique* (Paris: Présence Africaine; Dakar: Nouvelles Editions Africaines, 1976), pp. 157–167. Philippe Decraene, *Vielle Afrique, jeunes nations* (Paris: Presses Universitaires de France, 1982), p. 70.

53. Interview with Senghor, Dakar, June 14, 1973; Senghor, interview with Jean-Pierre Ndiaye, *Jeune Afrique,* no. 652, July 7, 1973.

54. Biarnès, *L'Afrique,* pp. 81–96.

55. Amin, *L'Afrique de l'ouest bloquée,* pp. 186–195; Colin Legum, ed., *Africa Contemporary Record, 1970–1971* (London: Rex Collings, 1971), p. B439.

56. Senghor, interview with *Abbia,* cited in Colin Legum, ed., *Africa Contemporary Record, 1976–1977* (New York: Africana, 1977), p. B694.

57. *Le Politicien,* no. 4 (April 1977); no. 12 (Dec. 1977); no. 38 (Dec. 1978); *Andé Sope,* no. 9 (March 1978); no. 11 (April 1978).

58. Colin Legum, ed., *Africa Contemporary Record, 1978–1979* (New York: Africana, 1980), p. B758. Biarnès, *L'Afrique,* p. 135.

59. Senghor. *Jeune Afrique,* no. 1022 (Aug. 6, 1980), pp. 14–17; Mar Fall, *Sénégal: L'état Abdou Diouf ou le temps des incertitudes* (Paris: L'Harmattan, 1986), p. 45.

60. Amin, *L'Afrique de l'ouest blocquée,* p. 305; *L'économie sénégalaise,* no. 5 (Paris: Ediafric, 1983), p. 8. Colin Legum, ed., *Africa Contemporary Record, 1980–1981* (New York: Africana, 1981), p. B603.

61. Robert H. Jackson and Carl G. Rosberg, *Personal Rule in Black Africa: Prince, Autocrat, Prophet, Tyrant* (Berkeley: University of California Press, 1982), pp. 77–78, 83–85, 74; for their analysis of Senghor as "prince," pp. 89–97.

62. Michel Vandewiele and Peter F. Merenda, "Senegalese Students' Perceptions of L. S. Senghor," *Perceptual and Motor Skills,* no. 154 (1982), pp. 131–134.

63. Hayter, "French Aid to Africa," pp. 236–251; Amin, *L'Afrique de l'ouest blocquée,* ch. 1 and pp. 297–304; Mamadou Dia, *Le Sénégal trahi, marché d'esclaves* (Paris: SELIO, 1988), pp. 9–31; Michel Aurillac, *L'Afrique à coeur* (Paris: Berger Levrault, 1987), pp. 94–97.

64. Colin Legum, ed., *Africa Contemporary Record, 1981–1982* (New York: Africana, 1982), p. B545. Diouf cited by Flora Lewis, *New York Times* (April 10, 1981).

65. Colin Legum, ed., *Africa Contemporary Record, 1985–1986* (New York: Africana, 1987), pp. B159, B153, and *Africa Contemporary Record, 1986–1987* (Africana, 1988), pp. B141, B139, B136; Dia, *Le Sénégal trahi,* pp. 32–36; *Le Monde* (Nov. 26, 1985).

66. Ass Malick, "Abdou Diouf, peut-il contenir le sopi?" *Africa International,* no. 204 (April 1988), pp. 29–30, 35; Francis Kpatinde, "Abdoulaye Wade: 'Diouf doit partir,'" *Jeune Afrique,* no. 1452 (Nov. 2, 1988), pp. 6–10; Albert Bourgi, "Pourquoi Wade hausse-t-il le ton?" ibid., pp. 8–9; Bourgi, "Sénégal: Diouf dans l'expectative," *Jeune Afrique,* no. 1447 (Sept. 28, 1988), pp. 30–31.

67. Saliou Mbaye, "Pour un Sénégal du 'Bok,'" *Le Soleil,* Nov. 10, 1988, and the film *Jom, the Story of a People,* directed by Babacar Samb (1981), are examples of attention to traditional concepts. On Islam, Magassouba, *L'Islam au Sénégal.*

13. Emeritus

1. Senghor, letter to Janet Vaillant, Feb. 24, 1987.

2. Institut de France, Académie Française, *Discours prononcés dans la séance publique tenue par l'Académie française pour M. Léopold Sédar Senghor, jeudi 29 mai, 1984* (Paris: 1984), p. 29.

3. *Fondation Léopold Sédar Senghor* (Dakar: Nouvelles Imprimeries du Sénégal, ca. 1981), p. 8.

4. Senghor, *Ce que je crois* (Paris: Grasset, 1988).

5. "Elégie pour Philippe-Maguilen Senghor," in Senghor, *Poèmes* (Paris: Le Seuil, 1984), pp. 285–289.

6. Senghor, letter to Janet Vaillant, Oct. 8, 1970. Interview with Senghor, Dakar, June 30, 1973.

7. Senghor, "Negritude and African Socialism," *St. Antony's Papers,* vol. 15 (London: Chatto and Windus, 1963), p. 13; "Messages," *Poèmes,* p. 107; "Elégie des eaux," *Poèmes,* p. 206.

8. Senghor, *La poésie de l'action: Conversations avec Mohammed Aziza* (Paris: Stock, 1980), pp. 233–234.

9. Ibid., pp. 235–236. René Maran made the observation about bringing the best of each to the other; cited in Jacques Louis Hymans, *Léopold Sédar Senghor: An Intellectual Biography* (Edinburgh: Edinburgh University Press, 1971), p. 85.

Index